The Complete Book
of Jewish Observance

Also by Leo Trepp

A History of the Jewish Experience

The Complete Book of

JEWISH OBSERVANCE

Leo Trepp

BEHRMAN HOUSE, INC./SUMMIT BOOKS
New York

Copyright © 1980 by Leo Trepp
All rights reserved
including the right of reproduction
in whole or in part in any form
Published by BEHRMAN HOUSE, INC.
1261 Broadway
New York, New York 10001
and SUMMIT BOOKS
A Simon & Schuster Division of Gulf & Western Corporation
Simon & Schuster Building
1230 Avenue of the Americas
New York, New York 10020
SUMMIT BOOKS and colophon are trademarks of Simon & Schuster
Picture editor: Tricia Grantz
Manufactured in the United States of America
1 2 3 4 5 6 7 8 9 10

Library of Congress Cataloging in Publication Data

Trepp, Leo.
    The complete book of Jewish observance.

    Bibliography: p.
    Includes index.
    1.   Fasts and feasts—Judaism.   2.   Jews—
Rites and ceremonies.   3.   Jewish way of life.
I.   Title.
BM690.T73   296.4   79-1352
ISBN 0-671-41797-5

Photographs Courtesy of: BILL ARON: pages 5, 20, 41, 37, 52, 69, 104, 104, 108, 122, 124, 145, 148, 149, 151, 165, 201, 223, 237, 243, 245, 251, 272, 284, 285, 289, 304, 316, 396; PHYLLIS FRIEDMAN: pages 130, 217, 264, 280, 286, 287; HEBREW UNION COLLEGE—JEWISH INSTITUTE OF RELIGION: pages 127, 275; ISRAEL OFFICE OF INFORMATION: pages 43, 135, 154, 195, 310; JEWISH MUSEUM: pages 4, 78, 84, 95, 116, 278, 303; JEWISH THEOLOGICAL SEMINARY: pages 17, 28, 97; PETER LERMAN: pages 176, 181, 183, 187; RELIGIOUS NEWS SERVICE: pages 74, 221; DR. LEO TREPP: page 340; WIDE WORLD PHOTOS: page 330; YESHIVA UNIVERSITY: pages 271, 309.

For my grandchildren
David Philip Greenberg
and
Amy Trepp Greenberg,
in love

מתנת אהבה
לנכדי דוד אורי בן מאיר וצפורה
ולנכדתי חנה בת מאיר וצפורה
לאי״ט

Contents

Preface

This book is intended to help Jews become celebrants of Judaism. "Celebrating Judaism" means studying our heritage and performing its commandments, its practices, ceremonies, and rituals. In this celebration we shall find meaning for our life, strength for our work, and comfort in our distress. At the same time, we earn respect for ourselves and recognition throughout the world, as we bring honor to our faith and people. In Judaism, faith and people are one. There is divinity in our faith, and we recognize divine providence in our survival.

This is what Torah tells us:

And now, Israel, give heed to the laws and the norms which I am instructing you to observe, so that you may thrive and be able to occupy the land that the Lord, the God of your fathers, is giving you. . . . Cleaving to Him, your God, you are alive, all of you, today. . . . See, I have imparted to you laws and norms, as the Lord my God has commanded me. . . . Observe them faithfully, for that will be proof of your wisdom and discernment to other people, who on hearing all of these laws will say, "Surely, that is a great nation of wise and discerning people." For what great nation is there that has a god so close at hand as is the Lord our God whenever we call upon Him? Or what great nation has laws and norms as perfect as all this Torah that I set before you this day? [Deut. 4:1–8]

Torah, "Instruction," is the visible bond between God and Israel.

It is God's Torah, but also ours to evolve out of our historical experience. It is given us every day anew. It is not in heaven, but here with us.

The word is very close to you, in your mouth and in your heart that you may observe it. [Deut. 30:14]

Standing at Mount Sinai, ready to receive Revelation, the people were given a divine pledge:

If you will obey Me faithfully and keep My covenant, you shall be My treasured possession among all the peoples. Indeed, all the earth is Mine, but you shall be to Me a kingdom of priests and a holy nation. [Exod. 19:5–6]

The people responded:

All that the Lord has spoken we will do. [Exod. 19:8]

A covenant was established for all times. We stand within that covenant to this very day.

THE WHOLE EARTH IS GOD'S.   From primeval times, humanity has attempted to understand and come close to the divine. Many beliefs and customs designed to give meaning to nature and the universe came to be absorbed by Judaism, which ennobled them.

WE ARE TO BE A KINGDOM OF PRIESTS.   We stand under God's special command. This "command" is Mitzvah. Through this command we establish our way of life. This is *Halakhah*, Jewish religious law.

WE ARE TO BE A HOLY PEOPLE.   Our ethical standards must always be higher than the standards of those not subject to Torah, higher than those of secular society. Halakhah rests on ethics and is designed to elevate the Jews to the highest moral plane. Undergirding Halakhah and springing from the covenant itself, from the idea of holiness, enshrined in *Aggadah*, ethical teachings, the spirit of ethics gives it strength. Transcending Halakhah, the spirit of ethics constantly challenges and judges it. Halakhah thus must serve to translate Aggadah into concrete action.

The covenant and the spirit of holiness dwell within the Jewish people. Halakhah is, therefore, accountable to the people, as the people are accountable to God, with whom the Jew stands in everlasting mutual relationship. There is a tension in the covenant between God and Israel, and this tension finds expression in dialogue. So long as the dialogue between Israel and God is kept alive, so long as the creative tension between ethics and Halakhah is permitted to operate, so long as Jews remain committed to Jewish survival, their attempts to find living solutions to current predicaments are legitimate. Today there are in America different approaches to Judaism. They are all "the words of the living God."

In prayer, we ask God for *binah*, understanding. The term is related to *bayn*, between. We have to understand that Judaism has always placed the individual "between." We stand between the poles of past and future, between our individual lives and the life of our people in Israel and the world. We are impelled by the love of our forefathers to fashion the future lives of our children. We are called upon to immerse ourselves in society and, at the same time, to retain our identity as Jews. Above all, we are placed between our actual selves and our ideal selves—as they ought to be and as, through Judaism, they can become.

Each Jew must look at himself or herself and ask, Where do I stand? With the help of the information and guidance provided by Torah, the Jew may find an answer to that question, to the demands of conscience and the issues of life. Ben Bag Bag said: "Turn it [Torah] and turn it again, for all is in it. Look in it, grow gray and old in it, never turn away from it for there is no better guide for you than it (Abot 5:25)."

This book is intended as an introduction to our heritage. It assumes no prior knowledge on the part of the reader; it is simple and self-contained. Its organization, following the Jewish year and the cycle of life, speaks for itself. I hope that it is a living book, not a report on what once was but a guide toward that which can be and will be as Jews find their way within their tradition.

The reader of this book may ask two fundamental questions that should be answered here. He or she may feel that following Judaism, as outlined here, will become a full-time occupation, leaving no opportunity in thought and action ever to move into the secular field of life, its challenges, enjoyments, and satisfactions. For non-Orthodox Jews in particular this is an important issue. The sense of being Jewish that accompanies us through life may sometimes be a negative feeling, a burden. Yet a full awareness of Judaism as a way of life, a meaningful and rewarding totality, will channel just such feelings into positive affirmation. Even if an individual Jew does not or cannot act in tune with the imperatives of Judaism at every moment or even for whole stretches of time, nevertheless, Judaism is there to meet all the issues. This is important.

A Jew may ask, Can I use this work to resolve *specific* issues or dilemmas that may arise in life? To this question the answer must be, for the most part, "No." Specific issues have always called for the decision of a rabbi in the individual case. This book, being general in character, omits details and differences of opinions. As a guide to Jewish living, it aims for accuracy. But as such a guide, it directs the individual to the rabbi to resolve issues of specific or personal import.

I am a grandfather, standing truly between the epochs. A European by birth, for a time an inmate of a Nazi concentration camp, I am one who lost my mother and many dear relatives in the Holocaust. My memory goes back to a Jewish world that exists no more and to Jewish martyrs who gave their lives for the sanctification of His Name. America has opened a new horizon for me and countless others: a new generation of Jews, standing between their own generation of transition and a future as yet unknown. But this we know: there will be a Judaism, and it will be an ornament to humanity. My grandchildren, David and Amy, to whom I dedicate this work, are its representatives.

I wish to express my thanks to the Jewish Publication Society of America for permitting me to quote from: *The Torah—The Five Books of Moses* (Philadelphia, 1962); *The Book of Isaiah: A New Translation* (Philadelphia, 1973); *The Book of Psalms; A New Translation* (Philadelphia, 1972); and *The Holy Scriptures* (Philadelphia, 1917). Whenever the translation deviates from theirs, it is my own, chosen usually to clarify a point of interpretation.

I am grateful to The Jewish Reconstructionist Foundation for permitting me to quote from Mordecai M. Kaplan's *Questions Jews Ask* (New York, 1956).

My special appreciation is expressed to my publisher, Jacob Behrman, who invited me to write this book and gave me the benefit of his knowledge and his friendship in its creation. I equally wish to thank all those who have read the manuscript and aided me by their suggestions. The responsibility for its content, its statements—and its errors—is mine.

1

The Covenant
and the
Jewish Way of Life

A t Sinai, God entered into a covenant, *B'rit*, with the people of Israel. *Torah* is the sacred writ of that covenant. Torah tells the story of how our forefathers were admitted into the covenant and how they struggled to construct their lives under it. It brings us into the presence of the prophets, who were granted an immediate vision of the divine and brought God's message to the people, admonishing and rebuking them, comforting them and holding out hope, all in the spirit of the covenant.

But the divine speaks to us directly as well. In Torah we are given *Mitzvot*, commandments. God's voice comes to us directly, and we respond through the act of *Mitzvah*. Every Mitzvah renews the covenant.

In Torah God speaks to us, but in human terms, through language. As human beings, we interpret God's utterance. Torah thus becomes the word of God *and* of man, reflecting human understanding. This understanding varies with times and circumstances. The Rabbis of the Talmud considered themselves authorized by divine mandate to interpret Torah for their times and for the future. They created a tradition which has been followed by untold generations of our people and which is, therefore, holy. But tradition does not absolve us of the obligation to read the eternal Torah ever anew in the human terms of our own time.

The covenant with Israel was not the first God made with His

2 THE COVENANT

creatures. After a cataclysmic flood had destroyed the earth, God made a pact with Noah, the only survivor, and through him with all of humanity:

I now establish My covenant with you and your offspring to come and with every living thing that is with you—birds, cattle, and every wild beast as well. . . . And I will maintain My covenant with you. . . . This is the sign of the covenant that I set between Me and you, and every living creature with you for all ages to come. I have set my bow in the clouds, and it shall serve as a sign of the covenant between Me and the earth. [Gen. 9:9–13]

All of nature and all of mankind stand under this covenant for eternity. Mankind and nature are interrelated; humanity is interrelated. By destroying human beings in war and conflict we destroy ourselves; by violating nature we bring destruction upon the human race. The Jew, therefore, pronounces a blessing when he sees a rainbow.

With the calling of the first Jew, Abraham, a new covenant came into being, initiating the Jew into his function within nature and humanity:

As for Me, this is My covenant with you: you shall be a father of a multitude of nations. . . . I will maintain My covenant between Me and you as an everlasting covenant throughout all times and spaces, to be God to you and your offspring to come. I give the land you sojourn in to you and your offspring to come, all the land of Canaan as an everlasting possession. I will be their God. . . . As for you, you shall keep My covenant, you and your offspring to come, throughout the ages. Such shall be the covenant, which you shall keep, between Me and you and your offspring to follow: every male among you shall be circumcised. [Gen. 17:4–10]

Circumcision is called *B'rit,* covenant. Bearing upon his flesh the seal of the covenant, the Jew knows that he is linked to every other Jew and stands with every other Jew in primordial relation to God.

Finally, superimposed upon the covenant with humanity and the covenant with the single Jew is the covenant made with the people at Sinai, constituting them God's treasured possession, a kingdom of priests and a holy people (Exod. 19:5–6).

SH'MA: AFFIRMATION OF THE COVENANT

As a people, standing under divine covenant, Israel is unique. No nation in the world can claim a similar distinction. Jews are aware of it and affirm it on the Sabbath:

You are One, your Name is One
where else is there on earth

a single tribe like Your people Israel,
one and unique?

The covenant makes us one people linked to the One God. We exist because God exists; we are one because God is One. Our being and our survival rest on the love of God, and this love commits us to love Him in return. This awareness and commitment are expressed in the great affirmation of our faith:

Sh'ma Yisrael: Adonai Elohenu Adonai Ehad! [Deut. 6:4]
   Barukh Shem Kevod Malkhuto le-olam va-ed!
Hear O Israel: The Lord our God, the Lord is One!
Blessed be His glorious Kingdom for ever and ever![1]
Love you then the Lord your God
with all your heart, with all your soul, with all your might!
Take to heart these words, which I command you this day,
impress them upon your children
by speaking about them
when you sit in your home and when you walk by the way,
when you lie down and when you rise up;
bind them as a sign on your hand
and let them serve as frontlets between your eyes,
inscribe them on the doorposts of your house
and upon your gates. [Deut. 6:5–9]

These verses are learned by Jewish children when they begin to speak; they are uttered by Jews with their last breath before they die. They accompany Jews through life, giving form and unity to their existence. They are known by every Jew in every land, have been spoken aloud by untold generations, and have accompanied thousands of martyrs into death. They give unity to the generations.

The first verse expresses our "acceptance of the yoke of the Kingdom of Heaven." God is One and unique. His oneness transcends all other forms of oneness. God's oneness is absolute. He is not composed of parts. There is no other oneness like His, and human beings cannot fathom it.

God's oneness guarantees the oneness of creation and hence the covenant with creation. Fashioned by the word of the One God, nature is an organism, each part in tune with every other part, each dependent on the next, the whole permeated by divinely ordained harmony. One law guides the entire cosmos.

Human society stands under one law. Ethics and nature are bound together. Any failure in human ethical conduct harms nature. Were it not so, the world could not exist.

If nature and society are to endure and prosper, human beings

---

[1]The passage "Blessed be His glorious Kingdom" is not in the Torah text, but is inserted in prayer.

The beginnings of both the covenant and the Jewish way of life are found in Torah. The Torah scroll used in the synagogue ritual is written by a scribe following carefully proscribed instructions. It is read aloud to the congregation to indicate that Torah belongs to all who give ear to it.

must base their lives on the awareness of God's oneness. We must place ourselves under "the yoke of His Kingdom." In pronouncing *Sh'ma Yisrael,* Jews affirm that they are conscious of this everlasting truth. In adding *Barukh Shem,* they declare that they understand it and that they will be guided by it in thought and action.

Traditionally, Jews cover their eyes as they recite *Sh'ma,* stretching out the word *ehad* in prolonged contemplation of God's oneness. Then they open their eyes, stepping out into the world as God's co-workers. In the following verses they are called upon to accept "the yoke of Mitzvot," as they stride open-eyed through life.

LOVE YOU THEN THE LORD YOUR GOD! This is the first Mitzvah. But love cannot be commanded; it springs from the heart. The command to love God is, in fact, a plea: as I love you, so love Me in return! The character of all Mitzvot has thus been established. The "yoke of Mitzvot" is not a burden, but an expression of mutual love. The Rabbis explain (Berakhot 54a):

WITH ALL YOUR HEART. Perform the Mitzvah wholeheartedly, with every one of your human drives and desires.

WITH ALL YOUR SOUL. Life must be totally dedicated to Mitzvah and, if need be, surrendered in martyrdom for His Name.

Rabbi Akiva, who openly defied the Roman interdict against the study and practice of Torah, became a martyr. The Romans tore his flesh from his body with iron hooks. Akiva smiled. "Should I not rejoice?" he asked his terrified disciples. "God has permitted me to serve Him with my soul, my very life" (Yerushalmi Berakhot 9:7). Millions of Jews throughout history have followed Rabbi Akiva,

4

and in his spirit have given their lives for the sanctification of His Name.

WITH ALL YOUR MIGHT. We must serve with every ounce of strength, with all the capacities of body and mind. We must equally serve Him with our worldly goods and possessions.

IMPRESS THEM UPON YOUR CHILDREN. Here sounds the call to education. Study of Torah is a form of worship, for Torah reveals the covenant. The child is to be initiated from the earliest age. Thus Jews have come to love learning (Sifri).

WHEN YOU SIT IN YOUR HOME AND WHEN YOU WALK BY THE WAY. The home is the fountainhead of Judaism. There are no "vacations" from Jewishness (see Berakhot 11a).

At times, Jews have been "at home" in their land; all too often they have been forced to "walk by the way," homeless and driven. Wherever their lot was cast, by impressing these words upon their children they have survived.

WHEN YOU LIE DOWN. This is the source of evening worship, which centers about the Sh'ma. It makes an end to the day's work and sanctifies the night's rest.

WHEN YOU RISE UP. This is the source of morning worship, which also centers about the Sh'ma. It places the day under God's command (Berakhot 2b).

BIND THEM FOR A SIGN UPON YOUR HAND. The hand is the instrument of action; it must be guided by. God's directive. This injunction is also the source of the rite of *Tefillin shel Yad*, the phylactery wrapped about arm and hand.

LET THEM SERVE AS FRONTLETS BETWEEN YOUR EYES. Our vision is to be synchronized with God's vision. This is also the source of the rite of *Tefillin shel Rosh*, the phylactery placed on the head (see Menahot 36–37).

INSCRIBE THEM ON THE DOORPOSTS OF YOUR HOUSE AND UPON YOUR GATES. The home and all its rooms are to be a sanctuary. The words spoken in it and the transactions performed in it must reflect an awareness of God's presence. This commandment is also the

The ceremony of dedicating a Jewish dwelling is not complete without the affixing of a Mezuzah. The Mezuzah is hung in a slanting position as a sign of respect for two great sages of the Middle Ages. One argued that it should be affixed vertically, while the other held that it must be horizontal.

source of the rite of *Mezuzah,* the scroll at the doorpost (see Menahot 34).

Sh'ma proclaims the covenant between God and man, between body and soul and mind and heart, between life at home and life in society, between parents and children, between the material and the spiritual. Under God's love, all become one.

THE CHARACTER OF THE JEWISH PEOPLE

We are a people and a faith, and both elements form an organic unit. The people have fashioned the faith, and the faith has sustained the people. This has been very difficult for non-Jews to understand, even those of goodwill. Most non-Jews can grasp the idea of Judaism as a *religion,* but cannot place peoplehood within the framework of theology. Yet the Jewish religion and Jewish peoplehood are one and inseparable.

In other faiths, separation from the church and its obligations cuts the bond to the community of the faithful; in Judaism, the neglect or even the denial of religion does not place a Jew outside the bounds of the people. There are many Jews who are not religious but who are committed to the survival of the Jewish people. Though lacking an essential element of Judaism, they are Jews. They remain members of the community of Israel.

During the Middle Ages, Jews *were* regarded as a nation. But with the Emancipation of the eighteenth century, it seemed to many legislators that Jews in western Europe were to be given civil rights and be made citizens of their respective countries only if they ceased to regard themselves as a people. "We will give everything to the individual Jew, nothing to the people," was the principle proclaimed in the French Assembly. Judaism was to become a religion only; synagogue, simply another "church." There were many Jews who were eager to embrace this doctrine. Equality in society was the goal for which they had yearned; and now that it had come, after centuries of oppression, the forms of Jewish life and worship could adjust themselves to meet the new social realities.

In eastern Europe there was no emancipation for Jews. During the nineteenth century, persecution continued and even increased. Some Jews came to the conclusion that "autoemancipation," as one thinker, Leo Pinsker, called it, was the only way to freedom. Jews must redeem *themselves*—as a people—and return to the promised land of their fathers. The Zionist appeal came to grip both the religious and those who, although not religious, were filled with the spirit of social justice implanted in Jews by the message of the prophets and proclaimed to the modern world by the ideals of liberal democracy and socialism.

The nineteenth century thus witnessed a divergence of roads in Judaism.

IN THE WEST.   The religious aspect of Judaism came to be stressed in the West; peoplehood receded into the background. And the Jewish religion itself came to be perceived in a variety of ways, giving rise to the forms and denominations familiar to us today.

IN THE EAST.   The bulk of Jewry remained in the embrace of Orthodoxy in the East, but within Orthodoxy some groups held that the work of redeeming Zion was permitted and desirable, whereas others maintained that only the Messiah could bring about the return of the Jews to *Eretz Yisrael.* Or again, one segment within Orthodoxy emphasized the study of Torah through logic and rational analysis, whereas another emphasized the mystical element in Judaism and redemption through living. Beyond Orthodoxy stood the adherents of *Haskalah,* or Enlightenment; many of them were deeply influenced by socialist ideology and fired by the desire to rebuild Israel, both as a sovereign people and as a sovereign state. From this group came the founders of modern Israel, men like David Ben-Gurion.

With all their divergent streams and internal differences, it can still be said that until the contemporary era the main distinction between eastern and western Jewry is that eastern Jewry unitedly upheld the idea of Jewish peoplehood, whereas western Jewry saw in Judaism primarily a religious experience. Under the impact of Zionism and, above all, the Holocaust, these divergent forces have begun to converge again. Religion and peoplehood have come to be fused once more.

VARIETIES OF JUDAISM

The Foundations of Normative Judaism

Traditionally, Judaism sees its origin in the revelation at Sinai. Torah is the foundation of doctrine, observances, and customs. We have the "written Torah," found in Hebrew Scriptures, and the "oral Torah," eventually laid down in the Talmud. An unbroken chain of tradition links Sinai to the Talmudic masters:

Moses received the Torah at Sinai, transmitted it to Joshua, Joshua to the elders, the elders to the prophets, and the prophets transmitted it to the men of the Great Assembly [the first great College of Rabbis]. [Avot. 1:1]

The Talmudic masters wrought a great reformation. They read ever new meanings into the written word and drew conclusions that were to affect the totality of Jewish faith and life. A *Midrash* states:

God brought Moses into the Academy of Rabbi Akiva. Moses sat at the end of the eighteen rows of the academy. He did not know what they were talking about, and his strength failed him. As Akiva arrived at a specific conclusion, his disciples asked him: "Whence do you know this?" He replied: "It was given to Moses at Sinai." When Moses heard this, his mind found peace [Menahot 29b].

It was indeed Moses' Torah, the word of Sinai, but translated into new meanings and new Mitzvot. The Rabbis wished to protect the people and the Torah; they wished to "build a fence around the Torah" so that it might never be violated. They succeeded in preserving Torah, and, through it, the Jewish people.

Throughout the millennia, Jews have studied Torah and followed its precepts. Next to the written word, the ordinances of the early masters carried great weight; those of their followers in history were of lesser, but still significant, prestige. It was believed that each generation of interpreters held less authority than its ancestors, being further removed from the Sinaitic source. The decisions of the earlier Rabbis could not be overruled, as only an assembly "greater in numbers and greater in wisdom" would have that power. Our own generation has no right, therefore, to tamper with the ordinances of the Rabbis.

The laws of Torah and the ordinances of the Rabbis form the Jewish way of life. They are Halakhah. Over the centuries they have been codified more than once, but above all in the *Shulhan Arukh* of Rabbi Joseph Karo (1488–1575), a work that has remained *the* guide for traditional Jewry. In addition, customs adopted by all of Israel or by individual communities have come to acquire the force of law. They are called *Minhagim* (plural of *Minhag*).

Thus protected, the Jew found historic stability. Every facet of life was minutely regulated within the covenant. Jewish destiny was seen as divinely ordained. God's reward for faithful performance was assured. The rebellious or neglectful Jew might expect divine retribution. The Jewish people would be redeemed and return home in the Messianic age.

One early codification of Jewish law was undertaken by Moses Maimonides. This fourteen-volume work, *Mishneh Torah* (Repetition of Torah), became the basis for over four hundred commentaries since its publication in 1180. The illustration shows one of many diagrammatic pages from a fifteenth-century Italian edition.

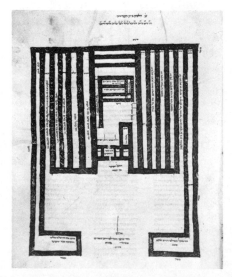

Orthodoxy

Orthodox Jews are guided by these principles. As in days gone by, they are protected by a strong spiritual bulwark against a hostile world and uplifted by the awareness that they dwell within God's presence.

When, in the period of the Emancipation, the outside world began to intrude and the power of the rabbinic leadership to enforce obedience was reduced, a German rabbi, Samson Raphael Hirsch (1808–1888), attempted a new interpretation that would leave Halakhah intact while allowing and even bidding Jews to immerse themselves in Western culture. Fearful that contact with Jews of other convictions might contaminate the Orthodox, Hirsch called for complete separation from non-Orthodox Jewish society and its institutions. At the same time, he undertook to synthesize Jewish tradition and modern insights. He created Neo-Orthodoxy, according to which Jews may contribute fully to the life of society without compromising Torah in the slightest.

In the United States, the prime center of Neo-Orthodoxy is the Rabbinical School of Yeshivah University. But there are other forms of Orthodoxy and other academies that transmit the ancient forms of Jewish tradition. A special place may be accorded to the Lubavitcher Rebbe, a great Hasidic leader who has developed a chain of schools fusing secular and Jewish knowledge and has set up student centers at numerous universities to reveal to all Jews the emotional appeal of Orthodox observance.

Fundamentally, Orthodoxy can make no basic concessions to modernity, nor can it recognize other forms of Judaism as legitimate.

Reform

With the Emancipation, the pull of the outside world became irresistible for many Jews. Leaders of western Jewry, therefore, came to believe that if Judaism were to retain its strength and its appeal for a new generation, it had to be reformed. To do so, they believed, was consonant with the idea of a living Torah, placed ever anew in the hands of Jews.

For the leaders of Reform, Jews were divinely called to be teachers of ethics, a life force for humanity. Here was the relevance of Judaism for all time. Halakhah was seen as a teaching tool and guideline. It brought to mind the function of the Jew in the world, but it was not binding. Observance of Halakhah was a matter of individual conscience.

In Germany, Reform was urged upon the Jews by various state and local governments as a means of acculturating them and perhaps in the hope that it would become a stepping-stone to conversion. Actually, it kept many within the Jewish fold.

But there were dangers. To many Jews, Reform offered an excuse for casting off the yoke of Torah. Resting on reason, its forms of worship often became cold and emotionless. Many of its original leaders, caught up in the spirit of the times, went so far as to deny the concept of Jewish peoplehood.

But today's Reform has once again reformed itself. It has long since embraced Zionism. It has sought to recapture the mystical elements in Jewish tradition, has called for ever greater observance, and has stressed the Hebrew language. The individual freedom it promises is the freedom to become increasingly dedicated to Judaism as a way of life.

In America, the original center of Reform was in Cincinnati, where many German Jews had settled. Here was established the Hebrew Union College, Reform's institution for the training of rabbis; as the scope of Reform Judaism has widened, new campuses have been opened in New York, Los Angeles, and finally Jerusalem.

Conservatism

Conservative Judaism also emerged in Germany and gained wide allegiance among the German Jews for whom Reform was generally too radical. It rests on the principle of "positive historical Judaism." Traditional values, including Halakhah, must be preserved. In Halakhah the divine is present. At the same time, the forces of history that operate within the people must be permitted to exert their influence. God and the people interact, and God gives assent to those changes that emerge from the consent of the Jewish people in its historical setting. Halakhah is to be read ever anew, with deepest reverence and consideration, but the people are the key to Jewish living.

Conservatism thus stands between Orthodoxy and Reform. While affirming the binding authority of Halakhah, Conservatism equally stresses Halakhah's ever-changing and evolving character. Internally, however, Conservatism has been the arena of many controversies. The main issue has been this: which is the authentic voice of the Jewish people? The synthesis between tradition and modern life is difficult to achieve. Even the rabbinical committee entrusted with the issues of Halakhah has not always succeeded in resolving problems satisfactorily. Unless a decision is unanimous, Conservative Jews at large may follow either the majority or the minority opinion, and this has resulted in a variety of practices among Conservative congregations.

Conservatism's greatest success has been in the United States, where its philosophy of adjustment and evolution seems to reflect the pragmatic spirit of America. Its fountainhead is the Jewish Theological Seminary of America at New York, with a branch, the University of Judaism, at Los Angeles and another branch in Jerusalem.

Reconstructionism

Diaspora Jewry lives in two civilizations, its own and that of the world of which it is a part. Orthodoxy once strove for centuries to erect a wall of separation between them; Reform once accepted the world and declared Judaism a mere religion, not a civilization at all. Reconstructionism attempts a synthesis, by seeing the *people* as creator of its religion and culture.

The movement originated in America and was fashioned by one of the towering personalities of our age, Mordecai M. Kaplan. Kaplan's starting point is the idea of Jewish peoplehood. As a people, we are endowed with a collective spirit, as are all the peoples of the world. The uniqueness of the Jewish spirit found historical expression in ethical religion and in the striving for ethical nationhood. As a people, the Jews developed a civilization that evolves in history. Judaism is "an evolving religious civilization," rooted in religion and including language, literature, art, folkways, even cuisine.

The Jews for Kaplan are not a chosen people, but they do constitute one organic unit, whatever their place of residence and citizenship. Israel is the hub of a wheel; Diaspora Jewry is its rim. Ethics, religion, and culture are the spokes, linking the two in mutual interaction.

Out of their collective spirit, the Jews found God, not a person, but a "transnatural power," which pulls us upward from the world and society as it is toward a world and society that "ought to be." The Mitzvot, fashioned by Israel's collective "élan vital," acquire through it a divine character. They are seen as *sancta*, holy symbols that make our task manifest. Therefore, they have to be reinterpreted. The Sabbath becomes a living call to justice, symbol of the right of every person to equal rest and renewal and to a life of rewarded labor and dignity. Those Mitzvot that no longer hold meaning serve no purpose. Jewish law has to be brought in tune with the ethical standards of our time.

Samson Raphael Hirsch (1808-1888), father of Neo-Orthodoxy.

Reconstructionism, which began as a school of thought rather than of "denomination," has nevertheless exerted a great influence upon non-Orthodox Jewry. Eventually, it grew into a "denomination" with headquarters in New York; its Rabbinical College is in Philadelphia, and it has membership congregations all over the United States and in foreign countries.

Interaction

In spite of its divisions, Judaism is one. Marriages between members of different Jewish "denominations" are common and legitimate. Actually, none of the varieties of Jewish thought exists in pure form. Conservative congregations may be closer to Orthodoxy or to Reform; Reform congregations may be very liberal or lean toward Conservatism. With changing membership, the character of a congregation may itself undergo change. Rabbinical bodies encompassing rabbis from all schools are common on local or regional levels.

The Nonreligious Jew

Jews affirm their Jewishness in nonreligious ways as well. Secular Zionists, nonreligious Hebrew scholars and educators, philanthropists or professional Jewish social workers who do not belong to congregations—all affirm an attachment to the Jewish people and a dedication to its survival. Many young Jews, in addition, have rendered enthusiastic service to social causes without knowing that their idealism derives from the wellsprings of Judaism.

Unfortunately, a number of young Jews, in search of meaning, have looked outside Judaism, often in religious organizations that are hostile to Jews and Jewish teachings. Those who regard themselves as committed Jews must assume a certain guilt in this development and must redouble their efforts to transmit to our children the spiritual beauty of the Jewish heritage. Only Jewish living has the power to hold future generations within Judaism.

2

Synagogue
and Home:
Two Focal Points

Jewish life revolves about two focal points, synagogue
and home.

The Torah states:

And let them make Me a sanctuary, and I shall dwell in their midst.
[Exod. 25:8]

The sanctuary bears physical witness to Jewish settlement in a
given environment. The Tent of Meeting that was built in the desert
was a temporary structure that could be dismantled when the people
moved on the road to their land. Only in the days of King Solomon,
when Israel dwelt secure, was a permanent temple erected. The
destruction of the First and Second Temples initiated a long period
of wandering that would only come to an end—as the people firmly
held—when a new Temple once again sanctified Israel's hallowed
place of inheritance forever. Synagogues built over the centuries in
many lands signified the people's expectation that they might dwell
secure there for long periods of time; but again and again these
synagogues were destroyed. Jews had to realize that no mere *place*
would ensure their survival. God, dwelling in "their" midst, gave
this assurance. He dwells in the family.

The family, existing in *time,* was indestructible. Refugees fortunate enough to escape with their families found strength in together-
ness and rekindled the spirit of Judaism in many lands, transplanting

13

The Venice Synagogue, an Italian Jewish work of art
dating from the seventeenth century.

it even to those countries where few Jews had existed before. Even
the Land of Israel was revived through the spirit of the family, the
spirit that imparts eternal life to our people.

THE SYNAGOGUE: FOCAL POINT IN SPACE

The synagogue announces to the world at large the Jewish desire
to proclaim the heritage of Judaism and to claim for it recognition
and respect. In antiquity, the Jewish house of worship was called by
the Greek word *proseuche,* whereas the term *synagogue* stood for
"congregation," the people who assembled in it. A structure has no
meaning, no name, until the people make it the center of their lives.

The synagogue is a forceful reminder that Jews are a covenanted
people. Individual piety by itself is insufficient, unless and until it
finds expression in community.

The house of worship is one of the gifts of Judaism to humanity.
The temples of antiquity, including the Temple at Jerusalem, were
conceived as dwelling places of divinity; they were small and incapable of holding large gatherings of people within their walls.
The people remained in the courts; only the priests entered the
holy precincts. The synagogue, as created by the Jews during the
Babylonian exile (sixth century B.C.E.), was the house of God *and*
man, a place of assembly for the people in the presence of God. All
other religions have copied this idea.

14

The synagogue has never been called the "House of God"—for who can contain God in an earthly abode?

The heaven is My throne
and the earth is My footstool:
what kind of house could you build for Me,
what place could serve as My abode? [Isa. 66:1]

The synagogue, rather, has been called *Bet Ha-Knesset,* house of assembly; *Bet Ha-Midrash,* house of study; *Bet Am,* the people's house. Early Reform chose the term *temple* for its synagogues. It wished to indicate by this choice that the yearning for *the* Temple in Jerusalem had been stilled by the Emancipation and that Jews could proclaim the land of their citizenship to be their everlasting homeland. This enthusiasm proved to be premature and mistaken, but the name *temple* stuck, and it is used today interchangeably with the term *synagogue.*

The ancient Temple consisted of three sections. The *Courts* were set aside for the people. Here they watched the priests in the performance of their sacred rites before the great altar that stood in the open. The *Sanctuary,* hidden from the people, held the seven-branched candelabrum with its eternal lights; an altar, upon which incense was offered; and a table with the twelve loaves of shew-bread, representing the twelve tribes of Israel. The priests performed their sacred office in solitude. The *Holy of Holies* was separated from the Sanctuary by a curtain. In it rested the Ark with the tablets of the Ten Commandments, and, according to the Rabbis, a scroll of Torah. At the time of the destruction of the First Temple, the Ark was hidden away and never recovered. During the period of the Second Temple, the Holy of Holies was empty. Only God's *Shekhinah,* His Presence, dwelt there. Not even the priests were permitted to enter, except for the High Priest, who stepped behind the curtain once a year on Yom Kippur to express in symbolic rites the people's allegiance to God.

Today's synagogue follows the structural pattern of the Temple and is divided into three sections. The *auditorium* corresponds to the *Courts,* the people's place of gathering. The *Bimah,* or pulpit, corresponds to the *Sanctuary.* Here an eternal light is kept alive—not a seven-branched candelabrum as in the Temple, but a simple lamp symbolizing that the light of Torah will never be extinguished and also that the synagogue is always lit to receive worshipers or learners. The *Holy Ark* corresponds to the *Holy of Holies.* Here the Scrolls of Torah, Israel's holiest possession, are kept. In many synagogues, a curtain separates the Ark from the rest of the building.

A synagogue must have windows: it is not a retreat from life, but a retreat for the sake of life. The ancient Temple had windows so constructed that, symbolically, its light poured unto the outside world. The ancient Temple rested on the top of a mountain, visible throughout the city of Jerusalem. The Rabbis, therefore, ruled that a local synagogue must be higher than all the other buildings in town. This, however, was frequently forbidden by non-Jewish authorities during the Middle Ages. If synagogues were permitted at all, they had to be humble and inconspicuous. Jews then used to place a pole, crowned by a six-pointed star, on the roof of their synagogue, to give it at least symbolic height.

There are several variations to indicate that the synagogue is *not* identical with the Temple.

The Temple at Jerusalem faced toward the West: Israel did not worship the sun that arose daily in the East, but rather offered homage and petition to the sun's Creator (see Sukkah 51b). Our synagogues, however, face toward Jerusalem, which in Western countries means that they face East. The prayers of all the people are thus gathered in at the hub of its being to be offered to God as one great prayer.

On entering the vestibule of a traditional synagogue, visitors will find a pitcher and washbasin for pouring water over their hands. Physically purifying themselves, they are reminded of their duty to be pure in conduct.

Who may ascend the mountain of the Lord?
Who may stand in His holy place?
He, who has clean hands and a pure heart. . . .
[Ps. 24:3–4]

One or several steps then lead down into the sanctuary proper. "Out of the depths I call you, O Lord . . ." (Ps. 130:1ff). There the visitor's eye is guided toward the eastern wall. Here the Ark rises, reached by steps. Before it glows the eternal light.

Below the Ark and level with the auditorium, we find the reader's desk, facing the Ark. The cantor, or leader of the service, is not an officiant, bringing the sacraments of God to the people; he is one of them; he is *Shaliah Tzibbur*—Messenger of the Congregation.

The traditional synagogue has a *Bimah*, a large pulpit, in the center of the room. It is raised by several steps. Here the Torah is read, with the scroll solemnly carried from the Ark to the Bimah before the reading and afterward returned to the Ark. The people gather around Torah, as they did once at Sinai.

The main sanctuary is reserved for the male members. The women sit in a balcony and are separated by a veil, a *Mehitzah* (division). It is entered by a separate door.

Judaism has no ordinances regulating the style of the synagogue building. Synagogues thus mirror the style of their periods. They were often designed by Christian architects, because Jews were

Folk arts such as woodcarving were often reflected in the synagogue building and its appurtenances. This wooden Holy Ark was crafted in Germany, c. 1760.

excluded from the guilds. Old eastern European synagogues, especially those made of wood, reflect the folk art of the people. In more recent times, many synagogues were built in Moorish style to set them apart from Christian houses of worship. Contemporary synagogues frequently exhibit the most daring modern style.

Modifications have also occurred within the sanctuary proper. In non-Orthodox congregations, the Bimah has been removed from the center of the auditorium and placed in front of the Ark. From an elevated platform, rabbi and cantor face the congregation. Here, too, we find the seats of the officiants and elders, the nine-branched Hanukah menorah, perhaps a seven-branched menorah, age-old symbol of the Jewish people, and the American and Israeli flags. Some synagogues feature two pulpits, one for the reading of Torah, the other for the liturgy.

Practically all non-Orthodox synagogues have found it desirable to seat men and women together and have eliminated the balcony. In the vestibule of contemporary synagogues, sometimes in the sanctuary itself, memorial tablets for departed members may be found and also a perpetual memorial to the six million who perished in the Holocaust.

Even the best-designed synagogue is never completed. New curtains, pulpit covers, Torah mantles and ornaments, menorahs, stained glass windows, wall designs, kiddush cups, and other needed appurtenances will give the house of God an ever new aspect and will become doubly precious as expressions of the people's dedication.

In many synagogues, an inscription over the Ark speaks clearly, though with silent voice:

Know before Whom you stand!

17

Jews have always felt at home in the synagogue and in the presence of their Father in Heaven, but this familiarity has at the same time been tempered by reverence and awe. Such is the balance struck by the synagogue, the focal point of Jewish life in space.

The Congregation

Traditionally, public worship requires a *Minyan,* a quorum of ten. If the quorum is present, the locale does not matter.

In Orthodoxy, only men are included in the Minyan. In Conservative Judaism, women may be included if the individual congregation so resolves. Reform does not require a Minyan for public worship (see Chapter 26). The Talmud requires a Minyan for all "holiness acts" (Berakhot 21b, Megillah 23b).

Only in the presence of a Minyan may Torah be read publicly, may *Kaddish* be recited, and may the sanctification, *Kedushah,* be pronounced: "Holy, Holy, Holy is the Lord of Host, the whole earth is full of His glory." God is fully hallowed only in the assembly of the people.

Individual prayer is, of course, commanded in Judaism, but communal prayer opens up a new dimension: it reflects the covenant of peoplehood. The Jews were the first in history to institute communal prayer. Before praying for himself or herself, the Jew prays for his or her people, for humanity. Communal prayer gives strength and solidarity.

Traditionally, the congregation assembles three times every day: in the morning for *Shaharit,* the morning worship; in the afternoon for *Minhah;* at nightfall for *Maariv,* the evening prayer.

The Sacred Scroll

The scroll of the Torah rests in its Ark, clothed in a precious mantle of silk or velvet. The poles, to which the parchment is attached on both ends, are taller than the scroll itself and may be adorned with crowns. The poles provide the handles for rolling the parchment. Some scrolls bear a breastplate and a pointer, both suspended by a chain placed about the poles, and crowns placed on the poles.

The scroll is holy because it contains the word of God. It links us to our past and makes manifest the covenant. The text may, therefore, never be changed. A group of Rabbis once counted every word, every paragraph, even every letter in it, to make sure there would be no errors or variations in the future; the text has never changed since.

Writing a Torah is a sacred occupation, requiring a highly knowledgeable and skilled scribe, a *Sofer,* who usually dedicates his entire life to this calling. He uses a special parchment, made from *kasher* animals, a special quill, made of goose feathers or turkey feathers, and special vegetable ink, which he prepares himself. He follows precise guidelines, setting down each letter in its exact, prescribed form. Some letters have little "crowns" on them; others do not; occasionally, a letter is larger or smaller than its neighbors.

The Sofer must write in a spirit of holy intent. As he sets to work, he proclaims: "I am writing with the holy intent of writing a Torah." He must be extremely careful that each letter fully stands on its own. If he makes a mistake, he may erase it with a small penknife; but he may never erase the Name of God once it has been written.

Because the writing "sits" on the parchment and the ink does not penetrate, letters may in time become chipped. This makes the scroll *patul*, unusable, until the letter is repaired. Similarly, if we were to touch the parchment, the moisture of our finger might lead to a smear, which would again make the Torah *patul*. For this reason and out of respect, the reader of the Torah uses a pointer, a long staff ending in a little hand with an extended index finger, to guide him in his reading. It is called *Yad*—hand—and is usually fashioned of silver.

The various Torah ornaments are not mandatory, but depend on the means of the congregation. The Torah crowns are purely ornamental, meant to signify that the Torah is for us our crowning possession. The breastplate, on the other hand, has a useful function. If a community has more than one scroll, each can be rolled ahead of time to the special section to be recited on those occasions when a special passage is read from the Torah. In order to know at a glance where a scroll has been set, we place a breastplate on it with a little window, in which we insert a silver tablet telling us the occasion for which the scroll has been set.

A Torah crown fashioned in Germany, 1771. Ancient Jewish sources speak of the "crown of Torah" figuratively, to mean the respect that accrues to a worthy student.

Although these ornaments may be fashioned of any material, we do not use gold. Gold once led the people into defection; it was the material of the golden calf.

Taking off the Torah mantle, we find a wrapper that holds the scroll together. In days gone by Jews used to fashion this wrapper out of the swaddling cloth on which a boy rested at his circumcision. It would be washed and cut into lengthy strips that were then sewed together, with the name of the child and his birthday embroidered on it, and the following inscription: May he grow up to Torah, a worthy marriage, and good deeds.

When the scroll is solemnly taken out of the Ark and carried to the Bimah and later returned, the congregation stands. By pious custom, many will kiss its mantle as it passes by. The act expresses not just the love for the scroll itself, but love for its message, for what is in it. When a scroll is dropped by accident, everyone who witnesses it must fast in penitence.

When a Torah gets so worn out that it can no longer be repaired, it is placed in a clay container and laid to rest in a Jewish cemetery. Very pious persons may be honored by having a Torah scroll buried with them.

A Torah should be transported from one place to another only if necessary and only with an escort of at least two people.

The Reading of Torah

Torah is publicly read at the morning and afternoon services of every Sabbath and Fast Day, including Yom Kippur; it is also recited during the morning service of every festival and half-holiday, on Hanukkah and Purim, on Rosh Hodesh, and on every Monday and Thursday. According to the Talmud, Torah reading on Sabbath and festival morning was instituted by Moses (Jer. Megillah 4:5).

As those called to honor the Torah look on, the reader chants a passage from the scroll. The Yad, or pointer, is held gently so as not to chip the ink of the letters while moving back and forth across the surface of the parchment.

The appointed portion is divided into sections, *Parshiot.* For each section a member of the congregation is "called up," receives an *Aliyah,* is an *Oleh.* This member recites a blessing, follows the reading from the scroll, and offers a second blessing as the reading comes to its close.

The sanctity of a festival determines the number of people called up. The Sabbath is Judaism's holiest day: seven people are called to the Torah; on Yom Kippur, six people are called; on the festivals, five; on half-festivals and Rosh Hodesh, four; on fast days, weekdays, and afternoon services, three members are given the honor.

During the reading, an elder stands at the left of the recitant, the Oleh at his right. On completing his final blessing, the Oleh remains on the Bimah until the following Oleh has completed *his* final blessing. In many congregations, a benediction is pronounced over the Oleh, and he may request additional benedictions for his family and friends. As this procedure can protract the reading period, it has been eliminated in many communities.

Traditionally, a Kohen is called first, followed by a Levi, thus honoring the descendants of the priestly family and of the Levites, who assisted them in the sanctuary. A Yisrael is third. If there is no Kohen present, anybody may go first; a Levi may receive this Aliyah, but may not be called after a common Yisrael. If there is no Levi present, the Kohen is called twice (Gittin 59a,b). Many non-Orthodox congregations have done away with this practice, and some also call women to the Torah and permit them to act as readers; in Orthodox communities only men receive the honor. Reform has greatly shortened the length of the portions read and, until recently, did not call members to the Torah; the ancient practice is gradually being reinstated.

It was ancient practice to have a translator standing next to the reader. This *Meturgaman* immediately rendered each verse in the idiom spoken by the people. The rabbi would also interpret the lesson. This Jewish practice is the origin of the *sermon* in all Western religions.

On being called by his Hebrew name, the member hurries to the Bimah and there invites the congregation to join him in praising God:

Ba-re-khu et Adonai ha-me-vorakh!
Bless the Lord who is to be blessed.

The congregation responds:

Barukh Adonai ha-me-vo-rakh le-o-lam va-ed!
Blessed be the Lord, who is to be blessed for all eternity!

The blessing follows:

Barukh attah Adonai Elohenu Melekh ha-olam, asher bahar ba-nu mi-kol ha-a mim, ve-na-tan la-nu et Torato, Barukh attah Adonai No-ten ha-To-rah.
Blessed are You, Lord, our God, Ruler of the universe He, who has chosen us from all peoples by giving us His Torah. Blessed are You, Lord, Giver of Torah.

Now the portion is read. At its conclusion, the recipient of the reading speaks the second blessing:

Barukh attah Adonai Elohenu Melekh ha-olam, asher na-tan la-nu Torat emet, ve-ha-ye o-lam na-ta be-to-khe-nu, Barukh attah Adonai Noten ha-Torah.
Blessed are You, Lord our God, Ruler of the universe, He who has given us a Torah of truth, thus implanting within us eternal life. Blessed are You, Lord, Giver of Torah.

The cycle of Torah reading begins in the fall, right after the festivals, and concludes in the fall, on Simhat Torah. Some congregations follow a triennial cycle to shorten the weekly readings; in doing so, they follow the practice of ancient Palestinian Jewry, whereas Babylonian Jewry adopted the annual cycle. Reform Jewry reads only short selections from each week's portion.

The Torah reading of Sabbath afternoon (claimed by the Talmud to have been ordained by Ezra, Jer. Megillah 4:5) is taken from the portion to be read during the morning Sabbath service of the following week, thus linking week to week.

Mondays and Thursdays used to be market days in ancient Israel, when the farmers brought their produce to the city. In their behalf, a portion of the coming week's section was read on these two weekdays. The custom, also ascribed to Ezra, has remained intact.

The Haftarah

On Sabbaths and other days of feasting and fasting, a portion, the *Haftarah,* taken from the Biblical books of the Prophets, is added to the reading from the scroll. The Haftarah is keyed in content to the message received in Torah.

The person who will recite the Haftarah is first called up to Torah. A portion of Torah is read to him, and he recites the blessings. Then the scroll is rolled up, and he reads the prophetic section of the day, together with the blessings that precede and follow it.

Sing unto the Lord

Torah and Haftarah are not simply declaimed; they are rendered in a form of recitative, following exact musical notations. Each has its own *trop,* or tune. This recitative may be the oldest form of liturgical music still in use. The Gregorian chant of the Catholic church derives from it, at least in part.

In the Torah scroll we find neither vocalization, nor punctuation, nor musical annotations. The reader must know these by heart.

Jews have always been a singing people. The Rabbis state:

Song in worship is ordained in Torah. [Arakhin 11a] He who sings unto God in this world will be permitted to do so in the world to come. In the days to come, all prophets jointly will sing a song to Him. [Sanhedrin 91b]

When Israel sang a song at their deliverance from Pharaoh's host at the Sea of Reeds, even the sucklings and the unborn in their mother's wombs raised their voices in praise [Sota 30b–31a].

Modern synagogue music shows the influence of Diaspora cultures and, in particular, the Romantic Movement. In our time, much new music has been composed both in the West and in Israel.

Instrumental music and women's voices are not permitted in Orthodox worship. In Temple days, many instruments gave color to the song, and there is no basic objection to instrumental music from the standpoint of Halakhah. Wind and string instruments may, in fact, be used in Orthodox synagogues on weekdays, for instance, at weddings. But the use of instruments on Sabbath and festivals was forbidden, as a sign of mourning for the Temple; no Jewish worship, it was held, should approximate the glory of worship in the ancient sanctuary. It was also forbidden on the Sabbath and festivals as it might lead to work, such as the repair of a broken string on a violin.

The dance equally played a role in Judaism. In antiquity, young men and women would dance in the vineyards on Yom Kippur and the fifteenth of Av. Dancing seems to have been a passion with Jews during the Middle Ages; each Jewish community had its dance house. But, in time, the segregation of the sexes came to be more pronounced. Orthodoxy prohibits mixed dancing; yet Orthodox men will dance with other men on Simhat Torah, right in the synagogue itself. At Orthodox weddings, men may dance with women, but they may not touch. Each grasps the corner of a handkerchief, which they hold between them.

The synagogue is a center of Jewish life in all its communal facets and expressions: Torah, prayer, study, debate, instruction, festive meals, mournful commemorations, song and dance and lamentation, remembrance and resolve. All who frequent it reap the rewards of life in community.

THE HOME: FOCAL POINT IN TIME

Jewish life is keyed to time. Upon reaching a juncture in time, the Jew pronounces a blessing, *Sheheheyanu*:

Barukh attah Adonai Elohenu Melekh ha-olam, she-he-he-yanu ve-kee-ye-manu ve-hee-gee-anu la-z'man hazin
Blessed are You, Lord our God, You are He who has kept us in life, has sustained us, and has permitted us to reach this moment.

There is no equivalent blessing for being permitted to reach a certain place. On completing a new house and taking possession, the Jew does not offer thanks to God for establishing a dwelling *place* for him, but rather recites Sheheheyanu.

Our home is our school of life. It exists in space and should be a holy enclave in space, but it earns its title of honor through the Jewish spirit that rests in it and is renewed constantly by those who dwell in it. It acquires its distinction by the way the members of the Jewish home shape their times together. The Jewish home makes time live and permits us to live in time that has meaning.

The Unity of Jewish Life

The Jewish day, the week, and, as we shall see, the year and even the lifetime of a Jew are not disconnected units in time. They form a strand of pearls, each valuable, each held to the next in holiness.

Life is a pilgrimage toward *shalom,* peace, perfection. Shalom is a name of God, Who is All-Perfect. Life is striving after God. To a Jew, setting out on a journey, family and friends extend the farewell *lekh le-shalom,* go *toward* shalom (I Sam. 20:42). Only when life's journey has ended, do we send our dear ones off with the wish *lekh be-shalom,* go *in* peace.

The Day: Celebration in Worship

The Jewish day begins with the preceding night:

And there was evening and there was morning, one day. [Gen. 1:5]

Were night to follow day, it would be a mere period of slumber, of emptiness. As it precedes day, it becomes *prologue,* its rest being not merely a pause in our work but a preparation for the tasks to come. Torah commands us, therefore, to affirm God's Oneness "when you lie down *and* when you rise up" (Deut. 6:7; *Sh'ma*). The Sabbath and every Jewish holy day begin with the preceding evening.

The active period of the day begins with dawn. Torah commands us to affirm God "when you rise up." On awakening, the Jew washes himself, gives thanks for restored life and strength, wraps himself in the Tallit, dons the Tefillin, and joins the congregation in prayer. He recites the morning prayer, *Shaharit*.

In the afternoon, the Jew pauses for an accounting of his work so far. The name *Minhah* has been applied to the afternoon worship. As three stars emerge, the time has come for *Maariv*, the evening prayer. A prayer at bedtime concludes the day with a plea for healthy rest and a joyful reawakening. Night is prologue.

Celebration Through Life's Pursuits

Life in the marketplace, the office, or factory must be Jewish in character. Our dealings with each other must be honest, just, and fair. The business hours of the day are moments in time between the hours of daily prayer, between birth and death, between expectation and fulfillment, between toil and redemption from want.

Earning a living is not an easy task; its success depends on God's blessing.

When the earth heard God's words: "I will make for man a helpmate" [Gen. 2:18], it objected with violence: "Lord of Time and Space, how can I possibly feed all the children of man?" God replied: "Let us share the burden, you provide your half, I shall provide mine." [Midrash Hagadol, Bereshit]

Our conduct in the world of work will be conditioned by our total experience of life; the rules governing that conduct will, therefore, be discussed as we deal with the cycle of life. But we should equally be guided by an awareness that, sooner or later, we shall die. We stand in judgment, not only after death, as the Rabbis held, but here and now: have we lived authentic Jewish lives? One proof lies in our dealings with our fellow man.

When men are brought to their divine judgment, each will be asked:
Have you been upright in your business affairs?
Have you set aside fixed times for the study of Torah?
Have you brought children into the world?
Have you been firm in your hope for Messianic redemption?
Have you searched after wisdom?
Have you engaged in study?
If "reverence for God has been your treasure, all is well with you" [Isa. 33:6]; if not, it is not well. [Shabbat 31a]

The guiding principle of Jewish life has been:
In all your ways acknowledge Him
and He will straighten your path. [Prov. 3:6]

We are called upon to celebrate Judaism in even the most worldly of our pursuits.

The Week

As the day has rhythm, so has the week. At *Minhah* on Sabbath we read a section of the next Sabbath's portion in the Torah, linking Sabbath to Sabbath.

Mondays and Thursdays have a special distinction: The Torah is read on these days.

Tuesday is regarded as a day of blessing. On this day during the week of Creation, God *twice* reviewed His work, and twice He expressed divine satisfaction (Gen. 1:10, 12). Tuesday, so uniquely distinguished, is therefore chosen by many Jews as a day for weddings.

Friday, Erev Shabbat, the eve of the Sabbath, is dedicated to preparations for this holiest of days in Jewish life.

3

Symbols
of the Covenant

TALLIT: ROBE OF RESPONSIBILITY

Judaism demands a commitment of the total person: it holds the Jew accountable for thought and action at home and abroad, in the house of worship and in the marketplace. It vests him with total responsibility; the Tallit is the robe of responsibility.

The Lord spoke to Moses saying: Speak to the children of Israel and enjoin them to make for themselves tassels (*Tzitzit*) on the corners of their garments throughout the generations; let them attach a cord of hyacinth-blue to the *Tzitzit* at each corner. That shall be your *Tzitzit;* look at them and recall all the commandments of the Lord and observe them, so that you do not follow your heart and eyes in your lustful urge. Thus you shall be reminded to observe all My Miztvot and be holy to your God. . . . [Num. 15:37–40]

Jews in antiquity commonly wore a four-cornered garment, as do the Bedouins to this day. Torah, therefore, commands that the robe be so fitted with fringes that it may serve as a reminder to its wearer at all times of the presence of God.

Today, we no longer wear four-cornered garments, but we make one for ourselves to wear at worship, hoping that the message emanating from it might be with us in our worldly work as well. Orthodox Jews also wear, underneath their regular clothes, a Tallit Katan, a small Tallit, also called *Arba Kanfot*, a four-cornered garment with Tzitzit.

27

The garb of prayer: Tallit, skullcap, and Tefillin.

A Tallit may be large or small. Some are so large that the worshiper can completely draw the Tallit over his head, to be in seclusion with God. A Tallit can be of any material, in any color; but it must meet two conditions: it must have four corners, and on each of these corners there must be a symbolic tassel, making four Tzitzit. (Ideally, the Tallit should be of wool and the Tzitzit of wool, but, as long as both are of the same material, the Tallit is *kasher.*)

The Tzitzit must be white. They consist of four long strands, looped through a hole in the garment's corner and knotted. In antiquity, by command of Torah, one strand had to be hyacinth-blue. The white stood for purity; the blue, for God's heaven.

From the colors of the Tzitzit the colors of the flag of Israel are derived: white and blue.

But the colors of the Tzitzit confer an additional distinction upon the garment and its wearer: Tallit is the robe of princes. In antiquity, only princes were privileged to wear the "royal blue." "Blue reflects the sky, and the sky resembles the colors of God's throne" (Menahot 43b). Blue is no longer used for Tzitzit—perhaps, as the Rabbis stated, because we no longer have the exact color or perhaps, as Mordecai Kaplan holds, because Rome objected to the wearing of royal blue by commoners.

Reform dispensed with the Tallit, but it is now coming back, at least in the form of a stole worn by the cantor or rabbi. The Tallit is the Jew's steady companion through life. He is to wear it once every day, usually at morning worship, whether at home or at the synagogue. It accompanies the departed in death; he is wrapped in it before being laid to rest, with one thread of one Tzitzah severed, to make it *patul,* signifying that the duty of Tzitzit no longer rests on him. The Tallit is to be worn at daytime only, as Torah rules: "you shall *see* them" by natural light. The reader of the service wears it on nights of holy days as a robe of honor.

Before putting on a Tallit Katan, the pious Jew offers blessing:

Barukh attah Adonai Elohenu Melekh ha-Olam asher kidshanu bemitzvotav vetzivanu al Mitzvat Tzitzit.
Blessed are You, Lord our God, Ruler of the universe.
You are He, Who has sanctified us by His commandments and commanded us regarding the Mitzvah of Tzitzit.

On putting on the Tallit, the Jew holds it at the top between his stretched-out arms. He offers blessing:

Barukh attah . . . vetzivanu le-hil'atef ba-Tzitzit.
Blessed are You . . . He, Who . . . has commanded us to wrap ourselves in Tzitzit.

Now the Tallit is drawn over body and head for a moment; the whole person is wrapped in it. Then it is placed on the shoulders.

As the Tallit is a garment it may not be worn upside down or inside out. Because all four sides look the same, one is given a special band, the *Attarah.* This band must always be on top and outside when the garment is worn. This Attarah is removed when the Tallit is wrapped about the dead.

May women wear a Tallit? Orthodox Jewry does not permit them to do so. Generally, women are freed from all those Mitzvot that call for an act of performance linked to specific times. Because the Tallit is put on as an act of performance and ordained only for the hours of daylight, women are under no obligation to wear it. But we do find in history that women have voluntarily resolved to place themselves under certain obligations. We also know that Rabbi Judah the Prince, the editor of the Mishnah, with his own hands put Tzitzit on his wife's apron (Menahot 43a). There is no basic prohibition against a woman's wearing a Tallit, though later ordinances may have hedged this right with restrictions. (See, however, S'ridei Esh III, 104.)

Making a Tallit or Tallit Katan is not difficult. The garment, of any material or color, must have exactly four corners. After reinforcing these corners, we put a hole in each, about one finger's width from the seam, and hem it. Now we take the four strands of the Tzitzit; one of them will be very long, for it will be wrapped about the others. We put the four strands through the hole, seeing to it that, except for the long strand, they extend equally on both sides. We now have a tassel of eight threads, seven of the same length and a longer one. We make a loop large enough for the corner of the garment to lie flat in it. This is done by a double knot. We now wrap the long strand *seven* times around the others and make a double knot with all of them. We must wrap the strand very firmly, and we may even tighten it by making a single knot of the strand itself after each revolution. Now we wrap the long strand *eight* times around the others and again make a double knot with all of them. Next we wrap the long strand *eleven* times around the others and make a double knot with all of them. Finally, we wrap the long strand *thirteen* times around the others and make a double knot with all of them. Our tassel is complete.

Various explanations have been offered for the number of spirals. Adding the first three $(7 + 8 + 11)$, we arrive at 26, a numerical value equivalent to the sum of the Hebrew letters in the name of God "YHVH": $10 + 5 + 6 + 5 = 26$. The Hebrew word *Ehad*—One —has the numerical value of the fourth spiral, 13: $1 + 8 + 4$. The sum total of the spirals is, therefore, equivalent to the total in the words: *Adonai Ehad*, God is One. Or perhaps the spirals remind us of the basic principles that must guide us on our way: *Seven,* reminder of the Sabbath, the seventh day; *eight,* reminder of the B'rit, the covenant of circumcision, to be performed on the eighth day of life; *eleven,* reminder of Joseph, before whom his eleven brothers bowed down, recognizing his superiority, attained through steadfastness in temptation; *thirteen,* reminder of God's thirteen attributes (Exod. 34:6–7). The four corners may then call to mind that wherever we may be "in the four corners of the world," our task is clear.

When we haxe affixed the four Tzitzit, our Tallit is complete; we add the Attarah to define its sides. May we wear it in pride. From time to time we have to check that none of the threads of the Tzitzit has been torn off; one severed strand within the loop, or two broken threads in the tassel, renders the Tallit unusable.

A Tallit should be purchased only from a reliable Jewish dealer. It may have blue stripes on the sides, a reminder of the blue thread; it may have black stripes, a reminder of the fall of the Temple. It may have a fringe around the entire four sides. All this is irrelevant; only the Tzitzit count.

TEFILLIN: BOND OF FAITH

The Tallit was originally an everyday garment, which had its use without Tzitzit. Tefillin, on the other hand, are of no practical use whatsoever; their worth is symbolic. The very term *Tefillin* points to their character; its root is *palal,* which is also the root of Tefillah—prayer, meditation. Tefillin are adjuncts to prayer and meditation, making its meaning visible and strengthening its impact.

During the morning prayer, we offer many blessings for the gifts of life, restored to us by God day after day. Among these are words of gratitude for Him "who girds Israel with strength," followed by thanksgiving to Him "who crowns Israel with glory." The Rabbis relate this blessing to the Tefillin, and as we pronounce the words, we touch the Tefillin and carry our fingers to our lips in a form of kiss.

Binding the straps of Tefillin around his arm, the Jew says:

And I will betroth you unto Me for ever;
Yea, I will betroth you unto Me in righteousness and in justice,
and in loving kindness and in compassion.
And I will betroth you unto Me in faithfulness;
And you shall know the Lord. [Hos. 2:21–22]

Tefillin are a "wedding bond" between God and Jew, the sign of a covenant that imposes mutual responsibilities on the partners and that deepens their love for each other.

Tefillin are a bond: the Jew binds his strength to God; he binds his mind and body; he signifies that he is "bonded" to God in all he thinks and does.

Halakhah bases the Mitzvah of Tefillin on four passages of Torah, each of which ordains as follows:

Bind them [God's words] as a sign on your hand,
let them serve as frontlets between your eyes.
[Deut. 6:8; 11:18; Exod. 13:9, 13:16]

Jewish tradition interpreted the words of Torah literally. Not only must God's word determine our actions and our vision in life; it must be inscribed and literally placed on arm, hand, and head. This is the origin of Tefillin.

In accordance with Halakhah, the four portions making reference to Tefillin are written on parchment with a quill and placed in two perfectly cubical containers, one for the head and one for the arm. To these containers, which are constructed of parchment and are also black, straps are attached, permitting one of the Tefillin to be placed on the head, and the other to be strapped about arm and hand.

There are differences between the two cubes. The cube, or *bayit* (house), for the head is divided internally into four compartments, their seams visible from without. Each of the four Biblical portions on an individual scroll is placed within its own compartment in the bayit. On each side of this cube, we find a convex letter *Shin*: ש ; the one on the right side follows the normal shape of the letter, with three prongs: ש ; the one on the left has four prongs: שׁ . An extension on the bayit allows for the insertion of the leather strap, which must be black and which—like all the parts of the Tefillin—must come from a kasher animal. The strap is formed into a circlet, its size conforming to the size of the wearer's head. The knot at the rear is rather complicated, having the form of a double *Daled*: ךּ . The rest of the strap, now in two bands, falls down the right and left side of the wearer's body, in front, and extends the length of his torso.

The set of Tefillin for arm and hand also has a bayit. It consists of only one compartment, in which the four portions, written on a single scroll, have been inserted. The outside of the bayit is flat. The strap has a loop on one side, tied by a knot in the form of a *Yod*: ' . Through this loop we can feed the rest of the strap, tightening it as we place it around our arm. The strap must be long enough to be wound about arm and hand.

The making of Tefillin is a job for experts. A violation of any of the complicated rules makes them *patul,* unfit. The reasons for these rules were unknown even to the Rabbis of old; they simply declare them to be an ordinance given Moses at Sinai. God Himself, they hold, showed Moses the knot as He passed before him. At that moment, permitted to behold God's "back," Moses noticed the knot of the Tefillin of the head (Exod. 33:23). God Himself, that is to say, wears Tefillin, both as a crown and as a sign of self-limitation through love and compassion.

The mystery surrounding the shape of the Tefillin suggests that they may have originated in primeval times, possibly as a magical protective device against evil forces. Placed on the head, they were a kind of helmet; on the left arm, they were a kind of shield.

The four-pronged Shin may be a trace or a reminder of the four compartments in which the individual scrolls are placed. Some masters of Jewish mystical tradition, the Kabbalah, held that the four-pronged Shin is the true Shin, as God writes it. We may not use it in Torah, as our knowledge of its ultimate meaning is faulty, owing to human limitations; but eventually, in His own time, God will reveal the meaning of Torah in its completeness and thus the character of the four-pronged Shin. In our present life and intelligence we should strive to proceed from the three-pronged Shin of limited insight and faulty understanding to the four-pronged Shin of complete knowledge of God. The two Shins thus point to our task. Seen in this way, the four-pronged Shin corresponds to the four-letter Name of God, YHVH, which we may not pronounce, in awareness of our limitations. In this spirit, the Shin has often been used in synagogue art as a symbol for God.

It has been held that the three-pronged Shin, when combined with the Daled of the knot of the headband and the Yod on the strap for the arm, spells the word *Sh-D-Y,* Shaddai, which is one of the names of God.

In our daily lives we hardly ever perform an affirmative act that signifies, even to ourselves, that we are Jews. We lead "ordinary lives" in a secular world. Placing Tefillin on hand and head, we give each day a Jewish character: we affirm our Jewishness before we start the day's routine. A Jew who *legt Tefillin,* as the Yiddish expression has it, is never alienated from the source of his being.

Tefillin must be worn on a clean body, for the body is now the bearer of the divine Name and word.

We first put on the *Tefillin shel yad,* on the left arm. (The Rabbis interpreted a variant spelling of "your hand" in Ex. 13:16 as referring to the "weak hand.") The bayit is placed on the flesh of the upper arm, opposite the heart. The strap is tightened by one circle about the upper arm. Then it is wound seven times around the lower arm and down to the hand; here it is temporarily wrapped diagonally

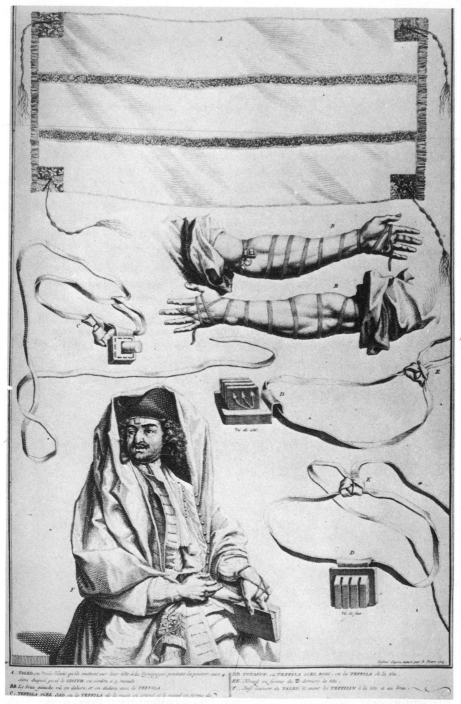

Tallit and Tefillin, an eighteenth-century engraving by B. Picard. Note the way in which the Tallit is pulled over the head to create a sacred space for devotion and prayer.

across the hand, working from the back to the space between thumb and index finger. Some Jews wind the Tefillin clockwise around the arm; others, counterclockwise, depending on their tradition.

Before tightening the loop at his upper arm, the Jew pronounces a blessing:

Barukh . . . vetzivanu le-ha-ni-ah Tefillin
Blessed are You . . . He, who has commanded us to wear Tefillin.

He then completes the circles about the arm and fastens the temporary strap on his hand.

Next he places the *Tefillin shel Rosh* on his head. The bayit must be between his eyes but above them, its front edge parallel to the hairline.

Before he completes the act, he recites the blessing:

Barukh . . . vetzivanu al mitzvat Tefillin
Blessed are You . . . He, who has commanded us concerning the Mitzvah of Tefillin.

He immediately follows the blessing by the words:

Barukh Shem kevod malkhuto le-olam va-ed
Blessed be His glorious Kingdom for ever and ever. (This verse is always recited when we have unnecessarily spoken the Name of God. As the Rabbis were not sure that *two* Berakhot were required for Tefillin, they added it as a precaution.)

After placing the Tefillin on his head, the Jew returns to those of the hand. He unwraps the section he has wound about his hand, and with it he first encircles the upper part of his middle finger twice; then he encircles the middle part of the finger once. Now he carries the strap to his fourth finger and thence back to the hand, wrapping the rest of the strap diagonally across his hand from the back to the space between thumb and index finger. He has made a Shin. In doing so, he recites the verse from Hosea that we have quoted above; the Shin forms the wedding band.

Putting on Tefillin may sound complicated, and a person doing it for the first time should ask a friend for assistance, but the procedure is learned very quickly. Once in place, the *Tefillin shel Yad* may be covered with the wearer's shirt sleeve. But the *Tefillin shel Rosh* may not be covered. It is a crown, to which the Rabbis applied the following verse in Deuteronomy:

And all the peoples of the earth shall see that the Lord's Name is proclaimed over you and they shall stand in fear of you. [Deut. 28:10] [Menahot 35b]

Tefillin touch head and eyes, heart, arm, and hand; all thoughts, desires, actions, and instruments of action are to be influenced by this touch.

Tefillin are worn in daytime. We customarily don them in morning worship, but the Mitzvah can be fulfilled at any time during the day. On Tishah b'Av, when we mourn the fall of the Temple and reflect on the agonies of our people, we do not put on Tefillin during the morning hours but in the afternoon, when hope springs forth again.

Tefillin are not worn on the Sabbath or on the full holy days.

Being donned only on weekdays, Tefillin fall into the category of active commandments to be fulfilled at specific times. This means that women are not subject to the commandment, but here again, as in the case of Tallit, there exists no basic prohibition against their fulfilling it. (See Chapter 26.)

MEZUZAH: GUARDIAN OF THE HOME

Twice in Torah we find the passage

Inscribe them on the doorposts of your house and upon your gates. [Deut. 6:9 and 11:20]

Taken figuratively, the commandment bids us make the love of God and the teachings of Torah our motto, in order that our home may become a small sanctuary. But the Rabbis took the injunction literally. The portions of Torah in which these words appear are to be inscribed on a small scroll and affixed to the doorposts of our homes: this is the *Mezuzah*, which means doorpost.

The Mezuzah is the guardian of the home in a twofold sense. It ensures that our home is more than just a physical residence and gives a spiritual dimension to our immediate physical environment. It also serves as symbolic protection against evil forces. Indeed, it may actually have had its origin as a protective device or amulet.

The Mezuzah has to be written on parchment in the same manner as is done for Tefillin. In addition to the passages inside the scroll, the Sofer writes the Name of God—Shaddai—on the outside. Here, the three letters are also thought to be an abbreviation for *Shomer Delatot Yisrael*, Guardian of Israel's doors. At the bottom of the scroll, on the outside, the Sofer writes in Hebrew Kh-V-Z-V B-M-V-Kh-SS-Z Kh-V-Z-V, a sequence of letters that is meaningless until each is replaced by the preceding letter of the Hebrew alphabet. Then we get: Y-H-V-H A-L-H-Y-N-U Y-H-V-H, *Adonai Elohenu Adonai*, the Lord our God is the Lord. The custom of writing these names of God in transposed letters may again suggest magical intent.

A Jew who acquires or rents a home must affix a Mezuzah to each of its doors (except bathroom doors) within thirty days; if he transfers the home to another Jew, he must leave the Mezuzah in place.

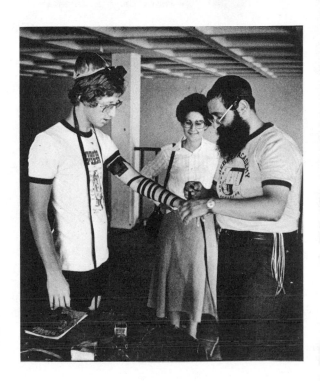

Just as it is a Mitzvah to wear the Tallit and Tefillin, it is a Mitzvah too to teach their proper use.

The Mezuzah is affixed diagonally to the upper part of the right-hand doorpost (as one enters). The top of the Mezuzah must incline toward the inside of the house or room.

Affixing a Mezuzah is a joyful occasion. Holding it in place, we pronounce the blessing:

Barukh. . . . vetzivanu likboa Mezuzah.
Blessed are You . . . He, who has commanded us to affix the Mezuzah.

Now the Mezuzah is firmly nailed to the door. If we are placing it on a new home, we also recite Sheheheyanu, giving thanks for being permitted to reach this beautiful moment in life.

In recent years, the custom has spread among Jews of wearing a small Mezuzah on a chain around the neck. It is not endorsed by tradition. The pendant must, therefore, *not* contain a handwritten scroll, as it will be worn in places where a Mezuzah should not be, and is otherwise exposed to moisture and other hazards.

Rabbi Eliezer ben Jacob stated:

He who wears Tefillin on his head and Tefillin on his arm, who carries Tzitzit on his garment and has placed a Mezuzah on his door, is sheltered.
He will not fall into sin, as we are told:
A threefold cord will not easily break.
[Eccles. 4:12] [Menahot 43b]

KIPPAH: COVERING THE HEAD

Orthodox Jews keep their heads covered at all times, wearing a skull cap or Kippah. Most non-Orthodox Jews wear it at prayer and in the synagogue. A Yiddish word often used for this cap is *Yarmulka*, supposedly an abbreviation of *Yare Me-Elohim*: "stand in awe of God." This may relate to a practice of Rabbi Honah ben Joshua:

He never walked four cubits with uncovered head, for he used to say: The Shekhina, God's Presence, resides above my head. [Kiddushin 31a]

Rabbi Honah's individual practice became universal in the course of time. It may have had its origin in accordance with the beliefs of ancient peoples, that an uncovered head was a symbol of freedom and human strength. For Rabbi Honah, the head covering thus proclaimed that man is subject to God, whose hand is over him. Firmly ordained in the Shulhan Arukh (Orah Hayyim 2:6, 151:6, 282:3) the head covering has become a symbol of Jewish self-affirmation in society.

4

Prayer:
Concentration
on the Ultimate

The Hebrew term for prayer is *Tefillah;* it is derived from the root "palal," which means "to judge," "to intercede," "to plead," "in concentration," "in anticipation." Prayer is concentration on the ultimate in anticipation of its realization through the efforts of man and the aid of God. Prayer is concentration on God in behalf of human attainment through divine help. It is a combined activity of heart and soul and mind overflowing into the spoken word. When Jacob was reunited with his son Joseph, whom he had long believed dead, and was even permitted to place his hands in blessing upon Joseph's sons, Ephraim and Manasseh, he exclaimed:

I never judged *(lo pillalti)* that I would see your face again, and now God has permitted me to see your children as well [Gen. 48:11].

We may see confession in these words: an event, so impossible for Jacob that he had given up praying for its realization, had come to pass through God. No doubt, he *should* have prayed, for in his heart he knew that his beloved son was not dead (see Rashi to Gen. 37:34–35), and perhaps the reunion might have come to pass much sooner. But even his unconscious concentration found compensation, the impossible became reality through God.

Prayer is contemplation on the meaning of life, viewed in the light of God's design. In this manner, the prophet Habakkuk reflects:

God, I have come to understand, an understanding of You;
filled with fear, O God, I have experienced Your working,
in the years that are near let it be revived;
in the years that are near let it be grasped;
in wrath remember compassion [Hab. 3:1–2].

Understanding leads to petition: that the purpose of life be recognized and, through it, that life be revived, reflecting God's work.

When King Solomon dedicated the Temple he had built, he garbed his dedication speech in the form of a prayer, explaining the meaning of the house for Jew and non-Jew alike, pleading for divine grace, for justice, for blessings and for peace, voicing the hope that from these sacred halls a divine spirit would emanate that would transform Israel and mankind. God responded:

I have heard your prayer [tefillatkha], and also your supplication. . . .
[I Kings 8:1–9:9]

Prayer is petition, directly addressed to God. When Miriam, Moses' sister, was stricken with leprosy for having slandered her brother, Moses pleaded for her in prayer:

Heal her now, O God, I beseech You. [Num. 12:1–13]

Miriam was healed.

In its very brevity, this petition reveals a great deal about the character of Jewish prayer. It is the shortest prayer found in Scripture, but it rests on a lifetime of experience. Moses had also offered the longest prayer ever to be uttered when he pleaded for 40 days in behalf of his people, asking for divine forgiveness for the sin of the golden calf (Berakhot 34a). His long prayer enabled Moses to utter his brief prayer later on. He had learned of divine compassion and knew that humans must imitate it; thus he could bear no grudge against the sister who had wronged him so deeply by her slander. He knew that it is better to pray for others than to pray for one's own needs and that such petition would lead to a divine response (Baba Kamma 92a). He realized that response does not rest on the multitude of words, but on the attunement of heart. This is Jewish prayer.

Prayer has been Israel's "sword and bow," its weapons of defense against a hostile world. Jacob revealed this truth to his son Joseph. He assigned to him a special inheritance, "shoulder high above your brothers" (Gen. 48:21). This was Shekhem, where Joseph was eventually buried (Jos. 24:32); he claimed to have taken it from the Amorites "with my sword and with my bow" (Gen. 48:21). In reality he had purchased it (Gen. 33:19). The translator of the verse into Aramaic (Targum Onkelos) therefore gives these words a new meaning. The Hebrew be-harbi ubekashti becomes b'zloti uv' va-uti, "with my prayers and supplications." The Talmud endorses this interpretation: prayer, supplication, and wisdom are the Jew's sword and bow (Baba Batra 123a). They link us to God, "guardian of Israel, Who never sleeps nor slumbers" (Ps. 121:4) and with Whom we are bound in an eternal covenant.

At the end of every public worship, we therefore recite a special Kaddish, including the plea:

May the prayers and supplications [z'lothon u-va-uton] of all Israel be acceptable unto their father in heaven.

As we are covenanted to Him, these are our weapons of survival.

CHARACTERISTICS OF JEWISH PRAYER

Even the few examples we have cited reveal to us essentials of Jewish prayer:

Prayer is *tefillah she-balev,* the contemplation of the heart. Words by themselves are insufficient.

Prayer is witness to the covenant. It confirms it and renews it. The Rabbis therefore declared:

God longs for the prayers of the pious [Yebamot 64a], for their ever-renewed affirmation of the covenant. Therefore, even an iron wall cannot separate God and Jew in prayer [Pessahim 85b].

Individual prayer is important, but communal prayer has greater worth. The community reflects in miniature the covenanted congregation standing before God. The individual Jew derives the meaning of his life from the eternal communion with his people under God. Having affirmed this covenant in communal prayer, the Jew may then add his personal petitions (see Berakhot 6–8). We may pray in any language; yet Hebrew holds a special significance. It is the holy tongue of Torah, the tongue of creation (Bereshit Rabba 18). It is the language in which the covenant was made between Israel and God and among the members of Israel's community themselves. Hebrew links us to our history; it constitutes our bond across all lands and seas. It is *lashon ha-kodesh,* holy tongue.

Prayer is encounter with the divine, to whom our heart reaches out. It must remain the language of the heart. We must be conscious that God's indwelling, the Shekinah, stands before us as we pray (Sanhedrin 22).

The Rabbis warn us:

Let not your prayer become a matter of routine, but let it be a plea for mercy and compassion. [Abot 2b, Berakhot 29b] Prayer must mean putting one's very soul upon our hands, offering it to God. [Taanit 8a]

The Talmudic masters, therefore, would spend an entire hour in meditation before they started their prayer. They demanded quiet, respect, and absolute decorum during worship, in order that there be no distractions (Megillah 28a).

As Jewish prayer evokes the covenant, it must be uniform and structured. It must be a tool for uniting Israel within itself, with its history and with God. We, therefore, have a firmly established liturgy for our daily prayers. Unity is created through prayer. At the same time, the structured prayers express the thoughts and emotions of our own soul more perfectly than individual prayers could possibly do. We are called upon to fill these prayers with a meaning of our own, thus acquiring them for ourselves. *Keva*, the appointed, is to be filled with *kavanah*, attunement.

Individual prayers may be added. The Rabbis of Talmudic times composed prayers of this kind that were so beautiful they came to be incorporated in our public worship (Berakhot 16–17). Medieval poets wrote *piyyutim*, liturgical poetry for special occasions and for the festivals. We may do so as well, but within the framework of the established pattern that has remained identical in all branches of modern Jewry. We may pray for our needs, but as we pray for others, our own concerns will be answered more readily.

In order to ensure that our prayers be more than the empty words of wandering minds, the tradition of Judaism has involved the human body as a whole in the act of prayer. We clothe ourselves in the Tallit, bind ourselves in heart and mind and hand as we don the Tefillin. At special moments during the year, we sound the Shofar, shake the Lulav.

All my bones shall say: Lord, who is like You (Ps. 35:10). From the days of Rabbi Akiva to the Eastern European synagogue, we find men so gripped by the fervor of prayer that their bodies shake. They speak with all their bones and sinews. Jewish prayer is encounter with God, an audience granted us by the divine.

Too frequent prayer might cheapen the act (Tanhumah Miketz); in principle, we should confine ourselves to the appointed times. Yet, in need, we may call upon Him at all times.

In distress as in joy, Jews have found in Tehillim, the Psalms, a vehicle of expression. Of course, every Berakhah is a prayer, an affirmation. Prayer is basically affirmation. Praise is more valuable than petition, and in the world to come, say the Rabbis, only praise will be offered, as all our needs will have been met (Vayikra Rabba 9). The larger portion of our worship consists of praise of God.

The Institution of Prayer and Prayer Book

In the days of the First Temple, prayer was sporadic. The average person felt that the needs of the community and of the individual

A prayer service at the Great
Synagogue, Tel Aviv.

were spread before God in the sacred service of the Temple. Here
the people's link with God was visually expressed. Occasionally, individuals did pray at moments of great distress or of great joy.
Hannah, Samuel's mother, poured out her heart in longing for the
child that had been denied her; as her petition was granted, she
jubilantly expressed her gratitude (I Samuel 1, 2). Such outpourings
of the heart in silent devotion were sufficiently rare that Eli, the
priest at the sanctuary, mistook Hannah's ecstasy in prayer for
drunkenness.

After the First Temple was destroyed and the people carried into
Babylonian exile, prayer became a necessity, not only in replace-
ment of the sacrifices but as a unifying bond for the people. Liturgy
evolved and was given shape by the Rabbis of Mishnah and Gemara.
Long after the rules had been laid down and practiced, they were
arranged in formal texts. The first actual outlines of the prayer book,
the Siddur (meaning "Order" of worship) were prepared by the
heads of the Babylonian academies, the Gaon Rav Amram and the
Gaon Saadia in the ninth and tenth centuries of the common era.
(Gaon, meaning "Excellency," was the title of the rectors of the
academy.) But the Siddur is so old in its true origins that we may
rightly call it the second oldest book still in use throughout the
world. The oldest is the Tenakh. Both are ours.

43

BERAKHAH: THE BASIC FORMULA OF BLESSING

Berakhah is a fixed formula of blessing for the various situations in life. A Jew, partner in God's covenant, is called upon to make his or her life authentic. He may not walk through his years routinely. He must develop *kavanah*, attunement, springing from an ever-renewed wonder at the work of creation and placing him in never-ending dialogue with God and the world. A Jew must feel himself addressed individually and constantly and may not shirk or evade his duty to respond.

Torah is one channel of communication: God speaks to the individual person through Mitzvah, which is both command and the response to command. For that reason, Jews have always rejoiced in Mitzvot.

Nature, in all its forms, animate and inanimate, is another channel of communication, sometimes awakening our sense of awe, sometimes demanding active participation. This call is ever renewed. As the morning prayer states:

You renew each day, and constantly throughout the day, the work of creation.

Not only are we called upon to be alert, but we must affirm the fact that we have seen and witnessed and absorbed the grandeur of creation, and we must do so in spoken words. This is *Berakhah*, the blessing.

We offer blessing:

over fruit growing on trees [before we eat them] . . . over wine . . . over fruit growing on the ground . . . over bread . . . over products that do not grow on the earth [like water] . . . after meals . . . [Mishnah Berakhot 6:1, 3, 6];

over comets, earthquakes, thunder, storm and lightnings, over mountains, hills, oceans, rivers and deserts . . . over rain and over good tidings . . . over evil tidings . . . over ills that conceal good as over good things that conceal ill . . . when we have built a new house, or bought new clothes . . . even on beholding kings and potentates, the sages of Israel and those of the non-Jewish world. . . . [Mishnah Berakhot 9:2, 3, 5ff.]

The Rabbis appointed a Berakhah, a blessing, in set form for every occasion. The origin of the Berakhah may be found in the Psalms:

Barukh attah Adonai lamdeni hukekha
Blessed are You, Lord, teach me Your statutes. [Ps. 119:12]

This formula came to be enlarged.

On beholding the world or partaking of its gifts, we say:

Barukh attah Adonai Elohenu Melekh ha-Olam. . . .
Blessed are You, Lord our God, Ruler of the universe.

This is followed by mentioning the specific gift for which we are offering thanks, for instance, over bread:

hamotzi lehem min ha-aretz
You are He, who causes bread to come forth from the earth.

On seeing lightning or the wonders of nature:

osseh maaseh bereshit
You are He, who performs the acts of the creation.

Before we perform a Mitzvah, we put ourselves "in tune" by speaking:

Barukh attah Adonai Elohenu Melekh ha-Olam
asher kid-shanu be-mitzvotav vetzivanu. . . .
Blessed are You, Lord our God, Ruler of the universe, You are He, who has sanctified us by His commandments, and commanded us. . . .

This is followed by the Mitzvah we are about to perform, for instance, on putting on the Tallit:

lehitatef ba-Tzitzit
to wrap ourselves in Tzitzit.

We have already mentioned a number of Berakhot in this book and shall mention many more.

Rabbi Meir held that we should recite one hundred Berakhot a day (Menahot 43b); there would thus scarcely be a single moment when a Jew lived a routine, inauthentic life.

The Berakhah allows us to take possession of the goods of the earth for our own use. Legally, we may own an item, but spiritually it belongs to God until we have asked Him for His leave to make use of it. We receive the gift from God, and we acknowledge it by blessing and giving thanks to the Giver.

DAILY PRAYER

The Rabbis instituted three prayers for every day, as we have seen: Shaharit, Minhah, and Maariv.

Shaharit and *Maariv* have their source in Torah, the ordinance of the Sh'ma to be recited evening and morning. *Minhah* is a rabbinic ordinance.

The Rabbis felt, however, that these three prayers had been instituted by the patriarchs themselves and confirmed by Israel's prophets and kings:

Abraham instituted the morning service:

Early in the morning, Abraham hurried to the place where he had stood before the Lord [Gen. 19:27].

"Standing before the Lord" means praying.

Isaac instituted the afternoon service:

And Isaac went out to meditate in the field toward evening [Gen. 24:63].

"Meditating" means praying.

Jacob instituted the evening service:

He came upon a certain place and stopped there for the night, for the sun had set [Gen. 28:11].

"Coming upon" means praying (Berakhot 26b).

Daniel prayed three times daily on his knees, but did not give us any specific hours (Daniel 6:11).

David gave us specific hours:

evening and morning and noon [Ps. 55:17] [Tanh.B. Miketz 98a–b]

The Rabbis wished to point out that prayer has been woven into Jewish history from the very beginning. But seeing in the patriarchs the archetypes of the Jew, they may have wished as well to reveal something of the character of Jewish prayer.

The occasion of Abraham's prayer was his setting out on his journey to sacrifice his son Isaac, as God had commanded. The morning prayer thus calls upon the Jew to render utmost obedience to God throughout the day, including the supreme sacrifice. It holds out the hope that this sacrifice may not be required of him, even as Isaac was spared. The day will test the Jew's convictions.

The occasion of Isaac's afternoon meditation was his anxiety about finding the right wife, who was to come from far away, as the women in his own environment were unsuitable to be true Jewish mothers. The afternoon prayer thus calls upon the Jew to review his work up till now and to remember that the purpose of his life is the family. It is his sanctuary, which he must sustain. It is the guarantor of the future. Toil for gain alone holds no meaning; toil in behalf of the Jewish family transforms mundane work into divine service.

Jacob's prayer was occasioned by fear for his very life. He had been forced to flee from his brother Esau, who had threatened to kill him. In prayer, he found strength and overcame his fear. The evening prayer reminds the Jew of the precariousness of Jewish life and the miracle of Jewish survival. Throughout our entire history, we have been threatened by those who, under God, should have been our brothers. We did not perish, for God was our shield and buckler.

Nineteenth-century engraving by Gustave Doré. Abraham has become a Jewish paradigm for the person of great faith, a faith which God tested. Abraham was commanded to bind his son Isaac upon an altar as a sacrifice. Only at the last moment did God send an angel to stay Abraham's hand (Genesis 22).

Daniel, the Diaspora Jew, prayed in allegiance to God, defying a royal edict, and was delivered by God.

David placed his rule under God's Kingship.

Our prayers are equally keyed to the ancient sacrifices in the Temple, the morning offering and the afternoon offering. We are reminded of the words, spoken by the prophet Hosea:

Take with you words, and return unto the Lord;
Say unto Him . . .
"We will render, instead of bullocks, the offering of our lips" [Hos. 14:3].

Finally, our prayers are in response to the commandment:

Recite the words [of the Sh'ma] when you lie down and when you rise up [Deut. 6:7]

We therefore find:

Shaharit, the Morning Prayer (from Shahar, Morning), traditionally instituted by Abraham, is also keyed to the morning offering in the ancient Temple. It may be recited at any time during the first quarter of the daylight hours, the period "when royal princes arise" (Berakhot 9b). Before God we are princes.

Minhah, the afternoon prayer, received its name from the meal offering in the Temple, Minhah being keyed to the afternoon sacrificial service. Traditionally, it was instituted by Isaac. It may be offered during the second half of the daylight hours, beginning at least nine and a half hours after daybreak, and as late as eleven and a quarter hours after daybreak.

The prophet Elijah was called upon to make manifest before an assembly of heathens and of doubting Jews, before king and people, the presence and power of the One God. At Mount Carmel he placed a sacrificial animal upon the altar he had built; poured water over the sacrifice and the altar; and then, staking his life on his faith, chided the people for "halting between two opinions," compromising between God and idols. Then he prayed, certain of divine response. At the moment the Minhah offering was presented in the Temple, his prayer was answered:

Then the fire of the Lord fell and consumed the burnt offering and the wood and the stones and licked up the water. [I Kings 18:38; see entire chapter]

Minhah bids us then to reflect: have we too been "halting between two opinions," worshipping God and the world? But Minhah, the Rabbis explain, is also a time of God's special compassion. The Jew who may have been denied the blessing of sustenance prays that it be granted him before the day is gone.

Maariv, traditionally instituted by Jacob, is offered after night has fallen and three stars have appeared in the sky.

In congregational worship, Minhah and Maariv may be combined during the last one and a quarter hours of daylight, in order not to burden the people with two visits to the synagogue. The individual then has to recite the Sh'ma once again, after night has fallen.

These hours are not clock hours; each hour is one-twelfth of the daylight period, longer in summer, shorter in winter.

In Orthodoxy and Conservatism, a special prayer is also recited on those festive days when an additional offering was presented in the Temple of old. This is the Additional Prayer, *Mussaf.*

On Yom Kippur, we add a special concluding prayer, *Ne-eelah,* the Closing Prayer.

The Structure of Prayer

The structure of our prayer is uniform throughout the year, symmetrical as far as morning and evening prayer are concerned and very logical.

The two pillars of prayer are the *Sh'ma,* to be recited every morning and every evening, and the *Amidah,* a set of petitions, offered while the worshipper stands (Amidah means "standing"). This Amidah will be explained in detail later.

These two key prayers are preceded and followed by lengthy *Berakhot.* The Rabbis ruled:

In the morning there are to be two Berakhot before (the Sh'ma) and one after (the Sh'ma); in the evening, there are to be two before and two after (the Sh'ma) (leading to the Amidah). [Mishnah Berakhot 1:4]

This is the core of our worship, around which a number of additions have been made.

We shall now briefly follow the structure of the worship service.

The Morning Prayer

1. Originally, the Jew, on arising, would give thanks for the new day; on putting on his clothes, he expressed his gratitude for being clothed by God; and so on. These prayers are now part of our structured worship.
2. The Jew dons Tallit and Tefillin.
3. Through Psalms, he puts himself in tune with the divine.
4. Now public worship begins. A Minyan, quorum of ten, is required in orthodox worship.

   a. The call to communal worship is issued: *Barekhu,* Praise ye God!
   b. The first Berakhah is offered. We give thanks to God for the day He has created.
   c. The second Berakhah spells out the meaning of each day: life in Torah. We give thanks to God for the gift of Torah.

    d. Guided by Torah, we now are ready for the affirmation of faith, as ordained in Torah: the Sh'ma.

    e. The Berakhah after the Sh'ma elaborates on the covenant. We have affirmed Him. He has rescued us from all our enemies throughout history. We praise God as our Redeemer.

    f. The Amidah follows; it is repeated by the leader. At that time, the sanctification is pronounced by the congregation:

Holy, Holy, Holy is the Lord of Hosts . . . [Isa. 6:3]

5. *On Weekdays:* We confess our sins. *On Special Holidays:* We express our praise, the Hallel (Ps. 113–118).

6. God speaks to us: The Torah is read. We read the Torah on Sabbath, Holy Days, Fast Days, and on Monday and Thursday, once market days, when the farmer was able to come into the city and listen to Torah.

7. On Holy Days the Mussaf is added here by Orthodox and Conservative congregations. In conclusion, we recite the *Alenu*, a poem composed by Rab for Rosh Hashanah, but of such beauty that it came to be incorporated into every service throughout the year. It speaks of God's greatness and His covenant with us; it evokes our dedication in response; and it holds out the hope of a united mankind in days to come.

The Minhah Service

The Sh'ma is not required by Torah and, therefore, not recited.

1. The service opens with Psalm 145, which will put us in tune.

2. On Sabbath afternoon and on fast days, the Torah is read. On Sabbath afternoon, the first section of the following week's portion is recited from the sacred scroll, thus linking Sabbath to Sabbath.

3. Kaddish, in abbreviated form (half-Kaddish), serves as call to worship. Kaddish requires a Minyan.

4. The silent Amidah places our concerns before God. It is repeated by the Reader.

5. On weekdays, confession of sins is silently voiced.

6. Alenu concludes the service.

The Maariv Service

Following the order laid down in Mishnah, the evening service is arranged in a manner symmetrical to the morning service.

1. A few verses from the Psalms put us in tune.

2. The call to worship is sounded: *Barekhu . . .* !

    a. The first Berakhah praises God for day and night, emphasizing the blessings of the night.

    b. The second Berakhah offers thanks for Torah, whose study

is to occupy us day and night. In Torah lies the meaning of our life.

c. Thus keyed to the commandments of Torah, we speak the affirmation of faith, the Sh'ma, as ordained in Torah.

d. The first Berakhah after the Sh'ma brings to mind God's covenant. God's love, responding to our own, has redeemed us from all oppressors throughout history.

e. The second Berakhah after the Sh'ma pleads for divine shelter throughout the night.
On weekdays, an additional Berakhah, paraphrasing the Amidah, is added.

f. The Amidah is silently offered by the worshipper; it is not repeated.

3. Alenu concludes the service.

A Word About the Kaddish

We shall discuss the Kaddish later on. It is, as the term indicates, a sanctification of God. In it, the leader of the service calls upon the congregation to bless the Name of God, and the congregation responds.

The Kaddish is recited at many occasions. It constitutes the call to worship at Minhah; it is used to mark the end of the required Aliyot in Torah reading, of a section in worship and its very end. It is also offered by mourners, about which we shall speak.

AMIDAH

The prayer called *Amidah*, offered while standing (Amidah means "the standing"), consists of a series of short petitions, each a Berakhah.

Originally, there were eighteen of them in the version offered on weekdays, hence the name *Shemone Esre*, the "Eighteen" (Prayer). During the period of early Christianity, a nineteenth Berakhah was added, directed against apostates.

The Amidah consists of three sections:

Section One: Contemplation of God: three Berakhot. This is recited on weekdays and on festivals.

Section Two: Twelve and, later, thirteen petitions, Berakhot. These are recited only on weekdays. On the Sabbath and the festivals, when no temporal concerns are to be uttered, there is only one Middle Berakhah: thanksgiving for the holy day.

Section Three: Thanksgiving and the plea for peace: three Berakhot. This section is recited on weekdays and on festivals.

Even the synagogue is not an absolute necessity for Jewish prayer. Any place fitting for "an encounter with the Divine" may be used.

The concerns of petition are arranged in logical order:

The first concern: contemplation of God.

1. *He is the God of history,* Who has been our shield since Abraham's days and will bring redemption to our descendants.
2. *He is our daily helper,* sustaining the living and faithful to the dead.
3. *He is holy.* In the repetition of the Amidah the congregation proclaims: Holy, holy, holy is the Lord of hosts, the whole earth is full of His glory [Isa. 6:3].

The second concern on Sabbaths and festivals: thanksgiving for the festive day, instituted by Him for our benefit.

The second concern on weekdays: our needs.

1. *Our Spiritual Needs*
   a. *Plea for understanding,* knowledge and insight.
   b. *Plea for guidance through Torah,* by which our knowledge is directed toward worthy goals.
   c. *Plea for forgiveness of sins,* putting us back on the road of Torah.
2. *Our Physical Needs*
   a. *Plea for reconciliation of conflicts* that divide society and disorient the individual, making us powerless in life.
   b. *Plea for physical health and healing of the sick* that they may again be given the fullness of life.
   c. *Plea for sustenance, our daily bread,* needed for survival.

52

3. *Israel's Needs*
   a. *Plea for Israel's rescue* from oppression and its ingathering from "the four corners of the earth," to be one again.
   b. *Plea for justice* and restoration of Israel's judges, acting under God's supreme rule.
   c. *Added plea for abolition of evildoers and slanderers,* inserted in a period of apostasy, when those who had left the fold became persecutors of the Jewish people.
   d. *Plea for vindication of the just and pious* that they may see their justification and be rewarded for their steadfastness.
4. *The World's Needs*
   a. *Plea for the rebuilding of Jerusalem* that it may once again be God's residence, David's capital, center of peace.
   b. *Plea for the coming of the Messiah,* bringing world redemption.
   c. *Plea for divine acceptance of all our prayers* in mercy.

The third concern: humanity's most precious goods.

1. *The Opportunity of Worship.* Worship leads us to recognition of true worth and true values. May our worship be pleasing to Him, and may it be restored in the "halls of His house," as we witness His Shekhinah's return to Zion.
2. *The Quality of Gratitude.* We offer thanks for God's abiding goodness.
3. *The Gift of Peace.* Peace alone assures the permanence of the blessings for which we have prayed. The Rabbis stated:

The Holy One Blessed be He found for Israel no vessel capable of holding blessing as peace, as is stated:
   The Lord will give strength unto His people
   the Lord will bless His people with peace.
   (Ps. 29:11) (Ukzin 3:12).

   Preceding this last petition, the priestly benediction is invoked upon the people, when the Amidah is repeated by the leader of the service: The Lord bless you . . . (Num. 6:24–26).

The order of the Berakhot of the Amidah was established by the Rabbis (see Berakhot 17b–18a). During the Shaharit, Mussaf, and Minhah services, the Amidah is first spoken silently and then repeated by the reader. The congregation responds with *Amen* after the end of each Berakhah. This was originally done in behalf of those who could not read and were thus able to identify themselves with the prayer by their *Amen.* Conservative and Reform Jews, basing themselves on this historical origin, frequently shorten or omit the silent Amidah. In the evening service, owing to a rabbinical question as to whether the Amidah is required or not, the prayer is recited silently by each worshipper but not repeated.

THE STRUCTURE OF WORSHIP

Morning	Afternoon	Evening	Mussaf
BENEDICTIONS ON ARISING—REFLECTIONS			
Psalms of Reflection	Psalm of Reflection	Psalms of Reflection	Psalm
CALL TO WORSHIP	Kaddish as Call to Worship and Affirmation of God	Call to Worship	Kaddish
AFFIRMATIONS			
God, Lord of Nature		God, Lord of Nature	
God, loving Giver of Torah		God, loving Giver of Torah	
The Affirmation of Faith:			
Hear, O Israel!		Hear, O Israel!	
God, Lord of History		God, Lord of History	
PETITIONS:			
		Evening Prayer and paraphrase of Amidah (on weekdays)	
Amidah	Amidah	Amidah	Amidah
Repetition of Amidah	Repetition of Amidah		Repetition of Amidah
Individual penitence (on weekdays only)	Individual penitence (on weekdays only)		
Festive Psalms: 113–18 (only on festivals)			
TORAH READING	(Sabbath and Fast Days)		
(Mon., Thu., Sabbath, Festivals, and Fast Days)			
CONCLUDING PRAYER			
Kaddish	Kaddish	Kaddish	
Alenu	Alenu	Alenu	
Kaddish	Kaddish	Kaddish	

5

Kashrut: Discipline Through Diet

he term *Kashrut* denotes a universe of laws, rules, and regulations and their observance in a manner that is in accordance with tradition. In a narrower sense the term is applied specifically to dietary laws. A *kasher* home is a home where these laws are faithfully followed in every detail.

Kashrut transforms the act of nourishment into a celebration of the spirit and the body into a vessel of the divine. Kashrut has sustained the Jewish people, setting it aside from the rest of the world. As Mordecai M. Kaplan has written:

In the course of the centuries, Kashrut has . . . served as a means of Jewish identification and distinctiveness. Kashrut has contributed to the perpetuation of the Jewish people and the retention of its way of life. . . . Kashrut is capable of becoming a means of generating spiritual values, in that it can habituate the Jew in the practice of viewing a commonplace physical need as a source of spiritual value. . . . We eat to live rather than live to eat. [*Questions Jews Ask*, p. 252]

At the end of the Kashrut laws in Leviticus, Torah admonishes:

. . . therefore become holy, for I am holy. [Lev. 11:45]

The term *holy—Kadosh* literally means "set apart"; the Jew sets himself apart from the world to link himself to God; he grows in holiness through discipline in his diet.

55

Although Kashrut has become widely neglected in modern times, large numbers of Jews still recognize its significance:

It is a bond, linking us to the generations of the past;
it is a distinguishing mark, linking Jew to Jew in the present;
it creates a Jewish style of life;
it is an act of discipline, strengthening character;
it is an affirmation of the Jewish people and its will to survive;
it is a bond between Diaspora Jewry and Israel;
it has hygienic value, preserving health;
it is an affirmation of the covenant, a law of God.

PERMITTED AND PROHIBITED FOODS

Most of the dietary laws are laid down in the Book of Leviticus, Chapter 11, and in the Book of Deuteronomy, Chapter 14. Some laws are found in other portions of Torah. And all these laws have been amplified by later rabbinical ordinances.

The following foods are *permitted*:

all vegetables and plants;
all four-footed animals that chew the cud *and* have parted hoofs,
    provided other regulations are met;
all fish having *both* fins and scales;
all fowl known by tradition to be kasher, provided other regulations
    are met.

The following foods are *prohibited*:

all animals and fish that do not meet the above requirements;
any animal, even of the kasher type, that has died of natural causes
    or been killed by other animals or by man, unless in accordance
    with the Jewish laws of slaughter. Any other method renders the
    meat *terefah,* torn, and therefore unusable;
any animal that has been found to be diseased when examined after
    kasher slaughter;
certain fats and sinews in kasher animals;
blood;
any of those birds enumerated in Torah as *tameh*—unclean; as we
    cannot today identify these birds, we consider ourselves permitted
    to eat only those birds which tradition has certified as clean;
all insects, reptiles, and the like;
any mixture of meat and milk, but not of fish and milk.

Definitely included in the *prohibited* category are pig, as it does not chew the cud; rabbit, as it has no parted hoofs; horse, camel, bear; all the beasts that live by destroying other lives. Equally included are all birds of prey. Among fish and seafood, the prohibited category includes eel and shellfish of all kinds. Nor may the products of any of these be eaten.

Blood is prohibited in Leviticus 3:17 and in Deuteronomy 13:23–25. In Leviticus we read:

you must not eat any fat or any blood.

The method for eliminating fat and blood will be discussed below.

THE SINEW OF THE THIGH may not be eaten. In his struggle against the "divine being" of darkness, the patriarch Jacob was lamed when the socket of his hip was strained.

That is why the children of Israel to this day do not eat the thigh muscle that is on the socket of the hip, since Jacob's hip socket was wrenched at the thigh muscle. [Gen. 32:33]

MEAT AND MILK constitute a forbidden mixture; three times we read in Torah:

You shall not boil the kid in the milk of its mother. [Exod. 23:19; Exod. 34:26; Deut. 14:21]

To the Rabbis, the threefold repetition indicated a threefold prohibition, namely:

Meat and milk must not be cooked together;
meat products and milk products must not be eaten together;
meat and milk products must not be used together.

The injunction was eventually extended to fowl as well, but not to fish. The consumption of fish and milk is permitted.

THE PREPARATION OF MEAT AND FOWL

By following the preparation of meat and fowl step by step, we may gain a fuller understanding of the law and the obligations it entails. *Shehitah*, or kasher slaughter, must be performed by a thoroughly trained, knowledgeable, religious person (a *Shohet*), who has undergone a course of study and received authorization from a rabbi. He holds a credential, called *Kabbalah*. The Shohet must use a knife without the slightest nick in it and must sever both the arteries of the neck and the windpipe in a single stroke, without exerting downward pressure. The sharpness of the knife leads to a rapid gush of blood from the animal's brain, which prevents it from registering any sensation of pain. Shehitah has been acknowledged as the most humane method of killing an animal; it testifies to Jewish concern to prevent the suffering of living beings.

BEDIKAH, the examination, is performed by the Shohet after the slaughter. A discolored brain, ulcerated stomach, diseased lung are among the symptoms that make the meat unfit for consumption. Torah is concerned with human health.

PORSHEN, as it is called in Yiddish (from *parash,* to separate), is performed by the butcher, who must be a knowledgeable, religious man. He removes the arteries and sinews. Generally, the hindquarter is not used by Jews, as the sinews are difficult to extract. In fowl, the neck artery must be removed by the housewife.

KASHERING, or eliminating the blood, is sometimes performed by the butcher and sometimes done at home. There are a number of steps:

The meat is soaked in water for about a half-hour;
the meat is covered with salt on all sides; fowl must be salted on the
    inside as well;
the meat is placed on a grate, permitting the blood to drain freely;
    it remains on the grate for about one hour;
the meat is washed thoroughly to eliminate all salt.

In preparing fowl, we first remove all intestines, which, if they are to be used, must be made kasher individually. Liver, which has more blood than the other organs, is made kasher by being broiled over an open grate. The same method may be used for other meat. The blood that is drained in this manner may not be used.

Meat that has not been washed and salted within three days after slaughter can no longer be used, for the blood will have congealed to a point where salting cannot remove it. If the meat has been soaked in water during the three days, it may be salted at any time during the following three days; this process cannot be repeated a second time, however.

Those who are medically forbidden to have salt in their diet should consult a rabbi.

Meat and Milk and Neutral

As meat and milk have to be kept strictly separate, a kasher household has to have at least two complete sets of cooking utensils and dishes. These may not be mixed or washed together. Glass dishes, which are not porous, may be used for both milk products and meat products, provided these dishes are *not* used for cooking. Of course, they must be thoroughly cleaned after each use.

Meat products and milk products may not be eaten together—for instance, no milk or butter may accompany a meat meal—and a waiting period has also been ordained between the consumption of meat and milk. After eating milk products, one should wait at least a half-hour before eating meat. After eating meat, one should wait at least

P.IV.

An engraving by J. C. Bodenschatzen, 1748, depicts ritual slaughter and the kashering of meat.

one hour—according to other traditions, at least three or six hours—before eating milk products.

PAREVE refers to those foods that are neutral, neither meat nor milk; fruit is an example.

KASHER AND NONKASHER

Items containing nonkasher ingredients may not be used, even for dishwashing; this includes soaps that may contain animal fats. (Detergents made of synthetics may be used.) Canned foods containing nonkasher ingredients may not be eaten. Generally, kasher foods can be recognized by the seal of several Orthodox rabbinical bodies that vouch for Kashrut. The buyer should look for the seal on the can or wrapper. Among these seals are: Ⓤ, ⓓ, Ⓚ, ⓐ, K, Ko, K.

There are divergences of opinion between Orthodoxy and Conservatism on several items. Hard cheeses are not eaten by Orthodox Jews; Conservative rabbinical authorities permit their consumption. Conservative Halakhists have also permitted sturgeon and swordfish; Orthodox Jews may be more restrictive. As milk from nonkasher animals is forbidden, Orthodox Jews frequently will drink only milk produced under rabbinical supervision and will not eat milk chocolate. Conservative Jews are by and large content to trust the state, which forbids the use of any milk but cow's and goat's milk for human consumption. Orthodox Jews will drink only wine that has been prepared entirely by Jews. Conservative Halakhic authorities permit the use of generally produced wine based on thorough Halakhic, historical, and technological investigations. They advise, however, that on Mitzvah occasions kasher, especially Israeli, wine be used.

The Origins of Dietary Laws

Orthodox Jewry has one simple and categorical answer regarding the origin of the dietary laws: they are the word of God. If, however, we take a historical approach to the evolution of Judaism, we may notice other origins as well.

Thus, the *sinew of the thigh* is forbidden because Jacob's thigh was lamed in his struggle with an unknown force. We seem to be dealing here with a taboo of a type frequently found among the ancients. The sinew of the thigh is thought to be capable of bringing harm to the descendants of the forefather who was injured in that place.

BLOOD has always been regarded as a special substance. The Torah echoes this belief:

But make sure that you do not partake of the blood,
for the blood is the life,
and you must not consume the life with the flesh.
You must not partake of it;
you must pour it out on the ground like water,
you must not partake of it,
in order that it may go well with you
and with your descendants to come,
for you will be doing what is right in His eyes.
[Deut. 13:23–25]

The ancients saw in blood a substance that might transmit the qualities of the dead to the living. Some tribes drank the blood of a slain hero so that his courage might fill their own bodies. Some used to consume the blood of their totem, an animal embodying their collective self, in the hope of being strengthened through this common ingestion of the fluid of life. To Jews, however, there was to be no other source of life and strength but God; other "life" was not to be ingested.

Among ancient peoples there was also a fear that the blood of an animal, if left on the ground, might vengefully pursue the person who killed the animal. The blood of wild deer and of birds had to be covered with earth and made harmless. To this day, under Jewish law, a small portion of the blood of deer and birds is covered with earth by the Shohet after slaughter.

The Egyptians and other ancient peoples regarded many animals as sacred. The mouse was considered an embodiment of the soul. These animals, holy to the heathens, became "abominations" to the Jews.

These meat stamps, used in nineteenth-century Europe, indicated to the buyer that the animals had been slaughtered and the meat prepared according to Jewish ritual law. They carry the simple legend, "Kasher."

The pig especially had a peculiar character in the minds of the ancients. The Egyptians both worshiped and abhorred it. It was known throughout the ancient world that the Jews despised the pig, but the false rumor that they worshiped it was equally widespread and persistent.

Heathen practices, sometimes followed, more often combated, may well lie at the root of many of our laws of Kashrut. Hygienic concerns also seem to have played a part, for instance, in the prohibition of diseased animals or of shellfish, which spoils very quickly in the climate of the Mediterranean region.

Ultimately, the consumption of food is a "religious" act. The symbolism of Kashrut invites us to be pure, inwardly and outwardly, in body and mind. The common meal is a form of worship, a communion; our choice of food should make it so.

GRACE AFTER MEALS:
SYMBOL OF MEAL AS COMMUNION

All the Berakhot were instituted by the Rabbis, but Grace after Meals is ordained in Torah, as the Rabbis explain. This emphasizes the sacred character of our meal. Torah states:

When you have eaten your fill, give blessing (*u-verakhata*) to the Lord your God for the good land which He has given you. [Deut. 8:10]

The Rabbis, who formulated our Berakhot, saw in this ordinance a command to recite four benedictions:

for sustenance, coming from God
for the Land, given us by Him,
for Jerusalem, His holy city
and for His goodness.

They held that Moses established the first Berakhah, when Israel was given manna in the desert; Joshua ordained the second benediction, after the people had entered the land; David and Solomon introduced the blessing for Jerusalem and "the House," for David brought Jerusalem under Jewish sovereignty and established it as Israel's capital, and Solomon built the Temple. Finally, after the terrible defeat of the city of Bethar—Beth-ther—in Bar Kokhba's days, the Rabbis ordained the blessing for God's goodness. The Romans had forbidden burial of the slain Jewish warriors, but their bodies did not decay until the Romans finally relented.

The Rabbis also ruled that the Sabbath and the festivals should be included in the grace pronounced at these days.

They ruled that in assembly of either three or ten, grace should be offered with special blessings in company.

Though Torah calls for a blessing only upon having eaten our fill, the Rabbis held that Grace should be spoken after eating as little as a morsel of bread the size of an olive (Berakhot 47b–49a).

The Order of Grace

By tradition, we put ourselves in the mood by a table song. On weekdays it is the sad remembrance of Zion (Ps. 137); on festive days it evokes the joyful anticipation of our return (Ps. 126).

The Summons of the Company

If three (or ten) have dined together, a leader is appointed, who summons the company to join him:

Leader: *Hav lan u-nevarekh*
Let us say grace
Company: *Yehee Shem Adonai mevorakh me-attah ve-ad olam*
May God's Name be blessed from now on and throughout all time and space
Leader: *B'reshut . . . nevarekh [Elohenu] she-akhalnu me-shelo*
With permission of those present, let us praise [our God] from Whose bounty we have eaten
Company: *Barukh [Elohenu] she-alkhalnu me-shelo u-v'tuvo hayinu*
Blessed be He [our God], from Whose bounty we have eaten and by Whose goodness we live
All: *Barukh Hu uvarukh Shemo*
Blessed be He, and blessed be His Name.

The first Berakhah

Leader recites; the company joins silently:

Blessed are You, Lord our God, Ruler of the universe. You are He who in His goodness sustains the entire world. In grace, kindness, and compassion He gives bread to all living beings, for His kindness extends throughout all time and space. In His great goodness, He has never let us lack food, nor will He let us lack food at any time, for the sake of His great Name. For He is God, who feeds and sustains all, doing good unto all, providing food for all His creatures, which He has created. Blessed be You, God, You are He, who feeds all.

The Second Berakhah

We give thanks for the "precious, good, and wide land" given to our fathers as inheritance, for our deliverance from Egypt, for the B'rit sealed in our flesh, for life and sustenance.

On Hanukah and Purim we include the *Al Hanisim* for the occasion.

The Berakhah concludes:

Blessed are You, God, for the land and for the food.

The Third Berakhah

We plead for "compassion with Israel and Jerusalem, Your city, for Zion, and [the coming] kingdom of David, the anointed [Messiah], and for the House [the Temple].

On Sabbath and festivals, the special portion, commemorating the special occasion, is inserted.

The Berakhah concludes:

Build Jerusalem, the holy city, soon, in our days.
Blessed are You, God, who in His compassion builds Jerusalem. Amen.

The Company, having joined in the singing of this part—as it frequently sings significant portions in unison—answers, "Amen" in one voice.

The Fourth Berakhah

God is praised, for "He did good to us, does good to us, and will do good to us."

Pleas

After completing the ordained portions of grace, we add pleas to Him who is "all compassionate"

to rule over us, to sustain us, to bless this company and our host, to send us Elijah, to bless all the members of our family, whom we name,
on special occasions: to make us truly appreciate the holy days that we be blessed.
to let us live to witness the coming of the Messiah.

Conclusion

We conclude on a cheerful note, as together we sing:

He accords great [on Sabbath: a tower of] victories to his King, showing compassion for His anointed unto David and his descendants for all eternity (Ps. 18:51—alternate version for Sabbath: II Sam. 22:51). He, who creates peace in His heights, may He make peace for us and for all of Israel. To that say ye: Amen.

Meditations

Silent meditation follows. One verse in it has given difficulties to some worshipers:

I have been young and am now old,
but have yet to see a righteous man abandoned,
or his children seeking bread (Ps. 37:25)

This does not seem to be true, as our own history has shown. A great rabbi, Joseph Carlebach of Hamburg, who became a martyr in the Holocaust, once explained to me:

This is how we have to understand the verse:

I have been young and now am old, but have never been able to stand by idly while a righteous man is abandoned. I had to come to his aid.

In this manner, the verse constitutes the climax of our grace, a call to action.

Conclusion

All sing:

Adonai oz le-amo yiten, Adonai yevarekh et amo bashalom
The Lord give strength to His people, may the Lord bless his people with peace.

Through song, grace becomes an exhilarating conclusion to a festive meal.

While the Rabbis held that women may not form a table round for purposes of pronouncing the summons, non-Orthodox Jewry permits them to do so. The traditional call, as voiced by German Jewry, states:

Rabbotai nevarekh—Gentlemen, let us say grace.

The call, in its eastern Europe version, as given here, does away with this distinction of sex.

In times of pressure, an abbreviated grace may suffice on weekdays.

6

Shabbat: Sanctification of Time

J udaism has given the world the awareness that time is sacred. It has also revealed the way of celebrating the sanctity of time: the Sabbath.

We read in Torah:

The heaven and the earth were finished, and all their array. And on the seventh day God finished the work which He had been doing, and He ceased on the seventh day from all the work which He had done. And God blessed the seventh day and sanctified it, because on it God ceased from all the work of creation which He had done. [Gen. 2:1–3]

Because God had ceased the work of creation, the blessing and sanctification bestowed on this final day were related to no specific process or product, but to time itself. With the sanctification of time, the work of creation reached its climax and its consummation.

The Sabbath was appointed that we might learn the meaning and the sanctity of time, experiencing time without exploiting it for work but simply as a holy gift out of the hand of God. No work may be done. With this sanctification of time, all relationships, between man and man and between man and nature, are transformed. Sabbath observance is, therefore, equivalent to observance of Torah as a whole (Yerushalmi; Nedarim 3:9).

The Sabbath is the only one of the holy days to be ordained in the Ten Commandments; it constitutes the Fourth Commandment. Two versions of the Ten Commandments exist in Torah, and there are variations between them in the presentation of the Sabbath commandment. The version in Exodus emphasizes the call for cessation from work in order that we may celebrate God's sacred time. The version in Deuteronomy places emphasis on the ethical implications: equality of man, man's stewardship over nature. In the following quotation, the variations are italicized.

In Exodus we read:

Remember the Sabbath Day and keep it holy. Six days you shall labor and do all your work, but the seventh day is a Sabbath of the Lord, your God; you shall not do any work—you, your son or daughter, your male or female servant, or your cattle, or the stranger, who is within your settlements. For in six days the Lord made heaven and earth and sea, and all that is in them, and He rested on the seventh day; therefore the Lord blessed the Sabbath Day and sanctified it. [Exod. 20:8–11]

The Sabbath was sanctified, because all work had been completed; there was only time, and it was hallowed.

In Deuteronomy we read:

Observe the Sabbath Day and keep it holy, *as the Lord your God has commanded you.* Six days you shall labor and do all your work, but the seventh day is a Sabbath of the Lord your God: you shall not do any work—you, your son or your daughter, your male or female servant, *or your ox or your ass,* or any of your cattle, or the stranger in your settlements, *so that your male and female servant may rest as you do. Remember that you were a slave in the land of Egypt and the Lord your God freed you from there with a mighty hand and an outstretched arm; therefore the Lord your God has commanded you to observe the Sabbath Day.* [Deut. 5:12–15]

The key to the second version is social justice. The servant is to rest "as you do"; he is equal to yourself. Work is a duty, but all work must be conducted in conscious relationship to the Sabbath principle: honesty in the spirit of stewardship, in an awareness that those who dwell with us in time are equals, in an affirmation that time is sacred and must not be defiled by wasteful or sinful action.

In the version found in Deuteronomy, the memory of Egyptian slavery is invoked. Egypt represents human conditions that are obnoxious to God: one human being transforms another into a mere tool and thereby degrades him or her. Slavery kills the human spirit. We must not tolerate it, for God despises it. The Sabbath is the road from slavery to freedom.

The Rabbis therefore claim: "Were Israel to observe but two Sabbaths, redemption would come" (Shabbat 118a). The beauty and peace of the Sabbath, its radiance pouring over the entire week, would create a world worthy of Messianic redemption.

For suffering Israel, the Sabbath has been an eternal renewer of hope; enslaved, we never became slaves. "As Israel has preserved the Sabbath, the Sabbath has preserved Israel."

The Talmud states that God pronounced the opening words of the two versions—"Remember" and "Observe"— in a single breath (Shabuot 20b). The dual injunction addresses the two poles of the Jewish soul, revealing the basic character of Judaism in general. *Zakhor*, "Remember," speaks to our emotions. The Jew is to embrace the Sabbath with his soul, celebrating it in joy, peace of mind, through meditation and festive meals. *Shamor*, "Observe," bids the Jew to observe with great care the concrete laws through which Sabbath rest is fully implemented. The two go together: the law, by restraining action, releases the soul to find its attunement. Isaiah expresses it clearly:

If you restrain your foot on account of the Sabbath, from pursuing your
    affairs on My holy day [observance],
If you call the Sabbath "delight,"
the Lord's holy day "honored" [remembrance],
and if you honor it and go not your ways,
nor look to your affairs, nor strike bargains,
then you will have delight in the Lord.
I will set you astride the heights of the earth,
and I will let you enjoy the heritage of your father Jacob—
For the mouth of the Lord has spoken. [Isa. 58:13–14]

Throughout our history, even the poorest Jew saw in the Sabbath a beacon lighting up and transforming the degradation of the week. When it arrived, he was able to shake off his worries and sorrows. Even the mourner laid aside his grief. The Jew experienced a "foretaste of the world to come," as the Sabbath cast out all earthly concerns.

The Sabbath is therefore a *sign* of God's eternal covenant with His people. We proclaim in prayer on the eve of the Sabbath, and in the Kiddush on Sabbath morning:

The children of Israel shall keep the Sabbath,
observing the Sabbath throughout their generations
as a covenant for all time.
It shall be a sign for all time
between Me and the Children of Israel.
For in six days the Lord made heaven and earth,
and on the seventh day He ceased from work
and was refreshed [Exod. 31:17]

The literal translation of the term *refreshed* (*vayinafash*) would be "reanimated." *Anima,* the soul of the divine, is restored to creation and man. The Rabbis, therefore, hold that on the Sabbath every Jew acquires *"neshamah yeterah,"* an additional soul, through whose strength he experiences a foretaste of the delights of redemption and gains endurance for the trials of the week to come.

A time-honored tradition: walking on the Sabbath.

The Sabbath as Israel's Gift to Humanity

The Sabbath is Israel's gift to mankind, perhaps the most revolutionary one in all the history of human progress.

The ancient Babylonians had a day called *Shappatu,* meaning "rest." But it was observed only once a month, on the day of the full moon, and regarded as unlucky. Our Sabbath is independent of the cycle of nature. Like the pulse beat of the heart, it sustains life and joy.

The ancient Greeks and Romans did not know the Sabbath and chided the Jews for laziness in observing one day of rest every week. Israel of antiquity had to be educated to understand and observe it, as Torah reveals (II Kings 4:22–23; Ezek. 20:12–14; Amos 8:4–5; Neh. 13:15–21, and so on). In trials, the Jews came to appreciate the Sabbath; it removed them from the world and immunized them against its poison.

The Sabbath became a unique day of meditation. Unlike Eastern religions, in which meditation is a separation from life, Judaism has placed meditation within life, affirming the need for it and balancing it against the obligations of work.

SABBATH OBSERVANCE

Sh' mirat Shabbat, "Observance of the Sabbath," entails a cessation from work. Torah lists only a few prohibitions explicitly:

Let no one leave his place on the seventh day.
[Exod. 16:29]
Whoever does any work on it [the Sabbath] shall die.
You shall kindle no fire throughout your settlements on the Sabbath Day.
 [Exod. 35:2–3]

69

Basically, no work is to be performed. But what is work? The Rabbis designated as work all those activities that were once performed in building the sanctuary in the desert. In this manner, they wished to indicate that the entire world is God's sanctuary (Isa. 66:1); we toil for Him and we cease from work at His behest.

They arrived at seven basic categories of prohibited work, subdividing them into a total of 39 prohibitions:

1. The growing and preparation of food; 11 prohibitions.
2. The production and preparation of clothing; 13 prohibitions.
3. Leather work and writing; 9 prohibitions.
4. Providing shelter; 2 prohibitions.
5. Kindling and extinguishing fire; 2 prohibitions.
6. Work-completion; 1 prohibition.
7. Transportation; 1 prohibition.

Included in category 1 are plowing, sowing, reaping, all agricultural work; also all cooking, baking, and broiling.

Included in category 2 are shearing, weaving, washing, bleaching, dyeing, spinning, making loops, and separating of threads.

Included in category 3 are catching an animal, slaughtering, flaying, tanning, salting, curing, preparation of fur, preparation of parchment, writing, and erasing.

Included in category 4 are building and demolition work.

Included in category 5 are kindling and extinguishing fire.

Included in category 6 is the final hammerstroke that completes the object.

Included in category 7 is transportation of goods outside the immediate confines of the home.

In addition, the Rabbis laid down injunctions that would prevent any violation of the laws of Torah.

1. MUKZAH: Tools used for work, such as pens, pencils, and hammers, may not be touched or moved.

2. SHVUT: Regulations imposed for the sake of ensuring true rest. They include prohibitions against sports, dancing, swimming, boating, and anything that interferes with the spiritual character of the rest.

3. UVDA DE-HOL: Anything that may give the Sabbath a workaday character, including the use of the telephone [Shabbat 150a, b].

Implications

This has led to wide implications and arrangements:
1. Objects other than clothing, be they as small as a handkerchief, may not be carried outside the home. Persons, however, may be carried—for instance, babies. A person may not carry a Tallit in its bag

to the synagogue, but may put it on at home, whereupon it becomes a garment. Jewelry may be worn. To alleviate hardships, the Rabbis also ruled that a whole city may become a private domain, within which carrying is permitted. This can be done by erecting a wall around the city; it may be a symbolic wall, such as a wire, but it must not have any holes in it. Thus the whole city becomes a condominium, an *Eruv*. Jerusalem is a city with such a wall, and carrying objects in it is permitted on the Sabbath.

2. Movement from city to city is prohibited. The limit for walking beyond the built-up section of town is 2,000 cubits, roughly 1,200 meters or 1,300 yards. If food is placed at the outermost limit of the 2,000 cubits, this spot becomes a dwelling place, and the person is allowed to walk another 2,000 cubits in the same direction. In Europe, farmers living beyond the 2,000-cubit limit from the synagogue found it possible to walk to the synagogue by this means, having established an Eruv.

3. Fire means any kind of flame. It includes the turning-on of electric light, of heat, or the use of the automobile, radio, or television; all are prohibited.

4. The law against providing shelter includes opening an umbrella.

5. A private letter may be read on the Sabbath, if it is already open; a business communication may not be read even if it is open.

6. Although cooking is prohibited, the use of food simmering in heat (though not on an open fire) is permitted. Jewish women customarily placed a dish in the oven on Friday afternoon, where it would simmer until Sabbath noon, serving as the midday meal. This was called *cholent*, a term derived from the French, *chaud*, hot.

The strictness of these rules called for the employment of a *Shabbes Goy*, a Gentile with whom it was arranged beforehand to turn out the light, heat the stove in the morning, milk the cows, and perform the essential chores.

The Jew who thus observes the Sabbath dwells on an enchanted island in time. He is removed from the world, serene and secure.

The Sabbath may be broken, and must be broken, if life is in immediate danger. Rabbi Jonathan ben Joseph stated: "Torah says: 'The Sabbath is holy for *you* [Exod. 31:14].' This means, it is given to *you* [man], not you to the Sabbath [Yoma 85b]."

Here we are dealing with a universal rule. Any Mitzvah of Torah must be broken in behalf of a human life in immediate danger. The Rabbis explain:

Whence do I know that danger to life pushes the Sabbath aside? Rabbi Judah in the name of Samuel explained it. It is written: "You shall keep My laws and My norms, by the pursuit of which man shall live; I am the Lord" [Lev. 18:3]. This means that he *lives* through them, not dies through them [Yoma 85b].

Unity and Diversity in Sabbath Observance

All of Jewry is united in the emphatic affirmation of the Sabbath as the cornerstone of Judaism. Interpretation of the Sabbath ordinances, however, reflects the variety of religious beliefs within Judaism. We shall cite but one example: kindling of fire.

Orthodoxy holds that any act even remotely falling under the prohibition is forbidden. Rather than use an automobile, the Jew should stay at home, even if this means that he will be unable to attend Sabbath worship in the synagogue.

In a split decision, the law commission of the *Conservative* rabbinate ruled that the use of the automobile is permitted to take a worshiper to the synagogue, but for no other purpose, and then only if there is no way for him or her to reach a synagogue on foot. Synagogue attendance is, after all a *duty* for men and women (see Berakhot 47b). It is permissive regarding the use of telephone, radio, television, music, and so on, if their message is spiritual.

Reform sees in the law an injunction warranted by the conditions of the time it was issued. Kindling a fire by rubbing sticks together or striking flint is indeed work, and it was thus forbidden. Today it is no longer work; indeed, without heat and light and transportation, the spirit of the Sabbath might actually be dimmed. It is this *spirit* that, according to Reform, has to be deepened.

SABBATH CELEBRATION: REMEMBRANCE

How may we create the atmosphere of holiness and joy that restores the soul? Let us follow the preparations and celebrations.

Friday

The Rabbis ruled that a short span of time be added to the twenty-four hours required for Sabbath rest. The holy day begins early and ends late. Actually, the entire sixth day, Friday, stood under the radiance of the Sabbath, and its hours became a crescendo of anticipation (see Pessahim 50b, Shabbat 117b).

The aroma of Sabbath food permeates the home on Friday.

The Sabbath bread has been given various names: *Hallah, Berches, Tatscher.*

Hallah is a small piece of dough taken by the baker. A blessing is recited, and the piece is burnt. Tradition links this regulation to the commandment in Torah (Num. 15:18–21), according to which the priests were to receive a portion of the bread, the Hallah, to serve them as sustenance. But this portion had to be consumed in ritual purity, and as this no longer obtains, the piece is burnt. Although the Hallah portion must be taken of all dough, its name came to be attached to the Sabbath bread.

We read in Proverbs:

Birkhat Adonai hee taashir—God's blessing makes rich. [Prov. 10:22]

Birkhat, a word pronounced *Birchas* by Western Jews, became *Berches,* and *Taashir* became *Tatscher.* Jews felt blessed and rich on the Sabbath.

Food tastes special on the Sabbath, not only on account of the love that has gone into it in honor of the holy day, but also because Sabbath itself forms one of its ingredients.

Once Rabbi Judah the Prince invited the Emperor to a Sabbath meal. "This food tastes like no other I have ever eaten," the Emperor exclaimed, "give me your recipe!" "I cannot do so," the Rabbi replied. "We have a special spice, it is called 'the Sabbath,' and it gives its special taste to every morsel consumed in Jewish homes on the holy day." [Sabbath 119a]

Our grandparents will tell us how they skimped throughout the week, putting aside every penny for the Sabbath meal. When the day arrived, poverty was forgotten, and they feasted like princes. The Sabbath was the spice of their lives.

While the food is on the stove, the family dresses.

On the Sabbath, the Jew is to put on special garments, set aside for it and for the festivals. [Ruth Rabba 5:2]

The table is set. Kiddush cup and wine, candlesticks and Hallah are placed on the gleaming white tablecloth.

By custom, family members taste a small portion of the Sabbath soup ahead of time, in line with the words they will later speak in worship:

Those who taste it [the Sabbath, ahead of its arrival] are granted life.

Could this be the origin of the reputation of the Sabbath soup, traditionally a chicken soup, as a universal and life-giving medicine?

Sabbath enters the home as the mother kindles the candles. There must be at least two candles, a contrast to the scanty light available during the week to our downtrodden ancestors. Candles must be lit before the sun has set, for then the kindling of a flame is forbidden. Jewish calendars usually list the correct time for every week of the year.

As soon as the mother has spoken the blessing, her Sabbath has arrived. Ordinarily, a blessing is pronounced *before* the act. On this occasion, it is not possible; so the mother lights the candles and shields her eyes in order not to see the light until after the Berakhah. (The placing of hands between eyes and light is *not* a blessing of

The Sabbath is ushered in with the lighting of candles and the recitation of a blessing on behalf of the children.

the lights; we do not bless the object; we bless God for the Mitzvah.) She speaks:

Barukh attah . . . vetzivanu lehadlik ner shel Shabbat
Blessed are You . . . He . . . commanding us to kindle the Sabbath light.

She may dwell for a moment in meditation or in prayer for her loved ones before opening her eyes. With the performance of this Mitzvah, the home has received the Sabbath.

Worship in the synagogue opens with *Kabbalat Shabbat*, the welcome of the Sabbath, while daylight still reigns.

Responsively, the congregation recites Psalms of joy (Pss. 95–99 and 29). The hymn *Lekhah Dodi*, "Come, my beloved," follows. The ancient Rabbis compared the Sabbath to a bride and Israel to her groom (see Shabbat 119a). They would walk to the city gates on Friday evening to welcome the Sabbath queen, their bride, as she entered. Rabbi Solomon Halevi Alkabetz, who lived in the sixteenth century, wrote the song expressing this emotion; it became one of the most beloved hymns of the synagogue.

The poem reaches its climax in the last verse:

Come then in peace, your bridegroom's crown,
in joy, jubilation, we make you our own,
amidst the faithful, your chosen folk abide,
Come, O Bride, come, O Bride!

74

As the congregation sings this verse, all stand and face the entrance
of the synagogue, as if Sabbath truly passed through the portal to
be welcomed. At this moment, the Sabbath has arrived for the worshipers. Immediately, the congregation intones the Sabbath Hymn
(Psalm 92, followed by Psalm 93). The welcome is completed, the
evening prayer follows. It includes the Sabbath proclamation:

The children of Israel shall keep the Sabbath. . . .
It is a covenant . . . it is a sign. [Exod. 31:16]

Worship ends with the Kiddush over the wine. It was originally
instituted for wayfarers, who were then fed in the hall. Children,
assembled around the celebrant, are given a taste of the wine.

Before departing, the worshipers shake hands, greeting each other
with *"Shabbat Shalom"* or *"Gut Shabbes."* The same greeting is
extended to the family at home: may this be a Sabbath of peace.

Legend has it that two angels accompany the father on his way
from synagogue to home. One is an angel of blessing; the other, an
angel of rebuke. If the home radiates the Sabbath spirit, the angel
of blessing pronounces: "May it be thus again next week." The angel
of rebuke, against his will, must respond "Amen—so be it." But if
the home lacks the Sabbath spirit, the angel of rebuke may voice
his wish for the coming week, and the angel of blessing, against his
will, must respond, "Amen" (Shabbat 119b). The family welcomes
the angels, often marching hand in hand, around the splendid Sabbath table.

Shalom Aleikhem. . . ! Peace be with you, Angels of Service to the All-
Highest! May your coming, your blessing, and your parting be unto peace.

The father now addresses his wife. In her honor he recites the
Praise of the Valiant Woman (Prov. 31:10–13). Father and mother
bless their children. One after the other, the parents place their
hands on each child's head, pronouncing the blessing found in
Torah:

Yevarekkha Adonai ve-yish-marekha
Yaer Adonai Panav elekhah veee-hu-nekha
Yissah Adonai Panav elekhah ve-ya-sem lekhah shalom

The Lord bless you and keep you.
The Lord make His face shine upon you and be gracious unto you.
The Lord lift up His face upon you and give you peace. [Num. 6:24–27]

Blessing their sons, the parents conclude with words reminiscent
of the blessing given by the Patriarch Jacob:

Yesimkha Elohim ke-Ephraim ve-khee-Menasheh
May God make you like Ephraim and Menasheh.
[Gen. 48:20]

The blessing of daughters is concluded with the words:

Yismekh Elohim ke-Sarah, Rivkah, Rahel, ve-Leah
May God make you like Sarah, Rebecca, Rachel, and Leah.

The family joins at the table. At the father's place stands the Kiddush cup; next to it are two loaves of Hallah, covered by a cloth. The cup is filled with wine. The father recites the Kiddush. He speaks of the completion of *Creation* on the seventh day (Gen. 2:1–3) and of God's sanctification of time. He gives thanks for the Sabbath. Kiddush, which means "sanctification," concludes with the words:

Blessed are you, God, You are He, Who has sanctified the Sabbath.

After each member has partaken of the wine, the head of the house turns to the bread. A double portion is placed before him, just as to our forefathers in the desert a double portion of manna was granted on the Sabbath. As the manna was covered by a layer of dew, the bread is covered by a cloth (Exod. 16).

The Berakhah over the bread is spoken as each member receives a portion. The meal follows.

Wine and bread, with which the feast has started, are special foods. In them God's dispensation and human ingenuity are equally represented. God gives the grape and the grain; man makes the wine and the bread. In wine and bread we recognize perfect balance; therefore, we use them for Kiddush. Table songs conclude the meal.

Psalm 126 and Grace after the meal round off the celebration.

The physical act of joy and creativity through sex is permitted on the Sabbath. According to some mystics, God rejoices when His children unite and mirror their Oneness with Him through the celebration of the Sabbath.

Sabbath Morning

This is the moment of *Revelation*: the Torah is read to the people. The liturgy speaks of the giving of the Torah and calls forth a remembrance of the service in the Temple of old.

Sabbath morning is usually the hour when Bar Mitzvah or Bat Mitzvah is celebrated. A young Jew, for the first time in life, steps to Torah, giving thanks for the Revelation, reciting from it, and placing himself or herself in the stream of the Jewish people and the Jewish tradition. On Sabbath morning, too, parents bless their children.

The meal that follows the service is introduced by the Kiddush. In it the Sabbath proclamation (Exod. 31:16–17) and the Fourth Commandment (Exod. 20:8–11) are recited, followed by the blessing over the wine and the two loaves of Hallah. Songs and Grace complete the meal.

Sabbath Afternoon

The mood changes from the solemnity of the morning to relaxation. Friends may gather for a period of Torah study. A father may review with his son the lessons learned during the week in the Jewish school. A nap after lunch is a hallowed tradition, as is the leisurely walk of the family in park or promenade, where friends meet friends in greeting and pleasant chat.

The afternoon service finds the people in synagogue once again. The first section of next week's Torah portion is read. The feeling of being *redeemed* now finds expression in earnest:

You are One, your Name is One,
where else is there on earth
a single tribe like Your people Israel,
one and unique?

As individuals, even as community, we are surely not redeemed. But as a people, though battered and bruised, we are eternal and indestructible. In this sense, we *are* redeemed. The Sabbath makes it manifest.

To guide us as individuals on our road, we read, after Minhah, during summer months when the days are long, a chapter each week of the *Sayings of the Fathers*, ethical pronouncements of the Rabbis.

As the shadows lengthen, the third meal, *Seudah Shelishit*, brings us once more together. (Three meals are ordained for the Sabbath.) This meal has no Kiddush. Hasidim assemble around the Rebbe's table for this meal, sharing a morsel of his food and listening in rapt attention as his mind delves in divine mysteries and his words reveal instruction. In Israel, the Seudah Shelishit is often given over to words of wisdom and to song, continued until nightfall and the Havdalah candle sheds flickering light upon the assembly.

The Sabbath Ends

Three stars have appeared in the sky. (Jewish calendars usually give the time of nightfall.) Loath to say farewell, the cantor stretches out the first words of the evening prayer:

Vehu rahum—He is compassionate
(Mystical tradition holds that even the dead enjoy special Sabbath rest up to the end of this introduction.)

The regular evening service continues. In it, we find *Havdalah*, the "Separation" of the holy day from the days of work. The service concludes with Torah passages and Psalm 128, a voice of encouragement for the week:

Eating the fruit of your hands' toil,
you are happy, it will be well with you. . . .
May God bless you from Zion,
May you witness Jerusalem's prosperity.

The solemn Havdalah is recited both in synagogue and at home. For it we need: a Kiddush cup, a plate on which the cup is set, a spice box filled with sweet-smelling spices, and a twisted candle. The cup is filled to overflowing, and part of the wine will spill over into the plate: may our cup be blessed, running over. The candle, held by a child, is lit.

The celebrant raises the cup. He recites:

God is my salvation, I will trust and will not fear. . . . [Isa .12:2–3; Ps. 3:9; 46; 12; Esther 8:16; Ps. 116:13]

He speaks the blessing for the wine; puts down the cup and takes the spice box, speaking:

Barukh . . . bore minei besamim
Blessed are You . . . He who is creator of all types of spices.

The spice box is passed around, and every member smells it. Symbolically, we take a last breath of Sabbath perfume to sustain us through the week. Frequently, the box is in the form of a tower, for "God is a tower of deliverance."

Spices were rare and expensive in medieval times and often stored in castle towers. Jewish craftsmen often adopted the tower shape for Havdalah spice boxes, as in this silver example from Frankfort on the Main, c.1550.

The spice box is put down. Taking the candle and holding it up, the leader speaks the blessing:

Barukh . . . borei meorei ha-esh
Blessed are You . . . Creator of the lights of fire.

Light was created on the first day of the week, now beginning; we give thanks for it. But because a Berakhah must precede *use*, the leader moves his hands in front of the candle, opening and closing them, to observe the play of lights and shadows. The candle is returned to the child: "Hold it high; your partner in life will be as tall as the candle!"

The celebrant takes the cup again for the actual words of "Separation." He praises God

Who makes separation between holy and secular,
between light and darkness,
between Israel and the nations,
between the seventh day and the six days of work.
Blessed are You, God, You are He, Who separates the
Holy from the secular.

He drinks from the cup, sharing it with the company. He takes the candle and extinguishes it in the overflow of the wine on the plate. The Sabbath is over.

"*Shavua Tov*," or, in Yiddish, "*A gute Voch*,"—"a good week"—is the greeting. Once again, parents bless their children. Once again, the family joins in a light repast, *Melave Malkah*, the "Escorting of the Queen."

It has been said that this meal was once King David's weekly supper of thanksgiving. He had been foretold that he would die on a Sabbath, but not when this Sabbath would arrive (Shabbat 30a/b). At the end of each Sabbath, David therefore gave thanks in reverent feasting for the additional week that had been granted him. In spite of toil and trouble, each week of life is a divine gift for every human being.

A mood of sadness, mixed with trust, pervades the atmosphere. One of the songs at the end of the Sabbath invokes the presence of the prophet Elijah:

Eliyahu ha-navi, Eliyahu ha-Tishbi, Eliyahu ha-Giladi,
bimhera beyameinu yavo elenu im Mashiah ben David
Elijah the Prophet . . . may he soon come to us with the Messiah, David's scion.

Elijah is regarded as Israel's guardian. According to tradition he never died, but ascended to heaven in a fiery chariot (II Kings 2:11, 12). It is said that he will return in the end of days, a time of cataclysmic struggles, to unite the people and to announce the forthcoming arrival of the Messiah and of eternal peace.

I will send you Elijah the prophet
before the coming of the great and terrible day of the Lord.
And he shall turn the heart of the fathers to the children,
and the heart of the children to their fathers. [Malachi 3:23–24]

But Elijah is also Israel's constant companion on its march through history. He protects Jews from dangers threatening without and from corrosive forces within. As "Guardian 'Angel' of the Covenant" (Mal. 3:1), he is invoked at circumcision, and at the Passover Seder a cup is set aside for him and the door is opened, in the hope that this Seder may initiate the ultimate deliverance of Israel.

At *Motzaei Shabbat*, the Exit of the Sabbath, we call upon Elijah to stand by us during the week, protecting us and helping us to succeed. And linked to our call for Elijah's coming at this time is our hope for the speedy arrival of the Messiah.

Beautiful Things for Sabbath Celebration

It is a Mitzvah to surround the Sabbath with beauty. We may choose our own designs for Kiddush cups and candlesticks, spice boxes and holders for Havdalah candle, plates for the overflow of the wine, even the twisted candles themselves. We may fashion tablecloths and Hallah covers, and the inventive cook may create new dishes for the Sabbath meal.

In this manner, the beauty of the Sabbath permeates the week and its work and deepens our Jewish spirit.

7

Calendar:
The Measure
of Time

T he primitives had no calendar. They knew only of
the eternal recurrence of the year's cycle from
sowing time to harvest time. Ancient artifacts, including early Greek vases, are decorated with geo-
metric designs portraying the cyclical movement of time, repeating
itself in eternal sameness.

Observation of the phases of the moon led to the knowledge that
twelve cycles of the moon correspond to one cycle of the sun: the
lunar year had been discovered. In the moon's waxing and waning
a message was perceived: we grow and decay, disappear and are
reborn.

Measuring the years called for greater sophistication. A king's
accession to the throne might be seen as the beginning of a new
period. The birth of a new religion, such as Christianity, was hailed
as the opening of a new era; we still count our own years in the
West by the supposed date of Jesus' birth. Muslims do the same,
taking the year of Muhammad's flight from Mecca to Medina as the
beginning of a new era (622 c.e.). Formal instruments of the United
States always refer to the date of our independence, for on this date
of liberation "a new order of the centuries" emerged, as every dollar
bill proudly announces.

Liberation is a logical beginning point for a nation's historical
counting. Every calendar day then becomes a reminder of liberation
and an appeal to the members of the nation to dedicate themselves

ever anew to its ideals. The Jews adopted such a calendar. Spring is the beginning of the year, according to Torah, for in spring Israel was liberated by God from Egyptian bondage. Spring also marks the rebirth of nature: human liberation and nature's rebirth go hand in hand, for both have their foundation in God.

In time, Judaism came to see itself as a world religion. As the moment of its own liberation had significance for the Jews, but not for the rest of humanity, an additional beginning date had to be introduced, with meaning for all, and this was the day of the world's creation.

Creation was conceived as having occurred in the fall. Using the genealogy found in Genesis, the Rabbis added together the life-spans of the early generations and combined them with the time that had elapsed since then to arrive at the age of the world. This is how our Jewish calendar came to be, and we still use it. Thus, the year of the American Bicentennial, 1976, corresponded to the year 5736 "since the world's creation." Though we know that this is not, strictly speaking, a true count, we maintain it out of pious attachment to our ancestors.

As Torah reveals, evening was created before morning. ("There was evening, and there was morning, one day" (Gen. 1:5ff). Hence we count every day starting with the preceding evening; Sabbath and holy days begin on the eve of the preceding day. And the Jewish year, too, begins in a kind of night,. in the fall, nature's evening, and at a time when the moon is "hidden" and just about to emerge again as a new creation.

God created the world at a time when night fell over nature. But God assures rebirth: the moon will rise again; the seed, slumbering in the soil, will sprout once more. God is the Lord of *nature*. All creatures stand in review before Him on this day of renewal. New Year's Day is the day of judgment.

As we have seen, we have a second New Year as well, in the spring. The spring festival tells us: we are God's people, witnesses to His liberating act. God is the God of *history*, and history is a march toward universal human freedom. Thus nature and history, day and night, new moon and full moon are linked and held in the hands of the Creator. This is the greater meaning of our dual New Year.

Inspired by ancient beliefs, the farmer saw in the moon's eternal renewal a reassuring sign that seed leads to harvest. In consequence, the Jewish year became a *lunar* year. But spring is brought about by the revolution of the *sun*. The festivals of the year had to be observed in their seasons; lunar year and solar year had to be adjusted so that all the feasts would fall in their appointed seasons.

Israel had been given divine authority to sanctify the seasons.

This was done by the Sanhedrin, the Supreme Court at Jerusalem. As soon as witnesses observed the emergence of the new moon, they went before the Sanhedrin, and the Court proclaimed that this was the first day of the new month, and messengers were sent throughout the land to announce the date. Jews outside the borders of the land of Israel, however, could not be properly informed, on account of the distances, and hence they adopted the practice of observing festivals for two days, just to be sure. This practice has had consequences to this day.

The Sanhedrin kept track of the discrepancies in length between the sun year and the moon year and saw to it that the two were balanced within a sequence of several years. When necessary, a leap year was proclaimed, adding an entire additional month to the year.

As the Sanhedrin was about to be disbanded, a permanent calendar had to be established to adjust moon year and sun year. This was done by the Patriarch Hillel II (around 350 C.E.). We have followed this calendar ever since.

THE LUNAR CALENDAR

The lunar year has 354 days; the sun year has 365 days. Hillel first of all adjusted the sequence of the months. They alternate in length between 29 and 30 days (with certain variations). He established 7 leap years in every period of 19 years, each leap year containing one additional month.

19 *sun* years of 365 days		=6935 days
19 *moon* years of 354 days	=6726 days	
plus 7 leap years of 30 days	= 210 days	
Total	6936 days	6935 days

Minor adjustments, such as alternating the length of the months between 29 and 30 days, took care of the remaining one-day difference and also provided for the elimination of other difficulties foreseen by Hillel. Yom Kippur, for instance, can never fall on a Friday or a Sunday; to have two consecutive days of work-cessation would create too much hardship.

Hillel's calendar firmed the dates of the festivals, but ancient practice was not easily broken. Jews in Israel had always observed one-day festivals, as Torah prescribes, and do so to this day. Yet in spite of the fact that we now know the exact date of the festivals, Orthodoxy insists that Diaspora Jewry observe two days of all the holy days. Reform considers such double celebration unnecessary. Conservatism gives individual congregations and their rabbis the option of observing one or two days.

Rosh Hashanah is different. Even in ancient times, it was observed for two days. It falls on the day of the new moon itself, and no one could know ahead of time when the witnesses might arrive with their sightings. Even in Israel, the message could not be received in time by all, and two days had to be kept.

Rosh Hodesh

The beginning of the month is celebrated as a minor holy day, for one day, if the preceding month had twenty-nine days; for two, if it had thirty. The day of Rosh Hodesh is announced in the service of the preceding Sabbath. It is celebrated in the synagogue by the recital of a shortened version of the Psalms of Praise, *Hallel* (Pss. 113–118, with the omission of Ps. 115:1–11, and Ps. 116:1–11). The Torah is read, and four persons are "called up." The festive prayer, *Mussaf,* includes a plea for a blessed month.

As there is no work prohibition, Rosh Hodesh lends itself to contemporary forms of recreation and celebration. Some Orthodox leaders have proposed it as a recreational holiday for Israel. Tradition has regarded Rosh Hodesh as a monthly "mother's day," honoring women for their superior piety by which the Jewish people is eternally re-created (see Rashi and Tossafot to Megillah 22b). It would be both beautiful and Jewishly meaningful were men to express their gratitude to wives and mothers by some token of appreciation each Rosh Hodesh.

Yom Kippur Katan: Introduction to Rosh Hodesh

To emphasize the spiritual character of renewal, a "little Yom

This schematic calendar for the Hebrew year 5036 (corresponding to the secular year 1276) was found inserted in a Bible manuscript of the thirteenth century. The inner wheel shows the lunar cycle; the outer, the cycle of the solar year.

Kippur," Day of Atonement, precedes the feast of the new moon. The congregation offers petitions for divine forgiveness, followed by confession of sins and *Sh'ma Yisrael* before the open Ark.

This practice originated with the mystics of the city of Safad and is keyed to a passage in the Talmud. When God created the two "great lights," sun and moon, the moon spoke up. There should be no more than one great luminary in the sky, the moon argued, hoping that the sun's light would be reduced. God reduced the moon's light in punishment for its jealousy and evil intent (Hullin 60b). Mindful of this lesson, we try to purge our souls from error and arrogance by observing a miniature Yom Kippur. The mystics held that the moon will remain reduced in strength until the coming of the Messiah. Through humility and repentance we try to make ourselves worthy of the days of Messianic fulfillment, praying that it may come to pass with the rebirth of the moon at this time.

Kiddush Levanah

The association of the moon's renewal with the restoration of Israel pervades the entire celebration of Rosh Hodesh (*Hodesh* itself means "renewal"). Nowhere does it find so full an expression as in the "Sanctification of the Moon." Several days after the sickle of the moon has reemerged, Jews assemble in the open to offer thanks:

Blessed are You . . . He, Who by His word has created the expanse of the universe . . . Who has told the moon to renew itself, a crown of glory to us, borne in the womb [of the divine] who will be renewed in the future, as it [the moon] has been renewed. . . . [Sanhedrin 42a]

The assembly repeats the phrase:

David, King of Israel, lives and endures.

It was once used as a password to announce the day and act of consecration of a new month (Rosh Hashanah 25a), possibly originating at a time when Jewish religion was proscribed by the Romans and practiced secretly. In choosing these words, the Rabbis might have wished to convey the additional message to the people: as the moon eternally emerges from its darkness, so will you; David, Israel's King and ancestor of the Messiah, lives. Be strong in faith and hope!

Upon recalling this message for the present, the worshipers greet each other in farewell:

Shalom Aleikhem—peace be with you;
Aleikhem Shalom—and with you, peace.

Kiddush Ha-Hamah

The ancients saw in the sun a divine power. Even Akhenaton, Pharaoh of Egypt, who proclaimed one god, identified this divinity with the sun. Torah, therefore, explicitly forbids sun worship (Deut. 4:19; see Job 31:26–28), and the prophet Ezekiel rebuked the people for this heathen practice (Ezek. 8:16f.). The Temple at Jerusalem was deliberately oriented toward the West to force the worshipers to turn their backs on the sun.

Still, the sun is accorded a blessing of its own. When the cycle of the heavenly bodies completes itself, at spring equinox, every twenty-eight years, we give thanks to God for the sun (Berakhot 59b). April 9, 1981, is such a date. We step into the open and recite:

Barukh attah . . . ose masseh Bereshit
Blessed are You . . . You are He, who performs the acts of creation.

On Leap Year

Leap year is, of course, an artificial institution, but tradition has regarded the period of the added weeks in spring as a time of threat and disturbance. During those weeks, pious persons will assemble every Monday and Thursday to recite the Book of Psalms in behalf of women in childbirth and the child being born. This is done only during leap year.

THE MONTHS

The names of our months come from Babylonia and Persia, where astronomy flourished. Some of these names are found in the later books of Holy Scripture, such as the Book of Esther.

Each month holds its own "lesson," through the events it commemorates; together, the months form a "catechism" of Judaism. In the following survey, we shall first list the months from spring to spring and then present a table (beginning now with Rosh Hoshanah, in the fall), showing the special days of observance.

The Months and Their Meanings

NISSAN, month of nature's rebirth, brings the call to freedom through Pessah; to modern Jews it commemorates as well, through Yom Hashoah, the six million martyrs of the Holocaust.

IYAR, month of ripening harvest, overture to the coming feast of Revelation, Shavuot. Freedom from restraint must lead to freedom under duty. We count the days from Pessah to Shavuot.

The Independence of Israel was achieved during this month, on the fifth day.

SIVAN, at the height of the harvest, commemorates through Shavuot the giving of Torah.

TAMMUZ reveals to us our failure to live up to our sacred vocation. Our own breach of faith is seen as a contributing force to the breach made in the walls of Jerusalem by Babylonian armies in 586 B.C.E. This happened on the seventeenth of the month. It is also the time of the summer solstice. Daylight begins to decline.

AV, month of deepest mourning, but also of comfort. On the ninth, both the first and second Temple went up in flames. But the very same day is seen as the birthday of the Messiah: our hope is never lost. On the fifteenth the tree harvest is celebrated.

ELLUL, month of preparation for the "Days of Awe"; the Shofar is sounded.

TISHRIE calls us to begin anew, starting a new year by acknowledging God as King, Judge, and Redeemer; this is the message of Rosh Hashanah.

We are given a period of probation during the ten Days of Repentance.

We are given a full day apart from the world in communion with God, to Whom we confess our shortcomings and Whose dominion we affirm: Yom Kippur.

Renewed in spirit and filled with resolve, we give thanks for harvest and shelter, pledging to sanctify the gifts of nature by using them to mankind's benefit. This is the meaning of Sukkot.

Before returning to our daily routine, we embrace Torah, our most precious heritage, our guide in life. *Simhat Torah* is our commencement.

MARHESHVAN has no special day of celebration. We have fasted and feasted; now we are to turn to the study of Torah.

KISLEV bids us to profess our Jewishness by placing the lights of Hanukah at our windows, visible to the world. It is the time of the winter solstice; daylight begins to grow.

TEVET marks the beginning of the siege of Jerusalem by the Babylonians, which began on the tenth day of the month. We must be vigilant in the defense of our people.

SH'VAT, tree-planting time in Israel, reminds us of our bond with our land. On the fifteenth of the month we celebrate the "New Year's Day of Trees."

ADAR I, the added month of leap years, complements the lesson of Sh'vat: we must catch up with the cycle of nature.

ADAR (II) brings us the fast of Esther on the thirteenth and Purim on the fourteenth.

MONTHS AND OBSERVANCES

Name and length of month	Begins between	Holy Days Hbr. Date	Name	Character	Biblical source
TISHRIE 30 days	Sept. 6–Oct. 4	1	Rosh Hashanah–New Year	major	Lev. 23:23–25
		2	Rosh Hashanah†	major	
		3	Fast of Gedaliah‡		II Kings 25:22–25 Zach. 7:5; 8:19
		4–9	Days of Penitence (includes entire period from Tishrie 1 through 10)		
		10	Yom Kippur–Day of Atonement	major	Lev. 23:33–36
		15	Sukkot, Tabernacles	major	Lev. 23:33–36 Deut. 16:13–17
		16	Sukkot*	major	
		17	Sukkot	intermediate	
		18	Sukkot	intermediate	
		19	Sukkot	intermediate	
		20	Sukkot	intermediate	
		21	Sukkot	intermediate	
		22	Sh'mini Atzeret–Concluding holy day	major	
		23	Simhat Torah–*	major	

Name and length of month	Begins between	Holy Days Hbr. Date	Name	Character	Biblical source
MARHESHVAN 29 or 30 days	Oct. 5–Nov. 4		Festival concluding Torah cycle of the year		
KISLEV 29 or 30 days	Nov. 5–Dec. 3	25 Hanukah		minor	none (Apocrypha: Maccabees)
		26 Hanukah			
		27 Hanukah			
		28 Hanukah			
		29 Hanukah			
		(30) Hanukah			
TEVET 29 days	Dec. 5–Jan. 2	1 Hanukah			
		2 Hanukah			
		(3 Hanukah) §			
		10 Fast Day‡			Zech. 7:5; 8:19
SH'VAT 30 days	Jan. 3–Feb. 2	15 Arbor Day–Planting season		minor	none (Talmud)
ADAR I (Leap Y. only) 30 days	Feb. 1–Feb. 11				
ADAR (Adar II; L.Y.) ‖ 29 days	Feb. 1–Mar. 13	13 Fast of Esther‡			Book of Esther
		14 Purim		minor	Book of Esther

Name and length of month	Begins between	Holy Days Hbr. Date	Name	Character	Biblical source
NISSAN 30 days	Mar. 13–Apr. 11	15 Passover (Pessah) –Exodus from Egypt		major	Exod. 12; Lev. 23:4–8 Deut. 16:1–8
		16 Passover*		major	
		17 Passover		intermediate	
		18 Passover		intermediate	
		19 Passover		intermediate	
		20 Passover		intermediate	
		21 Passover		major	
		22 Passover*		major	
		27 Yom Hashoah Commemoration of the Six Million martyrs of the Holocaust		minor, as it is a modern institution	
IYAR 29 days	Apr. 12–May 11	5 Yom Haatzmaut Israel Independence Day		minor, as modern institution[xx]	
SIVAN 30 days	May 11–June 9	6 Shabuot–Giving of Ten Commandments 7 Shabuot*		major	Exod. 19–20 Lev. 23:15–21 Deut. 16:9–12
TAMMUZ 29 days	June 10–July 9	17 Fast Day–‡Conquest of Jerusalem			Zech. 7:5; 8:19
AV 30 days	July 9–Aug. 7	9 Fast Day–Destruction of Temple‡			Jer. 52
ELLUL 29 days	Aug. 8–Sept. 6				

*These days are not observed in Israel and are not obligatory for Reform Jews. Their observance is optional for Conservative Jews.
†This day is observed in Israel but not obligatory for Reform Jews.
‡Fast Days are not obligatory for Reform Jews.
§The sixth, seventh, and eighth days of Hanukah can fall on the 30th of Kislev and the first and second of Tevet; or on the first, second, and third of Tevet, depending on the length of the month of Kislev.
‖This includes the beginning of Adar in regular years.
[xx]If this day falls on a Sabbath, it is observed on the preceding Thursday, the third of Iyar.

8

The Period of Teshuvah

Teshuvah means "Return." Teshuvah is a perennial task. It calls for a counting of our days and an accounting for our actions. The Psalmist pleads:

Teach us to count our days rightly
that we obtain a wise heart [Ps. 90:12]

Teshuvah is a daily obligation:

Be not sure of yourself till the day of your death. [Avot 2:5]

The act of Teshuvah consists of several steps: we must feel sincere remorse at our failures, we must confess our shortcomings, and we must redress them by doing right henceforth. Words of repentance are part of every one of our three daily prayers:

... bring us back into Your presence through wholehearted Teshuvah
... forgive us, Our Father, for we have sinned. . . . [Amidah]

The season of the year set aside for Teshuvah is not divorced from the rest of our days, but is designed to lead us to a pinnacle of fervor. The whole period is, therefore, structured step by step.

As the month of *Ellul* arrives, we sound the Shofar at the end of each service to awaken us from the routine of the past, and to alert us to the future.

Several days before Rosh Hashanah are the *Days of S'lihot.* We offer penitential prayers, recite the litany of God's thirteen attributes. and confess our sins.

91

On *Rosh Hashanah* itself the New Year begins. We are made conscious that we stand before God. We appeal to "our Father, our King" for a year of blessings and of peace, for forgiveness and a life unmarred by sin. But the main theme of Rosh Hashanah is the proclamation of God's presence and power. We bend our knee to Him in adoration.

During the week that follows, *Days of Repentance,* we offer S'lihot, confess, recite the litany of God's attributes, and voice our plea. The remainder of these days is given over to life's regular pursuits. They are days of probation. The Shofar is not heard.

Yom Kippur arrives; the probationers are led spiritually into the sanctuary itself. On Yom Kippur we experience our highest and deepest communion with God. On this day, we retrace the steps of Teshuvah taken since Ellul began. But time is telescoped; a sense of urgency prevails.

The Eve of Yom Kippur invites us to look back upon the past, as we did in Ellul, and then turn our gaze toward the future. With a plea for forgiveness of negligence (*Kol Nidrei*), we express our fervent hope that in this period, from eventide to eventide, reconciliation may be realized (*Yaaleh*). We offer *S'lihot,* the litany of God's attributes, confess our sins, and appeal to our Father our King for a year of grace and pardon.

The Morning recaptures the *Days of S'lihot* in prayers for forgiveness, the litany of God's attributes, confession and *Avinu Malkenu,* Our Father Our King.

At Noon, after reading the Torah, we are brought into the immediate presence of God, as we were on *Rosh Hashanah,* but now even closer. We relate the story of the service in the Temple of old, as the High Priest entered the Holy of Holies. At this celebration he pronounced the ineffable Name of God and the people prostrated themselves. *S'lihot,* the litany of God's attributes, and confession of sins reveal our will to become worthy of God's presence.

The Afternoon Minhah directs our attention to life, as in the *Days of Repentance.* But now it is a specific aspect of Jewish life: martyrdom. From ancient times to modern times, Jews have given their lives for their sacred heritage. This is true Teshuvah, the return of life itself to God, Who gave it. The *S'lihot* of the afternoon, the litany of God's attributes, and our confession reflect our determination to sanctify our lives. Remembering our own departed parents and dear ones, we hope their lives may serve us as example.

Finally, there is *N'eelah,* the closing prayer, as "the gates are about to shut." It has no like throughout the year. On the highest level of dramatic tension, expectation, and yearning, the whole road is traversed again: *S'lihot* and the litany of God's attributes, affirmation of His greatness and of our nothingness, confession of sins, *Avinu*

Malkenu. Each step is a surge, a gathering of the final resources of heart, soul, and mind. The sense of urgency is terrible.

The shadows lengthen, night falls. The Ark is opened. The congregation affirms: *Sh'ma Yisrael!*

It ends, as it all began, with the sound of the Shofar, the clarion call to life. The fasting congregation, physically and emotionally exhausted, is filled with inexpressible peace.

GOD'S KINGSHIP AND FATHERHOOD

A full understanding of the Penitential Season, its spirit and its forms, must rest on a knowledge of the traditional Jewish awareness of God, an awareness that finds fullest expression during these days. It has shaped the liturgy, which serves as vehicle even for those modern Jews, such as Reconstructionists, whose God awareness is not traditional.

The relationship between Jew and God has always been intensely personal. God is a person, but at the same time the Jew has understood that God has absolutely no human features, that His essence cannot be fathomed. He has willed that we understand Him as a person, while remaining ineffable.

God is both the King and the Judge of the universe. As King, He rules all of creation. As Judge, He judges the whole host of heaven and earth. But He is compassionate. He waits for even the slightest sign of Teshuvah, that He may grant pardon and mercy. Man, by his actions, inscribes his own record in the book of evidence; whatever the accusing testimony, Teshuvah wipes it out.

Moved by His great compassion, God has given us a period of repentance. It is the moment when the divine Court is convened. God, the Judge, is on His seat of judgment, but His quality of mercy moves Him to abandon this seat for the throne of kingship. As wisest of Rulers, He knows human frailties and human motivations, the good intentions thwarted by weakness. As King, He takes into consideration hidden evidence and inarticulate resolves that would be inadmissible in a court of law, but that may gain us a verdict of acquittal.

During the Penitential Season we therefore address God as *Melekh,* King. The morning services on Rosh Hashanah and Yom Kippur open with the call: *HA-MELEKH,* the King! Passages in our daily liturgy that speak of God as *El,* the God of Justice, are changed; He is invoked as *Melekh.*

God the King entered a covenant with Israel that binds the partners in mutual love. During these days, we invoke it.

Remember the covenant with Abraham,
the binding of Isaac.
Lead back the captives of Jacob's tent
and liberate us for the sake of Your Name.

An even closer bond unites us with Him: He is our Father.

Hail unto you, Israel: Who cleanses you, and before Whom do you cleanse yourselves? It is your Father in Heaven. [Yoma 85b]

On Rosh Hashanah, after the Shofar sounds, we pray:

Today the world is born, today in judgment there stand before You all the creatures of the world, as children or as slaves. If we may call ourselves [Your] children, show us mercy as a father shows mercy to his children; if we are [but] slaves, our eyes are focused on You that You may have compassion and decide our case in judgment as brightness in light, awesome and holy God. [Rosh Hashanah Mussaf service]

As the days of the season progress, anxiety yields to an ever-growing sense of intimacy, combined with reverence. We voice our petitions daily in the litany of *Avinu Malkenu*, "Our Father, our King": grant us our needs; vouchsafe us forgiveness, though we are not worthy.

Judaism places us in dialogue with God throughout the year, but never more so than during the Days of Repentance.

THE ANATOMY OF REPENTANCE

During the Penitential Period, we offer certain specific prayers and use specific adjuncts to prayer. These will now be explained.

The Shofar and Its Sounds

The Shofar is a ram's horn, a reminder of the ram offered by Abraham instead of his son Isaac (Gen. 22:13). The horn of a cow or steer may not be used (it might serve as a reminder of the golden calf). The animal from which the horn is to be taken must be *kasher*. The horn is softened by boiling for several hours; then the cartilage is removed, a hole is drilled into the end that will serve as mouthpiece, and the hole is then enlarged.

The root of the term *Shofar* is *sh-p-r*, hollow. It must, therefore, consist of a perfect, hollow shell, coming to life by the breath of man. No mouthpiece of any material may be added, nor may the Shofar be decorated with any foreign matter, though carvings on the horn itself are permitted. A Shofar should be obtained only from a reliable Jewish dealer and should have a certificate of Kashrut.

Although no foreign substance may be added as decoration to a Shofar, it is permitted to carve decorations into the horn. This example of an engraved and inscribed Shofar comes from eighteenth-century Europe.

The Shofar is symbol of revelation and of redemption. It was sounded at Sinai:

On the third day, as morning dawned, there was thunder and lightning and a dense cloud upon the mountain, and a very loud blast of the Shofar. [Exod. 19:16]
The sound of the Shofar grew louder and louder. As Moses spoke, God answered him in thunder. [Exod. 19:19]

It will be heard on the day of Israel's final ingathering.

And in that day, a *great* Shofar shall be sounded; and the strayed, who are in the land of Assyria, and the expelled, who are in the land of Egypt, shall come and worship the Lord on the holy mount, in Jerusalem. [Isa. 27:13]

Tradition links the Shofar to the Binding of Isaac, the *Akedah,* which is read from the Torah on Rosh Hashanah. The ram that Abraham substituted as a sacrifice in Isaac's place had two horns, which God preserved. The smaller horn was sounded at Sinai, but the *great* Shofar will initiate redemption.

The Shofar is also the herald of freedom. By its sound, the year of the Jubilee was initiated, when slaves went free and property was restored to its original owners. We read in Torah:

95

Then you shall transmit a blast on the horn; in the seventh month, on the tenth day of the month, the day of Yom Kippur, you shall have the horn sounded throughout the land and you shall hallow the fiftieth year. And proclaim liberty throughout all the land unto all the inhabitants thereof. [Lev. 25:9–10]

The last verse of this Torah section was aptly chosen as the inscription on the American Liberty Bell.

As the blasts on Rosh Hashanah are to be identical to the Shofar sound of the Jubilee, the notes to be sounded have been derived from that Biblical passage. We read in Torah:

Ve-haavarta shofar teruah, Transmit a blast on the horn.

Ve-haavarta, "transmit," signified to the Rabbis a *straight,* long sound.

Teruah, a blast, must then mean a modified or broken sound. The Rabbis ordained two different forms of broken sound, one a three-break sound, the sigh of a broken heart, and the other a nine-break sound, the whimpering of a weeping soul, and finally both combined. Thus they were sure to have captured the meaning of the injunction. As the term *Teruah* appears three times in Torah, they decided that the broken blast should be sounded three times, each time preceded by a straight sound and followed by a straight sound.

We call the straight sound *Tekiah;* the three-break sound *Shevarim,* and the nine-break sound *Teruah.* On Rosh Hashanah we sound:

three times: Tekiah/Shevarim=Teruah/Tekiah
three times: Tekiah/Shevarim/Tekiah
three times: Tekiah/Teruah/Tekiah,
stretching the last Tekiah into Tekiah Gedolah, a grand Tekiah.
The three sounds in each group must always be of equal length.

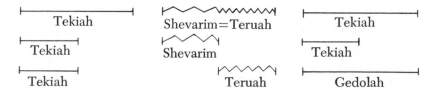

S'lihot and God's Attributes

S'lihot are prayers for forgiveness, penitential poems written over the centuries by numerous sages. During the week preceding Rosh Hashanah, and from then on until Yom Kippur except on the Sabbath, we hold special S'lihot services every morning, preceding the Shaharit service. This may mean at 4:00 A.M., or shortly after midnight.

We have seen that the morning service on Yom Kippur reflects,

on a higher level, the spirit pervading the days before Rosh Hashanah. This is expressed by the recital of the identical S'lihah on the
day before Rosh Hashanah and on the morning of Yom Kippur:

Judge of all the earth,
that now in judgment stands,
grant life and mercy
to a people poor, indigent.
May the prayer of the morning
take the place of sacrificial offering,
May the offering of the morning
be the sacrifice we make. [David ben Eleazar ibn
Pakuda; twelfth-century Spain]

A display of rare ritual objects for the High Holy Days,
including three ancient Shofarot, a nineteenth-century
German platter, a Mahzor for Yom Kippur, and an unusual brass plate which illustrates the sounds of the
Shofar.

S'lihot ascend to a cry:

Hear our voice, You, our God,
protect us, have mercy upon us;
accept in mercy and with favor our prayers.
Do not cast us aside, as we grow old,
as strength has waned,
do not desert us.

After each S'lihah, we recite the *Litany of God's Attributes.* According to Torah, these attributes were revealed to Moses at Sinai.

God passed by him and spoke:
The Lord! the Lord! A God compassionate and gracious, slow to anger, rich in grace and truth, extending kindness to the thousandth generation, forgiving iniquity, transgression, and sin—yet remitting all punishment [this He will not do]. [Exod. 34:6–7]

The Rabbis were so fully convinced of God's unconditional pardon that they omitted the words we have bracketed from the recital, thus reversing the meaning of the verse: God *will* remit all punishment, without condition.

Tradition has explained these attributes as follows:

The Lord!: I am with man before he sins.
The Lord!: I am with man after he sins.
God: I have absolute power to make My will effective.
Compassionate: I shelter you in love as a mother shelters her child in her
    womb [the term *rahum,* "compassionate," derives from *rehem,* womb]
Gracious: I hold you in grace, even if justice were to dictate punishment.
Slow to Anger: I am patient with sinners.
Rich in Grace: I rule the world in loving-kindness.
Rich in Truth: I will make truth prevail in the world.
Extending Kindness to the Thousandth Generation: I reward children for
    their fathers' merits; the good deeds of one generation will bear fruit
    in the following ones.
Forgiving Iniquity: I forgive though you transgressed knowingly.
Forgiving Transgression: I forgive though you transgressed in willful de-
    fiance of My will.
Forgiving Sin: I forgive your weakness, your unintentional transgressions.
Remitting all Punishment: I will grant you full pardon, if you return to
    Me in Teshuvah. [see Rosh Hashanah 17b]

These are God's terms under the covenant. S'lihot, therefore, conclude with an evocation of the covenant:

Remember the covenant with Abraham . . .

Then confession, the act of Teshuvah, follows.

Confession of Sins

There is a silent confession in which we may include individual transgressions against God and fellowman. But we also recite public confession, for we are responsible for one another and bear our brothers' and sisters' guilt to the extent that we fail to guide and admonish them. In this confession we list only those offenses committed against fellow human beings. In hurting others, we have simultaneously hurt God, our common Father. Upon making restoration, we straighten ourselves before God.

Rosh Hashanah and Yom Kippur as Festivals: The Wearing of White

Our High Holy Days are festivals. We light the festive candles and recite the blessings of Sheheheyanu as on all joyous occasions.

The Rabbis explain the reason for our joyful mood:

God speaks to Israel: When you appear before Me in judgment on Rosh Hashanah, and after you have been discharged in peace [at the end of Yom Kippur], I account it to you as having been re-created as new persons. [Yerushalmi: Rosh Hashanah 4:8]

Only Hallel, recited on other festivals, is forbidden us. These Psalms of Praise would be inappropriate as we stand in judgment. But our dress must be festive. As the Rabbis point out: May those who appear before an earthly court dress themselves in somber garments; we will appear in festive array, for we are sure of being pardoned.

The color of the High Holy Days is white. Torah curtains, Torah mantles, all coverings are white. In many congregations, particularly Orthodox ones, the women wear white; the men robe themselves in a white *kittel*. These are garments of death and reminders of the brevity of human life; they reinforce the call to Teshuvah. They are also symbols of equality; the distinction that dress may confer has disappeared: before God, all are equal. Finally, white is the color of purity, toward which we should aspire.

A kittel is made of linen, in the form of a long white shirt or monk's cowl. The collar may be attached or separate. A belt of white twisted linen strands completes the garment. By custom, an additional knot is added to the belt whenever a great joy enters the life of a Jew: marriage, the birth of a child, the arrival of grandchildren.

Self-Denial

On Yom Kippur, bodily wants must be denied, and the call to Teshuvah even includes castigation.

For it is a Day of Atonement, on which expiation is made on your behalf before the Lord your God. . . . It shall be a Sabbath of complete rest for you, and you shall practice self-denial. [Lev. 23:26–32]

Self-denial means complete abstinence from any food or drink. Ointments are not to be used; washing is restricted to the ritually required cleansing of fingers and eyes. Leather shoes are removed, with canvas shoes frequently worn instead. Torah insists on fasting. The human person is shown how little the body needs, how much denial it can bear; the smaller our concern with physical satisfactions, the greater will be the spirituality we attain.

9

The Celebration
of the
High Holy Days

ELLUL

Ellul was always a time of preparation for the act of divine grace. On the sixth of Sivan, Moses ascended the mountain to receive the tablets of the Ten Commandments. He spent forty days in communion with God, returning on the seventeenth of Tammuz. Finding the people enmeshed in the sin of the golden calf, Moses broke the tablets. For forty days, he remained with his people. Then he ascended Mount Sinai again; the date was the *first of Ellul.* On this second stay, he pleaded with God for forgiveness. On the fortieth day, God responded: I have forgiven the people's sin. The date was the tenth of Tishrie, Yom Kippur, henceforth and forever Day of Forgiveness. The letters אלול have been interpreted as acrostic: אני לדודי ודודי לי I belong to my Beloved, my Beloved to me (Song of Songs 6:3).

At the end of the Sabbath before Rosh Hashanah (or a week earlier, if Rosh Hashanah falls on a Tuesday), S'lihot begin.

Erev Rosh Hashanah, the day before the feast, calls the worshipers to early S'lihot. The binding of Isaac is the key theme. Some people will fast on this day, at least until noon. The Shofar is not sounded, as a break between the voluntary and the required sounding on the morrow. Preparations for the festival move forward, the food is prepared, and the table is set. Last letters are written. The family dresses for the evening service, the beginning of the New Year.

A Doré engraving. Seeing the people enmeshed in the sin of the golden calf, Moses shattered the tablets of the Law. It was on the first day of Ellul that he once again ascended Mount Sinai to plead with God to forgive the Jewish people. Forty days later, on Yom Kippur, God was persuaded, thus setting Yom Kippur forever as the Day of Forgiveness.

ROSH HASHANAH

The Eve

As the sun sets, the New Year enters. The service in the synagogue is just the regular evening service, but with the Amidah for Rosh Hashanah and the Kiddush of the festival.

New Year's greetings

Wishing each other well, members of the family, friends, and acquaintances use a traditional formula: May you be inscribed unto a good year. Following the grammatical rules of Hebrew, they say:

to a male: *Leshanah tovah tikatev*
to a female: *Leshanah tovah tikatevee*
to more than one male: *Leshanah tovah tikatevu*
to more than one female: *Leshanah tovah tikatavnu.*

A greeting applying to all and, therefore used on cards, simply says:
May the decision to be inscribed and sealed be good.

Ketivah ve-Hatimah tovah.

These wishes may be expressed only on Rosh Hashanah eve. After Rosh Hashanah eve our greeting takes the form of

G'mar Hatimah tova.
As God puts His final seal on you, may it be for good!

The truly pious are inscribed for good at the very beginning of the penitential season. Courtesy demands that we regard our neighbor as truly pious; God merely needs to put His seal on the decision (Rosh Hashanah 16b).

Family Celebration

On returning home, the parents bless their children. Mother lights the candles. (Unless Rosh Hashanah falls on a Sabbath, the rules of the festivals apply. They permit the transfer of a flame for lighting and cooking.) The mother speaks the blessing *first*, then lights the candles; she does not spread her hands.

Barukh . . . vetzivanu lehadlik ner shel Yom Tov
Blessed are You . . . He, Who . . . has commanded us to kindle the light of the festival.

Sheheheyanu follows.

The Kiddush for Rosh Hashanah is solemnly pronounced by the father; the blessing over the bread is spoken. Each person present gets a share.

The Hallah for Rosh Hashanah is round: a wheel. We are all bound to the wheel of fate. According to Jewish custom, the pieces of bread given to the members of the family are dipped in honey, that the year be sweet.

The same idea led to the practice of dipping a sweet apple in honey. After the Hallah each person gets a slice of the apple. Following the blessing for the fruit, a plea is offered:

May it be Your will, Lord our God and God of our fathers, to renew unto us a good and sweet year.

In many homes, it is the custom to distribute a morsel of the head of a fish, symbol of fertility. Before partaking of it, each person says:

May it be Your will, Lord our God and God of our fathers, that we be head and not tail.

Salads and sour dishes are eschewed. Nothing is to mar the sweetness of the first moments of the New Year, now begun under a happy omen.

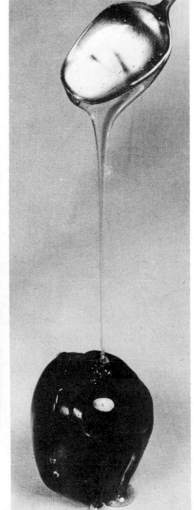

Two Rosh Hashanah customs: the round Hallah reminding us of the wheel of fate, and the apple dipped in honey reminding us of God's many blessings.

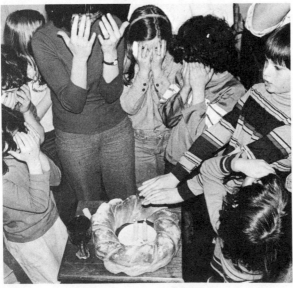

Rosh Hashanah Morning

The service commences early, with introductory meditations and Psalms. Then the cantor intones as in court:

THE KING! Seated on His Throne high and supreme!

Shaharit, embellished by liturgical poetry, finds its climax in *Avinu Malkenu.* But if Rosh Hashanah falls on the Sabbath, this great petition is omitted; the Sabbath spirit must banish all human concerns, even on such a holy day.

Torah is read. Five people are "called up."

On the *first* day of the feast (in Orthodox and Conservative congregations), Isaac's birth and youth are related.

The *Haftarah* consists of the song of thanksgiving, sung by Hannah, as she dedicated her long-yearned-for son, Samuel, to the service of God.

On the *second* day of the feast (in Reform congregations, on the first day) the story of the *Akedah,* the Binding of Isaac, is read. Isaac, in his willingness to submit to the supreme sacrifice, is prototype of the Jew throughout all generations (Gen. 22:1–24). The *Haftarah* offers assurance. The people will survive and will find favor. Rachel, mother of Isaac, is comforted:

Your children will come back from the land of the enemy . . .
Your children will return to their own land. [Jer. 31:1–20]

The *Shofar* service follows. The *Baal Tekiah* prepares himself in silent meditation; then he intones:

Barukh . . . vetzivanu lishmoa kol Shofar
Blessed are You . . . He . . . Who has commanded us to hear the voice of the Shofar.

Sheheheyanu follows.

In order that the *Baal Tekiah* might concentrate fully on his task, the name of each sound is called out to him, one by one.

Then the people proclaim:

Blessed are the people, who understand [the meaning of] the blast; they walk in the light of Your countenance.

If Rosh Hashanah falls on the Sabbath, the Shofar is not sounded (except in Reform congregations). Rather than run the risk that Sabbath law be broken by carrying a Shofar to the synagogue, the Rabbis omitted the rite.

The *Mussaf* is distinguished by three specially added proclamations: *Malkhiot*: Proclamation of God as King; *Zikhronot*: Proclamation of God, Master of absolute Remembrance and Judge of the universe; *Shofarot*: Proclamation of God Who will sound the Shofar of redemption, God the Redeemer.

The congregation reads the *Mussaf Amidah* silently; the cantor then repeats it. In the repetition, the Shofar is sounded after each of the proclamations.

Let us follow this second reading of the Amidah.

Unetane Tokef

After the opening benedictions, embroidered by poetry for the day, the cantor reaches the *Kedushah,* the sanctification. But before this is pronounced, a reflection on the meaning of Rosh Hashanah is introduced, the profound and powerful *Unetane Tokef.*

Unetane tokef kedushat hayom. . . . Let us acclaim the majestic sanctity of this day, for it is awesome and mighty. Your kingdom is triumphantly proclaimed, Your throne established in mercy, and You occupy it in truth. In truth, You are judge and prosecutor, knowing motives, giving evidence, writing, sealing, counting, measuring, remembering all, even things we have forgotten. You open the book of remembrances, and it speaks for itself, for every person's signature is affixed to his deeds.

The great Shofar is sounded. A muted small voice is heard. The angels too are frightened, fear and trembling seize them, and they declare: "This is the day of judgment, of mustering the host on high!" In Your sight not even they are exempt from judgment. And all that have come into the world pass before You as a flock of sheep. As a shepherd gathers his flock, making his sheep pass beneath his staff, even so do You make pass, count, and muster the souls of all the living. You determine the latter end of every creature and record their ultimate verdict. On Rosh Hashanah it is written down for them, on Yom Kippur it is sealed: How many shall leave [life] and how many shall be born, who shall live and who shall die, who shall attain his full span of life and who shall not, who shall perish by fire, and who by water, who by the sword and who by wild beasts, who by hunger and who by thirst, who by storm and who by plague, who shall have rest and who shall be restless, who shall find repose and who shall be wandering, who shall be free from sorrow and who shall be tormented, who shall be exalted and who shall be humbled, who shall be poor and who shall be rich. *But Teshuvah, Prayer, and Good Deeds can avert the severity of the decree.*

For your renown is as Your Name: slow to anger, ready to be soothed, You do not desire the guilty one's death, but that he turn from his way and live. You wait for him up to the very day of his death; if he returns You accept him at once. Verily You are their Creator and You know their inner drives; they are but flesh and blood.

As to man, his origin is dust and his end is dust, at the risk of his life he earns his bread, he is like a broken vessel of clay, like withering grass, a fading flower, a passing shadow, a drifting cloud, a fleeting breath, scattering dust, a transient dream,

But You are King, God, living and enduring!

The *Unetane Tokef* reveals the essence not only of the Days of

Awe, but of the Jewish concept of life. It was used by the Catholic Church in the Requiem Mass, but there it deals with God's inexorable judgment on those that have parted from the earth. The redeeming call to Teshuvah is not heard.

The majestic poem was written during the latter part of the eleventh century by Kalonymus ben Meshullam, head of the Jewish community of Mainz. With his family he underwent martyrdom during the first Crusade.

The Three Proclamations

From Kedushah the service moves to *Malkhiot,* the affirmation of God, the King. The introduction to this section is of such beauty that it has become the concluding adoration of every service throughout the year:

It is for us to praise the Lord of all . . . we bend the knee and bow, offering thanks to the King of Kings, the Holy One, Blessed be He . . .

At this moment the congregation kneels. It will do so again and three times more on Yom Kippur.

The selections from Holy Scripture reveal God as King, and end with our acceptance of "the yoke of the kingdom": *Shema Yisrael.*
The Shofar is sounded (except on Sabbath).

Zikhronot dwells on God's covenant from the days of Noah, but especially the covenant with His people. It concludes with the plea:

Remember this day the *Akedah,* the binding of Isaac, in mercy unto his descendants. Blessed are You, God, He, who remembers the covenant.

The Shofar is sounded (except on Sabbath).

Shofarot takes us from the sound of the Shofar that accompanied the revelation at Sinai to the day when the "great Shofar" will be sounded for our redemption, and Israel, in everlasting joy, will return to Zion.
The Shofar is sounded (except on Sabbath).
The concluding benedictions and the recital of the priestly blessing complete the service.

Rosh Hashanah Afternoon

Returning home, the parents bless their children. The Kiddush is spoken, the motto of the day:

Sound on the day of renewal, when the moon is hidden, the Shofar for our festival. It is an ordinance for Israel, a [time of] judgment for the God of Jacob. [Ps. 81:4–5]

The family joins in the repast.

Tashlikh

Later in the afternoon (except on Sabbath), the people go to a stream for *Tashlikh*, prayer. The word is derived from the verses that will be recited at the river banks:

Who is a God like You that pardons iniquity . . .
because He delights in mercy . . .
and You will cast [ve-*tashlikh*] all their sins into
the depth of the sea. [Mic. 7:18–20]

The custom may have originated in antiquity. The Romans had a similar ceremony. Objects representing human wealth, including stalks of grain, were thrown into the floods to propitiate the gods who might resent the wresting of food from the earth that belonged to them. Petrarch (1307–1374) relates a similar custom that he observed among the people of Cologne on the river Rhine. Among Jews, therefore, the custom may have had its origin in Christian practices in the Rhineland.

But whatever its origin, the pilgrimage into nature, held to have been created on this day out of the primordial waters (Gen. 1), is observed. The custom of throwing bread crumbs into the water was castigated as superstition and prohibited by Rabbi Jacob Moellin (Maharil) of Mainz (1365–1427) at almost the very time that it is mentioned by Petrarch.

Following Tashlikh, some Jews will spend the rest of the day in responsive recital of the Psalms.

Although some have disclaimed it as superstition—and one great rabbi attempted to prohibit it altogether—the custom of Tashlikh, casting bread crumbs into the water to vicariously cast one's sins away, continues to today.

The Second Day of Rosh Hashanah

The Rabbis were not certain whether the two days were not to be regarded "as one long day," which would make a second-day Sheheheyanu superfluous and hence forbidden. We, therefore, place fruit on the table, of which we have not yet partaken during the current season, in order that the Sheheheyanu of the Kiddush may relate to it. In the synagogue, large baskets of fruit are arranged next to the cantor, who speaks the Sheheheyanu in the evening Kiddush, and the children receive both wine and fruit. The liturgy of the morning service follows that of the first day, but new poetry is introduced.

THE WEEK OF PENITENCE

Between Rosh Hashanah and Yom Kippur a whole week elapses. The total season consists of ten days: *Aseret Yemei Teshuvah*, the Ten Days of Teshuvah. The week is a period of probation in action. S'lihot are offered; the *Avinu Malkenu* is recited every morning and afternoon.

TZOM GEDALIAH. The day immediately following Rosh Hashanah is a fast in commemoration of Gedaliah. He was a pious Jew, appointed governor of Judah by the Babylonians after the destruction of the First Temple. His confused countrymen held him responsible for their troubles and murdered him. With his death, complete disaster fell upon the unhappy community (see Jer. 40; II Kings 25:22–25). The fast reminds us not to blame others for our misfortunes, but rather to examine ourselves.

Some Jews will fast during the days of the week, at least for half a day. On Sabbath and the eve of Yom Kippur fasting is not permitted.

The Sabbath of the penitential week is called *Shabbat Shuvah*. The Haftarah, read on this day, begins with the words:

Shuvah Yisrael. . . ! Return, Israel, unto the Lord, your God. . . . [Hos. 14:2–10; Mic. 7:18–20; Joel 2:15–27]

Erev Yom Kippur

After S'lihot and morning services a number of rites are performed by Orthodox Jews on the day before Yom Kippur.

Flagellation

A maximum of 39 strokes is ordained in Torah in punishment for certain crimes (Makkot 3:10, based on Deut. 25:2–3). Some of us may have committed these transgressions. Pious Jews will, therefore, submit to the scourging, at least symbolically. Stretching out on the floor, the penitent receives 39 soft lashes on his back administered by a friend with a leather strap. Counting them, the executing Jew recites three times the verse: "But He, being merciful, will forgive iniquity and will not destroy; He restrains His wrath again and again and will not give vent to His fury" (Ps. 78:38). The verse, in Hebrew, has 13 words. It was originally offered as a prayer for those about to undergo court-appointed punishment, a plea that the convict might endure his punishment well. At the same time, the quotation offers comfort to the penitent. Children may never administer this rite to a parent.

Absolution from Vows of Religious Performance

A person may have imposed upon himself certain religious obligations, such as special days of fasting, and may have broken this vow. A court of three, a Bet Din, may grant absolution and annulment. Three men form a Bet Din, and a fourth pleads for remission, which is granted. Then they take turns. The Yom Kippur service will open with a similar formula of annulment.

Pledges *made to others* can *never* be dissolved.

Kapparot

This custom is based on the idea of ransom, the substitution of one living being for another. Later on we shall discuss the Scapegoat Ritual of the Yom Kippur service in the Temple, which rests on the same concept. The custom, first observed by Babylonian Jewry in the third century C.E. has been severely condemned by many of our great masters as superstition. It has nevertheless prevailed in circles of Orthodox Jewry.

A rooster is selected for males; a hen, for females. (These birds, never offered in the Temple, are selected in order that no suspicion may arise that we are re-creating a Temple offering, an act strictly forbidden.) The head of the house gathers the male members, takes the rooster and recites several verses from the Psalms (107:10, 14, 17–21), concluding with the quotation from Job 33:23–24:

If there be for him one angel
one intercessor among a thousand [accusers]
    to vouch for man's uprightness;
then He is gracious unto him and says:
    "Deliver him from going down into the pit,
    I have found a ransom."

The bird is then twirled three times over the heads of the group with the words:

This is in exchange for me [us, you], this is instead of me [us, you], this

Kapparot. The hen or rooster is twirled above the head in the symbolic act of substituting one life for another.

is ransom (*kapparah*) for me [us, you]. This rooster will go to its death, but I [we, you] may go forward to a good life and unto peace.

The same rite is repeated for the women, as the hen is used. Other living things, such as fish, even flowers in a planter, may be used, with substitution of the appropriate words. The practice of using money can be found, but is not encouraged. The bird is slaughtered by the Shohet, and the fish is killed and given to the poor.

A Universal Duty:
Seeking Forgiveness from Those We Have Wronged

Sins against our fellow human beings will not be forgiven by God unless we have obtained our neighbor's pardon. We are bidden to seek him or her out again and again and to make restitution for damages we have inflicted. At the same time, we must be forgiving of others when they come to us. Sins against another human being carry double weight: they are transgressions against God *and* violations of our neighbor's rights. After our fellow man has pardoned us, we may seek God's pardon on Yom Kippur.

An early meal is taken by the family. Then the congregation assembles for the weekday afternoon service. At this time, each individual recites the great confession of sins, as on Yom Kippur. The Rabbis felt that the heavy meal, to be consumed later, might disable a person from attending worship on the holy day itself. Early confession removes apprehensions during the final banquet.

The family dresses. The meal is served; it is sumptuous but usually bland, lest we become thirsty.

The parents bless their children, adding any thoughts their hearts may prompt.

111

One additional blessing reads:

May it be the will of our Father in Heaven to put into your heart love
for Him and reverence for Him. May the reverence for God accompany
you all the days of your life that you may not come to sin. May your
longing be for Torah and Mitzvot, may your eyes be directed straight,
your mouth speak wisdom, your heart strive for reverence, may your hands
be occupied with Mitzvot, your feet hasten to do the will of your Father
in Heaven. May He give you pious sons and daughters, who will occupy
themselves with Torah and Mitzvot all the days of their lives; may your
womb be blessed. May He vouchsafe your sustenance through legitimate
means, without stress and with profit, out of His hand that is wide open
and not through the handouts of other human beings, a sustenance that
will direct you toward the service of God. May you be inscribed and
sealed unto a good, long life, you and all the righteous of Israel. Amen.
[Kitzur Shulhan Arukh, 131:16]

A large candle is lit, to burn for 24 hours. The house may not be
dark. Memorial candles are kindled for the departed members of
the family. Now the mother ushers in Yom Kippur, as she does the
Sabbath. She lights the two Sabbath candles, shields her hands and
speaks:

Barukh . . . vetzivanu lehadlik ner shel Yom ha-Kippurim
Blessed are You . . . He, Who . . . has commanded us to kindle the light
of Yom Kippur.

Sheheheyanu follows.
The family departs for the synagogue.

YOM KIPPUR

The Vigil

The synagogue is ablaze with light; memorial lamps flicker. The
men, dressed in their kittels, are not unlike the priests of old. During this night, the High Priest, surrounded by a priestly court, kept
a vigil, preparing himself through the study of Torah for the great
task ahead (Yoma 1:6–7). For us, members of the "kingdom of
priests," this night is also a vigil. The "white fast" is about to
commence.

The beginning has the grandeur of simplicity. This is the only
evening service of the year when everybody wears the Tallit. It
must, therefore, start while the sun is still in the sky. The rabbi
loudly pronounces the blessing. Each of the men who will lead a
portion of the service in the next 24 hours sings the Berakhah while
standing in place amid the congregation. The sound floats anti-
phonally through the sanctuary; the congregation follows in unison.

Three Torah scrolls are carried from the Ark to the Bimah, and then the rabbi declares in a loud voice:

By authority of the court on high
and by authority of this court below
with the consent of the All-present
and with the consent of the congregation
we hereby permit prayer to go forward in the company
of transgressors.

This statement is based on a Talmudic teaching: "No fast is true, unless some of the sinners in Israel participate in it" (Ker. 6b). The declaration dispels arrogance. Who is a transgressor in this assembly? It may be I.

It has been held that the declaration is also meant to refer specifically to the Marranos, the secret Jews of Spain who officially had adopted Christianity but on Yom Kippur came furtively to join their breathren in plea for divine forgiveness.

Surrounded by three men, a Bet Din, holding the sacred scrolls, the cantor intones Kol Nidrei. The first time he renders it very softly, then he repeats it in a louder voice, and finally he sings with all his might. The statement itself, of no great import, is a collective annulment of vows we have imposed *upon ourselves*. Of course, no oath given in court, no pledge made to others, can ever be dissolved. Only pledges made to ourselves can be so annulled. This is worth stressing because over the centuries the Kol Nidrei has been falsely pointed to by the enemies of the Jews as an example of how Jews supposedly absolved themselves from oaths.

The formula is different in various rites. It may be retrospective, referring to vows taken in the past, or prospective, referring to the future. Our generally used version is a confusing mixture of the two.

Kol Nidrei originated in the East between the sixth and the tenth centuries. The tune for it was created in southern Germany during the sixteenth century. This tune is so haunting, voicing sorrow and suffering before rising triumphantly in hope and faith, that it has become dear to all Jews.

After the singing of the Kol Nidrei the community recites the words:

And all the congregation of the children of Israel shall be forgiven. . . . [Num. 15:26]

The cantor intones:

Forgive, we beseech You, the sins of this people. . . . [Num. 14:19]

The congregation responds:

And God said: "I have pardoned. . . ." [Num. 14:20]

Jewish faith is so strong that the people feel assured of divine pardon even before the service has truly begun. Their Father in Heaven cannot deny His children.

The scrolls are returned to the Ark.

Night has fallen, and the evening service may begin. It includes the supplication that grace may be granted us before the sun will set again:

May our supplication rise at eventide,
our pleas come to You from early morning
and our thanksgiving be seen tomorrow night.

S'lihot and confessions are offered; *Avinu Malkenu* concludes the service (on Sabbath it is not recited).

Some pious men will continue the vigil by reciting responsively the Book of Psalms.

Sexual intercourse is not permitted on Yom Kippur.

Yom Kippur Day: The Cleansing of the Soul

The Yom Kippur service lacks the drama of sight and sound of Rosh Hashanah. It leads instead to inwardness: the cleansing of the soul.

SHAHARIT.   S'lihot, confessions, and *Avinu Malkenu* (except on Sabbath) are the core of the morning service.

TORAH READING.   Traditional congregations read the portion ordaining the sacred service in the Temple (Lev. 16). Reform congregations read the portion reminding us of the eternal covenant that was made not only with our fathers but with us (Deut. 29:9–14; 30:11–20).

THE HAFTARAH, recited in all rites, reveals the meaning of the fast:

. . . this is the fast I desire
to unlock the fetters of wickedness
and unlock the cords of the yoke
to let the oppressed go free;
to break off every yoke.
It is to share your bread with the hungry,
and to take the wretched poor into your home,
when you see the naked, to clothe him
and not to ignore your own kin. [Isa. 57:14–58:14]

Social justice is the key to Jewish living.

In a number of congregations, the *memorial service* for our departed follows the Torah reading.

MUSSAF.   We reach the high point of the day. The core of the Mussaf service is the *Avodah*, the rehearsal of the Temple service. Four times the congregation kneels and prostrates itself. S'lihot and confessions frame the main section.

In many congregations, the Mussaf service includes a memorial to Jewish martyrs.

THE SECOND TORAH READING. Orthodox congregations read the portion on illicit sexual relationships (Lev. 18); non-Orthodox ones prefer to call attention to the positive side of Jewish obligation:

You shall become holy . . .
You shall love your neighbor as yourself, I am the Lord. [Lev. 19:1–18]

The prophetic portion, Haftarah, is again identical in all rites: the story of the prophet Jonah. Called to preach repentance to Israel's enemies, that they might save their lives, Jonah at first refused and then was forced to fulfill his mission. For Jews, even their enemies are children of God, our brothers and sisters.

MINHAH. In Western European rites, this is the hour when the martyrs are commemorated. It is a long tale, from Rome to Auschwitz. A burning theological question is asked and, in a sense, remains unanswered: why?

. . . The angels on high cried out bitterly: "Is this Torah, is this its reward . . . the enemy slanders Your holy and awesome Name, sneers and pours scorn on Your Holy Name?" A heavenly voice responded: "It is My decree, accept it. . . ."

Though we have no answer, we know that our suffering is not caused by God's absence or by His anger, but rather that it is His will that we be tried as no people has ever been tried in history.

YIZKOR. From the remembrance of the martyrs we turn (in many congregations) to the memory of our immediate dear ones who have died. We resolve to carry on where they have left off.

N'EELAH. The concluding prayer, offered only on Yom Kippur, raises emotions to their greatest fervor:

Open unto us the gate
at the gate's closing time,
for the day is almost over.
The day is passing fast,
the sun is going home and setting,
do let us enter Your gates.
Forgive us, pardon us, have mercy. . . .

The first verses of the main S'lihot, spoken throughout the entire season, are repeated; confession is spoken; God's attributes are invoked.

We pause for meditation: Man, as a biological being, is nothing. Only as he recognizes his divine mission does he acquire stature.

A Kittel clasp, a buckle used to close the white robe worn on the High Holy Days. Poland, nineteenth century.

God has called him to be this steward and thus to find reconciliation with himself and his fellow human beings.

In this spirit, the congregation speaks the *Avinu Malkenu*, even on the Sabbath. Where previously we have pleaded that God "inscribe" us in the book of blessings, now we ask that we be "sealed" in this book.

AFFIRMATION OF FAITH.   Night has fallen. Before the open Ark, repeating word for word the rabbi's intonation, the congregation speaks:

Sh'ma Yisrael Adonai Elohenu Adonai Ehad
Hear, O Israel, the Lord our God, the Lord is One.

As He is One, this affirmation is pronounced only once. We now say three times:

Barukh Shem kevod Malkhuto le-olam va-ed
Blessed be His glorious Kingdom for ever throughout all time and space.

The rabbi continues seven times, and the congregation responds:

Adonai Hu Ha-Elohim
He, Lord, He is The God!

Mystical tradition holds that, on Yom Kippur, God descends through the seven spheres of heaven to be with His people. Now He returns. As His Indwelling, His Shekhinah, departs, we call after Him our unshakable profession of faith.

THE SHOFAR.   One sound dismisses us: *Tekiah*. March onward in the new direction you have found!

THE WEEK ENTERS.   Evening prayers are recited, Havdalah is performed. The people greet each other, "*Hag sameah,*" or "*Gut Yontef,*" "A Happy Holiday to You." A festive mood pervades the crowd.

If the moon is clear, members will join outside for *Kiddush Levanah,* the blessing for the new moon.

After breaking their fast, they start preparations for Sukkot, to link Mitzvah with Mitzvah.

Morning prayers on the following day start a bit earlier than usual, "that Satan may not say to God: 'See, they have already slid back into their old ways.'"

Avodah: The Sacrificial Temple Service

Avodah means "Service." It was *the* service par excellence, performed by the High Priest on Yom Kippur. The Avodah follows step by step the instructions laid down in Torah: Leviticus, chapter 16. This passage, read to the people by the High Priest on this day, constitutes our Torah reading in traditional congregations.

In this chapter the purpose of the rites is also given:

Thus he shall purge the Holy of Holies of the uncleanness and transgressions of the Israelites, whatever their sins, and he shall do the same for the Tent of Meeting, which abides with them in the midst of their uncleanness. [Lev. 16:16]

When he made expiation for himself and his household, and for the whole congregation of Israel, he shall go out to the altar that is before the Lord and purge it. [Lev. 16:17–18]

Thus shall he cleanse it of the uncleanness of the Israelites and consecrate it. [Lev. 16:18]

He shall purge the innermost Shrine [Holy of Holies]; he shall purge the Tent of Meeting [Holy Section] and the altar [of incense]; and shall make expiation for the priests and for all the people of the congregation. This shall be to you a law for all time: to make atonement for the Israelites for all their sins once a year. [Lev. 16:33–34]

The Avodah had a *twofold* purpose: the purging of the sanctuary and the expiation of the people's sins. This testifies to its great age. It was held in antiquity that the divinity and the divine resting-place, contaminated and weakened by the people's sins, needed restoration, an "infusion" of spirit and of blood. Similarly, Jewish mysticism held to the idea that we influence God, and by our deeds we even redeem Him.

The Talmud devotes an entire tractate to Yom Kippur and the detailed rules surrounding the Avodah. It is the tractate *Yoma,* "The Day."

The rites were performed in all three parts of the Temple precincts.

In the courts, the High Priest took his ablutions, spoke confession, and slaughtered the sacrificial animals upon which he had placed the people's transgressions in his confession. Passing through the

Holy Section, he entered the *Holy of Holies* several times, conducting sacred offices in both. Additionally, a goat, consecrated in the courts to carry the sins of the people, was led into the desert and hurled from a mountain peak into a gorge, the goat of Azazel, the scapegoat.

At his *first* entry into the Holy of Holies, the High Priest restored the divine cloud that rested on the sanctuary [Exod. 40:34f.] and on the foundation of the universe. To that purpose he offered incense, whose smoke filled the space as a cloud.

At his *second* entry, he consecrated the divine precinct by sprinkling the blood of the sacrificed bull once in an upward direction. Before the reconsecrated Holy of Holies, he now sprinkled the blood seven times in a downward direction. This signified the pouring out of the "blood" of the sinful people, whose sins had been transferred to an animal, a symbol of humility and atonement.

At his *third* entry, he brought the blood of a goat, specifically designated "unto God," performing the same act of sprinkling and offering the "blood" of the people.

Returning to the *Holy Section,* he reconsecrated it in the same manner with the blood of both animals. Finally, he infused the incense altar with new blood. This altar, from which the cloud of the Presence arose every day, thus became once again a representation of the people, infused with the intangible essence of the divine spirit.

At a *fourth* entry, he removed the censer.

The idea of ransom, specifically expressed in the passage concerning the "scapegoat for Azazel," is also of great antiquity. The goat was a substitute for man. By "carrying off" man's sins, it may have allowed the people watching the ceremony to experience a catharsis, a release of aggressiveness and guilt. For us, the recitation of the Avodah service in its ancient and original form may serve much the same purpose.

The Date of Yom Kippur

The date of Yom Kippur, namely the tenth of Tishrei, becomes meaningful in the context of purification. It appears that each of the nature festivals was preceded by such an act of cleansing. Four such days occur at three-month intervals throughout the year.

The fast of the *tenth* of Tevet precedes the feast of the *fifteenth* of Sh'vat, the beginning of the tree-planting season.

The *tenth* of Nissan was appointed as the day when the Israelites in Egypt were to choose the sacrificial lamb, to be eaten during the night of the *fifteenth,* the night of liberation. Pessah, feast of liberation, marks the beginning of the harvest season. To this day, the house must be purged of all leaven, unclean remnants of the past, as an act of purification. The *ninth* of Av, and, if it falls on a Sabbath, the *tenth*, is a fast of deepest mourning. It precedes the *fifteenth* of Av, the climax of the tree harvest.

Yom Kippur, on the *tenth* of Tishrie, is a day of purification, preceding Sukkot, on the *fifteenth*, a feast celebrating the ingathering of the harvest. As we shall see, the structure of the Sukkot festival corresponds to that of the Ten Days of Repentance.

Yom Kippur as Folk Festival

In the Temple the solemn rites of purification were observed, but in the vineyards Israel's youth gathered for a joyful feast that testifies to the great age of the holy day; it was a fertility celebration:

Israel had no happier days of celebration than the fifteenth of Av and Yom Kippur. On these days, the daughters of Jerusalem would go out in borrowed white dresses, in order not to put to shame those that had none of their own. . . . The girls went out and danced in the vineyards, exclaiming: "Young man, lift up your eyes and look, whom you may choose; consider not beauty but family." [Taanit 26b]

And thus, "those who had no wife came" and chose and hoped that their marriage would be consecrated under a good omen.

Yom Kippur was the right day for this event; joy was undergirded by earnestness, and banter by an awareness of the day's sanctity. The young people were reminded that this was the moment the sanctuary itself was being consecrated; so might their home be a sanctuary, and their youthful exuberance tempered by a consciousness of the holy purpose that brings the sexes together.

In time, the "fertility" aspect of Yom Kippur came to be forgotten or transferred to the feast of celebration that follows it: Sukkot.

10

Sukkot:
The Harvest
Festival

THE FESTIVALS

Our Festivals—Pessah, Shavuot, Sukkot, and Rosh Hashanah—are periods of work prohibition. But this prohibition is not as complete as on the Sabbath and on Yom Kippur. Of the festivals it is stated:

. . . no work shall be done on them; only what every person is to eat, that alone may be prepared for you. [Exod. 12:16]

The preparation of food and the transportation of objects are permitted. Fire may not be created, but may be transferred from flame to flame. All this is forbidden on the Sabbath and Yom Kippur. Otherwise, the full degree of work prohibitions applies. This means that work, even cooking, may be performed only for the day itself, not in preparation for the following day. (It is permitted, however, to prepare a large amount of food each day, even if there are left-overs that will be eaten on the following day.)

Sukkot and Pessah are celebrated for seven days. Of these, only the first day of Sukkot and the first and the last days of Pessah are full holy days with work prohibition. On Sukkot the seven days are followed by a separate feast, the eighth day of the "Concluding Feast," on which work is equally forbidden. Diaspora Jewry observes two full holy days at the beginning and the end of the festivals, which extend Pessah to eight days and the Sukkot season to nine days among traditional Jews. The middle days have no work prohibition attached to them; they are *Hol-ha-Moed*—"Weekday-that-is-festival." The laws of dwelling in the Sukkah and, on Pessah, of eating Matzah apply during these days; festive worship is conducted in the synagogue.

We learn in Torah that the ancient Israelites were commanded to appear before God on Pessah, Shavuot, and Sukkot. These are the three "Pilgrimage Festivals," *Shalosh Regalim,* when the city of Jerusalem was thronged (see Deut. 16:16). We shall begin with Sukkot, as it follows directly after Yom Kippur.

THE HARVEST FESTIVAL

From earliest days, mankind has celebrated the ingathering of the harvest. This is the origin of Sukkot. But Torah gives a Jewish character to this celebration, linking the feast to events in history.

Mark, on the fifteenth day of the seventh month, when you have gathered the yield of your land, you shall observe the festival of the Lord for seven days; a complete rest on the first day, and a complete rest on the eighth day. On the first day you shall take the product of the *hadar trees,* branches of *palm trees,* boughs of *leafy trees,* and *willows* of the *brook,* and you shall rejoice before the Lord seven days. . . . You shall live in booths seven days; all citizens in Israel shall live in booths, in order that future generations may know that I made the Israelite people live in booths when I brought them out of the land of Egypt, I the Lord, your God.

And Moses declared to the Israelites the set times of the Lord. [Lev. 23:39–44]

After the ingathering from your threshing floor and your vat, you shall hold the Feast of Booths for seven days. You shall rejoice in your festival, with your son and daughter, your male and female slave, the Levite, the fatherless, and the widow in your communities. You shall hold festival for the Lord your God seven days, in the place that the Lord will choose; for the Lord your God will bless all your crops and all your undertakings, and you shall have nothing but joy. [Deut. 16:13–15]

On the fifteenth day of this seventh month there shall be the Feast of Booths to the Lord for seven days. The first day shall be a sacred occasion: you shall not work at your occupations; seven days you shall bring offerings by fire to the Lord. On the eighth day you shall observe a sacred occasion and bring an offering by fire to the Lord: it is a solemn "Concluding Feast"; you shall not work at your occupations. [Lev. 23:34–56]

These verses tell us in principle all we have to know.

Arba Minim: The Festive Bouquet

Four species are mentioned in connection with Sukkot; they form the festive bouquet for the holiday celebration.

ETROG, the fruit of the *hadar* tree, is a citron. A lemon may not be used. The fruit must be yellow, smooth, and, if possible, without spots. If the *pitum*, the pistil of the blossom, has been broken off, it is unfit. It should also have a stem. The *etrog* has to be handled with care. When not in use, it is placed in a container, wrapped in cotton.

LULAV, the branch of a date palm. It must be straight and strong, its ribs coming to a perfect point at the top. Only green branches may be used. The ribs may be tied by bands made of palm leaves. These leaves are first soaked in water to make them pliable, and then several of them are placed around the stem of the Lulav like rings, to keep the ribs from opening up. When not in use, the Lulav must be kept in water to preserve its greenness.

HADASSIM, boughs of leafy trees, are a special kind of myrtle that has three leaves sprouting from each knob of the stem. As Torah refers to it in the plural, we use three branches, tying them to the right side of the Lulav as its back or "spinal column" faces us. They are attached by means of rings made of palm branches.

ARAVOT, willows of the brook, are placed on the Lulav opposite the Hadassim. Two branches are affixed by means of a palm-leaf ring.

After putting the branches together in the right position, we may make a little basket of palm leaves, holding all of them firmly in place; it will have to be about 4 to 6 inches long, depending on the length of the Lulav and the branches. As with the Shofar, no extraneous materials may be used. The plants must touch the Lulav.

Selecting the Arba Minim is a precise art. One must be sure that the branches are not missing or defective, that the Etrog is nicely shaped and fragrant, and that its pistil, or *pitum,* is intact. And then, the price must be right.

If any of the four plants is missing or defective, the whole bouquet is useless and may not be used.

The Meaning of the Arba Minim

The plants represent a thanksgiving offering for the harvest, and each has its own special quality. *Etrog* has both smell and taste, offering perfume and nourishment; the date palm, rich in nourishment, produces fruit without smell; the myrtle exudes a sweet scent, but has no nutritional value; the willow of the brook, although without scent or nourishment, is also necessary for human satisfaction.

The Rabbis extended the symbolism of the four plants to human society. There are persons endowed with kindness and courtesy (smell) and with wisdom (taste), like the etrog. Others, like the date, may lack in courtesy (no smell), but are rich in wisdom (taste). Some, like the myrtle, may be filled with kindness (smell), but lack wisdom (no taste). Finally, many will have no distinctions at all, like the willows of the brook. But no single human individual is expendable (Vayikra Rabba Emor 30:12). If but one is slighted or excluded, the whole of society is *patul*, unfit.

The Rabbis equally found a resemblance to the Arba Minim within the human person: the etrog resembles the heart, seat of emotions; the lulav is like the spine, holding us straight; the hadassim are shaped like eyes, seat of vision; the aravot, like lips, instrument of speech. Only by placing these organs individually and jointly in the service of God can human beings expect to become whole.

The Mitzvah of the Arba Minim is one of the commandments of performance, linked to a certain point in time. Although women should, therefore, be excused from it, they have from the beginning insisted on the right to observe this Mitzvah, and they are bound by it.

Sukkah: The Booth

For seven days we are commanded "to dwell in booths." Actually, we are only bidden to take our meals in the Sukkah, but some pious men will sleep there as well. We may use it only if the weather is good, not when it rains.

Originally, the Sukkah was a simple hut in the harvest fields, a shelter for brief rests during labor and the center of celebration when work was done.

The essential element of the Sukkah is the roof, the *Skhakh*. The rest of the hut may be built of any material, as long as it is strong enough to withstand the wind. It is even permissible, by removing shingles from one's rooftop, to transform an attic into a Sukkah. In many European villages Jewish homes could be recognized by their special gable, whose covering was replaced by a Skhakh on Sukkot.

The walls of the Sukkah must be at least seven handbreadths long (approximately 30 inches), and ten handbreadths wide (approximately 45 inches), but nobody would build so small a Sukkah. The roof may not be higher than 20 feet from the floor.

The Skhakh, which makes the hut into a Sukkah, must be made of plants that cannot be used for food. These must be in their natural state (boards cannot be used) and must be detached from the ground (a natural bower may not be used as a Sukkah, nor may a Sukkah be built beneath a tree, with its branches serving as Skhakh).

This covering, usually consisting of branches with leaves on them, must be thick enough so that "the shade in the Sukkah is greater than the sunlight." There should be no gaps greater than a few inches. At the same time, those dwelling in the Sukkah should be able to see the stars. If the covering is so thick that a heavy rain cannot penetrate it, the Sukkah is not *kasher* (Mishnah Sukkah 1, 2).

The best way to place this foliage on the roof is by using a grating of latticework on which the branches may be laid. Straw and bamboo are suitable coverings. A roof cover should be placed over the Skhakh to protect it from rain, but care should be taken to remove the cover before the Sukkah is used.

The Sukkah should be decorated. The Jew is to consider it his main dwelling place during the feast, and some pious Jews will not consume anything outside of it, not even a drink of water. The decorations are left to the ingenuity of the family, but care should be taken not to affix any ornaments on the roof that will destroy its character. By tradition, the Sukkah walls are hung with tablets bearing the names of seven *ushpisin,* or special guests, whom we invite to be with us, one each day: Abraham, Isaac, Jacob, Joseph, Moses, Aaron, and David.

Decorating the walls and hanging fruit from the roof of the Sukkah is a part of the observance of the harvest festival.

The Meaning of the Sukkah

We dwell in the Sukkah because God sheltered our fore-fathers on their road from Egypt to the promised land. He built Sukkot for them. Some rabbis hold that He surrounded them with "clouds of glory"; others maintain that He made shelters for them out of natural material (Sukkah 11a). But as Sukkot reminds us of our liberation, which occurred in the spring, why do we dwell in the Sukkah during an autumn festival? As the Rabbis explain, in spring our faith would not be manifest to the world. Many people move into summer homes at this time of the year. But in the fall, when they return to the protective shelter of their sturdy homes, we demonstrate our faith by moving out of the house into the Sukkah. We bear witness to our faith that God is our shelter.

Sukkah thus becomes a symbol of Jewish fate. Throughout history, our people have been deprived of house and home while others dwelled secure. Our fathers raised their eyes to the stars, symbolizing God's presence; their homelessness was to them a trial of faith. This awareness is deepened by the presence of the *ushpisin*. Every one of them was homeless at one time or another during his life. All of them were protected by God.

Should it rain on Sukkot, sadness fills Jewish hearts. We are not permitted to enter God's sheltering hut on the appointed days. Perhaps He is dissatisfied with us on account of faulty allegiance shown Him throughout the year.

Celebrating Sukkot

You Shall Have Nothing but Joy

Torah ordains that we have joy on Sukkot. The festival is called "a time of our joy." Sukkot is a homecoming into the tabernacle of the divine. We read in the book of Nehemiah of the eager preparations for Sukkot made by the Jews just returned from Babylonia and of the great rejoicing that filled their hearts on the festival (Neh. 8:13–18). Physically and spiritually, they had come home.

All the "Feasts of Pilgrimage" are called *"Moadim le-Simhah,"* appointed times for joy. On every one of them a Jew must bring joy to his wife, children, and companions (Pessahim 118a), as every holy season has been given us by God that we be happy; and if we truly celebrate, then He will assign us the same happiness in the year to come (Tanhuma Bereshit). We are bidden to feast on food and wine, *after* we have served Him, for "one half belongs to God, the other half to you" (Pessahim 68b). The Hebrew term for festival is *Yom Tov*—"A Good Day."

ON THE EVE of the Yom Tov, festive services are held in the

synagogue. Most congregations have a communal Sukkah, and those members that have none of their own should recite the Kiddush in it on this first evening and break bread. Dwelling in the Sukkah on this night is commanded. On all other days, one need not be in the Sukkah except to eat.

The family moves into the Sukkah. The children receive their parents' blessing. Mother recites the blessing for the candles and Sheheheyanu. Father recites the Kiddush, adding:

Barukh attah . . . vetzivanu leshev ba-Sukkah
Blessed are You . . . He . . . commanding us to dwell in the Sukkah.

This blessing will be recited before every meal taken in the Sukkah throughout the seven days.

The family shares the wine. Father speaks the blessing for the bread and shares it with the family. The meal follows, accompanied by songs, and concluded by Grace.

In the morning the Arba Minim are carried to the synagogue. If it is a Sabbath, when carrying objects is forbidden, they are not used. (Reform congregations that observe only one day of the festival will use the Arba Minim even on the Sabbath.)

THE FIRST CELEBRATION WITH ARBA MINIM. The morning services are embellished by special poetry. Just before Hallel, the songs of praise for the festive days (Psalms 113–118), the blessing for the Arba Minim is spoken.

We take the lulav with the attached myrtles and willows of the brook in our right hand, the spine of the lulav facing us. We take the etrog in our left, its *pitum* facing downward. We must pronounce the blessing *before* using the bouquet in the right way. We speak the Berakhah:

Barukh attah . . . vetzivanu al netilat lulav
Blessed are You . . . He, Who . . . commanding us concerning the taking of the lulav.

The lulav is mentioned as it is the most visible of the four plants. On the first day Sheheheyanu is pronounced.

Now we turn the etrog, holding it the right way, and touching it to the lulav; the Mitzvah is being observed. We point the lulav three times in each of the four directions of the compass, then upward and downward (but *without* turning it toward the downward direction), shaking it a bit as we do so: east-south-west-north-up-down. In this manner we express thanks for the gifts that have come to us from the "four corners of the earth," from the sky above and the earth below. The six directions plus man, uniting the currents of life that reach him from all sides, add up to seven, a number of great symbolic significance in Judaism.

Holding the lulav, the congregation recites the Hallel. As they reach these verses, "Praise the Lord, for He is good, for His steadfast love is for ever," (Ps. 118:1), the cantor and then the responding congregation shake the lulav at each word. In Hebrew:

Hodu (east) *l'Adonai* (straight) *kee* (south) *tov* (west) *kee* (north) *le-olam* (upward) *hasdo* (downward).

The cantor recites the rest of the verses praising God's goodness (Ps. 118:2, 3, 4); the congregation, responding each time, shakes the lulav in concert.

The action is repeated as this plea is voiced: "We beseech You, O God, save now" (Psalm 118:25). As the verse has only three words, the lulav is pointed in two directions at each word:

Ana (east-south) *Adonai* (straight) *hoshee-ah* (west-north) *nah* (upward-downward).

Finally, reciting the repetition of the *Hodu* (Ps. 118:29), the congregation shakes the lulav as before.

On pronouncing the Name of God, we never move the lulav; God is the unshakable center of the universe.

The Torah Reading deals with the ordinances of the feast. The *Haftarah* of the first day introduces a new theme: the vision of the future.

And God will be the King over all the earth. On this day, the Lord will be One and His Name will be One. [Zech. 14]

Partaking of meals together in the Sukkah adds a special dimension to the holiday's observance. Some Orthodox Jews will not even drink a glass of water on Sukkot unless they can do so in the Sukkah.

THE SECOND CELEBRATION WITH ARBA MINIM follows the Mussaf. The Ark is opened; a Torah scroll is taken out and slowly carried along the outer aisles of the synagogue for its entire circumference. The cantor follows the Torah, his Arba Minim in hand. As the Torah passes by, each member with his bouquet joins the procession around the synagogue.

The cantor intones:

For Your sake, O our God . . .

The congregation completes the sentence:

Hosha-Na: save us.

The verses of the litany continue in the same manner.

This rite rests on a similar procession in the Temple around the great altar in the court. It takes up the theme of the Haftarah: mankind is on the march; may Torah lead us and God permit us to succeed in our effort to find the right goal—His kingdom.

The rest of the day is man's. Kiddush in the Sukkah ushers in the midday meal. The children are blessed. A period of leisure follows, up to the time of the afternoon and evening services.

THE SECOND DAY repeats the liturgy of the first with some variations in poetry, Torah reading, and Haftarah. If the first day falls on a Sabbath, the lulav ceremony is first conducted on the second day.

HAVDALAH concludes the feast and ushers in the Half-Holy Days.

Temple Celebrations

The festival of Sukkot was distinguished from all other feasts by three specific celebrations, partly contradictory, partly complementing each other: the water offering, unbounded merrymaking, and the manifestation of Israel's responsibility for the nations of the world.

The Water Offering

On Sukkot, a flask, filled with water from a nearby well, was carried triumphantly into the Temple and solemnly poured out on the great altar as an offering.

This was an expression of thanksgiving for the precious fluid and, at the same time, a prayer that God grant this life-giving substance again next year.

All the peoples of antiquity held water in great reverence. It was the primal matter out of which the earth had been wrested (Gen. 1:2). It was the universal mother, nourishing the plants in the soil and the seed in the womb.

Merrymaking

The people were jubilant as they watched the presentation of the libation. They had been put in the mood for rejoicing:

Joyfully shall you draw water from the fountains of triumph, and you shall say on this day: "Praise the Lord, proclaim His Name." [Isa. 12:3–4]

As soon as night fell at the end of the first day of Sukkot, a spectacular entertainment began in the Temple courts. Young priests lit gigantic candelabra, whose powerful light illuminated every courtyard in the city of Jerusalem. "The pious men of distinction danced with torches in their hands"; the trumpets blared. "He who has not witnessed the joy of the water drawing has never in his life experienced real joy" (Sukkah 5:1–3). The merrymaking lasted through the night.

These Temple celebrations have deeply influenced our rites. The willow of the brook relates us to water. On the last day of Hol ha-Moed, called Hoshana Rabba, we pray for water. On the following day, the eighth, a full day of rest, we pray for rain. The dancing and rejoicing were transferred to Simhat Torah, which concludes the season.

Israel's Responsibility for the Nations of the World

This found expression in the sacrificial offerings. On the first day, thirteen bulls were sacrificed; on the second, twelve; and so forth in descending order, to seven on the seventh day, a total of seventy sacrifices in addition to the regular ones. These were in expiation of the sins of the "seventy nations" of the world. Viewing itself as "a kingdom of priests" unto the nations, Israel assumed responsibility for their conduct. With each day, it was hoped, one additional nation would offer Teshuvah; hence the number of the offerings declined. Israel itself stood under probation, together with the rest.

The days of Sukkot, especially the middle days, thus assume a character akin to the Days of Repentance between Rosh Hashanah and Yom Kippur. Whereas, during the earlier period of penitence, primary emphasis is placed on our own cleansing, in the second period we plead for humanity as a whole, in all its political diversity.

Hoshana Rabba

On all the days of Hol ha-Moed Hallel is sung, the lulav is shaken, and Torah is read. We perform the procession through the sanctuary with the lulav, and we dwell in the Sukkah. The last of the Half-Holy Days is different.

Hoshana Rabba begins with a vigil the night before. Members of the congregation join to recite responsively the whole Book of

Traditionally every Jew brings the Arba Minim to the synagogue for the festival prayer service. The Talmud notes that even "a child who knows how to shake the lulav is obligated to do so."

Psalms and to study Torah. This resembles the vigil of Yom Kippur eve. The participants part with this wish, *G'mar Hatimah Tovah*: God set His final seal upon you for good! The same wish was voiced on Yom Kippur.

Hoshana Rabba is seen as a day of judgment, when God allocates water for the coming year. The curtain of the Ark is white; the Torah scrolls wear white mantles; the cantor is robed in the kittel.

After the Mussaf service, the special rites commence. Instead of one procession, there are now seven. Seven Torah scrolls are taken out; each one leads a circuit. Seven times we encircle the synagogue as an act of reconsecration.

The Arba Minim are now laid down, for they will no longer be needed. Each member has brought a separate bunch of willows of the brook. After the prayer—

Help Your people and bless Your inheritance, sustain and lift them up for ever,

—we strike the willows three times to the ground, so that the leaves fly off. The willow thus becomes a kind of substitute, a ransom, like the scapegoat. May *it* lose its leaves, but may our plants have abundant water. (The numerical value of the letters in *Aravah*, willow, and *Zera*, seed, is identical.)

130

Meditation concludes: Seal us up for good through the earth's yield.

Children and Sukkot

One of the great joys of childhood is decorating the Sukkah. On the festival itself, a visit to other Sukkot is both delightful and educational. "A child who knows how to shake the lulav is obligated to do so" (Sukkah 3:15). Beating the willows will be a special treat, and as willows are easily gathered, each child should have a bunch for the occasion. On Simhat Torah children will come fully into their own.

Sh'mini Atzeret: Concluding Feast of the Eighth Day

The final holy day is a new feast. Sheheheyanu is recited, as on all new festivals. The Arba Minim are no longer used. We still take our evening meal and lunch in the Sukkah, but without the blessing for the privilege of dwelling in it. Then we speak a farewell to the booth that has been our home.

The evening and morning services and home observances follow the order of all the festivals.

The *Torah Reading* consists of a review of all the festivals, concluding with the thought that, on appearing before God, no one is to come with empty hands, but is to give according to his means: K'matnat Yado (Deut. 14:22; 16:1). The reading leads to the forthcoming blessing of the congregation. The Haftarah concerns Solomon's prayer at the dedication of the Temple; we, too, have rededicated our sanctuary.

After the Torah reading we remember our departed (*Yizkor*). Then the rabbi, Torah in hand, blesses the congregation: men, women, and children. They have all been faithful in observance; they all will give a portion of their substance to worthy causes, each K'matnat Yado.

In the Mussaf, the petition for rain is included. Throughout Sukkot we could not utter it as we were hoping for sunshine, in order to dwell in the Sukkah. In a great poem attributed to Eleazar Hakaliri (seventh or eighth century), the events of history pass in review, revealing the blessing of rain. We conclude:

For You are the Lord our God,
causing the wind to blow and the rain to fall
 for a blessing and not for a curse   Amen
 for life and not for death   Amen
 for plenty and not for want   Amen

Henceforth, throughout the winter and until Pessah, we include a passage in our daily Amidah praising God, Who "causes the wind to blow and the rain to fall."

Kohelet

The Book of Ecclesiastes, *Kohelet,* a deeply pessimistic work, is read on the Sabbath of Sukkot. The Rabbis understood that inevitably the question would arise: We have fasted, we have prayed, we have celebrated—but will anything change, or is life going to resume in toil and trouble, cold and dark? Reading Kohelet allows such doubts to be voiced openly and candidly. Yet the book concludes with words that point to meaning in life:

Fear God and keep His commandments, for this is the whole of man. [Eccl. 12:13]

11
Simhat Torah
"Joy in Torah"

The name of the last day of the Sukkot festival, as observed by traditional congregations, is *Simhat Torah*, "Joy in Torah." On this day, the cycle of Torah readings is completed and immediately resumed for the following year. Great joy pervades the congregation; barriers fall between old and young, between rich and poor. Some eastern European communities even permitted women to join the men in the "men's *shul*" on this day.

The Eve

After the evening service, all the Torah scrolls are taken out of the Ark, and a joyful procession winds its way through the synagogue. Every member will get a chance to carry a scroll for a short distance. The children, bearing flags, make up their own procession, following the Torah. They are essential for the celebration. Without them, our ceremony might reflect a cyclical outlook on life: eternal recurrence, but no evolution. The presence and participation of the children show that we regard ourselves as marching onward in history, from generation to generation.

There may be dancing in the synagogue. Men will dance with the Torah in their arm; others will dance around them in a circle. The children are everywhere. As the dancing goes on, the young ones get sweets and cookies from all sides.

The Morning

At the conclusion of Shaharit, including Hallel, all the scrolls are once again taken out of the Ark, and the processions of old and young are held. Finally, three scrolls are placed on the Bimah.

From the first scroll, the end of the Five Books is read, except for the final paragraph. Today there is no limit to the number of people who may be "called up" to the reading. Over and over the section is repeated. In the end, all the children are called as a group, accompanied by an adult.

It is a high privilege to be chosen for the final paragraph of Torah, and it is one usually reserved for an older person, distinguished by learning and wisdom. He becomes *Hatan Torah,* the "Groom of Torah." Escorted by the children, he ascends the Bimah. The concluding portion of the "Five Books" is read.

Then the Torah is rolled up, and a second Torah opened for the "Beginning." It is a privilege just as great to be called up as *Hatan Bereshit,* "Groom of the Beginning." Escorted by the children, the person so singled out steps up to Torah, and the story of Creation (Gen. 1,1–2:3) is read to him. This honor is usually given to a younger man of proved promise.

A third scroll is unrolled, to be read to the person who will recite the Haftarah. In the Haftarah, Moses is dead, and Joshua has assumed his mantle. God calls out to him: *Hazak,* be strong, for you will conquer the land of promise. But you must obey the Torah, taught you by Moses. The people make a commitment to God and Torah; they accept Joshua's leadership. History marches on (Josh. 1). Now the dancing and marching continues

I will exult and jubilantly rejoice with this Torah;
it is our strength and light . . .
Abraham, Isaac, Jacob, Aaron, Joshua, Samuel, Solomon,
Elijah all rejoiced in the joy of Torah.
Torah is the tree of life; it is life unto all,
for with You is the fountain of life.

The Torah scrolls are returned; the Mussaf service is recited. It is hardly heard amid the noise of children scrambling for goodies. For some the dancing will go on a long time; others will repair home for Kiddush and meal.

As three stars appear in the sky, weekday evening services are held, and Havdalah is recited. The season is over. Soberness takes hold. A little aftertaste is left for one more day, called *Isru Hag*— "Bind the Feast" (based on Ps. 118:27).

Russian Jewry and Simhat Torah

Persecuted and harassed, the Jews of the Soviet Union have af-

Excitement pervades the synagogue: young and old; children, men, and women dance and sing in celebration of Torah.

firmed their Judaism ever more strongly. Many do not know what Judaism means, for they have been denied a Jewish education, denied even the right to celebrate Jewish holy days, by a brutal government. But in recent decades, under the eyes of a hostile police, these Jews have assembled on Simhat Torah in front of the synagogue in Moscow and other cities. They dance in the street, rejoice, give strength to one another. They may never see each other throughout the year, never enter the house of God, but they are Jews. On Simhat Torah, they make it manifest at great risk and with great courage.

Their dancing on Simhat Torah is the dance of life: *Am Yisrael hay*—the Jewish people lives!

TWO FESTIVE PERIODS—ONE SPIRIT

Like two movements of a symphony, the two festive periods, Days of Awe and Sukkot, develop the same basic themes. The first is a serious variation; the second, a joyful one.

In structure they are very much alike: a full holy day, followed by a sacred work period of probation and culminating in a full day of holiness, set aside for intimate communion with God in twosomeness. Both Yom Kippur and Sh'mini Atzeret are such days, the latter specifically designated by the Talmud as a moment of complete union of God and Israel (Sukkah 55b).

Both seasons open our hearts and souls by means of visible ad-

135

juncts to worship, the Shofar and the Arba Minim, discarding them
in the end, when no aids are needed any more to guide our minds
and inwardness has been achieved.

Both seasons call for Teshuvah. The first is an appeal to Israel as
priest-people of humanity; the second, as expressed in the seventy
sacrifices of old, is Israel's plea for the nations. This Teshuvah is vital
for mankind, in order that it recognize God as the giver of life, as
we do during the period of the Days of Awe, and as the giver of
the blessings of life, the water that quickens the seed and the harvest
itself, for which we offer both plea and thanksgiving on Sukkot.

In antiquity, the dance of youth on Yom Kippur served as a joyful
interlude amidst sober contemplation, a theme linking this season to
the coming one of joy and dancing.

Yom Kippur and Hoshanah Rabba are parallel in character as in
observance, from the vigil that precedes either of them to the solemn
service of the morning. On Yom Kippur, the Jew steps out of his
home and daily pattern; on Sukkot, he transfers them to the fragile
hut. On both occasions, the age-old custom of transferring human
sins unto other objects is revived. On Yom Kippur, it was the scapegoat and the offerings in general, reflected in the Kapparot rite,
where it is performed; on Sukkot, it is the willow, beaten to the
ground.

From primeval times, the farmer had to begin and end his work
in purity. He offered gifts to the deity. On Yom Kippur, we offer
ourselves; on Sukkot, our substance. The farmer equally performed
sacred rites to give new strength to the divine abode and to
strengthen its walls. The Avodah, performed by the High Priest
served this purpose on Yom Kippur. On Sukkot, the walls of the
Temple and the foundations of the altar were to be reinforced, as
the people's procession wound its way around them. Israel learned
this early in its history. When the people marched around the walls
of Jericho, the city's ramparts came tumbling down (Josh. 6), a
clear message that heathen gods were totally without power. The
God of Israel alone wields and does so freely. We merely express
our resolve to surround the world by His command: we walk in procession with the Torah. Jewish observance may thus have some of
its origins in ancient pagan rites. But it has transcended them.

The whole season reveals and affirms God's free-creating power,
man's duty to be His co-worker, dedicating to Him both life and
substance. Has man gone astray, he is to find his way back through
Teshuvah. Then he may expect that purification will lead to thanksgiving, and thanksgiving to dedication to mankind, and dedication
to restoration and renewal, both physical and spiritual. The common
theme of the season in its variations is:

For all comes from You, and of Your own have we given You. [I Chron.
29:14]

12

Hanukah: Festival of Consecration and Light

The month following Tishrei is called Marheshvan; "mar" means "bitter," bitter because there are no holidays in it, bitter because the days are getting shorter and the nights longer.

The first festival we shall encounter during the period of the diminished daylight will be Hanukah, followed by the Fifteenth of Sh'vat and Purim. Hanukah is observed roughly around the winter solstice; it is a feast of light. The Fifteenth of Sh'vat expresses joy at the planting of the trees. Purim occurs roughly at the spring equinox. They are all keyed to nature and express the yearning of man for the return of the sun that brings warmth and life.

In contrast to the summer festivals, which are all ordained by God in the Five Books of Moses, the winter festivals are human institutions created at various times in history and fashioned by the Rabbis into religious occasions. They are, therefore, minor holidays, and no work prohibition is attached to them.

HISTORICAL ROOTS

Hanukah is firmly documented in historical fact. It was instituted during the period of Hellenism and sprang out of the conflict between Jewish faith and Greek culture.

In 538 B.C.E., the Jews returned from Babylonian captivity; in 445 B.C.E., Nehemiah, a high official of the Persian court, soon to be joined by Ezra, led the revival of Jewish religion among the settlers and instilled its spirit and its practices in the people. Torah was restored.

During the centuries that followed, under the leadership of spiritual masters named the "Men of the Great Assembly," the Jews built a strong religious civilization.

In 336 B.C.E., Alexander the Great (356–323) appeared on the stage of history and soon brought the entire Middle East under his dominion. On his expeditions, he passed through Palestine and entered Jerusalem, and so gracious was he to the Jews that many named their sons after him.

The emperor, a high-minded and cultured man, saw in Greek civilization a tool for uniting the vast array of nations he had brought under his sway. Each people was to contribute to the whole, but the foundation would be that of Greece, its language and its culture. In Alexandria, his city, the emperor established a great library in which the works of all nations, translated into Greek, were made available to the scholar. Out of this interaction of Greek and non-Greek cultures came Hellenism.

The Jews derived cultural benefit from Hellenism. Holy Scripture was translated into Greek. Guided by Greek example, the Sanhedrin transformed itself from a judicial court that interpreted the law into a legislative court that made law. The Rabbis assumed the authority to issue ordinances and thereby changed the character of Judaism.

But Hellenism also had severe negative effects on many Jews, who became enamored of Greek culture to the point of abandoning their own tradition. In order to be accepted fully, one had to be Greek and adopt Greek ways. When Jewish law impeded this assimilation, it was cast aside.

With the death of Alexander, the empire was divided among his generals. The land of the Jews, which lay between Egypt and Syria, was first attached to Egypt (ruled by Ptolemy), then transferred to Syria, which was itself a vast empire under the rule of the descendants of Alexander's general Seleucus (Antiochus III, 200 B.C.E.). Jewish loyalty was divided: some clung to Egypt; others, to Syria. The governance of the province rested with the High Priest.

In the year 176 B.C.E., Antiochus IV ascended the throne of Syria. As a political measure he had himself deified, calling himself *Epiphanes*—"God made manifest."

The Hellenists among the Jews, led by the High Priest Joshua, who had changed his name to Jason, sought the emperor out, promising a complete Hellenization of the Jews in return for power. Antiochus agreed. The forced Hellenization progressed rapidly, spearheaded by the priestly caste. Gymnasiums were built, one next to the Temple; Jewish youth disported in the nude; many had the mark of circumcision removed by painful operation, in order not to be recognized as Jews.

Antiochus became embroiled in wars with Egypt (169 and 168 B.C.E.), and while he was thus engaged, a power struggle ensued in Jerusalem between Jason, favoring the Egyptians, and Menelaos. When the first Egyptian expedition ended in victory, Antiochus removed Jason and appointed Menelaos High Priest; in return, the emperor received permission to enter the Holy of Holies and was presented with the greater part of the treasures stored in the Temple treasury. The second expedition was aborted by the Romans. Antiochus, in a mood of humiliation and resentment, turned on Jerusalem. He entered the city and butchered the population, who did not resist as the massacre occurred on the Sabbath, when arms could not be taken up. He razed the city walls.

Antiochus focused his hatred on the Jews. Hellenization, he decided, was to be rammed down their throats.

Temple worship was exchanged for the adoration of Zeus, whose statue was placed in the Temple court. Other gods of the Greek pantheon, Athena and Dionysus in particular, were to be paid homage. Pigs were to be sacrificed on the high altar (167 B.C.E.).

To show his devotion to the emperor, Menelaos, the High Priest, proposed even more radical measures, which were enacted into law. Study of Torah was prohibited; Sabbath observance became a crime; circumcision was forbidden. In every town and hamlet, heathen altars were erected. There Jews were to prostrate themselves before the gods and offer swine as sacrifices. Disobedience was punishable by death.

Judaism was in grave danger of extinction. The Biblical book of Daniel, written at this time, reflects the agony of the Jews and their silent cry to God for help, as no human effort could prevail. But human efforts, buoyed by faith in the God of Israel, did prevail. It began with an incident in the little town of Modein. As a Jew approached the heathen altar, ready to prostrate himself before the idol, an aged priest, Mattathias of the House of Hasmon, in righteous wrath, struck him, killing him and the royal commissioner. To escape arrest, the old man fled into the desert. His five sons joined him there. Soon, an ever-increasing number of aroused "pious" joined him. They formed a guerrilla band. The leaders were called Hasmoneans, after the house from which Mattathias had sprung.

But the old man died shortly after his escape, and the organization of the army fell to his son, Judah. His exploits were to be so spectacular that he came to be called "Maccabee," the Hammerer, and his host came to be called the Maccabeans. According to another interpretation of the term, Judah and his men fashioned a flag, inscribed with the first letters of the verse:

The Book of Maccabees relates with awe the terror struck in the hearts of the Jewish soldiers as they first felt the earth tremble and then saw the great Syrian army with its mounted elephant corps. This engraving by Doré captures that moment as Judah raised his arms and called "upon the Lord that worketh wonders . . ." (II Maccabees15)

Mee khamokhah ba-elim YHVH
Who is like You, O Lord, among the mighty. [Exod. 15:11]

The letters spell *Maccabee.*

Initially, the government paid little attention to the uprising, believing it could be easily quashed, especially if the Jews were attacked on the Sabbath, a day when they would offer no resistance. But the Maccabeans issued a ruling that Jewish survival was so important that resistance on the Sabbath was legitimate (although an *attack* by Jews could not be launched on that day). Well-acquainted with the countryside, Judah the Maccabee lured the enemy armies into mountain passes, attacked them at night, and burned their camps. The enemy fled. Mustering its total strength, the Syrian army now made ready to engage Judah's band in battle, choosing the open terrain of the south.

Judah offered a settlement. In the year 164 B.C.E., Antiochus issued a decree of amnesty for the rebels and rescinded his edicts proscribing the teaching and practice of the Jewish religion.

In the Temple, however, Greek worship continued. Judah could not abide it. In the fall of the year he gathered his army again. In a surprise attack on Jerusalem, whose walls had been previously razed, he took the city. On the twenty-fifth of Kislev, Judah and his men entered the Temple, exactly three years after its defilement. The desecrated altar was torn down; the idols were smashed. The sanctuary was reconsecrated, and sacrifices were offered once again on a new altar and in conformity with the law of Israel. The people offered joy and thanksgiving to God, who had brought rescue, in a celebration that lasted for eight days.

As we review the events, we see in them an enduring message: Judaism may not isolate itself from other cultures. Hellenism introduced elements that actually helped to preserve the Jewish faith and people—specifically, it inspired the Rabbis to assume new authority and to "build fences around the Torah." Had Judaism rejected all outside influence, it might not have survived.

But Judaism cannot be preserved by a dismantlement of its basic structure. The High Priests of the time may have felt they could preserve the people by assimilation. They almost became the people's executioners.

Jewish survival is worth the supreme sacrifice of individuals. This is the example of the Maccabees. In times of emergency, Jewish survival supersedes specific laws; the Sabbath could be violated.

Religion and people are inseparable. Without faith, the people would have perished; without the people's military victory, faith would have been destroyed.

The Institution of Hanukah

The consecration of the Temple and dedication of the new altar were celebrated for eight days. This was not yet called *Hanukah* but rather "The Sukkot Feast of the Month of Kislev." The Jews, who had not been able to observe Sukkot while the Temple was still in enemy hands, now were permitted to gather within its walls for joyful assembly. As Sukkot was observed for eight days, the feast of consecration was equally observed for eight days. And there was an additional reason for regarding the feast as a second Sukkot: both the First and the Second Temples had been dedicated on the Feast of Booths (I Kings 8, 2:2–65; Neh. 8:13–18).

The name the holiday was eventually to receive was one that linked it to the consecration of the altar in the Tent of Meeting in the desert:

zot *Hanukat* ha-Mizbeah
This was the dedication of the altar. [Num. 7:60]

After the original celebration, an ordinance was issued and accepted by the people:

Then Judah and his brothers and the whole congregation of Israel established that the days of the consecration of the altar be celebrated for eight days at this period, namely beginning with the twenty-fifth of the month of Kislev, in joy and happy renewal. [I Macc. 4:36–61]

Letters to Diaspora, notably Egyptian, Jewry ordained the *Feast of Fire* and kindling of lights worldwide (II Macc.). But why lights?

The Strange Fate of a Feast

The people accepted Hanukah, but the Jewish authorities seem to have had second thoughts.

The Books of the Maccabees were not included in the canon of Holy Scriptures. (They belong instead to the Apocrypha, writings useful for inspirational reading but not for public recitation.) In the whole Mishnah, edited more than 300 years after the event, we find not a word about Hanukah.

One reason may have been that the Rabbis simply did not like the celebration of military victories. Another may have been that the Hasmoneans did not spring from the family of Zadok, which held the traditional *Yihus* (distinction) to provide the high priests; in other words, they were not regarded as worthy for this high office. Then, too, Rabbi Judah the Prince, editor of the Mishnah, may well have disapproved of the way the Hasmoneans, who were not descendants of King David but were priests, also crowned themselves kings of Israel, combining both offices in an absolute power that eventually corrupted absolutely (see Hatam Sofer: Taame ha-Minhagim, 847).

Rabbi Judah may have had additional compelling reasons. He was a friend of the Emperor Antoninus Pius and knew the mind of official Rome. The Romans had destroyed the Temple and State but recognized the Jews as a *religious* community. It would have been unwise to dwell on nationalistic liberation movements, especially because one of these movements, the Bar Kokhba rebellion, had ended not long before in disaster.

There may have been internal reasons as well. In introducing a new and perennial festival in commemoration of a great event, Judah Maccabee had adopted a *Greek* practice. The *eight*-branched candelabrum equally imitated heathen custom. The Rabbis were wary of such alien adoptions. Noticing however the great popularity of the ceremony of lights, they had to provide *Jewish* reasons and rules for it. Was the feast to be divorced from any festival ordained in Torah, or was it to be given sanction by being related to Sukkot? As we shall see, the schools of Hillel and Shammai argued the point.

Yet official esteem of the holiday also led to confusion among the people. Hanukah continued to be observed for eight days and as a festival of lights, but for a while nobody could really explain why. Josephus, who lived at the time of the destruction of the Second Temple, wrote:

[It is called] a feast of lights, because the free practice of our religion was to us like a rising day of light. [*Jewish Antiquities* XII, 7:7]

Later on, the Rabbis, overlooking the feast's relationship to Sukkot, perhaps even in a deliberate attempt to make a distinction between the feasts, explained:

Why do we kindle Hanukah lights? When the sons of the Hasmoneans, the High Priest, had defeated the Kingdom of the Syrians, they entered the Temple. There they found eight spears. They stuck them in the ground and put the lights on them. [Midrash Pesikta Rabbati 2]

This makes little sense, however. If the Hasmoneans wished to create a temporary substitute for the golden candelabrum, they should have kindled *seven* lights, corresponding to those on the Menorah.

Ultimately, the matter was settled in the Gemara:

What really is Hanukah? The Rabbis taught: On the twenty-fifth of Kislev the days of the Hanukah feast commence. There are eight of them, during which eulogies for the dead and fasting are prohibited. When the Syrians entered the Temple, they defiled all the oil stored in it. After the Hasmoneans had established their rule, and prevailed, they searched and found but one single cruse of oil, still sealed with the seal of the High Priest. But there was only enough oil in it to last for one day. A miracle occurred, and the supply lasted for eight days. In the following year, they appointed these days as *Yamim Tovim*, festivals with Hallel and thanksgiving. [Shabbat 21a]

By the times of the Gemara, after Judah the Prince, Hanukah had become so firmly anchored in folk custom that the Rabbis could no longer ignore it. But they gave it a new meaning: it was not a victory celebration but a festival that made manifest the spirit of Judaism. Pointedly, they chose as Haftarah for the Sabbath of Hanukah a selection from the prophet Zechariah (2:14–4:7), climaxing in the words:

Not by might, nor by power, but by My Spirit [shall you prevail], says the Lord of Hosts. [Zech. 4:6]

Hanukah as Celebration of the Winter Solstice

But why did Hanukah exert such a hold on the Jewish people? Why did it become connected with the kindling of lights? Hanukah was the feast of the winter solstice. It expressed the yearning for spring at the moment when the sun's light began once again to wax.

Plutarch relates that the Egyptians celebrated the winter solstice by fastening rows of lamps to the outside of their houses; fed by oil, they burned all night. The Jews, filled with longing for the return of the sun like all other peoples, adopted this practice in conjunction with Hanukah. But the custom had to be made Jewish. This led to a debate between the School of Hillel and the School of Shammai. Shammai held that the number of lights must decrease from night to night, just as the bulls offered on Sukkot decreased in number from day to day. The School of Hillel held the opposite, for "we must grow in holiness and not decrease." Judaism must increase its light in order to dispel the darkness in the world. Hillel, who understood the common folk, may have also known that as the lights were symbolically expressing the lengthening of daylight, now that the sun had passed its nadir, the people would simply not diminish their hope. He, therefore, joined that hope to the desire for increased holiness, and thus it has remained in Jewish tradition.

The Hanukah Menorah

The holy lamp in the Tent of Meeting and in the Temple was of gold, in the form of a tree, and had seven branches; it burned olive oil. Its shape is described in the Book of Exodus (Exod. 25:31–40 and 37:17–24). A representation that approximates its design can be found on the Arch of Titus; it was one of the spoils taken to Rome by the conqueror of Jerusalem. The Hanukah menorah has nine lamps to meet the requirements of the feast. Eight of these hold lights to be kindled; the ninth is the *Shamash,* the server that brings them to life. The Shamash must be separated from the other lights and cannot be in the same row with them. We are not permitted to make any practical use of the Hanukah lights; yet they do aid us in

Lighting the Hanukkah candles.

our work by illuminating the house; having the Shamash permits us to ascribe the light to *it*, not to the sacred eight.

There is no rule regarding the shape of the Menorah or the material from which it is to be fashioned; neither is there for our purposes any regulation concerning the kind of light we are to kindle. Oil is the most beautiful and meaningful; it requires small bowls and wicks. Candles are equally acceptable. They must be able to burn for at least one-half hour. Electric lights will *not* do. Traditionally, we find two designs of the Menorah. One follows the pattern of the sacred candelabrum, with four branches on each side of the stem and the Shamash affixed to the front and detachable for use. The other consists of eight small candle holders set in a row on a common foundation, with the Shamash raised. Behind the row of lamps is a screen, sometimes beautifully sculptured, permitting the Menorah to be hung on the wall and serve as a decoration during the year.

Although the Menorah is the center of our attention, the whole house should be filled with a Hanukah atmosphere. Buntings and streamers in blue and white will remind us of our bond with Israel.

HANUKAH OBSERVANCE

In the Synagogue

Every evening, the lights of Hanukah are kindled after a solemn blessing. Many synagogues own large and precious Menorot for Hanukah use. This kindling does not take the place of the home

145

ceremony, but was introduced "to spread the message of the miracle" in public assembly. Every morning Hallel is recited. The Torah is read, specifically the portion telling of the dedication of the Tent of Meeting. The whole section (Num. 7:1–89) is divided into eight lessons, one for each day. On the last day we hear the words: "This is the dedication of the altar, *Hanukat ha-Mizbeah.*"

In our daily Amidah and in Grace after meals we include *Al Hanissim,* offering thanks "for the miracles" of Hanukah and the events leading up to them.

Home Observances: The Lighting of the Menorah

The center of Hanukah celebration is the home; it is a family feast. The Talmud lays down the rules:

The Mitzvah applies from sunset up to the time when traffic in the streets ceases. . . .

One [set of the] Hanukah lights [is sufficient] for the head of the house and his entire household; but those who wish to beautify [Torah] have one for each person. . . .

It is our Mitzvah to place the Hanukah light at the door, outside; he who lives in an upper story shall place it at a window, facing the street. In times of danger it is sufficient to place it on a table. Raba said: He also must have a second lamp, as a source of the light he needs for use. If there is a flame in the room already, this is not necessary. . . . [Shabbat 21b–22a]

We are to kindle the lights when it gets dark, that their light may illumine the night around us. Ordinarily, we will light the candles as soon as night falls; if necessary, we may fulfill the Mitzvah any time before dawn.

On Friday evening, we cannot light the Hanukah candles at night, for the Sabbath forbids it. We, therefore, rely on the ruling that they can be kindled at dusk and do so *before* mother lights the Sabbath candles. But these Hanukah candles must be long enough to burn for at least one-half hour after nightfall.

At the end of the Sabbath, we cannot kindle the lights before Havdalah; but, knowing that the lights can be lit throughout the night, we kindle them immediately *after* Havdalah.

The Rabbis taught that there must be at least one light per household. If a Jew were very poor, one single candle would suffice. We no longer place the Menorah at the door; it is too dangerous. But we do place it at the windows. Let the world see that we are Jews and that Judaism means light.

The first candle must be at our *right,* as we face the Menorah; subsequent candles are lit from the *left.* The new light is always kindled first. We light the Shamash, take it in our hand, and speak the Berakhot:

Barukh . . . vetzivanu lehadlik ner shel Hanukah
Blessed are You, . . . He, Who . . . has commanded us to kindle the light
of Hanukah.
Barukh . . . she-asah nissim la-avotenu bayamim hahem ba-z'man hazeh
Blessed are You . . . Who has performed miracles for our fathers in
ancient days, at this season.

Sheheheyanu is recited on the first night.

After the flames have been brought to life, we contemplate their
light, speaking:

We kindle these lights on account of the miracles, the rescuing deeds, the
wars You carried out for our fathers through the hands of Your holy
priests. And throughout all of these eight Hanukah days these lights are
holy and we are not permitted to make use of them, only to look at them,
in order to give praise to Your Name for Your miracles, for Your rescuing
deeds, and for Your marvelous acts.

Hanukah has thus been completely spiritualized: the Hasmoneans
were but divine instruments; the victory was God's alone.

Home Observances: Customs

After the kindling of the lights, the family marches around the
room to the tune of *Maoz Tzur*. The melody originated in western
Europe. Its Hebrew text takes us through a number of events in
Jewish history, on each of which Israel would have perished without
God's help. The free English rendition begins with the words:

Rock of Ages, let our song praise Thy saving power.

Card playing and games are permitted and common. The "dreidel"
is spun.

The Dreidel

A dreidel (from the German: *drehen,* to spin), is a top,
containing four letters, one on each of its four sides: N–G–H–S:
ש,   ה,   ג,   נ   . If the top, after being spun, falls on *N*, the
player gets *N*othing out of the kitty; if it falls on *G*, he or she *G*ets
everything in it; if it falls on *H*, *H*alf of the kitty is his or hers; but
if it falls on *S*, he or she has to *S*et, put money into the kitty. The
four letters are an abbreviation of the sentence: *Nes Gadol Hayah
Sham.* A great miracle happened there. In order to play, children
receive some coins, *Hanukah Gelt,* Hanukah money. This used to
be the extent of the gifts.

In eastern Europe, children were allowed to cast their own
dreidels out of lead. Today, dreidel-making in other media will in-
volve children in the feast and prepare them for its coming.

In its many observances, Judaism includes nearly all forms of human activity—even gaming and gambling. The dreidel game played on Hanukah provides a gentle outlet for these human drives.

Card Playing

Some hold that card playing has always been a passion with Jews. But the professional gambler was considered an undesirable person, not trustworthy as a witness in court. In some communities, card playing was, therefore, put under ban for the entire year except the period from Hanukah to the Fast of the Tenth of Tevet. By permitting it during this time, the Rabbis may have wished to give people an opportunity to get their hankering out of their system.

Special Celebrations and Special Dishes

The fifth day of Hanukah was set aside by eastern European Jewry as the night for a special feast for family and friends. This was the night when light had positively triumphed over darkness; five lights were burning; only three unlit candles were left.

It is customary to serve pancakes, *Latkes,* on Hanukah, and some families make it a point to serve milk dishes during the festival. Both these customs are connected with the special role of women at the Hanukah season.

Women and Hanukah

When there is no man in the house, the women light the

Hanukah Menorah. There is no reason *not* to have a Menorah for every woman and girl (if they so desire), even when the men and boys are at home and kindle the lights. Actually, women were given special consideration on Hanukah. It was held that the victory had come to pass largely through their devotion and assistance.

Women are, therefore, not to do any work while the lights are burning.

WOMEN SET AN EXAMPLE OF SACRIFICE. Hannah was a widow, who had seven sons. They were all brought before the emperor and told: "Worship the idol or die." Encouraged by their mother, they chose death. When it came to the seventh son, still a child, the emperor himself felt pity. "I will drop my ring on the floor, you pick it up, the people will think you have bowed to the idol, and I will save your life!" The boy proudly refused and went to his death. Hannah then went up to the roof, jumped off, and died. A heavenly voice was heard at this moment: "Joyful mother of sons!" (Ps. 113:9) (Gittin 57b).

WOMEN SUPPORTED THEIR HUSBANDS. It was told that the Maccabee women had baked pancakes, a stable food, and had taken them to their husbands on the battlefields. We, therefore, eat Latkes.

WOMEN RESCUED THE PEOPLE. In the Apocryphal Book of Judith, we hear of a maiden, Judith, who brought deliverance to her people. She went to the tent of Holofernes, a general of Nebuchadnezzar, who was encamped before Jerusalem.

She prepared a meal for him, including many milk dishes that made him sleepy. Once he was asleep, she chopped off his head and brought it in triumph to her people. The enemy army retreated in

Foods, too, play special parts in Jewish ritual, and the making of potato latkes fills the kitchen with the special smell and sense of a true Hanukah celebration.

disarray; Israel was saved. Therefore, many families have milk dishes on Hanukah.

Its serious historical flaws—Holofernes was *not* Nebuchadnezzar's general, and, far from failing in his mission, he inflicted a gruesome bloodbath on his defeated enemies and returned home in triumph— may have kept the Book of Judith from being admitted into the canon of Holy Scriptures. The story was, rather, a legend fashioned after an event related in the Book of Judges, when a woman, Jael, actually killed an enemy general in her tent after drugging him with milk dishes (Judges 4:17–24). But historicity does not matter that much on Hanukah, when Jews wished to honor their women as examples of dedication, as sustainers, and as rescuers.

Hanukah and Christmas

Hanukah and Christmas are two holidays that have one feature in common: they celebrate the winter solstice. But then they move far apart: Hanukah celebrates Jewish self-affirmation, staunch resistance to non-Jewish religious influences; Christianity celebrates the birth of Jesus and the breaking away of the new faith from its Jewish mother.

Judaism sees in the lights of Hanukah a public demonstration of the Jewish spirit, Jewish tradition, and Jewish pride. Christianity sees in the lights of Christmas a reflection of the light that came into the world with the birth of Jesus, superseding the light of Judaism. The Star of Bethlehem is the crowning feature of every Christmas tree.

When Jews introduce a Christmas tree into their homes, rationalizing that it is, after all, a secular custom, based on the ancient celebration of the winter solstice, they are doing exactly what the Hellenists did, against whom the Maccabees rose. That is to say, they introduce alien customs that are detrimental to Judaism solely on the grounds that they happen to like them. At the same time, they denigrate Christianity, in voiding the religious significance the tree has attained. As Jews, we can affirm our faith and demonstrate our respect for the faith of our Christian neighbors only by refraining from bringing a Christmas tree into our homes. And as for our children, surely we may deny them certain satisfactions in the interests of strengthening their personalities as Jews.

Many Jews have sought to "compensate" their children for the supposed "loss" of Christmas by giving them lavish presents, spread over the eight days of Hanukah. True compensation would mean, rather, giving our children the experience of the joys of Judaism throughout the year. There is nothing wrong and much good to be derived from asking our children to deny themselves certain things in return for these joys.

It should be remembered that our society may be secular in character, but its foundations and its permeating spirit are Christian. At no time of the year is this as evident as it is at Christmas. The Jew who steps out of his or her Jewish environment enters not a neutral world but a world still very much based on Christianity. Effort and self-discipline are required of Jews who wish to remain Jews and transmit the warmth and beauty of Judaism, its power to bring peace of mind and soul, to the next generation. This is what Hanukah is all about.

13

Milestones
on the Road
to Spring

With anxiety and hope, the ancient farmer followed the gradual unfolding of spring, observing the rain; noticing the lengthening of the daylight; preparing himself for plowing, seeding, and planting. Midpoints during the winter season were milestones on the road to spring and were so celebrated. But each celebration had to be preceded by a purification; the gloom and darkness of winter, which had beclouded the soul, had to be removed; gods and men had to be reinvigorated. The *tenth* of special months, after the rising moon had overcome darkness but not yet reached its fullness, became the day of purification; the *fifteenth*, when the moon, in its full glory, illuminated the sky, was the date of subsequent celebration.

The Jewish farmer followed the same routine of purification and celebration, but for him the officially appointed fasts and feasts had to reflect historical events as well and were somewhat shifted to meet this need.

On the road to spring we, therefore, find:

the *feast* of the winter solstice, shifted to the twenty-fifth of Kislev, to commemorate the victory of the Maccabees and the rededication of the Temple.

the *fast* of the tenth of Tevet, a day of purification, followed by

the *feast* of the fifteenth of Sh'vat, beginning of the tree-planting season;

152

the *fast* of the thirteenth of Adar, shifted by a few days for historical reasons, to precede

the *feast* of Purim on the *fourteenth* of Adar, again shifted by one day for historical reasons.

the preparatory day for Pessah, as ordained for the Israelites in Egypt, on the *tenth* day of Nissan (shifted partly to the fourteenth, fast of the firstborn), followed by

Pessah, festival of spring on the *fifteenth* of Nissan.

The whole period marked an ascent from winter to spring. We shall find a similar structure for the summer season, this time in descent, as we shall see later (see Chapter 17).

the *ninth* of Av (shifted by one day for historical reasons), a day of fasting and mourning, followed by

the *fifteenth* of Av, celebrating the tree harvest;

the *tenth* of Tishrei, Yom Kippur, day of general purification, preceding

the *fifteenth* of Tishrei, feast of ingathering and thanksgiving.

THE TENTH OF TEVET AND THE FIFTEENTH OF SH'VAT

The Tenth of Tevet

The day of fasting on the tenth of Tevet commemorates the beginning of the siege of Jerusalem by Nebuchadnezzar (586 B.C.E). Reference to it and to other fast days can be found in Zechariah, who prophesied that all of these days of mourning would some day be converted into times of rejoicing (Zech. 8:19). It has served as a cutoff date for the merrymaking that accompanies the Hanukkah session.

The fast begins with dawn and ends at nightfall. In the synagogue, S'lihot are offered, confession is spoken, and in Torah reading we recite God's Thirteen Attributes of Mercy (Exod. 32:11–14; 34:1–10). There is no work prohibition. Reform Judaism does not observe the day.

The Fifteenth of Sh'vat

One month later, the "New Year's Day of Trees" is celebrated. In Egypt, it was forbidden to injure any fruit trees because the god Osiris dwelt in them. We find a similar prohibition in Torah, which finds it necessary to reject any belief in a tree's human, much less divine, character, holding instead that a tree sustains life and is to be preserved even in warfare.

Jewish agricultural celebrations have traditionally been tied to the climate of the land of Israel, but none more so than the holiday of Tu B'Shvat, which comes at a perfect time for tree-planting in the Holy Land. Throughout the years of wandering, Jews continued to celebrate this occasion at its appointed time; and today once again the children of Israel go out to plant saplings in honor of the "New Year of the Trees."

Are the trees of the field human, to withdraw before you under siege? [Deut. 20:19–20]

In joy, the awakening of the trees' life is observed. The fifteenth of Sh'vat is a pure festival of nature; it has no historical meaning.

Once important, the feast is of minor significance today. The Torah is not read in public.

We are, however, bidden to partake of the fruit with which the land of Israel is especially blessed, for it is

A land of wheat and barley, of vines, figs, and pomegranates, a land of olive oil and [date-] honey. [Deut. 8:8]

In Israel the children go out to plant saplings, and in this country the custom has developed for children to plant trees indigenous to Israel in the garden of the synagogue. The festival thus comes to reveal the significance of the restoration of Israel as a sovereign nation.

Tu B'Shvat (the Hebrew letters *Tet* and *Vav* have the numerical value of 15, hence the name) was once fiscally important (Rosh Hashanah 1:1). It was the cutoff date for determining the year when the fruit of the tree was to be tithed. If planted before this date, its tithe had to apply to the previous year; if planted afterward, its tithe was applied to the following year. Beyond that, the day was observed in joy as a stepping-stone to spring.

154

TOWARD SPRING

First Harbingers of Spring

Spring has to be understood not merely as a time of budding, but as the onset of fulfillment. Judaism has seen it that way. Spring reaches its climax with the harvesting of the first sheaf of grain. Spring also brings release from the confinement of narrow houses; it heralds freedom. Spring celebrates *Israel's* freedom, its liberation from Egyptian bondage, and its birth as a nation. In spring, also, the new State of Israel declared its independence. Pessah is the culmination of spring. It commemorates the Exodus and, in Temple days, the first offering of the new harvest.

The road from the darkest day of the year, Hanukah, winter solstice, to Pessah is long and arduous. More than a month has to pass from the tenth of Tevet, fast of purification, to the fifteenth of Sh'vat, New Year of the Trees. But now the pace increasingly accelerates. Within less than two weeks, the first of the four special Sabbath days, heralds of spring, arrives; a few days later, the happy month of Adar begins. A second special Sabbath is observed, bringing a new message of growth. Within the week, the fast of purification, preceding Purim, is observed, leading directly to Purim on the following day. Purim is the human anticipation of Pessah, a reflection of the feast of liberation. Another two special Sabbath days follow in rapid succession. Then Nissan, the month of spring, arrives. The tenth of the month was the day of preparation for the feast when Israel dwelt in Egypt. It is observed on the "Great Sabbath." The fourteenth saw the sacrifice of the Pessah lamb, offered in the Temple by the multitudes; today it is a day of purification for the firstborn. The eve of the fifteenth brings us the Seder; the fifteenth sees exultation at liberty through God. The night leading to the sixteenth witnessed the cutting of the first measure of new barley; on the sixteenth, it was offered unto God in the Temple of old. Fulfillment had come.

The increased crowding of events truly reflects nature. The beginning is slow and invisible, but from the moment when the first buds appear, nature surges forward with greater speed and energy, from bud to leaf to blossom. During the weeks anticipating Pessah, the Jew will have occasion to praise God for this joy. Seeing the first trees in blossom, he speaks a blessing:

Barukh . . . shelo hisar be-olomo davar, uvara bo b'riot tovot v'ilanot tovim l'hanot bahem b'nei adam.
Blessed are You . . . He Who has not omitted anything in His world, but has created in it goodly creatures and goodly trees, to give delight through them to the children of man.

We shall now trace in greater detail the steps from the fifteenth of Sh'vat to Pessah.

Advent of Purim

The Talmud rules:

With the advent of Adar we are to increase joy. [Taanit 29a]

The season begins with the Sabbath of the new month's proclamation. It is one of the four on which a special *Parshah* is read from a second scroll after the weekly reading. This week it is *Parshat Shekalim,* dealing with the half-Shekel everybody was to pay as a poll-tax (Exod. 30:11–16). Winter rain and storms had attacked the Temple; it needed repairs. Now that spring had come, these could be carried out. The half-Shekel was used for this purpose. No one could pay less or more, for the Temple belonged to all equally. The "half-Shekel" was designated as an instrument of both personal purification and restoration of the sanctuary.

The second of the Four Parshiot is *Parshat Zakhor.* As Israel, just emerged from Egypt, wearily plodded the uncharted desert, it was suddenly attacked in the rear by the Amalekites. In a fierce battle, led by Joshua, the Israelites chased away the attackers. During the fight, Moses, at the peak of a nearby hill, raised his arms heavenward, and the people prevailed; if he lowered his arms for a moment, Amalek would prevail. Moses served as a banner: by taking their strength from God in heaven, the people overcame the enemy; trusting in themselves only, they were beaten (Exod. 17:8–16).

At this time the people were admonished to heed the truth learned in battle with the Amalekites. The warning is repeated in the Book of Deuteronomy:

Remember, what Amalek did to you. . . .
You were faint and weary and he did not fear God. . . .
Therefore . . . you shall blot out the memory of Amalek from under heaven. Do not forget. [Deut. 25:17–19]

This is the portion read on the Sabbath before Purim. The Rabbis hold that Haman, the villain of the Purim story, was a descendant of Amalek.

In Parshat Shekalim, the people learned that they must unite and center their collective and individual life around God's Temple. Only then could they expect prosperity from the wellsprings of nature. In Parshat Zakhor this idea is reinforced. The Israelites were "faint and weary," which meant, according to the Rabbis, that they were weak in faith. They became easy victims to Amalek, who did not fear God at all. History has repeatedly shown that nations lacking the will to resist can be brutally attacked and destroyed. Only by subjecting themselves to ethical values can they survive. At the same time, freedom-loving nations must put their energy to work to bring an end to latter-day Amalekites and the aggression for which they stand, until their "memory will be wiped out."

Fast of Esther

On the thirteenth of Adar, a fast is observed from dawn to nightfall. S'lihot are offered, confession is spoken, and God's Thirteen Attributes of Mercy read from Torah (Exod. 32:11–14; 34:1–10). Preceding Purim, it is called the "Fast of Esther," for Esther fasted before engaging in the most dangerous action of her life.

Purim may be regarded as a human replica of Pessah, which it precedes by one month. Just as purification was required for the Pessah feast, so it was ordained for Purim. This is the meaning of the fast. Esther did not fast on this day.

14

Purim:
The Foreshadowing
of Pessah

THE PURIM STORY

The Purim story is found in the Biblical book of Esther. Although it has no real foundation in history, it offers a penetrating psychological analysis of the sources and workings of anti-Semitism.

King Ahasverus, ruler over Persia and Media, had cast out his queen, Vashti, for her public refusal to obey his command and appear at a banquet. A new queen was found by means of a contest to which all the young girls of the realm were bidden. There were many Jews in the kingdom, for the story is placed during the period of the Babylonian exile. Among them was Esther, ward of a Jewish sage by the name of Mordecai. She, too, had to participate in the contest. When she appeared before Ahasverus, he was so taken by her beauty and character that he immediately acclaimed her queen. She did not reveal her background.

As Esther moved into the palace, Mordecai made it a habit to spend his days at the palace gate, where he might be available to her for advice and counsel. There he also overheard the talk of courtiers, and thus he learned one day of a conspiracy among two officers to assassinate the king. He reported this to Esther, who reported it to the king, naming Mordecai as the source of her information. Investigation proved the matter to be true, the officers were executed, and Mordecai's good deed was recorded in the king's chronicle.

Shortly thereafter Ahasverus elevated a vicious, spiteful man, by the name of Haman, to be viceroy of the empire. Haman immediately ordered everybody to prostrate himself before him as he passed by. Mordecai refused to fall on his face before a man decked out with heathen idols; as a Jew, he could not do so. Haman sought revenge. He did not know of the relationship between Mordecai and Queen Esther, which neither had revealed. Haman, seeing in Mordecai the noxious stereotype of the Jew, decided that all Jews throughout the entire empire were to be exterminated. But for this genocidal action, Haman required the king's authorization.

In the month of Nissan, Haman cast lots to determine the most propitious date for the extermination of the Jews. (According to the Book of Esther, the Persian term for "lot" is *pur*, hence the name "Purim"—Feast of Lots.) The date of the massacre was to be the thirteenth of Adar. Then Haman went to the king, armed with the perennial argument of Jew-haters:

There is a certain people scattered abroad and dispersed among all the
    provinces of your kingdom;
their laws are different from those of every other people;
they do not obey the king's laws;
there is no gain for the king in tolerating them.
If it therefore appears good to the king, let it be ordained in writing that
    they are to be exterminated;
and I will weigh out ten thousand talents of silver into the hands of the
    officials to be delivered into the royal treasuries. [Esther 3:8-9]

Ahasverus declined the gift, but without any personal investigation gave Haman power to proceed and made him keeper of the seal on the royal ring.

On the thirteenth of Nissan the edict was issued, ordering the populace to strike down all the Jews on the thirteenth of Adar and granting them the spoils.

Consternation gripped the city of Shushan. Mordecai sped to the royal palace. Through a messenger he conveyed the news to Esther, urging her to see the king immediately. But she sent back word that she could not enter the audience chamber without being summoned. Such an act would jeopardize her life. Mordecai replied: You must go to save your people and yourself. Esther, therefore, bade Mordecai call a fast of three days for all the Jews; she, too, would fast, and on the third day she would go in to the king,

And if I perish, I perish. [Esther 4:16]

On the third day, royally dressed, she entered the audience chamber. The unexpected happened; the king admitted her. This was the sixteenth day of Nissan, Pessah. She invited Ahasverus and Haman for dinner that evening.

As he was leaving this banquet, Haman encountered the obstinate

Mordecai, who again would not bow to him. Enraged, Haman built a gallows, on which he vowed to hang Mordecai before twenty-four hours had elapsed.

During that night, unable to sleep, Ahasverus had an attendant read to him from the royal chronicle. He learned there of Mordecai's having saved his life, without ever having received any reward for it. At this moment, Haman's restless pacing was heard in the anteroom. He had come to obtain royal permission for Mordecai's hanging. He was summoned into the presence of the king. "What shall be done to a man whom the king wishes to honor?" Ahasverus asked. Haman, thinking the honor referred to himself, advised that the person thus to be honored be dressed in royal robes, placed on a royal horse, led through the city in procession, preceded by a dignitary of the realm who would call out: "Thus shall be done to the man whom the king wishes to honor." To Haman's dismay, the king agreed to the suggestion but ordered *him* to be *Mordecai's* herald in the procession through the city.

Hardly had he returned from his public humiliation when Haman was summoned to a second banquet with the queen. The king asked her if there were any royal favor he might grant her. Now Esther revealed the plot and pleaded for her people and, important to Ahasverus, for her own life. The king, shocked, realized that he had been duped. Learning from a courtier that Haman had built a gallows for Mordecai, Ahasverus curtly commanded: "Hang him on it."

Mordecai was thereupon appointed viceroy. Although a royal edict, once issued, could not be revoked, a new one was issued on the twenty-third of Sivan, ordering the Jews to arm and defend themselves. When the thirteenth of Adar arrived, the Jews overcame their attackers. In fact, many among the population stood in such awe of the Jews that they converted to Judaism rather than fight. Haman's sons, the ringleaders, were hanged.

Mordecai and Esther ordered that the Jews of the realm celebrate forever the fourteenth of Adar and, in the cities, the fifteenth also, as

days of feasting and gladness, and of sending portions one to another and gifts to the poor. And the Jews took upon themselves, to do as they had begun, and as Mordecai had written unto them . . . they called these days Purim, after the name of pur. . . . [Esther 9:20–28]

Historicity of the Book of Esther and the Origin of Purim

It is widely believed that the book of Esther was written during the Maccabean period; the "Day of Mordecai" is mentioned in the Second Book of Maccabees (15:36). The author of the work had a certain acquaintance with Persian conditions, such as the Council of Seven, consulted by Ahasverus on the expulsion of Queen Vashti;

Gustave Doré imagined the scene in which Esther, in Persian garb, against a Persian background, accused Haman of plotting against the Jews. As the Book of Esther records, "Then Haman was afraid before the king and the queen . . ." (Esther 7:6).

such a council is also mentioned by Herodotus. It is not impossible that a persecution of Jews did occur or was planned in some part of the empire at some time. But we have no record of a Queen Esther or of a Jewish viceroy Mordecai, although the Book of Esther states that the events were recorded in the royal chronicle (10:2). Finally, the term *Pur* meaning "lot" cannot be found in Persian or related languages.

It may thus be assumed that we are dealing here with a feast dear to Babylonian Jews, who wished to introduce it into general Jewish practice. To achieve this purpose they may even have adjusted the date of the battle between the Jews and their enemies to coincide with an event that took place during the Maccabean period: the Syrian general Nicanor, sent out to capture Judah the Maccabee, was defeated and killed in battle on the thirteenth of Adar, and the anniversary was subsequently celebrated. In light of the Jewish aversion to victory celebrations, which we observed in connection with Hanukah, we can understand how such a feast would be transformed into a glorification of God's power.

We have seen in connection with the observance of Ellul, preceding the Days of Awe, and the fast of the tenth of Tevet, in relation to the fifteenth of Sh'vat, that a thirty-day period of purification preceded certain festivals of renewal. Purim, preceding Pessah, would initiate such a period, and the story would make them edifying reading. Perhaps it was even performed as a kind of morality play. The Book of Esther gives us the dialogue between the actors in great detail and, in fact, reads like a script of a play. Most significantly, it never mentions the Name of God, for His Name could not be pronounced in nonliturgical discourse.

Purim as a forecast or foreshadowing of Pessah is characterized by the following features. Like the Biblical feast, the event occurred on Pessah; it occurred outside the Land of Israel; the Jews came close to extinction; they were rescued through the sacrificial leadership of great personalities, who risked their lives in appearing before the king (see Exod. 2:11–15); in the end, the evildoers perished, and the Jews gained the goodwill of their neighbors.

Both celebrations reveal the truth expressed at the Seder:

Not just one [Pharaoh] rose against us to exterminate us, but in every generation did they rise against us to exterminate us, and each time, The Holy One Blessed Be He has rescued us from their hands.

But there are significant contrasts as well between the two holidays, pointing to differences in degree. Moses, a man, represents the Jewish people before Pharaoh himself; on Purim, Esther, a woman, and by long tradition a member of "the weaker sex," defends the Jews against the king's underling. Behind Moses stood God; behind Esther stood Mordecai, a mere human being. In Egypt, visible miracles occurred; none were wrought in Persia, where "natural" events brought relief. Above all, the events in Egypt are to impress the people with the presence of the divine; in the Purim story, God is only alluded to. Purim puts the people in tune for the forthcoming Pessah.

Purim can be traced to non-Jewish sources as well. Thus we read in Mesopotamian mythology of the goddess Ishtar [Esther], forced to enter the realm of the netherworld in fall; as she descends, she sheds all her garments (the trees lose their leaves), and many sicknesses befall the earth. Eventually, the god of the netherworld is persuaded to let her return to earth, and happiness sprouts again. In our story, Esther enters the gates of danger as great distress befalls her people. At Pessah time, she emerges victorious, the evil overcome.

Haman is the demon [of winter], trying to dupe king and people; he is caught and hanged. Mordecai and Esther, both royally robed in the Purim story, become king and queen of fertility.

From these roots, many of the customs surrounding this season have sprung. Jews observe Purim with dances, mummery, costumes, and a banquet, during which drinking is a duty; in Israel, there is a parade. The children are taken to the synagogue armed with noisemakers. Whenever the name "Haman" is read from the *Megillah,* the Book of Esther, they are to stomp and make much noise to drive him out.

THE OBSERVANCE OF PURIM

THE EVE OF THE FEAST finds the congregation still fasting; it is the end of the Fast of Esther. (If Purim falls on a Sunday, the fast is kept on the preceding Thursday.) The mood is joyful.

At the entrance of the synagogue are two plates: one for the half-Shekel, the other for free-will offerings for the poor. The half-Shekel must be a silver coin, itself half of a silver coin; in our case, a half dollar.

The evening prayer is recited. *Al Hanissim* is included in the Amidah and will be included in Grace after meals. As on Hanukah, it retells the events in a few sentences, giving thanks for God's help.

Now the Reader holds a handwritten scroll (Megillah) of the Book of Esther. He folds it to resemble a letter, following Esther's injunction that "this letter" be complied with (Esther 9:26). He speaks the Berakhah:

Barukh . . . vetzivanu al Mikra Megillah
Blessed are You . . . He, Who . . . has commanded us concerning the Reading of the Megillah.

Handwritten manuscripts of the Book of Esther were often decorated in the most highly elaborate fashion. This scroll and its silver case comes from Palestine, c.1930.

Sheheheyanu follows. Then the whole book is read.

The children, with their rattles, wait for each recurrence of the name of Haman; then they break forth, and, as the Rabbis state, "the sacred noise of children casts out the enemy." Youth exorcises Israel's destroyers.

A brief recapitulation ends the reading. The congregation speaks:

The lily of Jacob [the Jews] was jubilant and joyful as together they beheld the hyacinth-blue of Mordecai [his robe in the procession]. You have been their Deliverer and their Hope from generation to generation. To make known that those that trust in You will never be put to shame, nor will those who put their faith in You suffer reproach. Cursed be Haman, who plotted to wipe me out, blessed be Mordecai, the Jew. . . .

The royal blue was also attached to the Tallit; it gives us equal dignity. Of "cursed Haman and blessed Mordecai" we shall speak later on.

At dinner and throughout the day, *Hamentaschen* are eaten, three-cornered pastries filled with fruit or poppy seed. The three-cornered cookie is supposed to represent Haman's hat, and it stands as well for the headgear of many potentates of later ages who tried to destroy us. The word for poppy seed in Yiddish is *mon*; add the Hebrew article *Ha* ("the"), and you get *Ha-mon*, Haman. This pun is very much in the spirit of Purim, a feast of fun.

IN THE MORNING Hallel is not recited, as it is replaced by the Megillah. Torah is read: the story of Amalek's attack on Israel (Exod. 17:8–16). Then the whole Megillah is once again recited from the scroll.

After services, gifts of food are exchanged. According to the Book of Esther, there must be at least two gifts between friends and gifts

164

unspecified to the poor. The proud but poverty-stricken Jew thus need not feel humiliated; he receives his gift not as charity, but because he is a friend.

In Israel, a great Purim parade follows in early afternoon. In the *shtetl*, the children, costumed and masked, would go from house to house. In many Jewish schools today contests are held for the best-looking Esther, the most royal Mordecai, the most evil-looking Haman. Dances, beauty contests, and Purim plays are generally held a few days earlier or later. There is too much to do at home on Purim itself.

IN THE AFTERNOON a great family banquet is held, as ordained by Esther (9:22). It is accompanied by much drinking, for there is a special ruling for Purim:

He must get so drunk that he no longer can distinguish between "Haman be cursed" and "Mordecai be blessed." [Megillah 7a]

"That he no longer can distinguish" is in Hebrew *Ad delo yada*. This is the name given the feast by Israeli Jews.

The Fifteenth of Adar, Shushan Purim, ordained for the Jews in Persia's capital and in big cities, has no special observances for us. It merely provides a lingering fragrance of the jolly feast, now past, and gently leads into the routine of daily activity. Now the great housecleaning for Pessah will start in earnest.

Costumes and merriment make Purim festive for adult and child alike. Puppet shows depicting the story of Haman's defeat and the triumph of Esther and Mordecai are very much in the spirit of the day.

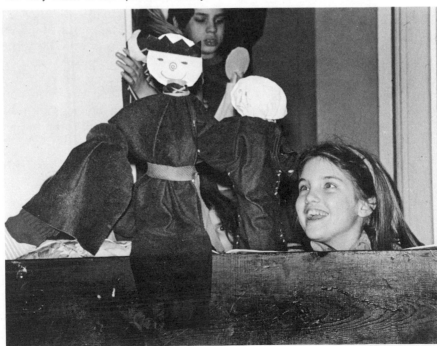

THE ADVENT OF PESSAH

On special Sabbath days that follow, the ideas expressed at Purim are taken up again: casting out the impurities of the past, ushering in the spirit of the future.

Parshat Parah, third in the sequence of the Four Parshiot, brings us the ordinance of the "Red Heifer." After slaughter and burning, its ashes were used for purification of those who had been in contact with the dead (Num. 19:1–22).

Purification rites were common among the ancients at this time of the year. The key message of this Sabbath is: exorcise the impurity of a year that has about died.

Parshat Hahodesh, the fourth special Sabbath, proclaims the future; it precedes the arrival of the month of Nissan and proclaims:

This month shall mark for you the beginning of the months. . . . [Exod. 12:1–20]

The nation was born in Egypt at this moment and is ever reborn.

During these weeks, the cleansing of the house takes its course; beginning on the first of Nissan, the Temple was cleansed.

Shabbat Ha-Gadol

"The Great Sabbath" is observed immediately before Pessah. In Egypt, the Israelites, cowering slaves, found the courage to select the lambs of their masters as Pessah sacrifice. As these animals were worshipped as gods, the Israelites thus rebuked Egyptian idolatry.

No special portion is read in addition to the weekly one. But on this day, the rabbi in the shtetl would preach. (He did so only twice a year.) Later in the afternoon, the rabbi would present a Talmudic discourse, a *sugya.* The subject was announced several weeks ahead of time and the sources given in order that members might prepare themselves. The subject was then analyzed by the rabbi from its earliest sources in Torah, through Talmud and later works, and an effort was made to conciliate differences of opinions by rabbis of various centuries. As Pessah meant freedom and Torah means freedom, the two belong together:

When Torah came into the world, freedom came into the world. [Bereshit Rabba, Vayery 53:7; see also Abot 6:2]

Erev Pessah

The day before Pessah is a day of fasting and purification, but not for all Jews, only for firstborn sons—they were protected when the firstborn of the Egyptians were slain by God. The fast is so minor that a S'udah shel Mitzvah, a banquet in connection with a Mitzvah, can cancel it. Thus the rabbi will conclude the study of a tractate of Talmud on this day, and a Mitzvah breakfast held in the morning to honor the event releases the firstborn from the fast.

15

Pessah:
Celebration
of Liberation

P essah celebrates the liberation of Israel from Egyptian slavery. It is the national birthday of the Jewish people.

The Significance of Pessah

Pessah Means Life. The slave has no life. He exists as the tool of his master who determines how he shall think, what he shall do, how long he shall live. Only the free have life.

Pessah Means Liberty. The isolated individual person has no liberty. He finds himself surrounded by the hostile forces of nature and the enmity of fellow humans. Liberty begins when individuals begin to cooperate, supporting one another; it grows as they establish laws to which they submit freely, knowing that only an ordered society, justly regulated, can assure freedom in justice for all.

Pessah means the Pursuit of Justice. Unless each member of society actively pursues the happiness of every other member, none is happy. The outcry of the disinherited will turn into rebellion, and happiness, rooted in peace, will vanish.

Pessah Means Inalienable Rights at the Hand of the Creator. The rights to life, liberty, and the pursuit of happiness are inalienable. They are an endowment given us by the Creator. The fathers of our country, framers of the Declaration of Independence, knew this. They had learned it from the Bible, from Israel.

On Pessah the Jewish people were made into a nation. They were granted freedom, not merely *from* slavery but *for* the task of establishing justice in their midst and to set an example to the nations. On Pessah, it was revealed to them that human rights are God-given and that law, national and international, must be in tune with the will of the Creator. This means that God enters history, and man is challenged to be God's co-worker.

Pessah is eternal revelation and everlasting challenge. The first sentence of the Ten Commandments makes this manifest, demanding that all our actions be placed under God's direction:

I the Lord am your God who brought you out of the land of Egypt, the house of bondage. [Exod. 20:2]

The call is repeated endlessly in Torah and liturgy.

The commandment of Tzitzit is linked to the reminder:

I the Lord am your God, who brought you out of the land of Egypt to be your God. [Num. 15:40–41]

In every Kiddush, on Sabbath days and festivals, we speak:

in remembrance of the Exodus from Egypt.

And when Torah speaks of the treatment of strangers or of ethics in business practice, it again makes reference to Egypt and to the lesson of the liberation from bondage (see Lev. 19:33–36). We are free, as we are bonded to God (Lev. 25:55).

In every generation, every individual person is to view himself as having been personally rescued from Egypt. . . . [Haggadah]

For Jews, history is an eternal present.

Pessah as Prologue. The feast of liberation must lead directly to the celebration of Torah, the Revelation at Sinai. As our Sukkot festival, thanksgiving for the harvest, leads to the feast of Sh'mini Atzeret, so does Pessah, beginning of the harvest, lead after seven weeks to our most portentous encounter with God: Shavuot.

BIBLICAL-HISTORICAL BACKGROUND

In its long history, Egypt underwent many upheavals. Important for us is the Hyksos invasion around 1700–1600 B.C.E. The Hyksos were a Semitic people who overthrew the ruling dynasty and assumed power. Eventually, in a revolution, they were cast out by the natives, who had always regarded them as usurpers.

This may explain some Biblical reports. We hear of Joseph, sold to Egypt, enslaved, imprisoned, and suddenly elevated to the highest rank in the realm. If the Pharaoh before whom Joseph stood to interpret his disturbing dreams was of the Hyksos dynasty, it is not quite so surprising that this Semitic "relative" should have empowered Joseph to direct the measures to be taken against the famine he had predicted. Nor is it quite so surprising that Pharaoh should have shown graciousness to Joseph's family, when, during the famine, they wished to migrate from the Egyptian colony of Canaan to the heartland of the empire.

When the Hyksos dynasty ran into trouble, conditions changed abruptly. There was fear that the new immigrants might make common cause with an invader. They had to be enslaved and their sons drowned at birth, for they had become too numerous:

Now a new king arose over Egypt, who did not know Joseph, and he said to his people: "Look, the Israelite people are much too numerous for us. Let us then deal shrewdly with them, lest they increase, and, in the event of war, join our enemies in fighting against us and gain ascendancy over the country." So they set taskmasters over them to oppress them with forced labor; and they built garrison cities for Pharaoh: Pitom and Raamses. [Exod. 1:8–11]

Archaeological research has confirmed the building of these cities; historical research has shown that the Israelites threw off the yoke of slavery under Rameses II (appr. 1292–1225 B.C.E.) and left Egypt, probably in the year 1280 B.C.E., on their homeward trek to Canaan, where some of their relatives still lived.

Now Torah elaborates (Exod. 1:1–15:21). It introduces Moses, whose historicity is not seriously questioned. Moses confronted Pharaoh in the Name of God, demanding freedom for his people. He challenged Pharaoh's divinity and the divine rights of all kings. He denied the divinity of the Nile. Ten plagues came over Egypt; Pharaoh himself was hit by them, and the Nile was the source of several of them. The tenth plague was the most severe: all the firstborn sons of the Egyptians, including the royal prince, were slain. Now, after a long resistance, Pharaoh let the Israelites go.

The Israelites, untouched by the plagues, were told to prepare themselves for the Exodus. On the tenth of Nissan, they were to choose a lamb for each family. It was to be carefully guarded up to the fourteenth; then it was to be slaughtered, roasted, and, at night, consumed in a family gathering, together with unleavened bread and bitter herbs. With this meal, they were to be ready for immediate departure, for this was to be the night of the slaying of the firstborn. As a distinguishing mark for their homes, they were to place a portion of the lamb's blood on the posts and the lintel of their

Engraving by Doré. Among the great events recounted in the Passover *Haggadah*, none is more significant than the crossing of the Red Sea. The chariots of the Egyptians were trapped in the mud; and the soldiers of Egypt were drowned beneath the closing waters. Then Miriam led the daughters of Israel in song and dance (Exodus 14).

doors. When the time came, the avenging hand of God *passed over* their homes. This has given our feast its name: Passover, Pessah.

When the frightened Pharaoh chased the Israelites out of his land, they were prepared and unprepared. They burned the leftovers of the lamb, as they had been commanded, took their belongings and the precious gifts many Egyptians had given them and which they had packed, gathered their families, and departed in haste. But the dough they had made and set aside for rising could not be baked. They put it on their heads, and the sun eventually baked it, transforming it into unleavened bread.

Three days later, Pharaoh regretted his hasty action. With his chariots, he chased after them. He reached them on the seventh day as they faced the Sea of Reeds, deprived of any route of escape. But the sea parted, they were led through, and the waves closed again over the pursuing Egyptians, drowning Pharaoh and all his host. The redeemed Israelites united in a great song of thanksgiving: the Song at the Sea of Reeds (Red Sea).

Subsequent Ordinances

Torah then ordained that the feast should be celebrated forever. It was to be observed for seven days, for on the seventh the miracle of the parting of the sea occurred.

During the first night, the people were to observe a Lord's Supper. A lamb, sacrificed in the Temple, and roasted over an open fire, was to be consumed together with unleavened bread—Matzah—and bitter herbs. The unleavened bread was to remind them of their hasty departure, when their bread had no chance to rise. Later, it was also interpreted as the bread of slaves. The bitter herbs were to give them the bitter taste of slavery, lest they inflict it on others. It was ordained that this supper be accompanied by a rehearsal of the events of the Exodus, as a lesson for the child (Exod. 12:26; 13:8; 13:14; Deut. 6:20).

This has given us the Seder. But we do not partake of a lamb, which was done only in Temple days.

Connected with the feast was the ordinance of complete elimination of all leaven from table, home, and possession (Lev. 23:5–8; Deut. 16:1–9). This prohibition may lie in the feast's character as a celebration of nature.

Pessah: Festival of Nature

Torah ordains that Pessah be observed "in the month of Aviv— the month of 'Green Corn' " (Exod. 13:3–8; 23:15; 34:18). An even clearer indication of the feast as a celebration of nature can be found in Leviticus:

In the first month on the fourteenth day of the month, at twilight there shall be a Passover offering to the Lord, and on the fifteenth day of that month the Lord's Feast of Unleavened Bread. You shall eat unleavened bread for seven days. . . . [Lev. 23:5–6] When you enter the land which I am giving to you and you reap its harvest, you shall bring the first sheaf of your harvest to the priest. He shall wave the sheaf before the Lord for acceptance in your behalf; the priest shall wave it on the day after the day of rest. [Lev. 23:10–11]

. . . You shall keep count [until] seven full weeks have elapsed . . . then you shall bring an offering of new grain to the Lord. [Lev. 23:15–16]

The whole chapter, outlining the festivals, relates them exclusively to agriculture and in no way mentions their historical connotation.

The regulations reveal the sources of the festival in universal, early nature rites. These took various forms.

The leftovers of last year's harvest were gathered and burned, lest they contaminate the new harvest. Sometimes they were buried to fertilize the earth and make it prosper. We, too, gather the leaven, "Hametz," and cast it out of the house. On Erev Pessah, a great bonfire consumes the leftovers of the "impure." Death is driven out; life is affirmed.

In pastoral societies, a young animal was eaten by the members of the clan, gathered for the feast. It was the shepherd's sacrifice of thanks. In agricultural societies, bread was broken and shared, the gift of the field. Our Seder, with its paschal lamb in Temple days, and the unleavened bread, reenacts this rite.

The solemn supper served as a prelude to the offering of the new harvest to the gods. In the same spirit, sheaves of the new grain were solemnly cut during the night following the first day of Pessah, and a measure of them, an *Omer* (roughly 0.4 liter), was offered in the Temple on the following day in culmination of the celebration: the new harvest had been consecrated. Barley was offered, the oldest cereal cultivated by man. From then on, a period of counting, fifty days, led to and linked this offering to the offering of wheat that had ripened in the meanwhile; the two feasts were united.

Pessah and Sukkot as Pillars of the Seasons

The rites we have discussed reveal a parallel between Pessah and Sukkot, constituting these two feasts as pillars of the seasons.

Pessah commemorates the Exodus, wrought by God; Sukkot commemorates divine protection in the desert.

Pessah calls for cleansing the house, that it be a pure abode; Sukkot calls for an abandonment of the house for God's Sukkah.

Pessah witnesses the offering of the new harvest: lamb and Omer; Sukkot witnesses the presentation of the completed harvest: Arba Minim.

Pessah calls for a preceding spiritual cleansing, the fast of the firstborn; Sukkot is preceded by the great cleansing of Yom Kippur.

Sukkot is followed by an eighth day of observance, a feast of communion with God: Sh'mini Atzeret; Pessah is followed after an interval of seven weeks by Shavuot, when the greatest of all communions took place between God and Israel: the Revelation at Sinai. The two events are bound together by the "Counting of the Omer."

Throughout the seasons, from festival to festival, there is an overarching structure that gives meaning to Judaism as an organic way of life.

HAMETZ AND ITS REMOVAL

Torah ordains:

From the fourteenth day of the month at evening, you shall eat unleavened bread [*Matzah*] until the twenty-first day of the month at evening. No leaven [*Hametz*] shall be found in your houses for seven days. [Exod. 12:18–19]

This injunction is permanent:

throughout the generations as an institution for all time. [Exod. 12:17]

Severe penalty is attached to its violation:

For whoever eats what is leavened, that person shall be cut off from the assembly of Israel, whether he is a stranger or a citizen of the country. [Exod. 12:19]

This punishment cannot be imposed by any court; it will be meted out by God Himself.

Analyzing the law, as the Rabbis did, we come to the conclusion that: only Matzah may be consumed; no Hametz may be consumed in any way; and possession, ownership, and storage of Hametz are forbidden ("it shall not be found with you in your houses").

What Is Hametz?

Any product of five types of grain—wheat, rye, barley, oats, and spelt—becomes Hametz if the grain has been in contact with water for eighteen minutes without being handled before baking. The burden of proof, that the grain has had no contact with water, rests on the Jew. This means that a product made of these cereals is permitted for use only if it has been subjected to constant supervision from cutting through milling, sifting, transportation, kneading, and baking, and has been prepared according to law, for example, Matzah. Anything in which even a minimal admixture of Hametz is found or may be assumed to exist is forbidden. This includes bread, cake, cereal, beer, grain alcohol, even medications containing alcohol or tablets having flour as a binder. (Jews who need special medicines should inquire of the rabbi about their use.) Cosmetics may be Hametz; chocolate and candy may have Hametz as ingredients. But even foodstuffs ordinarily prepared *without* Hametz are suspect, as some particles may have got into them during production or storage.

All Pessah foods, therefore, have to be prepared under special supervision to exclude any possibility of even the most accidental contact with Hametz. Foods that may be kasher throughout the entire year (such as canned foodstuffs) and may even have the kasher label on them are not automatically usable on Pessah unless they are so certified. They must have the seal: *Kasher le-Pessah.* Even Matzot must have this label.

Regional traditions have imposed additional restrictions. In Germany, fowl was not eaten for fear that some of the contents of the stomach might have spilled over in cleaning; the stomach usually contains grain. We do not have such a restriction in this country. Various other traditions prohibit lentils, beans, and other foods closely akin to the prohibited cereals. As these differ, a rabbi should be consulted.

Our pots and pans, silverware, dishes, and glasses also have absorbed Hametz during the year. Therefore, complete sets of meat and milk utensils and dishes have to be provided for Pessah; they are not used throughout the rest of the year. (See below, Erev Pessah.)

The Removal of Hametz consists of several steps. A great, *general housekeeping* extends over many weeks: every nook and cranny is scraped out; every crevice in upholstered furniture is vacuumed; every carpet cleaned and every floor washed. Subsequently, the members of the household, especially the children, are watched lest, while carrying Hametz, they enter the rooms already cleaned. In the Middle Ages, when the general populace permitted dirt to accumulate from year to year, Jews derived a special benefit from this housecleaning. They frequently found themselves protected from the germs that brought ravaging diseases to other people.

During the housecleaning, Hametz items, such as liquor, are stored away in a closet that can be locked.

Some *kitchen utensils* may be made kasher for Pessah. Glasses can be soaked in water for three days. Metal utensils, if made of one piece, may be made kasher for Pessah by total immersion in boiling water. Pots used for cooking may be filled with water, which is then brought to a boil; if we throw red-hot coals in, we make the water spill over without cooling off, thus kashering the

Everyday dishes and utensils are set aside on the holiday of Passover, as they become Hametz. In general, Passover has been the occasion of "Jewish spring cleaning" for thousands of years.

rims. Items used for broiling can be cleansed by being brought to red heat. All these items must first be thoroughly cleaned and may not be used for several days before the kashering. The rules that apply are very detailed. Glazed items cannot be kashered; china cannot be kashered; items that are liable to crack or fall apart cannot be kashered, nor can those that are made of several parts, glued together. The rabbi should therefore be consulted in all these matters. A good, basic principle is: when in doubt, do not use.

The kitchenware that cannot be used is thoroughly cleaned and put in a closet that can be locked (but not the one with the Hametz). (The Jew was permitted to retain possession of these Hametz-soaked utensils by an ordinance of the Rabbis, designed to prevent price gouging by pottery merchants after Pessah, if the Hametz pottery were ordered destroyed before the feast—an example of rabbinical power and socioeconomic concern [Pessahim 30a].)

The Search for the Hametz

The Talmud rules:

Before the light of the fourteenth [arises] we must search for the Hametz at the light of a flame. [Pessahim 1:1]

As the night falls on the thirteenth of Nissan, the head of the house goes with a light through every room, cupboard, and drawer, look-

176

ing for Hametz that is then removed. He speaks a blessing before this act:

Barukh . . . vetzivanu al Biur Hametz
Blessed are You, . . . He, Who . . . commanded us regarding the removal of the Hametz.

After the search and the collection of Hametz, he declares:

Everything leavened in my sphere of influence that I have not seen and have not removed shall be regarded as a non-existing, ownerless entity, as the dust of the earth.

He has formally renounced ownership over these Hametz items.

Prohibition of Consumption and Possession

On Erev Pessah, Hametz may be consumed up to one-fourth of the daylight hours and may be owned up to one-third of the daylight hours.

SELLING OF THE HAMETZ. Before this time, the owner of the home places all the Hametz of any value in the Hametz closet, locks it, and "sells" the whole store to a non-Jew by contract and a down payment. The closet is rented to the non-Jew, who receives the key. The contract stipulates that the non-Jew truly owns the goods and that he is to make final payment after Pessah, but that he may sell them back to the owner at that time if he so desires. In many communities, the rabbi buys the Hametz from the people and sells it collectively to a non-Jew. The clean Hametz dishes are locked away, but not sold, as we have seen.

BURNING THE HAMETZ. The rest of the Hametz, leftovers from breakfast, and so on, are burned, often at a great bonfire in the synagogue court. By this time, all dishes have to be made kasher.

The head of the house now makes a second, all-inclusive declaration, separating himself completely from all ownership and possession of any Hametz inadvertently left over:

Everything leavened that is in my sphere of influence and ownership, whether I have seen it or not seen it, whether I have removed it or not removed it, shall be regarded as non-existing, ownerless entity, as the dust of the earth.

The Hametz is gone.

What Can We Eat on Pessah?

There is no shortage of products bearing the Kasher le-Pessah seal.

The Conservative rabbinate permits the use of commercially produced, uncertified coffee, sugar, and salt, as state and federal laws provide for absolute care in preparation. The Orthodox rabbinate does not permit them. Green vegetables have to be carefully washed.

Pessah offers a challenge to the creativity of the Jewish cook and baker. There may be new inventions. Jewish cookbooks will give guidance, but their reliability in regard to Kashrut has to be checked.

What Is Matzah?

Matzah is the only grain product we may eat on Pessah. It is unleavened bread, baked under supervision by a Jewish bakery. Its ingredients are water and flour; the exact proportion of the ingredients is laid down by law. It is quickly kneaded, flattened for rapid baking, stamped out in round or square sections, and baked at a high temperature.

Matzah Shemurah is no different from any other kind except that the grain has been "watched over" from the time of its growth in the fields. It is baked by the people themselves, or at least it used to be, under the rabbi's direction. It is used for the Seder nights.

As Matzah is produced commercially all year 'round, the package will indicate whether the Matzah in it has been baked for Pessah use or not. This should be noted.

After the Matzah has been baked, it may be used with water—dunked into coffee, put in the soup, used for the "gefilte fish," and so on. Matzah meal is ground Matzah, usable for frying, cooking, and baking.

What About the Pessah Lamb?

We are often asked by non-Jews, do we eat a lamb at the Seder? The idea of the sacrificial lamb has played a great role in Christianity. Jesus is seen as the Lamb of God, bearing the sins of the world. But Torah says:

You are not permitted to slaughter the Passover sacrifice in any of the settlements that the Lord your God is giving you; but at the place where the Lord your God will choose to establish His name there alone shall you slaughter the Passover sacrifice, in the evening at sundown, the time of day when you departed from Egypt. You shall cook and eat it at the place which the Lord your God will choose; and in the morning you may start back on your journey home. [Deut. 16:5-7]

The Passover lamb could be offered only in the Temple and be eaten only in the holy city by the pilgrims, who returned home the next day.

Many families will carefully refrain from eating any roasted meat on the Seder night, to avoid even the impression that they are partaking of an "imitation." This is why chicken, which was never used as a sacrifice in the Temple, is often eaten.

We no longer offer sacrifices. Indeed, the great philosopher Maimonides (1135–1204) held that God only granted the privilege of sacrifice to the Jews because at that time in history, when all other peoples offered them to their gods, it would have been too much to prohibit it. But from the beginning God intended to lead Israel to the true worship, prayer. Therefore He ordained that sacrifices could be offered only in *one* place, the Temple, whereas prayer and supplication may be offered at any place and at any time (*Guide for the Perplexed* III, 23). Maimonides thus sees Judaism in a process of ethical evolution, leading it to outgrow the dependence on sacrifices and the need for them. Non-Orthodox Jewry shares this view.

Erev Pessah

There is no busier time during the year.

ON THE EVE of the day, the father with his candle goes through the house to search for the Hametz. The family follows in his steps. The children have been given some feathers, and crumbs have been deliberately placed on window sills for them to find and place in a container.

EARLY IN THE MORNING, after services, the *Siyum* for the first-born is held in the synagogue, allowing them to break their fast (see The Advent of Pessah, Chapter 14). As the Mitzvah breakfast consists of Hametz food, it must end quickly. At home, a hasty breakfast is eaten; then the table and surroundings are carefully cleaned so that no Hametz remains. In a short time, bread may be consumed no longer.

LATER IN THE MORNING, the kitchen stove and utensils are made ready for Pessah use; they are kashered. (Sometimes the synagogue offers this service to members, who bring their kitchenware.)

The Hametz is sold. This has to be done within the first third of the daylight hours.

Now the great bonfire is lit, and the children throw their Hametz into it.

The father of the house makes his final declaration, annulling his ownership of all Hametz.

At home, the mother has cleaned all the Hametz dishes and stored them away, locking the closet and removing the key.

Even though she has thoroughly cleaned the kitchen, she may place boards or sheets on the counters, as these may be deeply permeated with Hametz. She puts new linings in the cupboards. Now she gets out the Pessah dishes.

Her first task is to make lunch. It cannot have any Hametz in it, but, on this day, neither may Matzah be eaten. It is to be reserved for the evening. Lunch is prepared in the Pessah dishes.

In the afternoon, after feeding her family, the mother has to turn immediately to the preparations of tonight's festival meal. Helped by her family, she makes the special dishes for the Seder plate and sets the table. Much is to be remembered. Now, all get ready for the greatest family celebration of the year: the Seder.

(The detailed regulations for Erev Pessah when it falls on a Sabbath should be obtained from a rabbi.)

SEDER: THE SUPPER BEFORE THE LORD

Ever since the night preceding the Exodus, Jews, on divine command, have celebrated a supper before the Lord. In time, a special "Order" for the ritual evolved: the Seder. It is an old rite. To guide us, we have a book containing the "Story," the *Haggadah*.

The core portions of the Haggadah can be found in the Mishnah (Pessahim 10); later generations have added to it. We are permitted to include new interpretations, features, and rites and have done so over the years. But the Seder is not confined to a mere storytelling and meal. We use a number of adjuncts, symbols that visualize the meaning of the event, and, in particular, are designed to impress it upon the children. As we have seen, Torah ordains that we tell the tale of the Exodus to our children, thus drawing them into the stream of Jewish experience. The child plays a great role in the Seder, asking the questions around which the Seder revolves.

The "Order" carries us from the past through the present into the future. Tale and symbols oscillate between a representation of future freedom and a commemoration of past slavery. We are to use the

The Seder ritual is contained in the *Haggadah*. *The New Haggadah,* a Reconstructionist version, appeared in 1942. Early editions of this *Haggadah* carried poignant references to the plight of the Jews in the face of Nazism. Later editions mourn the victims of the Holocaust and make reference to the problems faced by Jews in the Soviet Union today.

One Seder plate is set aside for the Matzah which is then covered; another plate contains the five commemorative symbols recalling various aspects of the Passover story.

bitter memories of enslavement to promote freedom and build a better future for Israel and mankind.

The youngest child asks four questions:

Why is this night different from all other nights?
On all other nights, we eat Hametz and Matzah, on this night only Matzah;
on all other nights, we eat all kinds of herbs, on this night we eat bitter herbs;
on all other nights, we need not dip our food into condiments at all, on this night we have to do so twice;
on all other nights, we may take our meal sitting up straight or in a reclining position, on this night we are all reclining.

The child's *first* question refers to the three Matzah, ceremonially displayed on the Seder Plate. We break them and partake of them. They symbolize the food of slavery, for there was never time to bake decent bread, but they also remind us of the moment of freedom that came so suddenly that the Israelites could not bake bread in advance. By their number, they represent the three divisions in Jewry: Kohanim, the priests; Leviim, the Levites; Yisraelim, the common folk. All were redeemed; all are of one people.

181

In our days, a fourth Matzah has been widely introduced. It stands for our brothers and sisters in Russia, who are still enslaved and frequently denied the right to have Matzah on Pessah. They are part of our people, and we pledge our utmost to bring them to the day of deliverance.

The child's *second* question refers to the *bitter herbs,* the *Maror,* also placed on the Seder plate, which we eat ceremonially. They reflect the bitterness of the life our forefathers had to endure. As they cling to our tongues, bringing tears to our eyes, we resolve to cast out any kind of slavery from the world.

The first two questions emphasize the memory of slavery; the next two, the symbols of freedom.

The child's *third* question refers to the fact that we dip green herbs in salt water and Maror or lettuce in *Haroset.* These two elements are also on the Seder Plate.

At the banquets of wealthy patricians in antiquity, many sauces were offered. Dipping herbs in condiments reflects our status as a free people, patricians before God, who has given us liberty.

But even this act is not without its allusions to slavery. We dip parsley or spring onions in salt water, which stands for the tears our ancestors shed in Egypt. Yet it may equally stand for the salty waters of the Sea of Reeds, which parted to open the road to liberty. We dip our bitter herbs, or lettuce, into Haroset. Lettuce is not really bitter, but is mentioned by the medieval commentators. *Haroset,* a mixture of apples, nuts, cinnamon, and perhaps some wine, blended into a creamy sauce, reminds us by its color of the mortar the Israelites had to make to build Pharaoh's garrisons. An additional reminder comes with these foods: it is springtime, and these are the plants of spring.

The child's *fourth* question relates to the fact that we are supposed to eat in a *reclining* position. At least the leader of the Seder is to have an armchair, on whose left side a pillow is placed for comfort in leaning. It was the habit of the rich in ancient days to take their great banquets reclining on couches, their left arm on the cushions, their right hand holding the food or wine. On the Seder night we revive this custom.

There are other ceremonial elements on our Seder Plate. They are of purely commemorative character. A *shankbone* reminds us of the ancient Pessah sacrifice. It is, therefore, roasted. It cannot be eaten. A roasted *egg* reminds us of free-will sacrifices offered by the pilgrims to Jerusalem. It may also stand for spring: as the egg, in its shell, can produce new life, invisible to the outside until the shell breaks and the chick emerges, so does the earth shelter the germinating plants that pierce its surface in spring. The egg represents Temple sacrifices and is, therefore, roasted; it cannot be eaten.

Although the child does not ask about the meaning of these elements, they will be given an explanation in the course of the Seder.

Another very important item not alluded to in the child's questions is the *wine*. We are bidden to drink four cups of wine. The cup, as we have seen, symbolizes the gifts that God has "measured out." Wine is the perfect beverage, in whose preparation God's gifts and human ingenuity are applied in equal measure. The cup of wine is the cup of salvation.

When the Israelites were in Egypt, God made four promises, all of which were kept immediately.

I will *free* you from the burdens of the Egyptians
and *deliver* you from their bondage
I will *redeem* you with an outstretched arm . . .
and I will *take* you to be My people. [Exod. 6:6–7]

In remembrance of this fourfold redemption, we fill our cups four times, give blessing to God, and partake of the wine. The ceremony of the four cups is so spaced throughout the Seder that the first marks the beginning; it is the Kiddush; the second marks the end of our review of the past, offering thanks to God for help in ages gone by; the third comes after dinner, as thanksgiving for the blessings of the present; and the fourth, toward the end, is a toast to the future that lies in God's hands.

But God also made a *fifth* pledge, not yet fulfilled, but one that we know He will keep:

I will *bring* you into the land which I swore to give to Abraham, Isaac, and Jacob, and I will give it to you for a possession, I the Lord. [Exod. 6:8]

The Rabbis were not agreed as to whether we are bound to drink to a promise not yet translated into reality. In general, when they could not come to any conclusion, they would state: Let us wait for Elijah, herald of the Messiah; he will decide. They, therefore,

Elijah's cup. It is filled, but left untouched. This modern example recalls the story of the spies sent into the land of Canaan who returned bearing a single bunch of grapes so heavy that it had to be carried on a pole suspended from their shoulders.

ruled that the fifth cup be placed on the table and filled, but that no one drink from it. It is the cup of Elijah.

The word of the Rabbis came to be embellished. Even today the right to the Land of Israel has been widely challenged. Perhaps absolute security will have to await the coming of Messianic times. Elijah, guardian of Israel, invoked at the end of every Sabbath, at every circumcision, is equally the herald of the new age of God (Mal. 3:23–24). The cup of Elijah has come to demonstrate both our firm trust that this age will come and our determination to work for it. As we reach the third section of the Seder, revealing the vista of the future, we open the door for Elijah. Perhaps he will come tonight.

Preparations for the Seder

Our preparations are of two types: long-range and short-range.

Long-Range Preparations

Throughout the year our table is set without ostentation. At the Seder, we give it the fullest splendor we can afford. Heirlooms, especially Kiddush cups, are displayed and used (if they are kasher for Pessah). Special white tablecloths are reserved for the event.

We may buy or fashion in advance the plate on which the ceremonial foods are to be displayed. It can be of any material and should indicate the exact place for every item. Highly artistic plates have been created throughout the ages.

The three Matzah must be covered and separated from each other; and an embroidered "envelope" of silk or satin, with three compartments, serves this purpose.

We acquire an appropriate Haggadah. The traditional Haggadah is based on Talmudic discussions. There are many new Haggadot available, bringing the ancient story to us in modern form. Whichever we use, we ought to have a copy for every member of the company.

We purchase enough kasher wine for the family. Red wines, reminders of the Red Sea, have been customary but are not required.

Short-Range Preparations

We select three perfect Matzah for the plate.
We get parsley or green onions for the first dip.
We prepare the salt water.
A shankbone is roasted.
An egg is roasted.
We need lettuce (or horseradish) for Maror.
We need Haroset, made of apples, cinnamon, nuts, almonds, wine, and other ingredients.

We need ground horseradish for the "Hillel Sandwich."

We arrange these items on the Seder Plate, together with the Matzah. The best way to place them is in the order in which they are used.

We set the table, with a cup and a Haggadah for each member.

We prepare the special seat for the leader, with his cushion.

We place a pitcher filled with water and a small bowl on a little table or stand next to the leader for washing his hands. He also needs a towel.

We place the Seder Plate in front of the leader.

We provide the leader with additional napkins, one to wrap the *Afikomen.*

We remember the special cup for Elijah; it should be the best cup we have.

We place our best candlesticks on the table; the mother will kindle the lights of the festival.

We add the table settings for each participant.

Flowers and heirlooms may give our table special beauty.

THE ORDER OF THE SEDER

Before the art of printing had been developed, few people owned a Haggadah. (Those that were produced were lavishly illuminated and today are priceless.) In order to conduct the Seder in the prescribed manner, the leader of the celebration followed a series of cues, which he learned by heart. We shall list them, as they provide us with the sequence of action.

The Opening Ceremonies

The parents bless their children; the family gathers around the table; the mother speaks the blessing for the candles and Shehehe-yanu and kindles the lights.

The Supper Begins

KADESH—SANCTIFY. The leader recites the Kiddush, and each member of the family partakes of the *first* of the four cups.

REHATZ—WASH. From the pitcher at his side the leader pours water over his hands and dries them, for he will distribute food by hand.

KARPAS—PARSLEY. The leader takes the parsley from the Seder Plate, dips it in the salt water, and distributes small sprigs to the members. After speaking the Berakhah, the members eat it.

YAHATZ—DIVIDE (THE MATZAH). The leader takes the

middle Matzah from the Seder Plate. It reminds us of the bread of poverty. He breaks it into two parts, a larger and a smaller. The larger portion he wraps in a napkin for later use. The little package is hidden somewhere in the room. He elevates the other portion in sight of the company and says: "This is the bread of affliction, which our fathers ate. . . ." Reminding himself that even now there may be Jews that have found no table for the Seder or lack the means, he extends an invitation: "Anyone who is poor, may he come to eat with us. . . ." He concludes with the hope that next year may find us in the Land of Israel and witness the freedom of all those still enslaved.

The Reform Haggadah now introduces the blessings and the eating of Matzah and Maror, and the next part of the Haggadah thus becomes table talk; the traditional Haggadah postpones this rite.

Maggid—Tell the Story: The Past Is Rehearsed

MAGGID. The youngest child asks the *four questions: Mah Nishtanah . . . ?* to open the narrative.

The leader begins his answer: "Our fathers were slaves to Pharaoh in Egypt. . . ."

He digresses:

There are four types of sons: the wise, the obstinate, the slow learner, and the child incapable of even asking questions. We must deal with each of them on his own terms.

Now the story of the past is continued: We hear of the Ten Plagues, and at their recital we dip our finger in the wine and flick out a small drop; when our enemy suffers, our cup is diminished. We learn compassion.

Dayenu is sung by the company. The gifts of God to His people are recited. Much less "would have been enough for us." We have received above our deserts.

The Great Summation Follows

According to Rabbi Gamaliel, it is our specific duty to explain the meaning of "Pessah," the sacrifice of old, of "Matzah," and of "Maror."

The leader elevates the shankbone in the sight of the company, asking: Why Pessah? They answer: God passed over the doors of our forefathers in Egypt, when he slew the Egyptians. The leader puts down the shankbone.

He elevates the Matzah, asking: Why Matzah? The company responds: because the dough of our ancestors could not rise, owing to the suddenness of their liberation. The leader puts the Matzah back.

Partaking of Matzah on the holiday of Passover is a Mitzvah shared by young and old alike. The strength of Jewish family life grows out of such special times, so much so that many otherwise ·assimilated families still set aside Passover for a Seder meal.

The leader lifts the Maror from the Seder Plate, showing it to the company. He asks: Why Maror? They respond: Because the Egyptians made our lives bitter. The leader puts the Maror down.

All raise the cup, joining their voices:

Therefore we must thank God in every way for all the miracles—let us recite the Hallel:

The cup is set down.

The first part of Hallel (Ps. 113–114) is recited in unison or responsively.

Again the company raises the cup in thanksgiving for the *gifts of the past*. The blessing is spoken.

Everybody partakes of the *second* of the four cups.

The Present Enters

RAHATZ—WASHING. The leader once again washes his hands; the company follows, as is ordained before eating bread.

MOTZI-MATZAH: BLESSING FOR BREAD AND THE MITZVAH OF MATZAH. Over the two unbroken Matzah in the Seder Plate the leader speaks the Berakhah for bread.

He immediately follows it by the blessing of God,

Who has commanded us the eating of Matzah.

He breaks a piece from each Matzah for himself and for each member at the table.

187

They repeat the two blessings.
All eat the Matzah.

MAROR—BITTER HERBS.   The leader takes a portion of the lettuce, the Maror, symbol of bitterness; dips it in Haroset, symbol of the mortar our fathers had to make; and blesses God,

Who has commanded us to eat Maror.

He gives a portion to each member, who recites the blessing and eats it.

KOREKH—PUTTING TOGETHER A SANDWICH.   The leader takes a piece of Matzah, places some horseradish on it, and puts another piece of Matzah on top of it; he makes a sandwich.
He gives one to each member at the table.

Hillel held that the word of Torah—"with Matzah and Maror shall they eat it [the lamb]"—meant that it must be swallowed together. As we always abide by Hillel's ways, we do so at this time.

At this time, a memorial to Russian Jewry may be included. A Matzah, not included in the three in the Seder Plate, is elevated in sight of the company. The leader speaks:

This is the Matzah of oppression, inflicted on our brothers and sisters in Russia. . . . We hold them dear, and shall strive with all our might to lead them from slavery to freedom, from darkness to light. . . .

SHULHAN ARUKH—THE WELL-SPREAD TABLE.   The meal is now served. The custom in many families of offering boiled eggs in salt water as a first course calls to mind that Pessah is a festival of spring and of fertility.

During the meal, perhaps even before, the children are permitted to roam the room, looking for the Matzah previously wrapped and hidden after Yahatz.

TZAFUN—THE HIDDEN.   At the very end of the meal, each member of the family receives and eats a portion of the previously hidden Matzah, without any benediction. This Matzah is called Afikomen. Before it has been eaten, the Seder cannot continue; after it has been consumed, no additional food is permitted for the rest of the night.

The term Afikomen comes from the Greek and is mentioned in the Talmud (Pessahim 10). Its meaning is not quite clear; it may mean "dessert" or "after-dinner songs." It represents the Pessah lamb, after which no dessert was allowed; hence we may eat no food afterward.

Before it can be eaten, the child who has found it must surrender it. He or she will do so upon receiving a reward. (The custom is to give an equal gift to all children, including those who failed to find it, so that a child will not be disappointed on the Seder night.)

BAREKH—SAY GRACE.   Grace after meals, with its surrounding-ing songs, is joyfully recited. With it the meal, celebration of the present, comes to its end.

The family raises the cup, speaks the blessing, and partakes of the *third* of the four cups, in thanksgiving for the bounties of the *present*.

The Future Enters

OPENING THE DOOR.   We open the door for Elijah, the Prophet, herald of ultimate redemption, and sing:

Elijah, the prophet . . . may he come to us with the Messiah. . . .

We also recite a passage from the Psalms (Pss. 79:6–7 and 69:25) and from Lamentations (Lam. 3:66).

Pour out Your fury upon the nations that do not know You. . . .

The door is closed.

There are several reasons for this rite. As guardian of the covenant, Elijah visits every home where the cup is prepared for him at the Seder. Were he to enter now, proclaiming the arrival of redemption, we would be ready to follow him at a moment's notice, as were our forefathers in Egypt when the call to departure and freedom reached them in their Seder night.

The scriptural passages remind us of tragedy. In the Middle Ages the Jews were often accused of using the blood of a Christian child for the Seder. Their accusers might place a child's dead body at the door of a Jewish home during the Seder as "evidence" of ritual murder. The Jews, therefore, opened the door at this time to look around and make sure that no such "evidence" had been planted.

Hallel—Praise

The rest of Hallel (Pss. 115–118) followed by the "Great Hallel" (Ps. 136) and the great Sabbath, holy day hymn, "The breath of all living creatures shall praise Your Name," are included. They are recited and sung in unison or responsively.

The vision of the future has been invoked; our faith in it has been renewed.

The family raises the cup, speaks the blessing, and partakes of the *fourth* cup, a toast to the *future*.

Nirtzah—Optional Songs

Among the hymns of this final portion are:
"*Adir Hu,*" freely rendered as "God of Might." Its tune has become the "theme song" for Pessah.

"Ehad Mi Yodea"—"Who Knows One." The song was conceived as an entertainment for children. They are to associate the numbers 1–13 with basic Jewish principles and historical facts. "One" stands for the one God; "two" for the two Tablets of the Covenant, and so on.

"Had Gadya"—"A Little Kid." The song is based on a German ditty of the Middle Ages, which was secular in character. Here, the little (Pessah) kid stands for Israel, attacked by enemies, who, in turn, are devoured by *their* enemies. In the end, however, God, just and loving, sets everything aright. Mindful of the "lamb's" sacrifice, He wipes out death forever. The lamb, Israel itself, is revived. The lighthearted folksong carries us through all of history to its ultimate resolution.

It is left to individual option to add poetry and song, citations from modern literature, or individual interpretations, so long as they deepen the meaning of the celebration.

We conclude the Seder with *L'shanah habaah b'Yerushalayim:* "Next year in Jerusalem," and may add *"Hatikvah"* and "America" or "The Star-Spangled Banner."

RULES, CHARACTERISTICS, AND CUSTOMS

Women are obligated to partake fully in the rites, although the Seder belongs to the commandments of positive observance linked to a specific point in time.

Children are given wine, diluted in water.

The members of the family take turns in leading portions of the Seder, men and women alike.

Traditionally, the Seder has been conducted not only in Hebrew but also in Yiddish, with each paragraph being translated in turn. The use of English is appropriate; the essential point of the Seder is "to tell."

In some German traditions, only white wine is used, as red wine could be mistaken for blood. The effects of the blood libel are still etched in Jewish memory.

Significantly, we never find the name of Moses mentioned even once in the Haggadah, although he was the people's leader. All praise is to be given to God. He is forever *Shomer Yisrael,* the Guardian of Israel. This night, when His guardianship became fully manifest, has thus become for us *Lel Shimurim,* the night of protection. We may sleep undisturbed. On the Seder night, the prayer at bedtime asking for protection during the night is not recited.

The Days of Pessah in Observance and Worship

We have noted that Pessah is one of the three Pilgrimage Festivals, *Shalosh Regalim* (Deut. 16:16), and is to be observed for seven days. Diaspora Jewry, by tradition, has observed it for eight days. The first and last day are full festivals, with work prohibition; tradition-oriented Diaspora Jewry observes the first two days as full festivals and adds the eighth day as full festival as well. The middle days are *Hol Ha-Moed,* when essential work may be done. The rules of Matzah apply throughout.

As rites and patterns of worship slightly change during the festival, we shall briefly follow the sequence of days.

The Eve. On this night, the Kiddush is not spoken in the synagogue. It is one of the four cups of the Seder and may not be separated from the other three.

The First Day. The Torah reading deals with the institution of the festival in Egypt, the slaying of the firstborn and Israel's hasty departure (Exod. 12:21–51). As on all festivals, it is followed by a reading from a second scroll, dealing with the ordinances concerning the sacrifices of the feast in the Temple (Num. 28:16–25).

In the Mussaf, we pray for dew, as we have pleaded for rain on Sh'mini Atzeret. Eleazar Kalir (eighth century C.E.) is the poet of both these corresponding prayers.

The Second Eve, celebrated with a Seder among traditional Diaspora Jews, introduces the counting of the Omer, which shall be explained.

THE SECOND DAY follows the pattern of the first. In Torah, we hear of the institution of the festivals (Lev. 22:26–23:44).

The Third Day and the Days of Hol Ha-Moed. Beginning with the third day, we omit part of the Hallel (portions of Psalms 115, 116, namely, 115:1–11 and 116:1–11). This reveals the compassionate nature of the Jew. We shorten our songs of praise out of pity for the Egyptians who suffered so much during this period. (We do the same at the Seder, when we pour out a drop of wine while reciting Ten Plagues that came over Egypt.) They were our enemies, but Scripture warns:

Do not rejoice, when your enemy falls. [Prov. 24:17]

The Sabbath of Hol Ha-Moed brings us a Torah reading that speaks of God's Thirteen Attributes of Mercy, ending with a brief review of the festivals and setting the rules for the redemption of the firstborn (Exod. 33:12–34:26).

On this Sabbath, we read the Song of Songs. It speaks of love and spring and renewal. The earth, too, was dry and lifeless; by the divine breath of spring it is brought back to life.

The Eve of the Seventh Day does not usher in a new holy day (as did the eve of Sh'mini Atzeret). Sheheheyanu is, therefore, not spoken either in kindling the lights or in the Kiddush.

The Seventh Day was the time when the Egyptians were drowned in the sea. The story is told in Torah, and the people hear the magnificent hymn of thanks sung by the people after their rescue (Exod. 13:17–15:26).

The Eighth Day (in the Diaspora) is *Matnat Yad.* The Torah lesson speaks to us of the ordinance setting up the three Pilgrimage Festivals. Everyone is to go up to Jerusalem; no one is to appear empty-handed; each is to offer *K'Matnat Yado* according to his means (Deut. 15:19–16:17). By ancient custom, we remember our departed on the last day of the festivals (*Yizkor*) and receive a special blessing, pronounced by the rabbi.

The Haftarah of this day leads us beyond Pessah, which is but prologue, to the very end of history, opening the most grandiose of vistas, that of the Messiah:

And a shoot shall grow out of the stump of Jesse [David's father] . . .
The spirit of the Lord shall alight upon him
Justice shall be the girdle of his loins
The wolf shall dwell with the lamb,
the leopard shall lie down with the kid
and the lion, like the ox, shall eat straw.
A babe shall play over a viper's hole,
and an infant pass his hand over an adder's den.
In all of My sacred mount
nothing evil or vile shall be done;
for the land shall be filled with devotion to the Lord
as water covers the sea. . . . [Isa. 10:32–12:6]

Three Haftarot and a Song

The Haftarot of the first day, of the Sabbath within the feast, and of the last day, are each placed at a different locale and speak of a different period in time. Together they trace Israel's historical road, beginning at Pessah and finding its goal at the end of days. The Haftarah of the first day (Josh. 3:5–7; 5:2–6; 6:27) places us in the Holy Land and just at the moment when the wanderings through the desert, begun on Pessah, had reached their destination. A new task looms, calling for a renewal of the covenant.

The Haftarah of the Sabbath, from the book of Ezekiel, takes us to the time and place of the Babylonian Exile: the vision of the valley of dry bones (Ezek. 37:1–15). The people feel "dead." Is God with them even in an alien land? They are told that His spirit truly dwells with them and that by it they will be revived and redeemed. Exile is not the end; there will always be a new Pessah, for whose coming we must prepare.

The Haftarah of the last day leads us to the ultimate future; its message is worldwide. A Messiah of the House of David will come.

Natural enmity will cease to exist. Israel shall be mankind's counselor. The historical pilgrimage, begun in that Seder night long ago in Egypt, will then have reached its destination.

Israel and God are both in a bondage of mutual love, which makes eternal renewal possible and real. This is revealed in the *Song of Songs*, read on Pessah. It speaks of love in the most intimate terms, of sensual love, the love between a man and a woman, each yearning for the other, each seeing the physical beauty of the other, not only the endowment of heart, mind, and soul. This is not platonic love or mere "intellectual" love. It is passionate love. Thus is the love of Israel for God, Whom we cannot see; thus is the love of God for Israel, upon whom His eyes rest at all times. Out of this love comes His pleading command: "Love me then with all your heart and all your soul and all your might!"

This love must be so deep in us that it makes us transcend every hatred, even against our enemy, and even at a time when circumstances force us to fight him. This we show on Pessah.

Love in this most intimate form is the foundation and guarantor of our existence. Pessah is its signpost. Spring is the assurance of its power to bring us resurrection.

THE OMER PERIOD: A TIME OF JOYS AND SORROWS

Counting the Omer

By ordinance of Torah, we are to count the days and weeks from Pessah to Shavuot (Lev. 23:15–16; see above, Pessah and Sukkot as Pillars of the Seasons). We are to link the festival of freedom to the festival of Torah, as freedom without Torah may turn into license. No society can exist without law. The Rabbis held that Israel counted the days from the Exodus to the moment when liberty would be crowned by law.

The farmer equally counts the days, as he goes out into his fields, observing the ripening grain.

From the second night of Pessah, the counting takes place.

We speak a Berakhah:

Barukh . . . vetzivanu al Sefirat ha-Omer
Blessed are You . . . He, Who . . . has commanded us concerning the counting of the Omer.

Then we count both the days and the weeks. Thus, for instance: "Today is the fifteenth day, that is, two weeks and one day in the Omer count." Jewish calendars give us the count.

The Mitzvah is to be performed each night. If we have forgotten it at night, we may still perform the count during the day, but without the Berakhah. At the following night, the Berakhah may be recited again. But if we have forgotten the count for an entire twenty-four-hour period, we may no longer speak the Berakhah for the rest of the season.

The Omer weeks were seven happy weeks, a looking forward, day by day, to the celebration of a new feast, a new offering from the harvest, in which the harvest gift of the Omer would find its complement and culmination. But these were also weeks of anxiety, as, day by day, the farmer watched his ripening wheat, hoping that no unexpected quirk of nature might spoil it. It was the joy-in-apprehension of a mother in pregnancy.

The farmer trembles in his happiness everywhere. In some cultures, sexual intercourse was forbidden in this period; it might deflect into human fertility a portion of the total that should be allocated to the growing harvest. The Roman poet Ovid relates a commonly held belief that marriages contracted during these weeks of the ripening corn would be unhappy.

Judaism equally prohibits marriages during this season or a part of it. Opposed to heathen beliefs and superstitions, the Rabbis found their own reasons and transformed these weeks into a time of sadness and semimourning pierced by moments of joy.

The Talmud relates that Rabbi Akiva had twelve thousand disciples of the highest intellect. But their arguments were not confined to points of interpretation; they extended into life. "They did not render honor to one another." Therefore, they were carried off by a plague that lasted through the Omer period, up to its thirty-third day, when it stopped (Yevamot 62b).

Historians believe that these disciples were not felled by a plague, but were slain during the abortive Bar Kokhba rebellion against the Romans, an uprising some believe was supported by Rabbi Akiva. The large number of twelve thousand, an unlikely student enrollment, suggests an army. Considering themselves leaders and strategists, they may have failed to submit to the discipline and orders of their officers and have thereby contributed to the defeat. Jewish losses were disastrous. The Jewish religion came to be proscribed for some time, and Judaism came to the edge of extinction. We have reason to mourn.

During the first Crusade (1096), the great Rhenish centers of Jewish learning were wiped out by the rabble, who wished to get at the infidels in their own midst before attacking the Turks in the Holy Land. But their main objective was booty. The Jews of Mainz put up heroic resistance, but were overcome. They were slaughtered on Shavuot.

A moving liturgical poem for the Omer period, used by Polish Jewry, speaks:

Our years have been consumed in need and vanity;
we yearned for light; and see: we met contempt, abasement.
Slaves dominate us; we are in exile.
Help us, O God, in You rests our strength.
For Your Name's sake, grant us a sign of grace!
O God! How long! When will there be an end to our being mocked?

During World War II, in the last days of Pessah, a handful of Jews in the Warsaw Ghetto rose up in arms against the Nazis. They knew their cause was hopeless, but they wished to die with honor rather than as lambs led to the slaughter. Only through great effort and with their well-known ruthlessness did the Nazi armies succeed in destroying the heroic Jews.

In glorious contrast, one majestic ray of light falls upon us during this season out of the pages of history. On the fifth of Iyar 5708, the State of Israel was proclaimed. Its rebirth brought new life to all of Jewry, throughout the world.

Observances

YOM HASHOAH, HOLOCAUST DAY, is observed on the twenty-seventh of Nissan. Being of recent origin, it has not yet become rooted in Jewish practice. The day commemorates our six million brothers and sisters who were murdered in Nazi extermination camps. Here was total annihilation of body and spirit. The reservoirs of Jewish learning and piety were wiped out. Close to half of our people were murdered amid unspeakable torture. It is to be hoped that Yom Hashoah will become a major occasion in our collective life as Jews.

Celebrations in Israel for *Yom Ha-Atzmaut*, Israel's Independence Day, include a military parade in the heart of Jerusalem. This is not seen as a show of might, but as a symbol of the renewed presence of a Jewish government and a Jewish nation free in its own land.

YOM HA-ATZMAUT—INDEPENDENCE DAY OF ISRAEL—is observed
on the fifth of Iyar or on the preceding Thursday if the anniversary
falls on a Sabbath. It, too, has yet to become a universal holiday for
Jews. On May 14, 1948, surrounded by the massed armies of the
enemy, the leaders of the Jews in the ancient homeland met at Tel
Aviv to proclaim the independence of the State, which they named
"Israel,"

trusting in the Rock of Israel

as their Declaration of Independence concludes. After more than
two thousand years, land and people were once again united in
Jewish sovereignty. "Jerusalem, destroyed by fire, will have to be re-
built by fire," the poet says in a poem for the ninth of Av. This trial
by fire continues. But from the moment Israel declared its freedom,
a new sense of freedom entered the heart of every Jew.

Lag B'Omer: The Thirty-third Day of the Omer Count

The numerical value of the Hebrew letters L–G is 33. This is an
ancient folk festival. On this day the plague that had decimated
Rabbi Akiva's disciples supposedly came to an end.

The celebration in the eastern European shtetl centered around
the children and evoked the memories of Bar Kokhba's heroic deeds.
For days the children made bows and arrows in class. Now school
was closed for a day, and the children went into the woods for a
merry chase of imaginary enemies. But the lesson of Akiva's disciples was also brought to mind. Throughout the year, the older
pupils, who had already started the study of the *Chumash*, the Five
Books of Moses, lorded over the little ones, still occupied with
learning the *aleph-bet*, the alphabet. Today the young ones could
get even. They are permitted to tell off the older ones and push
them around, and the older ones have to obey. A balance was established. Jews have to be leaders, but must also learn to submit to
leadership—the lesson forgotten by Akiva's disciples.

This day is also considered the anniversary of the death of Rabbi
Simon ben Yohai, who lived in Israel during Roman times. His outspoken opposition to Rome compelled him to flee and seek refuge
in a cave, where he spent many years, miraculously sustained by
God (Shabbat 33b). Rabbi Simon was a mystic, to whom the great
mystical commentary to Torah, the *Zohar*, was long but erroneously
ascribed. On the thirty-third of the Omer, the Rabbi's followers,
the Hasidim, gather at Meron, where his grave is to be found. Bonfires blaze through the night; torch dances express joy and allegiance
to the master's teachings. Dancing and prayer continue all day.

Shelosha Yeme Ha-Gbalah—The Three Days of Setting Bounds. Three days were appointed by God for the people to make themselves clean for the Revelation. A boundary was set, not to be trespassed. Moses was to build a fence around Sinai lest anyone approach the mountain on which God was to descend (Exod. 19:10–13). The three days before Shavuot have become days of anticipation, offering a foretaste of the coming festival. They are joyful days.

Weddings during the Omer Period. Weddings are performed on *Lag B'Omer.* For the rest of the period, practices vary within Orthodox Jewry. Reform Judaism does not impose any restrictions at any time.

16

Shavuot: Feast of Weeks

S havuot is one of the Three Pilgrimage Festivals. The Torah states that Shavuot is to be observed on the fiftieth day after the first day of Pessah. It is the concluding feast of the season that opens with Pessah and is, therefore, called *Atzeret* in the Talmud. As we have seen, it resembles Sh'mini Atzeret.

Shavuot is nowhere in Torah designated as the Feast of Revelation. It was purely a festival of nature. However, a little arithmetic, based on Scripture (Exod. 19), reveals that the fiftieth day after the Exodus was the moment when God descended to Mount Sinai.

Two special events took place in the Temple on this day: the offering of wheat and the offering of the first fruits.

Torah states:

You shall bring from your settlements two loaves of bread as a wave offering; each shall be made of two-tenths of a measure of choice flour [wheat], baked as Hametz [leavened], as first fruits to the Lord. [Lev. 23:17]

This offering was called a "wave offering" because the priest waved the loaves before the altar. This was the only time when an offering made of flour was Hametz; it had to be, as it gave expression to the people's willingness to give their well-prepared bread in offerings. That they refrained from doing so throughout the year was on account of the law and not because they were stingy.

On this day, also, the farmer brought his first fruits to the Temple, although he could do so at other times as well. He followed the ordinance of Torah and recited a "theological" statement that reviews history and culminates in thanks for the land and its fruit, of which the first yield is brought into the House of God (Deut. 26:1–11).

The Talmud tells us:

When a farmer saw a beautiful fruit ripening on his trees, he tied a ribbon around it, setting it aside as an offering. . . . In accordance with the ordinance of Torah, he placed all the fruit in a basket and brought it to the Temple. [Mishnah Bikurim 3:1–8]

As a festival of nature, Shavuot would have withered away with the destruction of the Temple and the separation of the people from the soil. As a Feast of Revelation, it has retained its strength and impact.

What is revelation? At Sinai, God spoke:

If you will obey faithfully and keep My covenant you shall be My treasured possession among all the peoples.
Indeed, all the earth is Mine
but you shall be to Me
a kingdom of priests and a holy nation [Exod. 19:5–6]
All the people answered as one, saying:
"All the Lord has spoken we will do!" [Exod. 19:8]

Thereupon, the people experienced God's Presence and received the Ten Commandments. They affirmed:

The Lord our God has just shown us His majestic Presence and we have heard His voice out of the fire; we have seen this day that man may live through God has spoken to him. [Deut. 5:20–21]

Revelation consists of several elements. It is the incursion of God into history *and* the human awareness of His Presence. It is the word of God *and* the understanding of this word, as it is given to human beings to understand and to interpret it. It is God's call to man *and* man's affirmation that "man may live though God has spoken to him," leading to the conviction that "man can live *only* because God has spoken to him." Whatever happened at Sinai leads beyond Sinai. It means that God enters *my* life to make it authentic. This belief is an existential necessity for every Jew, incentive for Jewish survival. It is covenant.

In this sense, Torah could later say:

You stand this day, all of you, before the Lord your God— . . . to enter into the covenant of the Lord your God, which the Lord your God is concluding with you this day with its sanctions . . . I make this covenant, with its sanctions, not with you alone, but both with those who are standing with us this day before the Lord our God and with those who are not with us here today [the as yet unborn]. [Deut. 29:9–14]

Covenant rests on the reaching out of God *and* the acceptance by man. Revelation is the foundation of covenant, and covenant assures ever-renewed Revelation. A covenant with God is eternal. It gives Israel distinction as priest-servant on the earth; eventually, all the earth's inhabitants will come to recognize that they are His.

We may not claim, nor may the world expect the individual Jew to show, "priestly" perfection. We are ordinary people, but we must be conscious of our special obligation to act ethically.

OBSERVANCE OF SHAVUOT

Shavuot is to be observed for one day, according to Torah; Orthodox Diaspora Jewry celebrates it for two days.

The synagogues are decorated with flowers and plants. Nature is brought into the sanctuary.

On the *eve* of Shavuot, after services, blessing of children, candles, and Kiddush, many families partake of a supper of milk dishes, climaxed by a cheesecake. Torah is compared to milk; it is our "mother milk," and thus we express it.

DURING THE NIGHT, a vigil is held. The people assemble in the synagogue hall to read together portions from all sections of Holy Scripture and the first and last Mishnah of each of the tractates of the Talmud. Instituted by the mystics of the 16th century, this vigil prepares the "marriage feast" of the morrow. Unlike the vigils on Yom Kippur and Hoshana Rabba, this one is relaxed and happy. It includes a splendid repast of cakes made with milk. It is permissible to replace the set order, the *Tikkun* for the readings, by a general discussion of Torah. Frequently, the study continues until dawn and is followed by the morning prayer.

THE FIRST DAY is observed with the usual prayers for the festivals, including the Hallel.

Then we read the *Book of Ruth*. Ruth, the Moabite, member of a neighboring nation, married a Jewish man. He has died, leaving her childless and desperately poor. Her mother-in-law, Naomi, also

Ties between the holidays and nature are often expressed through foods used as a part of the celebration. Shavuot is tied up physically and metaphorically with the season of harvest, as this table of nuts, fruit, and wine suggests.

widowed and poor, decides to return home to her people, but advises Ruth to stay in her own homeland, where eventually she may find a husband among her own people. But Ruth has decided to cast in her lot with the Jewish people. She tells Naomi:

Entreat me not to leave you and to return from following after you.
Where you go, I will go . . .
your people shall be my people,
your God shall be my God. . . . [Ruth 1:16–18]

In the land of Judah, Ruth gathers fallen sheaves in the fields at the time of the harvest. The owner of the fields, Boaz, falls in love with her, marries her, has children with her. Proudly the author of the book tells us that Ruth became the great-grandmother of King David (Ruth 4:17–22).

The reading of this lyrical story on Shavuot may have been appointed because the events take place largely at harvest time. But there may be a deeper significance. Righteous proselytes, casting their lot with Torah and people, are a precious harvest to Israel.

The Torah reading brings us the Revelation at Sinai and the Ten Commandments (Exod. 19–20).

Ordinarily, the reading may not be interrupted while it is proceeding. Today, however, after reading the first verse of the portion, the reader rolls up the scroll, covers it, and leads the congregation in a hymn, sung responsively: *Akdamut.*

Before the [ten] words I shall read,
for permission will I plead,
in lines, voiced in hesitation,
to praise Him, sole Lord of creation.
Though all the sky of parchment be
and pens were made of ev'ry forest's tree
and made of ink were sea and water's every collection,
Though all earth's inhabitants were scribes of great perfection,
the Cosmic Power that is in Him,
cannot be described. . . . [Meir ben Isaac, eleventh century]

The Talmud mentions that King Hezekiah (715–687 B.C.E.) had been designated by God to become the Messiah, but was later rejected because he never sang a song of gratitude for God's many gracious acts and for His Torah (Sanhedrin 94a). This may be the reason we offer a hymn before receiving the Ten Commandments, thus proving our worthiness to welcome the Messiah.

THE SECOND DAY, as observed traditionally in the Diaspora, is *Matnat Yad.* The memory of our departed is evoked (*Yizkor*); the rabbi blesses the people as each has made an offering according to his or her means (*K'Matnat Yado*).

The Torah reading, as on all last days of the *Shalosh Regalim,* speaks of the duty to appear before God in His Temple at these days and to bring free-will offerings.

The Haftarah, a selection from the prophet Habakkuk, is a prayer concerning human error. Habakkuk reviews the events at Sinai, speaks of disasters that may befall nature and society, and praises God, who protects Israel. Fear that error may keep us from following the divine word, as we heard it again yesterday, is dissolved in a song of triumph at God's protection.

CONFIRMATION on Shavuot is a custom that was adopted by Reform Judaism, following the practice of the Protestant church. It started in Germany in the nineteenth century and was meant to replace the Bar Mitzvah celebration by a collective initiation of boys and girls. Today confirmation has been widely adopted among the various branches of religious Jewry, and Bar Mitzvah and Bat Mitzvah celebrations have returned to Reform. But our young people are not *being* confirmed; rather, they *confirm* their allegiance to Torah as did their ancestors at Sinai. Hasidic tradition tells:

Once they asked the Kotzker Rebbe: "Why is this feast called the time of the *giving* of our Torah, not of our *receiving* the Torah?" He replied: "The *giving* was on Shavuot, the receiving must take place *every day*."

Summer:
Decline and Distress

S ummer has been a period of bitter woes for the Jewish people. It is bisected by a three-week period of deepest mourning. Amid the glories of nature, we withdraw into a solitude filled with tears. In the summer the Jew commemorates the breach of the walls of Jerusalem and the fall of the Temple, events that mark the beginning of an agony stretching across thousands of years.

SHIVAH ASAR B'TAMMUZ

The "three weeks" of distress begin with the fast of the seventeenth of Tammuz, *Shivah Asar B'Tammuz*.

According to tradition, five catastrophic events took place on this day:

1. Moses returned from Mount Sinai, bringing the Tablets of the Covenant, and found that the people had already broken the covenant and were dancing around the golden calf. He cast down the Tablets, and they broke.

2. The enemy army succeeded in breaching the walls of Jerusalem.

3. The daily sacrifices came to an end, owing to the lack of animals.

4. The Torah scroll was burned by a villain.

5. Jewish traitors erected an idol in the Temple (Taanit 26a).

Some of these events go back to the beginning of our history. At least two of them, the golden calf and the idol, are related to heathen fertility cults. All of them brought either spiritual or physical desolation or both.

The day has agricultural associations as well. The ancients always observed turning points of the sun. This was one of them: summer solstice. According to Mesopotamian mythology, Tammuz, god of fertility, now had to descend to the netherworld. With his departure, the streams dried out, fertility of field and womb ceased, and sickness began to plague humanity.

The Jews took the name of this month from the Mesopotamians. The date of the fast is revealing. On the seventeenth, the moon was in decline, and the sun had begun its descent. It was a day of pessimism. This is the only occasion of Jewish observance throughout the year that begins and ends during the declining moon. In appointing this date, the Rabbis may have wished to tie it to an already existing observance that had been hard to eradicate. The prophet Ezekiel had already been outraged at the sight at the Temple gate of "the women weeping for Tammuz" (Ezek. 8:14). The Rabbis transformed the meaning: yielding to alien cults leads to the breakdown of the moral law, written on the tablets, and to the breach of the walls that spell Jewish security.

The seventeenth of Tammuz thus corresponds to Hanukah: both celebrate the sun's solstice. But Hanukah witnessed the restoration of the Temple through faith; the seventeenth of Tammuz, the beginning of its fall as a result of lack of faith.

Observance

A fast is ordained from dawn to nightfall. S'lihot are offered; God's Thirteen Attributes are invoked; confession is spoken. The Torah reading, both morning and afternoon, reveals these Thirteen Attributes of Mercy from the text of the Torah. The Haftarah of the afternoon calls for Teshuvah:

Seek the Lord while He can be found . . .
Let the wicked give up his ways,
the sinful man his plans;
let him return to the Lord
and He will pardon him;
to our God,
for He freely forgives. . . . [Isa. 55:6–56:8]

The Three Weeks

Shivah Asar b'Tammuz initiates a period of mourning, leading to the ninth of Av. No weddings may be performed. No new dresses may be worn for the first time; no fruit, previously not eaten this year, may be enjoyed. The hair should not be cut.

The Nine Days

During these three weeks, the month of Av arrives. Its first nine days, including the day of fasting itself, are for the Jew the period of greatest distress during the entire year. No meat may be consumed, and no wine may be drunk except on the Sabbath. In sharp contrast to Adar, we are told, "When Av arrives, we decrease joy" (Taanit 26b).

During these three weeks, a special Haftarah of rebuke is read after the Torah reading. The third one on the Sabbath before Tishah b'Av, called "black Sabbath," *Shwartz Shabbes* in Yiddish, is filled with the harshest words hurled against the people by the prophet Isaiah (Isa. 1:1–27). This Haftarah begins with the word *Hazon*— "The Vision." The Sabbath is, therefore, also called *Shabbat Hazon*.

Then comes *Tishah b'Av.*

TISHAH B'AV

This day, when the Temple was destroyed, has been called "the black fast," in contrast to "the white fast" of Yom Kippur.

According to the Rabbis, five tragic events happened on this day:

1. The generation of the Exodus was told that they all had to die in the desert, for they had despaired of God's power to lead them into the land of promise.

2, 3. Both the First and the Second Temples went up in flames.

4. The city of Betar (Beth-ther), Bar Kokhba's fortress, was captured by the Romans; thousands were slain; Jewish resistance ended and, with it, the hope for a speedy restoration of the Temple; Jewish religion was proscribed.

5. The city of Jerusalem was plowed under, to be rendered uninhabitable (Taanit 26a).

We cannot exclude the possibility that even this day may have connections with nature rites. Around this time the people of antiquity lit bonfires to drive away the demons of destruction that winter might bring. We are also reminded that each festival of nature was preceded by a day of purification, usually observed on the tenth of the month. We shall find that the fifteenth of Av was observed as the feast of the tree harvest; it may well have been preceded by purging.

As a day of purification, preceding the tree harvest, Tishah b'Av would then correspond to the tenth of Tevet, the fast preceding the fifteenth of Sh'vat, New Year of Trees, tree-planting time. One was observed as the days lengthened and nature awakened; the other, as the days grew shorter and nature had yielded its gifts.

Observance

The fast lasts from evening to evening. As the sun sets, a final meal is taken on the *eve*, a meal of mourners: eggs and bread, dipped in ashes, consumed sitting on the floor. Like the bereaved children of a departed parent, we take off our leather shoes and will not put them back on until the fast is over. As the egg is mute, has no opening, it is a mourner's first food after a funeral.

We go to the synagogue. It is dimly lit. All curtains and covers have been removed. After the evening prayer, the worshipers, sitting on low stools or on the floor, like mourners, recite the heartbreaking lamentations of Jeremiah over the fall of the First Temple: the Book of Lamentations.

In the *morning*, we do not wash or groom ourselves; only a ritual cleansing of fingertips and eyes is permitted. Tallit and Tefillin are not worn.

The Torah reading is taken from Deuteronomy (4:25–40).

Should you, when you have begotten children and children's children and are long established in the land, act wickedly and make for yourselves a sculptured image in any likeness, causing the Lord, your God, displeasure and vexation, I call heaven and earth to witness against you this day and you shall soon perish from the land. . . .

The Haftarah (Jeremiah 8:13–9:23) opens with the words:

I will utterly consume them, says the Lord. . . .

After the Torah has been returned, the congregation begins the *Kinot*, dirges, that will continue until noon. Sitting on the ground, one member after another takes his turn. All the tragedies of the Jewish people's history are permitted to pass in review: the destruction of the Temple, the defeat of Bar Kokhba, the interdict of Jewish religion by Hadrian, the martyrdom of the Rabbis, the slaughter of the Jews during the Crusades, the burning of Torah scrolls and precious, handwritten Talmud tomes during the Middle Ages. All had their beginning with the expulsion of the Jews from Jerusalem, after the Temple lay in ashes. In the words of Judah Halevi, the congregation cries out:

Zion, will you not ask about your captives' peace? A remnant of your flock they are,
suing for your peace. . . .
To weep your woe my cry waxes strong.

In the *afternoon,* hope is rekindled. Curtains and covers have been restored. Tallit and Tefillin are now put on. Tradition holds that the Messiah will be born on Tishah b'Av; out of travail, redemption will come. In the Amidah, God is praised:

He will comfort Zion and rebuild Jerusalem.

With the rising of the stars, the fast ends. But meat may not be eaten until noon of the following day; the Temple was still in flames on the tenth of Av. An exception is made on Friday, as the Sabbath cancels out all mourning.

After breaking their fast, the members assemble for *Kiddush Levanah,* the blessing of God for the moon, now in ascent.

Shabbat Nahamu

The Sabbath following the fast of Av has as its Haftarah the words of Isaiah, beginning:

Comfort, oh comfort my people
says your God. . . . [Isa. 40:1–26]

The Sabbath has, therefore, been given the name "Sabbath of Comfort," *Shabbat Nahamu.*

The Fifteenth of Av

We know very little about the origin of this happy day, but in ancient Israel it was a moment of exuberant joy:

There were in Israel no days more filled with joy than Yom Kippur and the fifteenth of Av [Taanit 4:8].

Boys and girls would dance in the fields and celebrate nature. The Rabbis themselves seem to have been at a loss for an adequate explanation of the feast's origin. They offer a variety of reasons for the celebration (see Taanit 30b–31a). One of their explanations was that this was the climax and completion of the wood harvest for the eternal flame on the Temple's altar, an occasion for great celebration.

It may indeed have been an age-old, pagan celebration of the tree harvest, a nature feast, now given by the Rabbis a new meaning that incorporated it in Jewish belief.

But, like all other feasts, the fifteenth of Av had to have a historical meaning as well. The Rabbis, therefore, stated that on this day death among the generation of the Exodus came to an end. We learn in Torah that Moses sent out twelve advance scouts to explore Canaan and the strength of its population, prior to its conquest by the Israelites. But ten of these scouts came back with a dismal report: the land could not be taken, even with the help of God. Lacking in faith, the people accepted this report. In punishment, the whole people had to remain in the desert for forty years until the entire generation of the Exodus had died (Num. 13–14). Each year, so we are told, on the ninth of Av, anniversary of their faintheartedness, those who had reached the age of sixty dug their graves and placed themselves in them, never to awaken.

When the fortieth year came, those who placed themselves in their grave on the ninth of Av arose again on the morrow. "Perhaps we have miscalculated the date," they thought and entered their graves again during the following nights. But when the fifteenth came, and the moon's full disk appeared in the sky, they knew that Tishah b'Av had passed. A new generation had arisen, which would live to enter the land. The ordeal was over (see Taanit 30b–31a). They celebrated. Tishah b'Av and the fifteenth of Av are clearly keyed to each other: the first as day of purgation; the second, as celebration of those who have been cleansed of guilt.

At the same time, the advent of the "Days of Awe" is subtly announced. Two weeks after the fifteenth of Av, the Shofar of Ellul will be sounded.

THE DESCENT OF THE YEAR

As winter feasts celebrate the rise of the sun, observances during the summer mourn its decline.

Purim, at the end of winter, is observed at roughly the time of the spring equinox. It leads us upward.

Pessah is the feast of spring, of the first harvest offering: barley.

Shavuot concludes the season; spring has matured into early summer: an offering of wheat was made; the first fruits were presented to the Temple.

Now, decline is marked.

Shivah Asar b' Tammuz, at roughly the time of the summer solstice, means a tearful farewell to the sun.

Tishah b'Av calls for rites of purification (on the ninth and tenth of the month), preceding the feast of tree cutting.

The Fifteenth of Av celebrates the end of the tree harvest.

Rosh Hashanah is commencement of the New Year, at eventide of the summer: sunlight and darkness have begun to mix.

Yom Kippur is the day of the great purification, preceding the harvest feast.

Sukkot, at roughly fall equinox, brings in the harvest and closes the agricultural season.

Sh'mini Atzeret offers a last moment of relaxed rest before winter envelops us.

The purging character of Yom Kippur and its sacrifices causes the Rabbis of the Talmud to debate whether the other festivals and

Rosh Hodesh with their sacrifices have an equal power to purge "the sanctuary and its holy elements from uncleanliness" and the human beings from their sins. In Rabbi Jonah's opinion, "all festivals are comparable to each other" (see Shevuot 2a, b; 9b–10b; Rosh Hashanah 4b).

While the Rabbis do not separate the day of purging from the feasts themselves, we nevertheless recognize their underlying concept of a periodical purging of the sanctuary itself, combined with an atonement for human sins.

18

Observances
of the Year
in Perspective

O ur days of observance reveal a cyclical and a historical view of life, fused into one.

The farmer's year is cyclical; there is everlasting
return. Being a peasant people, the ancient Jews,
like the rest of mankind, celebrated the milestones of the year by
adopting rites widely held by their non-Jewish neighbors.

Becoming a historical people, the Jews learned to see meaning
in history: it follows a time line, leading toward a goal. Individuals
and nations live within the stream of history and can shape its
direction. Jewish celebrations thus become linked to historical fac-
tors in the destiny of early Israel.

Every human being needs moments that transcend the moment,
times of reflection and inwardness. Such occasions arise for the
farmer after the gathering of the harvest, for others at the beginning
of a calendar year. On these occasions the temporal is transcended
in meditation, and the self is explored in the light of eternity.

We can readily see the relationship between the agricultural and
the historical foundations of our feasts and fasts and the symmetry
of summer and winter milestones, if we list them beginning in the
spring:

> *First of Nissan*: National New Year, month of liberation, New
> Year's Day for kings, counting the years of their reign
> (Rosh Hashanah 1:1). Spring has come.
> *Tenth of Nissan*: Removal process of last year's decayed har-

vest in preparation for the new one. The Israelites choose the sacrificial lambs for the Passover celebration in Egypt. The home, a "sanctuary," is to be cleansed.

Pessah: Offering of the new harvest, a new era has begun. Israel is freed from the dross of Egyptian ways and placed under divine protection. Beginning of a seven-week period of growth.

Shavuot: Peak of the harvest season. Wheat is offered in the Temple. It is the peak of Israel's spiritual harvest: revelation at Sinai, communion with God. It is called *Atzeret*, concluding feast after the seven-week period of expectation.

Seventeenth of Tammuz: Summer solstice, beginning of the sun's decline, commemorates the fall of Jerusalem's walls; the national decline has started.

Ninth of Av: Purification day preceding the end and climax of the trees' cutting season. Israel was felled as the Temple was destroyed.

Fifteenth of Av: Celebration of the tree harvest for the Temple altar; no historical meaning (though the Rabbis attempt to give it one).

Rosh Hashanah: Nature's New Year at the end of the harvest season, elevated into spiritual stocktaking by every individual. The King of Kings begins a new year of His reign in judging His creation.

Tzom Gedaliah: Mourning at the defeat of the sun at fall equinox; given a historical meaning as it also mourns a leader, whose death by murder brought untold hardship to the people.

Yom Kippur: The cleansing of the sacred house, the sanctuary, in acts of purification and sacrifices preceding the harvest feast, becomes a day of our soul's cleansing: purification through fasting.

Sukkot: The farmer's harvest feast was given a historical meaning: God gives His people divine protection by building huts for them.

Sh'mini Atzeret—Simhat Torah: A time of intimate communion with God and of rejoicing with Torah, His revelation. Concluding feast after the seven-day period of celebration.

Hanukah: Joy at the reemerging light of the sun at winter solstice is linked to an historical event of restoration after decline: the Maccabees.

Tenth of Tevet: Preliminary to the New Year's Day of Trees; as a time of purging, it is given a completely new meaning: the siege of Jerusalem began on this day.

Fifteenth of Sh'vat: New Year's Day of Trees, celebration of tree planting, no historical meaning.

Fast of Esther: Purification before spring equinox is given a historical meaning: Esther fasted, although not on this day. A leader had emerged to rescue the people.

Purim: Celebrating the triumph of the sun at spring equinox, combined with the driving out of "old man winter" and his demons. It is translated into a historical event by means of a story.

Tzom Gedaliah, at fall equinox, is not followed by any celebration. It mourns the descent of the sun. At spring equinox, we have both purification and celebration, the Fast of Esther and Purim.

In emphasizing the historical character of our celebrations, the Jewish people became a light unto the nations. Although the basic tasks of all nations are the same, Israel is to set an example in meeting them. In their historical aspect, our days of observance hold a message for all nations and all peoples. Through them, the universal character of Judaism is symbolized and demonstrated. One need not be a Jew to understand the call of these days. One need not even be a believer in God. The obligation revealed through Jewish celebrations is universal.

Pessah: Each nation and person has the right to be free.

Shavuot: No society can exist without just law and morality.

Tishah b'Av: A nation has the right to sovereignty on its own soil.

Rosh Hashanah: Individuals and nations must account for their actions in the light of history; their sovereignty is limited by ethical law.

Yom Kippur: Reconciliation within society and of the individual within himself is essential for survival and prosperity.

Sukkot: Only an open society guarantees peace; within society no member is expendable; none may be cast aside.

Sh'mini Atzeret: Societies and individuals have to find themselves, turning inward to regain their values.

Hanukah: Freedom of religion is a person's natural right; no government may establish religion or infringe on any.

The Sabbath stands alone, forming the foundation of the whole edifice, national and international: social justice, consecration to transcendent values, respect for the order of the universe.

19

The Stages
of Life

R abbi Judah ben Tema used to say:

At five [the child is ready] for the study of Torah.
At ten for Mishnah.
At thirteen for (responsible performance of) Mitzvot
At fifteen for Talmud. (This is the period of education through Torah
and Mitzvot.)
At eighteen (the youth is ready) for marriage.
At twenty for the pursuit of a livelihood.
At thirty (a person is at the fullness of) strength.
At forty (he reaches the time of) understanding.
At fifty (he reaches the years of giving) counsel.
(This is the period of procreation and of social responsibility.)
At sixty he enters his senior years.
At seventy he attains old age.
At eighty (his survival reflects) strength.
(This is the period of wisdom and of counsel.)
At ninety he is bent in anticipation of the grave.
At one hundred he is dead and past, withdrawn from the world.
(This is the period of preparation for the end, the time when
a wise person will withdraw to permit a new generation to act
without interference.)

ON BEING A JEW

Judaism is a religion; Judaism is a civilization. Jews live apart;

Jews live at the center of history. These are strange contradictions. They have made it very difficult for non-Jews to understand us. They have made it very difficult for us to understand ourselves. Our Christian friends, for instance, have little difficulty seeing Jews as adherents of a specific religion, corresponding to their own affiliations. They have problems seeing us as a people. Confronted with such an anomaly, they may even regard Judaism as an ossified fossil of the past, as Arnold Toynbee declared it to be. Others have historically considered us a monstrosity, evil, cursed. But even the most determined efforts to reduce us or wipe us out have somehow never succeeded. The heathen seer Balaam, once called to curse Israel, found it impossible to do so.

How can I damn whom God has not damned
how doom when the Lord has not doomed? . . .
There is a people that dwells apart,
not reckoned among the nations. [Num. 23:8–9]

Our liturgy in the Amidah on Sabbath afternoon echoes these words:

You are One, Your Name is One
where else is there on earth
a single tribe like Your people Israel,
one and unique?

We are not simply a "religion." Unlike the Christian, who is admitted into his faith by the act of baptism, the Jewish child belongs to Jewry from the moment of his or her birth. The child is of the people.

A convert to Judaism affiliates not merely with a faith, but with a folk.

Yet we are not simply a "people" either. Throughout history, we have been able to endure for long periods without a soil of our own. All other nations perished when soil and language were taken from them. We did not because our "religion" upheld us.

We are not a "race." As early as Abraham, we have admitted others into our fold. A "mixed multitude" of many non-Jews joined the Exodus (Exod. 12:38). We have already read about Ruth, a Moabite convert, ancestress of King David. There was widespread missionary activity among Jews in the days of Jesus. We know of the Khazars, a whole nation that merged into Judaism (about 740 C.E.). Today there are black Jews and yellow Jews, Mediterraneans and Nordics, all integral parts of the Jewish people. We are not a race.

What are we, then?

Torah makes it clear:

You stand this day, all of you before the Lord your God—
your tribal heads, your elders and your officials,
all the men of Israel, your children, your wives,
even the stranger [convert] within your gates,

from woodchopper to waterdrawer—
to enter into the covenant of the Lord your God,
which the Lord is concluding with you this day. . . .
I make this covenant, with its sanctions, not with you alone,
but both with those who are standing here with us this day
before the Lord your God
and with those who are not with us here this day. [Deut. 29:9–14]

According to the Rabbis, "those not with us today" means the souls of all future generations unto the most distant future, including the souls of the converts destined to become Jews. They all were present.

We are a *covenanted people*, a mystical body, unique among the peoples of the earth. We are a family, a household, *Bet Yisrael*. The covenant makes us both a religion and a people.

A Jew merely has "to be." His existence alone is witness to the covenant. The authentic Jew accepts "Being" as challenge, survival as obligation, the enhancement of Judaism as duty and the fight against the forces of erosion as perennial task.

Yihus

Historicaly, one way of combating the forces of erosion within Judaism was the striving for *Yihus*, distinction.

Actually, one had Yihus or one did not have it. The aristocrats in the shtetl had it by distinguished ancestry and inherited status. But there were ways of acquiring it. The best of them was learning. The *Talmid Hakham*, Disciple of the Wise, had it regardless of his social background. He had earned it.

A *Kohen*, member of the priestly caste, who spread his hands on every festival to pronounce the divine blessing over the congregation, had Yihus. The *Levi*, who poured water over the Kohen's hands before the latter ascended the Bimah to pronounce the blessing, had Yihus, too. (This blessing, still performed in Orthodox congregations, has been largely eliminated from non-Orthodox ones.)

Yihus could be acquired through marriage to the son of a Talmid Hakham or to an otherwise distinguished personality. Its refraction gave status to the parents and relatives of the bride.

Yihus was an intangible. It rested on aristocratic descent, but it expressed itself by the person's way of life. Of such a "fine Jew," much was expected: charity, concern, advocacy of Jewish causes, study of Torah, and performance of Mitzvot. In contrast to the *Am Ha-Aretz*, the "earthy folk," untutored and unrefined, the man of Yihus had qualities of knowledge and wisdom, of Torah and manners, which set an example. A family that had Yihus was bound to bring up children true to Torah, filled with the joy of it, and, in turn, willing to accept the obligations of aristocracy.

Ultimately, the whole community of Israel has Yihus.

It pleased the Holy One Blessed Be He
to grant Israel the means of acquiring merit;
He therefore multiplied for them Torah and Mitzvot.
As it is stated
  It pleases the Lord for His vindication
  that [His servant] magnify and glorify
  Torah. [Isa. 42:21]
[Makkot 3:16, recited every Sabbath afternoon in summer]

UNTO US A CHILD IS BORN

Children are *the* blessing for the Jew. "Each child brings a blessing all his own," our ancestors would say. We rejoice in children because we are a people, a historical people.

The study of Torah is for us a paramount obligation; yet were we just a fellowship of scholars, we might find children a nuisance and their rearing a burden, as Aristotle felt. We are a religion, but were we merely a religion, we might emphasize the hereafter to such a degree that the here and now became but preparation; our ideal would be the monk. As we are a people, standing in history, we live in the fullness of this world, duty-bound and emotionally motivated to preserve and perpetuate ourselves, to increase and not to diminish. We are to bring children into the world, and we wish to do so, that the ideals of Torah in study and action may never cease, that we may gain both *Olam Haba*, the world to come, and *Yemot ha-Mashiah*, the Messianic age, consummation of history on earth.

Science has told us that the earth's population is growing so rapidly that it will choke humanity unless it is controlled. Jews have been among the first to heed this message and to limit the number of children in their families. As a consequence, our growth has been proportionally much smaller than that of the general populace. This, however, holds dangers. Some Jewish leaders have felt that we are becoming "an endangered species." We lost six million in the Holocaust. The future of Russian Jewry is in jeopardy. Even in this country there exists the possibility that our decreasing strength in numbers may make the defense of Jewish interests more difficult. We have been fortunate in gaining a number of converts, but this gain is relatively small and offset by those among our youth who are drifting out of Judaism, including those doing so through intermarriage.

There is no easy solution to the problem.

In trying to increase our population, at least to the point of retaining our proportionate strength within society, we should surely not consider ourselves guilty of contributing to the world's over-population. Our losses within this century alone have been staggering, and we have a long way to go before they will have been replaced.

20

B'rit Milah:
The Covenant
of Circumcision

J udaism, by tradition, is paternalistic. There was always greater joy at the birth of a boy than at the birth of a girl. The male studied Torah, ascended to it in public, and joined with other male members to form a congregation. As he went into the marketplace, he alone could assume the duties of leadership, of official and judge.

The son bore the seal of the covenant, *Milah.*

Among ancient nations, circumcision was frequently practiced. Yet we notice significant differences between the usual rites of circumcision and the Jewish ones.

Among people that practiced circumcision, the rite was usually performed at puberty. As some psychologists have pointed out, this may have been done to demonstrate the father's and the tribe's power over the son: they could castrate him, but chose not to do so. The son learned that his manliness depended on the will of the father and of the tribe, that he was forever bound to them by an individual covenant. At the same time, the young man had to show his unflinching endurance during the operation, his manliness in trial. The exposed glans henceforth represented the male's undisguised strength, his leadership, and his superiority.

The Jewish child, by contrast, is circumcised on the eighth day after birth, at a time of utter dependence. He grows up knowing of no conscious state in his existence when this dependence was not there. Of course, circumcision also confirmed the boy's manliness: he bore the seal of the covenant. But this seal meant submission; it brought the awareness of duty rather than the arrogance of power. The Jew, in saying Grace after meals, affirms that the food he has

219

eaten comes from God, to Whom he is bound; he acknowledges gratitude to the Giver of all, including:

For Your covenant which You have sealed in our flesh.

LAWS PERTAINING TO CIRCUMCISION

The Jewish child enters the fold of Judaism at birth. He enters the covenant on the eighth day of his life. Through this rite, Abraham became party to the covenant (Gen. 17:9–14, 23–27). His son Ishmael was thirteen years old when the commandment was issued and obeyed. Isaac, born later, was circumcised on the eighth day, and all later generations were to be initiated on this date (Gen. 21:4; 17:12). The commandment was extended to the people:

When a woman at childbirth bears a male . . .
on the eighth day the flesh of his foreskin shall be circumcised. [Lev. 12:1–2]

Circumcision is a Mitzvah. A Jew who fails to perform it in the course of his life (assuming it was not done at the appointed time) remains a Jew, yet a sinful one. A bleeder, however, need not be circumcised if two earlier brothers have died in consequence of the act. The duty of entering a son into the covenant rests upon the father; if he has failed, it comes to rest on the son himself.

Circumcision may not be performed before the eighth day. If the child is sickly, it must be postponed. The general practice today, whereby male children are routinely circumcised by the physician while the mother is still in the hospital, usually on the third day after birth, is not admissible under Jewish law.

The eighth day is counted from birth. If a child is born on a Monday during the daytime, even in the afternoon, the B'rit is held on the Monday a week later, and in the morning. If the child is born on a Monday after nightfall, the B'rit takes place on Tuesday of the following week.

If the eighth day falls on a Sabbath, even on Yom Kippur, the B'rit *is* performed. This shows its importance and the significance of the eighth day. If, however, it has been postponed owing to the condition of the child, it may not be performed on a Sabbath or holy day.

The B'rit is done by a *Mohel,* a religious person well versed in the laws of Milah (circumcision) and the techniques of the operation. He need not be a rabbi, nor need he be a physician. Today, a Mohel receives a fee for his services, but in the past, pious Jews would not only perform the service free but might even provide for a poor family's celebration in order to have the great privilege of bringing a boy into the covenant.

By Halakhah the act consists of three parts:

Milah: cutting the foreskin from the penis;
P'riah: a sub-incision of the remaining skin, which is folded back that it may not grow over the glans;
Metzitah: the sucking or wiping off of the blood. In earlier days this was done by mouth; now a small glass pipette is used by Orthodoxy.

In earlier days, the Mohel used a clamp, a kind of shield, through which he pushed the foreskin; the glans itself was thus protected, and he used a knife for cutting. Modern surgical instruments may be used to facilitate the operation. If the Mohel is not a physician, the presence of a physician may be advisable to guard against unforeseen emergencies.

In earlier days, circumcisions were frequently performed in the synagogue. If the mother is still in the hospital on the eighth day, the rite may be held there; if she has gone home, the child may be returned, or the act may be performed in the physician's office. Ideally, it is carried out in the home. A Minyan ought to be present, if possible. A B'rit at home permits a celebration to follow.

Taken from the Ladies Section of a Brooklyn synagogue, this unusual photo shows members of the congregation straining to watch a B'rit being performed. The child is held by a *Sandek*, or godfather, during the rite.

PREPARATIONS

Preparations begin at the child's birth; this is his week. The duties fall mainly upon the father. It is his duty to bring his son into the covenant, and were he skilled and courageous enough, he could perform the operation himself.

The baby's mother is not supposed to work on these preparations, merely to advise. Traditionally, she does not attend the B'rit; it might be a strain that might affect the flow of her milk.

The parents determine who is to be *Sandek*, godfather (*Kvater* in Yiddish), to be godmother (*Kvaterin*). (Sandek from *syntekhos*—"he who accompanies the child"—in the Greek church, points to Christian origin.) The godmother brings the child into the room; the godfather holds him during the benedictions; the Sandek has the most distinguished honor of holding the child during the operation. Henceforth, they will be the child's special guides and counselors. The honor can, therefore, be bestowed only once, as each child has to have his own godparents.

Guests are invited.

The house is made beautiful with flowers and candles. A festive table is set for the Mitzvah meal to follow the event. Wine and Hallah are needed.

A cup is set aside for the celebration of the rite itself; sometimes it is an heirloom, sometimes a gift to the child (perhaps by the Sandek), to be used at all the special occasions of his life.

Relatives will either select or make the outfit to be worn by the boy at his B'rit. They will also choose a piece of especially fine linen in which he will be wrapped and on which he will rest during the operation.

The first Sabbath in the child's life revolves around him. On Friday night, after dinner, relatives and friends assemble in the home of the boy's parents for a study of Torah and a light repast. It is called *Zakhor*, "Remember."

Some families conduct a similar session on the eve of the B'rit. On Sabbath morning, the father is called to the Torah.

THE OBSERVANCE

AT THE MORNING SERVICE, the father is given a seat of honor and called to the Torah if Torah is read on this day.

As the portion of daily worship is reached when the Song at the Sea of Reeds is recited, preceded by introductory passages, Mohel and Sandek rise in their seats to sing in antiphonal recitative

You have made a covenant with him to give to his descendants the land . . .
and you have fulfilled Your words. [Neh. 9:8–11; Exod. 14:30–15:18]

A B'rit may also be performed at home, in which case the opportunity for a celebration is rarely neglected.

IN THE HOME, the B'rit takes place early in the day. Before the Mohel two chairs have been placed. On his left is the chair on which the Sandek will sit, holding the child. On the Mohel's right is the chair of Elijah, guardian of Israel, invoked at all the significant moments in Jewish year and life.

The godmother brings the child into the room. Everybody rises and calls out:

Barukh Haba—Blessed be he who cometh.

The godmother hands the child to the godfather and withdraws to be with the mother. The godfather gives the child to the father, who hands him to the Mohel, who will act as his agent.

The Mohel places the child on Elijah's chair; he speaks:

This is the chair of Elijah, his memory be blessed. I trust in Your help, O God . . .
Elijah, angel of the covenant, see, your own is before you; stand at my right hand and sustain me.

The mysterious quality of Jewish being and survival is invoked. The Sandek, who may be dressed in the Tallit, takes his seat next to Elijah's chair. The Mohel hands the child to him and arranges the little boy on his lap for the operation.

The Mohel pronounces the blessing:

Barukh . . . vetzivanu al ha-Milah
Blessed are You . . . He . . . Who . . . has commanded us concerning the
Circumcision.

He quickly performs the cut. (In modern method, it may take a
little longer.)

Immediately after the Mohel's blessing, the father speaks:

Barukh . . . vetzivanu lehakhniso bib'rito shel Avraham Avinu
Blessed are You . . . He . . . Who . . . has commanded us to initiate him
in the covenant of our father Abraham.

The assembly responds:

*Keshem shenikhnas la-Brit, key yikhanes le-Torah, le-Huppah u-le-Maasim
Tovim*
As he has entered the covenant, so may he enter (into the realm of)
Torah, marriage, and good deeds.

A small sponge filled with sugar water or a pacifier has kept the
baby slightly anesthetized. But the child does suffer. In consideration for his pain, Sheheheyanu is not spoken at the B'rit. The child
is bandaged and handed to the godfather.

Raising the cup of wine, the Mohel (or a rabbi present) offers
prayer and blessing. At that moment, the boy gets his Hebrew name.

Our God and God of our fathers: Preserve this child unto his father and
his mother, and may his name in Israel be called: . . . son of . . .

The reader calls out to the child, now having been named:

When I passed by you and saw you in your blood, I said to you: "In your
blood live!," and again I said to you: "In your blood live!" [Ezek. 16:6]

At this time, the Mohel places a drop of the wine on the child's
lips, doing so twice, using a spoon or a small sponge. On his eighth
day of life, the boy has tasted of Jewish pain; may he equally taste
the cup of salvation.

The Sandek drinks some of the wine, some of the boys present
are allowed to partake of it, and the rest is sent to the mother. She,
too, has suffered the pain of apprehension and deserves her share of
the cup of joy. If a rabbi is present, he may place his hands on the
child's head for the Torah benediction: "The Lord bless you and
keep you. . . ." The boy is then returned to his mother.

A joyous meal of thanksgiving follows.

The Wimpel

It was the custom in western Europe to take the baby's linen
wrap, worn at the B'rit, cut it into long strips, each about six inches
wide, sew the strips together, and write or embroider on them the

boy's name, his birthday, and the wish that he grow up to a life of Torah, marriage, and good deeds.

This "Wimpel" was presented by him at the synagogue after his first birthday. He was brought in for a moment and taken to the Bimah to deliver his gift and receive the rabbi's blessing. He arrived on a Sabbath just after the Torah reading, when the scroll was about to be wrapped, for his "Wimpel" would be used as the Torah wrapper.

As new generations brought ever-new wraps, the old ones were preserved in the synagogue archives, where they eventually became a most valuable source for historical research. Most of them disappeared when the Nazis burned the synagogues to the ground. The custom did not exist in eastern Europe.

What About Girls?

When a girl was born, the father was called to the Torah and received a special blessing after his portion had been read to him. His wife was included in the blessing, as was the newborn child, who was given her name at that time. Thus it has remained in Orthodox Jewry.

Many modern Jews have felt strongly that there should be an initiation rite for girls, combined with thanksgiving. No definite rituals have been generally adopted, except for Reform Judaism, which includes a ceremony called "The Covenant of Life" in its *New Union Home Prayer Book.*

Actually, the traditional ceremonial surrounding the B'rit lends itself well to adaptation and merely requires a change in the text from a masculine form of the Hebrew to a feminine one.

Father and mother (instead of the Mohel) ask for divine assistance in bringing up the child.

The father speaks the blessing, jointly with the mother:

In Reform it is phrased as

Barukh . . . vetzivanu al Kiddush ha-Hayim
Blessed are You, . . . He, Who . . . has commanded us to sanctify life.

As there is no pain involved for the child, the parents might recite the Sheheheyanu. The response of the assembled guests remains the same. The blessing over the wine would follow. Then the name would be bestowed, and the child would receive a drop. The festive meal would follow.

Reform has appointed the eighth day for this celebration. But as a B'rit may be postponed, this observance may equally be postponed, perhaps to the thirty-first day after birth, when a child is considered viable according to Jewish law.

Even some Orthodox parents have evolved ceremonies consisting of readings and a prayer of thanksgiving as well as a plea for the child's growth under God. These contain no Berakhot, except those for wine and bread, on the grounds that a Berakhah may be spoken only if ordained by ancient Halakhah.

Holegrasch

Under Napoleonic rule, all Jews had to adopt secular family names. At the same time, many gave their children a secular first name, in addition to the Hebrew one. The occasion was celebrated in a Jewish manner.

The children of the congregation assembled in the home of the new child. The crib was placed in the center of the living room. The father of the baby then read to the children selected verses, including the *first* verse of each book of the Torah, the blessing of Jacob, and the last verse of Torah (Gen. 1:1; 2:1; 48:16; Exod. 1:1; Lev. 1:1; Num. 1:1; Deut. 1:1 and 34:12). They repeated each verse word for word. Then the crib was raised three times. Each time, the father asked: "Holegrasch, how shall we name the baby?" Each time, the children responded by giving the child's secular name.

The word *Holegrasch* reveals its Napoleonic background. It is most likely a corruption of *haut la crèche,* raise the crib high. This was "delivery" from the grip of the earth to the realm of the spirit. (In death, the act is reversed.)

The children came to understand that they had to support each other in life. They were given bags of sweets.

Originally, the celebration was designed for boys only. It was eventually extended to girls as well. The Minhag reveals the legitimacy of a rite for girls.

It created a bond among children, teaching them that they had to help each other and were responsible for each other.

In our search for meaningful observances hallowed by tradition, we may find the Holegrasch ceremony valuable for our time.

21

The Importance
of Names

At the moment a Jewish child enters the covenant, he or she is given a name and becomes a person in his or her own right. The name is important for a person's development. It makes its bearer both identifiable and unique.

Jews have thus always felt that one name, the Name of God, supreme Master, may not be spoken. We cannot enter the essence of the divine. When Moses asked God to reveal His Name in order that the people to whom Moses was sent might know whose mandate their leader held, God did not comply. He merely gave Moses an indication of His power: *Ehyeh Asher Ehyeh*: "I-Am-Who-I-Am" or, according to others, "I-Am-Who-Brings-into-Being" (Exod. 3:13–14). This revealed what God could *do* for the people, as His power was eternal and unlimited, but it did not give the people any power over Him. The Name of God is regarded as ineffable; it may not be pronounced. *YHVH* was replaced, wherever it appears, by *Adonai*—"Lord." He is Master; we are servants. He calls us by name; we may not do so in return.

Holy Scripture reveals to us the significance of personal names. We find in the Bible both changes of name and interpretations of names. A few examples:

When God made a covenant with Abraham, He changed his name from *Abram*, "Father of Aram," to *Abraham*, "Father of a Multitude of Earth Tribes" (Gen. 17:3–5). At the same time, Sarah's name was changed. Originally, she was called *Sarai*, meaning "My Prin-

A Doré engraving, 1865. The essential nature of a name is revealed in the importance attached to changing it. With the new name comes new life, new personality, new understanding. This is one lesson of the story of Jacob's struggle with the angel, at the end of which his name was changed to Israel, the "one who struggled with God."

cess"; Abraham's wife was *his* treasure. But as he became patriarch of multitudes, she became princess of multitudes, and her name was changed to *Sarah*, simply "Princess."

Jacob, emerging from his mother's womb at the heel of his twin brother Esau, was simply called "The Heel"; that is the meaning of *Jacob*. In later life, after many trials, he was encamped with his family on the road when a man arrived out of the darkness of the night and wrestled with him until dawn. Jacob prevailed.

Said the other: "What is your name?" He replied: "Jacob." Said he: "Your name shall no longer be Jacob, but Israel, for you have striven with God and men and have prevailed." [*Sarita . . . El*, you have striven with God, forms Israel.] Jacob asked: "Pray tell me your name." But he said: "You must not ask my name!" And he took leave of him there. [Gen. 32:28–30; also Gen. 35:9–10]

Jacob readily gives his name; the stranger refuses. Jacob may have prevailed in combat, but has also met the divine, whose name and power must escape him. A victor over the forces of adversity, be they of God or of man, Jacob may no longer be called "a heel," a designation that may expose him to scorn and warp his courage. He becomes "God's Knight."

Jacob had a wife, Rachel, whom he loved with all his soul. She gave him two sons: Joseph and Benjamin. She died giving birth to her younger son. With her last breath, she named him: *Ben-oni*, "Son of My Suffering." Rightly considering the feelings of guilt the name would evoke in the child throughout life, reminding him that he caused his mother's death, his father renamed him: *Benjamin*, "Son of the Right Hand" (Gen. 35:18).

Jewish tradition has held that God inscribes each person's destiny in His record by name. A rite of the synagogue is based on this teaching. If a person is so critically ill that there is no hope for him or her, *Shinui Ha-Shem* is performed. The name is changed. A copy of Holy Scripture is opened at random, and the first name that appears is given to the dying person to replace the old name. If God had determined that "A" should die, his decree need not affect the new person, called "B" henceforth. With the change of name, a change of personality has occurred.

NAMES FOR JEWS

Up to the period of the Emancipation, Jews had no family names, merely those bestowed upon them at the B'rit or naming of girls. A Jew carried this name and his father's name. Moses, in Scripture, might thus be called Mosheh ben Amram (Moses, son of Amram); Miriam would be Miriam bat Amram (Miriam, Amram's daughter).

For internal, Jewish use, this practice has been retained. Jews are called to Torah, recorded in their marriage certificate, and commemorated after death and on tombstones by their own and their father's Hebrew names. (It may well be appropriate in our day to give recognition to both father and mother by considering adding the mother's name to the father's in calling Jews to the Torah and in official documents. Isaac's name would thus be Yitzhak ben Avraham ve-Sarah.)

Under an edict of Napoleon I, Jews had to adopt family names, a ruling that spread as far as Russia.

Jews might call themselves after the caste to which they belonged. If a Jew were of the priestly family, a Kohen, he might choose Cohn, Cohen, Cahn, Kahn, or Katz (an abbreviation of *Kohen Tzedek*, "A Loyal Priest").

If he belonged to the tribe of Levi, he might call himself Levi, Levy, Levitt, Leven, but also Siegel or Segal, an abbreviation of *S'gan Levaya* ("Overseer of the Levites").

Their hometowns often provided the names for Jews: Posner, from Poznan; Warshawsky, from Warsaw; Kissinger, from the German town of Kissingen. A distinguishing feature of their houses might provide them with a name: the Rothschild family got its name from the Red Shield on its house. As early as 1671, we have documents referring to a Jew *uff der Trepp;* he had a house with a large flight of stairs (*trepp*) in the city of Fulda.

Sometimes the government assigned names. Jews with the means to bribe officials could get beautiful names, such as *Greenberg*, a green mountain; *Blumenthal,* a valley of flowers; *Rubenstein* or *Bernstein,* reflecting precious stones; or *Margulis,* Hebrew for "pearl."

Upon coming to the United States, many Jews changed their names. Some names were too hard to pronounce; some were impediments to employment in a prejudiced world. Sometimes immigration officials, simply changed a name for the sake of convenience. Yet Jewish family names link us to our roots and should not be changed lightly or without forethought.

CHOOSING FIRST NAMES

Our Hebrew names link us to our immediate past and that of our people. Ashkenazic Jews, therefore, give their children the name of a departed member of the family, whose memory may thereby guide the new generation.

Sefardic Jews name their children after a living member of the family, that he or she may be the young one's model and guide. Jewish children are given their father's name only when the father has died before the child's birth.

As a rule, the English name is adapted to the Hebrew name, unless a Hebrew name (such as Abraham, Rachel, and so on) is chosen. Sometimes an English name is selected on the basis of the meaning of the Hebrew name. (Thus, as *Judah* is compared to a lion in Gen. 49:9, the secular version of it is often Leo or, in Yiddish, *Leib.*) A common practice has been to choose a name beginning with the same letter as the Hebrew one.

REDEMPTION OF THE FIRSTBORN

No rite reaches so deeply to the archaic roots of Judaism as *Pidyon Ha-Ben.* Torah states:

The Lord spoke further to Moses, saying: "Consecrate to Me every first-born; man and beast, the first issue of every womb among the Israelites is Mine." [Exod. 13:1–2]

The Rabbis explain that God had desired the firstborn to be the people's priests, but when Israel committed the sin of the golden calf and the firstborn joined in orgiastic adoration of the idol, they were found unworthy of the privilege. It was given instead to the tribe of Levi, which had remained aloof from this act of aberration. The firstborn son, therefore, has to be released from his obligation, and a ransom paid to the priest who takes his place.

Origins

Actually, the rite goes back to the very beginnings of human awareness. The gods, it was believed, were entitled to the first yield of field and womb, and the firstborn of cattle and of man were sacrificed to them.

Abraham accepted the divine claim to his firstborn, Isaac, without question, and prepared to surrender the life of his child. The *Akedah* episode shows us that Judaism early transcended this primitive and brutal concept. Isaac was not to die but to live; belonging to God means leadership in service. In thus transforming a very ancient practice, Judaism proclaimed the right to life and dignity of every human being.

It also affirmed the special obligations of the firstborn within the family. He is to set an example, and his younger brothers and sisters owe the elder brother a measure of respect (Ketubot 103a).

A Rare Celebration

A Pidyon Ha-Ben can only be celebrated if a mother's first child is a son. If she has had a daughter first or even if she has had a miscarriage preceding the present birth, there is no reason to perform the rite.

As Torah speaks of the first issue of the womb, it has been held that the child must actually "issue." There is no Pidyon Ha-Ben if the child was born by cesarean operation.

If the father is a Kohen or Levi, his son need not be ransomed; he will belong to the special caste of ministers. Also, if the mother is a descendant of a Kohen or Levi, the rite is not performed.

The Observance

The observance may take place after the child's thirtieth day of life. He is then considered a viable child. It should take place immediately. The table is set; Hallah and Kiddush cup are placed on it. The mother brings the little boy, carrying him on a pillow. In front of the table stands the father. He has obtained five silver coins (paper money will not do).

A Kohen, member of the priestly caste, faces him.

The mother hands the child to the father.

The father places the child, still on the pillow, on the table.

A dialogue ensues between father and Kohen.

Father: My wife has borne me a son, first issue of the womb.
Kohen: You have a choice: do you wish to surrender your son [for priestly service] or ransom him for five pieces of silver?
Father: I prefer keeping my son.
Father speaks the blessings:
   Barukh . . . vetzivanu al Pidyon Ha-Ben
   Blessed are You . . . He, Who . . . has commanded us concerning the redemption of the [firstborn] son.
      Sheheheyanu follows.
Father gives the Kohen the five silver pieces.
Kohen accepts them and speaks:
   Your son is redeemed, your son is redeemed, your son is redeemed.
Kohen then blesses the child with the priestly benediction, adding some additional verses. [Num. 6:24–26; Ps. 121:5; Prov. 3:2; Ps. 121:7]
Kohen speaks the blessing over the wine and the bread.

A Mitzvah meal follows for the friends and relatives who have been invited.

Extensions

Some non-Orthodox Jews hold that, as no distinction should be made between boys and girls and as the caste system is obsolete, this ceremony should express the parents' gratitude at the gift of a first child, whether boy or girl, their joy that he or she has survived the first critical month, and their hope that the child be vouchsafed a long and creative life. They would pledge to raise this child to be an example for those who follow.

Such a ceremony would be observed even for Kohanim and Leviim, for boys and girls, and for the first child after a miscarriage.

No Kohen would be needed; no money would be displayed. The money would be given to charity. (Actually, the Kohen does the same in a traditional Pidyon Ha-Ben or provides a gift for the child.)

Naming the Child in the Synagogue

Girls have always been named in the synagogue in connection with the blessing the father receives on the Sabbath after birth. Boys receive their name at the B'rit and a blessing in *shul* as well. There is ample precedent for naming in the synagogue, but it should not take the place of a B'rit at the correct time.

The practices of individual congregations will determine how the celebration is performed and whether the child is to be brought into the sanctuary.

22

Education
in Judaism

T he first wish extended to a boy at his B'rit is: "May he enter [the realm of] Torah." Torah is the tree of life. It is the key to life.

The goal is not mere knowledge, but Jewish living:

If fear of sin undergirds wisdom, wisdom will endure. . . .
If deeds surpass wisdom, wisdom will endure. . . . [Avot 3:11, 12]

Pursuit of Torah carries its own reward:

He who takes upon himself of the yoke of Torah, will find the yoke of the world removed from him. [Avot. 3:6]

The purpose of study is not honor, wealth, or power:

If you have learned much Torah, do not take credit for it; you were created for this purpose. [Avot. 2:9]

But with the life of Torah comes the striving for peace:

Love peace, pursue peace, love all creatures, bring all to Torah. [Avot. 1:12]

Torah study is not a mere academic pursuit, nor is it a profession:

It is good to combine Torah [study] with a worldly occupation; toil in both casts out sin; Torah without worldly work may be a waste and may lead to sin. [Avot. 2:2]

The man of Torah must never be removed from the common folk.

The man of Torah must stand within the community, not above or beyond it, and he must have humility:

Do not separate yourself from the congregation, do not be confident of yourself to the day of your death. [Avot 2:5]

He must be gracious:

As the untutored cannot be truly pious, so will the rude man never learn the fear of sin. [Avot 2:6]

He must have a good heart:

In it are included all the other qualities. [Avot 2:13]

He must stand up and be counted:

In a place where there are no men, strive to be a man. [Avot 2:6]
You may not be able to finish the work, but you are not free to desist from it. [Avot 2:21]
If I am not for myself [at my post], who will be for me? If I am but for myself, what am I? And if not now, when [will it be done]? [Avot 1:14]

From these spring love of fellowman and respect for government:

The honor of your fellow must be as dear to you as your own. [Avot 2:15]
Pray for the welfare of the government, for without the fear of it people would swallow each other alive. [Avot 3:2]

In sum:

Make His will your will; may He make your will His. [Avot 2:4]

The great philosopher Aristotle stated that the pursuit of reason was the human being's true source of happiness. Aristotle thought of philosophy; the Rabbis, of Torah. Aristotle accepted the conditions of life that denied to the majority the ultimate happiness of study. The masses had to devote their time to earning a living or otherwise lacked the requisite intellectual capacity. To the Rabbis, as Torah was the greatest source of happiness, all other demands of life paled before it and had to be reduced to a minimum. But *everyone* should have Torah.

This is the way of Torah: Be satisfied with a morsel of bread and a bit of salt, drink water in small measure, sleep on the ground, accept a life of hardship, but toil in Torah. If you lead such a life, "you will be happy, it will be well with you" (Ps. 128:2). "You will be happy" in this world; "it will be well with you" in the world to come (Avot 6:4).

THE ROAD OF EDUCATION

We read in the Haggadah that each child has a personality of his

or her own and should be given individual attention. This is based
on a scriptural verse:

Bring up the child according to his [destined] way, and even as he gets
old he will not depart from it. [Prov. 22:6]

The way destined for the child is determined by his character and
his capacities, his surroundings and his prospects, but above all by
his Jewishness.

Learning starts early. An environment has to be created that
places the child into an atmosphere of Jewish living from earliest
moments. On these foundations, parents are the first to erect the
structure of knowledge. It used to be the father's duty to teach his
child reading and writing. From the mother he might learn the
"Sh'ma," the blessings, and prayers for morning and night. He came
to know the benedictions for food long before entering school.

The Rabbis held that a child was ready for school by the age of
five. A minority felt a child should not enter until six, for if he entered too early, he might remain sickly for the rest of his life. "Let
him be sickly in body and strong in mind," their colleagues retorted
(Ketuvot 50a). This remained the rule in eastern European Jewry:
a powerful mind in a weakly body was not uncommon.

Public education among Jews was established in the days of the
High Priest Joshua ben Gamla, ca. 63–65 C.E. (see Bava Batra 20b–
21a). He may have been influenced by Plato, who, in his *Republic,*
advocated public schools for all children. Joshua set up schools for
Torah and was praised for this by the Rabbis.

The Rabbis discussed the proper size of classes. For each group
of twenty-five children there had to be at least one teacher; if the
number rose to forty, a teacher's aide was to be employed. If it
reached fifty, an additional teacher had to be engaged.

Who was best equipped to teach? A thorough teacher, progressing
slowly, or a fast-moving one, covering much but permitting errors
to creep into the children's minds? The slow, thorough teacher was
regarded as more desirable (Bava Batra 21a, b).

The Rabbis' method would not find approval among modern educators: "Fill him up like an ox," push a child to his limit, and stuff
him full with knowledge (Bava Batra 21a).

In line with the teaching of Scripture, the rod was not spared:

If foolery is found in the heart of a child the rod of correction shall drive
it out of him. [Prov. 22:15]

But what should be done if the child simply could not learn in spite
of all the thrashings he got?

When you castigate a child, beat him only with a [soft leather] strap [to
avoid lasting harm]. If he learns, well and good; if not, let him keep company with the others. [Bava Batra 21a]

Modern Jewish educators have adapted many of the methods of secular schools, as exemplified by the open classroom situation seen above. Yet the content of Jewish education has not changed, and the central message of Torah has remained Judaism's elemental teaching.

Secondary Education

In contrast to contemporary practice, public schools were established for older children first and then expanded downward. It was held that the father had an obligation to teach his child as far as the parent's ability and knowledge permitted him to go (Bava Batra 20b–21a). Even with the establishment of schools for all age levels, Judaism does not permit parents to be satisfied with education delegated to an institution. *They* are the teachers through word and example.

Higher learning began at the age of ten. The boy was introduced to Mishnah. It may have been quite a jolt, and the father (or teacher) was to have patience for a while:

A father may have patience with his son up to the age of twelve. From then on, he shall go after him for dear life. [Ketuvot 50a]

If the boy succeeded, he would be able to demonstrate his learning through a public discourse delivered by him in connection with his Bar Mitzvah at the age of thirteen. If he did not, he would remain an *Am Ha-Aretz* for the rest of his life, uneducated but observant.

The "University"

The gifted and diligent boys would eventually enter the Academy at the age of fifteen. Here a young man would study at the feet of a renowned master. It was hoped that he might truly become a *Talmid Hakham,* a Disciple of the Wise. After many years of un-

237

relenting work, he might be ordained Rabbi, becoming a master himself and empowered to raise a new generation of disciples and to interpret Torah authoritatively.

Secular subjects were not part of this curriculum. They were not regarded as necessary, for everything was contained in Torah, as one rabbi put it:

Turn it [Torah] and turn it, for all is in it. [Avot 5:25]

Torah gave life; it assured length of days and gave beauty, strength, wisdom, honor, and riches. (Avot 6:7–8). Above all, it brought freedom:

When Torah came into the world, freedom came into the world. [Gen. Rabba, Vayera 55:7]

Having found such freedom, the Jews needed no other, and could feel free even amid enslavement.

EDUCATION IN EASTERN EUROPE

The Jews in the shtetl had a definite goal for their children's education. They were to be replicas of their parents, but it was hoped that the sons might surpass their father in learning; perhaps one might even become a *lamden*, a person truly versed in Talmud.

Little boys dressed like their elders. They wore black caftans, a garment originating in medieval Germany, where it was the stately robe of Christian patricians. The little boy's hair was cropped on the crown of the head in preparation for the day when he would put on Tefillin that should sit directly "between the eyes." But the ear-

The riches of the eastern European Jew were the treasures of learning. Parents and grandparents continually sought to educate their childen. In the case of boys, every elder's prayer was that the child would grow to become a scholar.

locks at the sides were never cut, in strict conformity with an injunction of Torah that was interpreted in its most rigorous sense:

You shall not round off the side-growth of your head, or destroy the side-growth of your beard. [Lev. 19:27]

Later in life, when the youth had a beard, no razor would ever touch it, though it might be trimmed with scissors.

The little girl, dressed like her mother, helped in the kitchen and was gradually and thoroughly instructed in the laws of Kashrut. She might learn how to read in order to say her prayers and the meditations in the *Techinah,* a Yiddish book especially written for women. Later she would be instructed in her obligations as a woman. This was the extent of her education.

The children learned the blessings. An abbreviated form of prayer was arranged for them. It contained the Sh'ma and other selections, including:

The Torah, with which Moses has charged us, is the heritage of the congregation of Jacob. [Deut. 33:4]

Hear, my son, the words of discipline of your father, do not reject the instruction of your mother. [Prov. 1:8]

Soon the little boy would get his *Arba Kanfot,* the garment with Tzitzit, to be worn always. The Tallit would come later.

At five, the child was ready for *Heder,* the school where a poorly trained and often ill-tempered *Melamed* would drill his unruly pupils from morning to night, teaching them the aleph-bet and other elementary subjects. If a boy showed promise, he would be promoted to the *Yeshivah Ketanah,* the preparatory school for the academy, the *Yeshivah.* If he was not well equipped intellectually, he might have to go to work at an early age. Like his father, he would go daily to the *Bet Ha-Midrash,* House of Study, to learn or to listen to popular discourses.

But the school was not the only center of education. Environment and, above all, the home, were major forces. Here the child was permitted to share the joys and sorrows of the Jewish year and take part in the rituals, the celebrations of Sabbath and holy days. He saw how deeply his parents cared about their tradition. Shared values and shared aspirations united parents, children, and community.

The gifted child, having completed Yeshivah Ketanah, went to the Yeshivah. Frequently, this meant being away from home; the small town had no such academy.

The term *Yeshivah* comes from *yashav,* "to sit." Here the young men would sit from morning to night, studying heavy tomes of Talmud. Each small group would follow its own course, preparing for the rabbi's lecture and reviewing it. Some studied alone. The

Yeshivah student lived in a world of his own, far from sunlight and flowers. His cheeks lost their bloom. But he found sunlight in Torah and flowers in newly discovered "fine points."

The method of study, called *Pilpul*, was aimed at finding ever new meanings *within* the text. As it was held that all the great masters of the past knew everything, their conflicting opinions had to be reconciled, even if they lived centuries apart. This became possible only by means of a hairsplitting logic. It must be remembered that this method of interpretation was common among all scholars during the Middle Ages, not only Jewish ones. Through it, history came to be transcended; various periods spoke to each other and to the student across the centuries. Judaism became a living organism, beyond time and space and circumstances.

The students were poor, and many remained poor for life, being supported upon marriage by a father-in-law and, later, by the wife.

Psychologists have pointed out that every person stands in need of certain rituals, be they rationally explainable or not. The Jews of the *shtetl* were no psychologists, but they gave their children love and ritual, meaning and purpose, security and emotional stability through the observance of God-ordained rites; for this was their understanding of the ceremonies and practices they followed. The child was part of these. Learning and sharing of rituals imparted unmatched strength.

American parents share with their children the rituals of America, from holidays to football and baseball. As Jewish parents, hoping to retain the love and loyalty of our children, we might learn from our ancestors by building Jewish forms of shared experiences into our routine of life. We may not wish to follow the educational program of eastern European Jewry, but we have much to draw from their way of combining study with celebration. Providing the warm spirituality of the Jewish home, we need not fear the loss of our youth.

23

Bar Mitzvah
and Bat Mitzvah:
Gate to
Adult Responsibility

A t thirteen years and one day, the Jewish boy reaches the age of accountability for the performance of Mitzvot.

At thirteen, he is ready for Mitzvot. [Avot 5:2]

The girl attains this stage at the age of twelve years and one day. He is Bar Mitzvah, Son of the Commandment; she is Bat Mitzvah, Daughter of the Commandment.

This transition to responsibility is automatic. It does not depend on any special initiation rites. But Jewish wisdom has seen fit to surround this moment with celebrations that have become fully incorporated in Jewish life.

Circumcision, ordained in Torah, and Bar Mitzvah, established by custom, have become inviolate for most Jews. Actually, there is a relationship between them, intuitively recognized by Jews. Any child of a Jewish mother is automatically a Jew. Circumcision formally seals him in this status. As it occurs, the father assumes his responsibility to bring him into the covenant. Bar Mitzvah, equally automatically, concludes the first stage of the child's life. As it is observed in celebration, the father proclaims that he is now relieved of the responsibility for the religious conduct of his son. The young Jew now has to stand on his own feet. Circumcision and Bar Mitzvah are the two pillars of the structure that bridges the years of childhood.

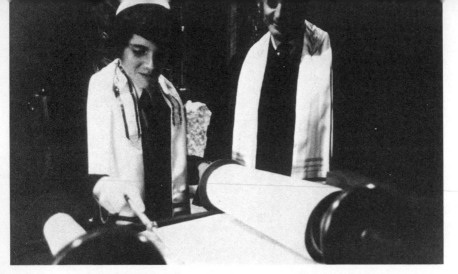

Since medieval times, Bar Mitzvah has been a central
ceremony in the life of a male. Years of training cul-
minate in the boy's reading from the scroll of the
Torah and reciting the prophetic portion of the week
before the assembled congregation.

Bar Mitzvah most likely originated in ancient initiation rites.
But for the people of antiquity, it was an initiation inflicted by others
and causing great pain. For Jews, it is the completion of an initiation
that began at birth, that led to a gradual immersion of the child in
Jewish ways, and that ends with an acceptance of commitment.
There is no pain. Where the suffering son of the ancients required
time to recuperate, the son of the commandment takes his place
immediately in the ranks of responsible adults.

Bar Mitzvah is an act that brings the child's early years to formal
conclusion. At the same time, it publicly opens a new chapter in
life. The boy and the girl are about to enter adolescence, a difficult
period. In many ways they are still children, but increasingly they
wish to be recognized as adults. And they wish to know how parents
and society view them. Judaism tells them where they belong: true,
they are still dependent, but in the context of religious life, as participants in worship, they are adults. They have to assume the burdens that go with adulthood and can equally claim the respect that
is due an adult. They know where they stand.

According to historians, the Bar Mitzvah celebration, as we know
it, originated in the Middle Ages. Yet we find that as early as the first
century c.e., boys of the age of thirteen were brought before the
sages for blessing, admonition, and encouragement. According to
Torah, the age of twenty constitutes maturity (Exod. 30:14; Gitin 65a).
But for purposes other than legal majority the onset of puberty was
regarded as the milestone in the young Jew's life and was set at
thirteen for boys and twelve for girls. This, according to the Rabbis,

was a Halakhah handed down to Moses by God at Sinai. Scripture does not mention it.

BAR MITZVAH IN THE SHTETL

In the shtetl, Bar Mitzvah long remained an event of minor importance. The boy would be called to the Torah on a day following his thirteenth birthday. This could be on a Monday or Thursday. A small repast might follow; the youngster received the good wishes of the assembled congregation.

If the boy was an *ilui,* a prodigy in Talmud, he might deliver a discourse at the home of his parents, to which friends and relatives and, above all, the learned of the community were invited.

About six months before his Bar Mitzvah, a boy began to put on Tefillin under the guidance of his father.

Beginning at the age of ten, both boys and girls began to fast, first on Yom Kippur and Tishah b'Av, then, gradually, on other fasts. At the beginning, they were permitted only a few hours of fasting, but as their strength increased, the time was extended to accustom them to both the meaning and the practice of the observances. Only after Bar Mitzvah did they fast the full prescribed time. This practice is still observed in Orthodox Jewry.

The celebration of a Bat Mitzvah ceremony for females—patterned after the Bar Mitzvah—is a recent development, still limited to non-Orthodox synagogues. It has gained prominence in the American Jewish community.

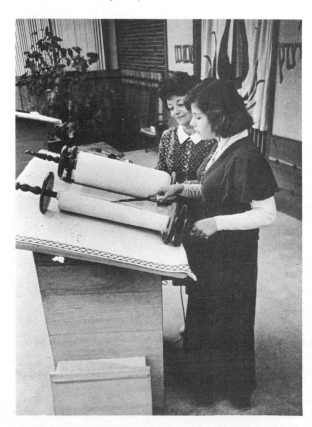

CONTEMPORARY OBSERVANCE

Although a Bar Mitzvah may be celebrated whenever the Torah is read to the people, Sabbath morning is the truly appropriate time.

THE CORE of the Bar Mitzvah is uniform in all congregations. The Bar Mitzvah is called to the Torah, speaks the Berakhot, reads a portion from the scroll, and, if he is gifted, several portions or the whole section of the week. He may also recite the Haftarah with its blessings and usually does. His father, godfather, and relatives are all called up. He may be permitted to lead parts of the service. By widespread custom, he delivers a short speech after the Torah reading, then receives a charge from his rabbi and the blessing.

ADDITIONAL PRACTICES depend on the religious affiliation of the congregation. In non-Orthodox synagogues, the parents may participate in the service; the mother may even be called to the Torah. Sometimes the father will place the Tallit on the shoulders of his son before the service commences. Some communities present the Bar Mitzvah with a certificate and a gift, a volume of Holy Scriptures or a prayer book or Kiddush cup.

THE FATHER'S BLESSING is spoken silently, as the son has completed his benedictions of Torah:

Barukh shepatrani me-onsho shel zeh
Praised be He, Who has freed me from responsibility for this [son].

In non-Orthodox congregations, Sheheheyanu may be added, perhaps recited by both parents.

The celebration concludes with a Kiddush and reception after the service. The young man receives congratulations and gifts. These should have Jewish significance. A family dinner rounds off the happy event.

CELEBRATING BAT MITZVAH.   Orthodox congregations do not permit special rites for girls, as Halakhah does not sanction them.

In non-Orthodox congregations, forms have been introduced that are patterned after the Bar Mitzvah of boys but not identical with it. In some, girls are given a Bat Mitzvah identical with the celebration for boys.

CONFIRMATION, introduced in adaptation of church practices by the Reform movement during the last century, has spread widely. It provides motivation for young people to continue their Jewish education after Bar Mitzvah up to an age when they can be given a more mature presentation of our heritage. It is conducted usually at the time of graduation from junior high school, when youngsters are about sixteen years old.

Some Regulations

Bar Mitzvah follows the birthday according to the Jewish calendar.

A boy or girl born in Adar of a regular year will observe Bar Mitzvah or Bat Mitzvah in Adar II, if Bar Mitzvah falls during a leap year. In some communities, no Bar Mitzvot are held during the holy days or during the entire holy-day season in the fall. Instead the ceremony is postponed to the earliest regular Sabbath.

The newly developed practice whereby mature people who did not have a Bar Mitzvah celebration at the age of thirteen celebrate the fact of their being sons and daughters of the Mitzvah at a ceremony later in age has merit. There are no Halakhic objections to it.

OBJECTIVES IN JEWISH EDUCATION

Many congregations insist that boys and girls attend at least three to four years of formal religious education and participate in religious activities if they wish to be Bar Mitzvah or Bat Mitzvah in their synagogue. The Jew must *know* about his people, its destiny, its ways of life, its creativity, and its forms of expression in ritual, life, and ethical conduct.

The Jew must *positively identify* with his people, be emotionally attached to it, derive orientation through its wisdom, guidance through its teachings, satisfaction from his sense of belonging, and peace of mind through his involvement.

The Jew must be *inspired to action* in behalf of his people, in a spirit of love for all its members and in a spirit of dedication to the people's collective aspirations.

Jewish education, therefore, must be dedicated to knowledge and wisdom, to theory and practice. It must touch the mind and the heart, the intellect and the soul. It must lead to a lifelong immersion

Jewish education is a lifelong pursuit. One is never too young nor too old to begin. It is the pursuit of Torah, which the rabbis called "a tree of life . . ."

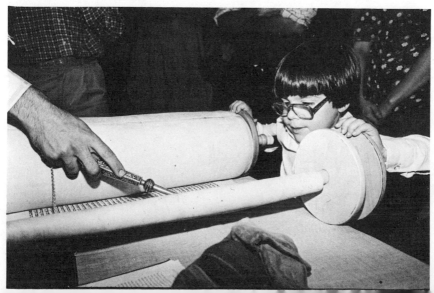

of the Jew in his people and heritage, in study and action, and to a contribution to Jewish survival.

The American Jew must come to link himself to Israel while recognizing the probability that he and his children will live out their lives in America. Though he draws strength from Israel, he may not make it the vicarious keeper of his heritage. He must rather evolve a living and vibrant Judaism in the context of American living through a synthesis of Jewish and American ideals and ways. He should acquire at least a basic knowledge of Hebrew, the language of Torah, Tefillah, and modern Israel.

Jewish education is not training, for training is mechanical. It is *e-ducare*, a "to lead out." Judaism is a living tree; it needs tending if it is to produce new fruit. Its yield is rich and blessed. Thus it is said of Torah and its wisdom:

It is a tree of life to those who take hold of it,
and those who support it will be enriched. [Prov. 3:18]

24

Conversion: Joining the Household of Israel

T he transformation of the native-born Jew into a fully responsible member of the community is slow and gradual. For the convert, it is sudden and dramatic. This transformation is a form of rebirth, and it is irreversible. The convert's new status is identical in rights and obligations to that of the native-born. Can such sudden change be expected? How does Judaism feel about conversion and converts?

JUDAISM AND CONVERSION

Conversion to Judaism is naturalization. The convert accepts the faith of Israel, but is also admitted into its peoplehood.

In Talmudic times, the Jews engaged in widespread missionary activity. We find but one Rabbi who opposed proselyting for fear that the convert might lead others astray, being himself not fully acculturated (Yevamot 47b).

The majority knew that, to the contrary, converts often show a deep attachment to their newly found allegiance and that their fervor frequently surpasses that of native-born Jews (see Isa. 56:6–8). It, therefore, might even be a badge of honor to be a descendant of a proselyte. Was not David's greatness attributable in part to the influence of his great-grandmother Ruth, the convert, on whose lap he sat as a child?

Among the descendants of converts the Talmud lists: Sh'maya and Avtalyon, teachers of the great Hillel, Rabbi Meir, Rabbi Akiva; even "descendants of Haman taught Torah in [the academy of] B'ne B'rak" (Sanhedrin 96b; Gittin 57b; see Maimonides, Introduction to Mishneh Torah). The Book of Ruth may have been written to counteract Ezra's harsh actions and resolutions against converts (Ezra 9, 10).

During the period of the Roman Empire, Jewish missionary activity was widespread. Two categories of converts were established: "adjunct proselytes," who did not submit to circumcision, and "righteous proselytes," who underwent all the prescribed rites and became full-fledged members of faith and people. Nero's wife Poppaea may have belonged to the former category; Queen Helena of Adiabene, who belonged to the latter, settled in Jerusalem and was praised by the Rabbis for her generosity toward the Temple and the people in times of need (first century B.C.E.). Much later, around 740 C.E., the entire nation of the Khazars, a country around the Crimean Peninsula, joined Judaism and merged with it.

When Christianity became the state religion of the Roman Empire, conversion of a person to Judaism became punishable by death for the proselyte and his sponsors. This may have contributed to the extreme caution, exercised to this day by Orthodoxy, in admitting converts to Judaism. Believers in One God, such as Christians and Moslems, stand in no need of conversion.

Judaism knows of no race, of no color. The convert is our brother or sister. It is, therefore, wrong to view a convert with suspicion, as is sometimes done, as if he or she did not "belong." The Rabbis have held that it is a sin even to remind a convert of his or her former state, lest he or she be hurt. Having freely left their former allegiance and joined the Jewish fold, they must be given great love and recognition. Their descendants may be our future leaders.

LAWS AND PRACTICES

During the period of the Second Temple the regulations regarding conversion became fully formalized.

The postulant had to demonstrate and declare that he or she was seeking admission on conviction alone, being motivated by no other consideration, and had to pledge full and unreserved commitment to all the laws and ordinances of Judaism.

The Rabbis fashioned the laws of conversion after the regulations of Torah relating to purification after occurrences that render a person ritually unclean. These are outlined in Leviticus 15. An offering had to be brought. A male wishing to bring such an offering had to

When one converts with a full heart, the entire covenant becomes the convert's possession. This is exemplified by the Bible's most celebrated convert, Ruth, as she spoke to her mother-in-law, saying, "Entreat me not to leave thee . . . for whither thou goest I will go; and where thou lodgest, I will lodge; thy people shall be my people, and thy God my God . . ." (Ruth 1:16).

be circumcised. Both male and female had to undergo immersion as an act of cleansing. At the same time, the Rabbis explicitly affirmed that a conversion was fully valid even without the sacrificial offering, now that the Temple no longer existed.

The Rabbis taught: In our time, should a person wish to become a proselyte, one must say to him: "What prompts you to become a convert? Do you know that, in our time, the Jews are scorned, oppressed, humiliated, and made to suffer?" If he replies that he is aware of it, one shall admit him immediately, and acquaint him with some of the lighter and some of the heavier commandments. . . . He is to be told of the punishment that follows transgression of Mitzvot. . . . "Until now, you were permitted to work on the Sabbath, . . . henceforth you will incur punishment for such an offense. . . ." As he is told about punishment, he should equally be told about rewards. He should be told: "Know that the world to come was created solely for the sake of the saintly. Israel, in our time, cannot bear too many good things, nor too much suffering." But one must not overdo the argument, nor be too painstaking. If he agrees, let him be circumcised at once. [Yevamot 47a–b]

The set of questions was derived from the conversation between Naomi and her daughter-in-law, Ruth, paragon of the true, righteous proselyte. Her words were interpreted as replies to her mother-in-law's searching questions:

Naomi: Return to your people.
Ruth: Entreat me not to leave you and to return from following after you.
Naomi: Have you considered the stringent Sabbath laws, forbidding us to walk beyond a certain limit?
Ruth: Wherever you go, there I will go [and no further].
Naomi: You may not spend a night in the same room with any man, except your husband.
Ruth: Wherever you take lodging, I will take lodging.
Naomi: You must fully identify with our people. This implies conscientious observance of the 613 commandments given us.
Ruth: Your people shall be my people.
Naomi: You must renounce your former faith and may not worship your present gods, even in conjunction with God.
Ruth: Your God shall be my God.
Naomi: Some violations of Torah carry death penalties.
Ruth: Where you will die, I will die [through nature's course and not by a court's verdict].
Naomi: Even the graves of the offender are separated from those of the rest of the people.
Ruth: [Where you will be buried] there I will [be worthy to] be buried.
And when Naomi saw that she was steadfastly minded to go with her [on the Jewish road of life], she ceased talking to her [and no longer tried to dissuade her]. [Ruth 1:16–18; Yevamot 47b]

There was no lengthy period of instruction in those days. It was a Mitzvah to initiate a convert. It had to be performed right away.

MODERN PRACTICE

The ancient Rabbis would not admit a postulant if there were any possibility that ulterior motives, such as love for a man or a woman, might have influenced the decision to convert. We today have become more lenient, realizing the necessity of keeping the family within the Jewish fold. Children of mixed marriages are most likely to be lost to us.

Generally, it can be found that the non-Jewish partner seeks admission not merely for practical reasons, but for very important spiritual ones. He or she will frequently be attracted by the closeness of the Jewish community and its family spirit and will seek for himself or herself the gift of belonging. Many have found Judaism attractive as it does not burden them with dogmas. As the incidence of divorce is much higher in interfaith marriages than in those in which the partners belong to the same religion, conversion may help a marriage to become stabilized. The children of such a marriage will be surrounded by the warmth of the Jewish home and its celebrations.

Yet there are problems that have to be faced and overcome: guilt feelings that may emerge at later stages of life at having renounced one's former religion; questions about "salvation"; fissures that may develop between the convert and his or her parents and

The exact ceremony for conversion differs from one Jewish "denomination" to another. Yet in all conversion rites, the bestowal of a new Hebrew name upon the convert marks the transition and seals the conversion.

family, especially if the family is strongly rooted in *its* faith; regret as dearly loved customs are abandoned; and the temptation to maintain them. The disabilities that attach to a Jew even in contemporary society and the uncertainty of the Jewish future both have to be pointed out, for conversion is irreversible. The special tasks imposed by Jewish living and by the rearing of children as Jews have to be clearly presented.

The practice has, therefore, developed of sending the postulant home three times for serious thought. Although this practice was most likely not followed by the Rabbis of old, it is based on the thrice-repeated appeal of Naomi to Ruth to return home (Ruth 1:8, 11, 12; Ruth Rabba 2:17).

In addition, a lengthy period of instruction is required of prospective converts. In large Jewish communities, courses for converts are conducted regularly, offering group instruction and discussion. The actual rite of conversion varies widely among the "denominations."

ORTHODOXY insists on strict Halakhic procedures. The convert undergoes a period of instruction. Here Orthodoxy may, in fact, be more lenient than the other movements, basing itself on the practice of the Rabbis and their directive that conversion take place as quickly as possible (Yevamot 47a).

Orthodoxy demands circumcision for males, by a Mohel and in the presence of a rabbinical court of three. It also requires of a male already circumcised the act of *Hatafat Dam B'rit*, the extraction of a drop of blood at the place of the Milah, as the earlier circumcision had no religious significance. The postulant is then given time to recover. Both males and females have to undergo submersion in a Mikvah (which shall be explained), also in the presence of the rabbinical court. If it is a woman, the rabbis wait until she is full submerged. Her companion then indicates the fact and the rabbis quickly verify it. Some hold that it is sufficient for the rabbis to be in an anteroom and listen to the ripple of the water.

On emerging from the water, the convert speaks the blessing:

Barukh . . . vetzivanu al ha-Tevilah
Blessed are You . . . He who has commanded us concerning immersion.

Some will call for a second submersion, now performed by the newly created Jew after having pronounced blessings for the first time. The blessing thus precedes the act.

In a benediction, the new Hebrew name is bestowed upon the convert. Ninety-two days after conversion, the proselyte may marry a Jew. This applies to women, in order to make certain that a child to be born after nine months will be the Jewish father's child. Basing itself on an interpretation of a verse in Ezekiel (44:22; see also

Lev. 21:7f.), Orthodoxy will not permit a converted woman to marry a Kohen.

CONSERVATIVE JEWRY basically follows the same rules. It insists on a lengthy period of instruction and demands circumcision and *Tevilah*, immersion. Opinion is divided on the need for Hatafat Dam B'rit. When it comes to immersion, the use of some type of swimming pool and the wearing of loose-fitting garments by women may at times be permitted. The rite begins at a session of three rabbis, at which the convert is examined on knowledge and conviction, and often ends in the synagogue, where the convert is publicly blessed and receives his or her name.

In relation to immersion, the Talmud requires the presence of the rabbis for males; in the case of females, it states that "they stand without" (Yevamot 47b). The Conservative rabbinate is following this rule rather than the more restrictive and embarrassing one, laid down by post-Talmudic authorities. A female convert is equally permitted to marry a Kohen under Halakhah as interpreted by the Conservative rabbinate. No taint of any kind, it is held, may attach to any convert.

Conservative Jewry may permit elders of the congregation to serve as the rabbi's associates on the rabbinical court.

Owing to the permissive changes sanctioned by the Conservative rabbinate, in general, its rabbis and the conversions over which they preside are not recognized by the rabbinate of Israel.

REFORM JUDAISM insists on thorough instruction, but has dispensed with the requirements of Milah and Tevilah.

The convert appears before the rabbinical court, composed of three rabbis or one rabbi and two elders. He or she is examined. The person then makes an oral and written declaration of commitment and is admitted. A public ceremony of blessing and bestowal of name usually follows.

The elimination of circumcision for males in this rite has created consternation among Jews of all circles in Israel, not only the religious ones. Conversions performed by Reform rabbis are not recognized by the Israeli rabbinate.

Hebrew Names for Converts

The convert is given a Hebrew name. As Abraham was the father of all Jews and brought many into the fold, a male convert usually receives the name: Avraham ben Avraham Avinu; Abraham, son of our father Abraham. Women are called: Sarah bat Avraham Avinu; Sarah, daughter of our father Abraham. But other names have been used and may be used. The Talmud tells us that an Edomite who became converted assumed the name Obadiah; he became the prophet known by this name (Sanhedrin 39b).

Children

Children born of a non-Jewish mother need conversion even if the father is a Jew. They require Milah and Tevilah. This can be done while they are minors *al Daat Bet Din,* in accordance with the judgment of the court. It is based on the principle that one may do another person a favor, though he may be unaware of it. When such a child attains the age of judgment, he or she can renounce Judaism, but not later.

Reform and Reconstructionism hold that a child brought up as a Jew by his or her parents needs no further rites of admission, even if the mother is not Jewish. Bar Mitzvah constitutes the declaration of faith.

The Baal Teshuvah

A person who deserts Judaism by *accepting another faith* is required by Halakhah to immerse himself or herself for full restoration of his privileges if he or she wishes to return. In practice, the change of will is frequently regarded as sufficient. This applies only to Jews who have formally *renounced* their faith, not to those who have moved away from religious observance without formally repudiating their Jewish affiliation.

25

The Family:
Atom of the Faith

I n the vision of Judaism, the family is more than a mere
social unit; it is the atom of the faith-people. As, within
the atom, particles move in well-appointed orbits around
a nucleus, held to it and to each other by the pull of
eternal forces, similarly, within the family, members interact not
for reasons of self-interest and gain, but through harmony. They
submit freely to each other and to the whole and carry out their
assigned obligations by means of an inner attunement. The individuals transcend themselves, forming a unity that is more than the
sum of the members. This unity is based on the great mysterious
force of love. The family is equally the source of the act that leads
human beings to the very limit of human power: the creation of
life. Here we approach the divine.

Torah and our Rabbis understood the character of the family.
The *Song of Songs* expresses that understanding. It is the song of a
love that mysteriously draws a man and a woman together and has
been seen as symbolizing the love of God for Israel and mankind.
Of this song, Rabbi Akiva was to say:

All the books of Holy Scripture are holy, but the *Song of Songs* is the
holiest among them. [Shir Ha-Shirim Rabba l]

An atom can be split. This can happen to the family. It then
becomes a mere community of interests, serving the self-centered
concerns of the members. This has happened frequently in our days.
The home, no longer a source of inner strength, becomes a physical

base of operations. Love itself may disappear, especially if it is originally based on a mere search for satisfactions. Parents get divorced; children become alienated. The restoration of the family amid the dangers that beset it is a primary task of Jews if the fabric of Judaism is to endure.

In his work *Centuries of Childhood,* Phillippe Ariés has advanced the theory that the family as we know it in the West did not come into being until the late Renaissance and that even then it was confined to the upper classes, with the rest of the population forming households for the practical purpose of dividing labor and placing children in the world who would add to the support of the unit as soon as they were capable of doing so. If this is correct, then Jews have formed a historic exception.

We can actually trace the emergence of the family among Jews in the events surrounding the life of Abraham, as told us in Scripture.

EMERGENCE OF THE JEWISH FAMILY

Abraham was translated from an urban environment to a rural one, from "Ur of the Chaldeans" to Canaan (Gen. 12:1–7). His homeland, a well-developed culture, was governed by the Code of Hammurabi, whose underlying principle was the protection of property rights. In such an urban surrounding the family could not emerge.

Abraham began his trek as master of a large clan, to which he added new members (Gen. 12:5). It was essential that a large, cooperative unit be created, in which every member had a share in production. Yet Abraham's wife was set apart. She was "Sarai," my princess, mistress of the home and priestess of its spirit. The family became a spiritual unit.

Gradually, layer after layer of self-interest was removed. Lot, Abraham's nephew, who had joined the clan for his own benefit, saw greener pastures for his flock elsewhere and departed (Gen. 13:5–13). Ishmael, Abraham's son, destined to be a hunter and regarding the family as a mere base of operations rather than a workshop of the spirit, had to be removed (Gen. 21:9–21). There remained only the sacred family, father, mother, and son. Isaac was the heir of Abraham's estate, as he was the heir of Abraham's spirit. Sarah had been the mover in Ishmael's expulsion and that of his mother, Hagar, Abraham's concubine. Abraham was told by God:

Whatever Sarah tells you, do as she says. [Gen. 21:12]

The last remaining dross of self-interest was removed in the *Akedah,* the Binding of Isaac (Gen. 22:1–15). The divine entered visibly. Both father and son accepted that their love would find fullest realization through obedience to the will of God. In sacrifice, they would affirm His love from which their own sprang, though His command was as mysterious in claiming a life as it was in permitting it to be created. We know that Isaac was spared and the family reborn in all its mystery, in all its love, and deriving its unity from the divine Being that guided it.

The family stands at the beginning of Jewish history, and throughout the millennia it has not changed its assigned character.

Family Versus Sexuality

When Sarai, "my princess," became Sarah, "*the* princess," she was established as the sacred vessel of the future. She became the prototype of the Jewish wife. Sexuality was to be adjusted to holiness, curbed for the sake of *Taharat ha-Mishpahah,* the purity of the family.

But Jews always had strong sexual urges and were proud of it. It is stated of Moses that even at the time of his death, at an age of 120 years

his eyes were undimmed and his sexual strength had not abated. [Deut. 34:7]

Torah acknowledged these urges by permitting men to marry concubines. Abraham married again after Sarah's death (Gen. 25:1); Jacob had four wives, two of whom were concubines (Gen. 29:14–30). David had several wives and Solomon a multitude.

Extramarital sex was not uncommon. We find Jacob's daughter, Dinah, pregnant out of wedlock (Gen. 34:1–5). Judah, Jacob's son, could not resist the lure of a prostitute (Gen. 35:15ff.).

Worse, David was led to adultery with a married woman, Bathsheba, and there was incest in his family (II Samuel 11–13).

In the time of the Rabbis, polygamy was generally no longer practiced, although it was not formally banned for Ashkenazic Jewry until Rabbenu Gershom of Mainz put it under interdict in the tenth century.

The Rabbis had to struggle with their drives. They were not always successful, and sometimes they were saved only by a supreme act of will or by divine grace (see Kiddushin 81a–b; Avoda Zara 17a). They came to the conclusion:

Temptation attacks the Disciples of the Wise most of all, but everyone may be ensnared by it. [Sukkah 52a]

But temptation had to be removed. How?

The basic solution of the Rabbis was through elimination of contact between the sexes, combined with study of Torah and early marriage.

The heroes of the Bible are depicted as having had strong sexual urges, urges which sometimes ensnared and destroyed them. The story of Samson, as told in the Book of Judges, recounts how he fell in love with the Philistine woman Delilah and how her attractions led him to betray the secret of his own strength (Judges 16). Read metaphorically, this narrative speaks to the issues involved in extramarital relations.

Torah itself was a source of purity. And as study of Torah was to be combined with the pursuit of a livelihood, a man would be left with neither time nor energy for mischief.

Outside of marriage, contact between the sexes was to be reduced to the absolute minimum required for business transactions.

Woman was seen as a temptress, not by design but by nature. Every limb of her body, her hair, her voice in song were "nakedness," indecent exposure (Sukkah 24a). A man should, therefore, not look at a woman or walk between two women or be in a room alone with a woman at any time. He should not talk too much even with his wife (Avot 1:5). Strictly Orthodox Jews abide by all of these rules.

The best solution was *early marriage.* A youth was warned that premarital sex would lead to God's punishment, namely the denial of a worthy wife (Kohelet Rabba 11). At the same time, he was urged to get married early, for God would withdraw His providential care from him were he to wait too long, in those days beyond the age of twenty (Kiddushin 29–30).

Marital Partners

A wife had several functions. She was to give her husband sexual satisfaction, but, more than that, she was to guide and inspire him. She was to be a spiritual force in his life, leading him to Torah. She also had to minister as "princess" by giving her husband children and bringing them up worthily. Her house was to be a sanctuary.

The Rabbis offer some guidelines for the choice of partner.

PHYSICAL SATISFACTION is keyed to beauty and mutual consent. Torah endorses the value of beauty. Rachel, with whom Jacob fell in love at first sight, was "shapely and beautiful"; Leah, whom her cunning father gave to him instead, had "weak eyes" (Gen. 29). Beauty was, therefore, important in a woman (Taanit 24a), and a young man should take warning from Jacob's fate and never marry a girl he had not seen (Kiddushin 41a). Nor could a girl be married off by her father against her wish, as had been done in the past. The girl had to be old enough to express her agreement: "I want this man" (Kiddushin 41a). There had to be reasonable hope that they would give satisfaction to one another.

COMPATIBILITY was of greater importance than beauty. They should complement each other physically (Bekhorot 45b). Ideally, both should come from the same social stratum, but in any event the woman should not be of higher status than the man. They should be of similar age. A father who married off a young daughter to an old man or a mature daughter to a child groom actually turned them into prostitutes (Sanhedrin 76b). Money should not be the decisive factor. A man who married an unworthy woman only for her money would have worthless children (Kiddushin 70a). Materialism would breed marital conflict, affecting home life.

CONCERN FOR WORTHY CHILDREN was the overriding consideration. Worth was more important than beauty. Both partners should truly be suited to each other (Yevamot 63a) that they might rear children on the basis of shared parental values. As the mother was the prime educator of the younger children, her background and upbringing were of primary importance. "Investigate the girl's mother and brothers," was the Rabbis' advice (Ketuvot 43a). Moses was not concerned with his wife's background; he married Ziporah, daughter of a Midianite priest, and his sons did not amount to much. Aaron married the sister of a prince in Israel, and his sons became priests (Bava Kamma 109b–110a).

A young man should make every effort to find the daughter of a *Talmid Hakham*, Disciple of the Wise. Should he die young, she would then be able to bring up the children in the hallowed tradition of her family. A father who married off his daughter to an *Am Ha-Aretz,* an ignorant person, "throws her to the lions" (Pessahim 49b).

If both are worthy, Elijah kisses them and God loves them. [Derekh Eretz 1]

Ultimately, the meeting and matching of a man and a woman were mysteries. God Himself assigned partners.

Every day, a voice is heard from on high: "This person's daughter is destined for this man, and that person's daughter for that man." [Moed Katan 18b]

MARITAL RELATIONS

Sexuality is to be enjoyed, but its goal—the creation of children—may never be forgotten. As a creative act, sex becomes holy. In the course of Jewish history we witness a gradual shift of emphasis from enjoyment to purposiveness in the sex act.

THE ENJOYMENT OF SEX is clearly expressed and sanctioned in the Talmudic statement:

Every man may do with his wife whatever he wishes to do. [Nedarim 20b]

It is reflected in the permission to use contraceptives under certain circumstances such as when a woman is still nursing a child, as her milk might dry out through a new pregnancy (Ketubot 39a). And it is reflected in the fact that a woman could ask for a divorce if her husband consistently denied her sex (Ketubot 61b).

THE CREATIVE PURPOSE OF SEX was, however, paramount. A healthy woman was not permitted the use of contraceptives.

It was felt that Israel should always be conscious of its sacred calling, even during the sex act.

If husband and wife are worthy, the Shekhinah dwells among them [during intercourse], if not, the fire [of passion] will devour them. [Sota 17a]

The rewards for sanctified sex were to be healthy children; the penalties for wanton sex and wanton positions in the act were weak or deformed ones (Nedarim 20a, b; Pessahim 112b).

If he sanctifies himself at the time of intercourse, he will be granted male offspring. [Shavuot 18b]

Under the impact of rabbinic teachings, physical satisfaction came to be more and more devalued. Eventually, Rabbi Joseph Karo, sixteenth-century author of the *Shulhan Arukh*, wished to see intercourse entirely robbed of sensuality.

Every action should be directed toward the service of the Creator. . . . This applies to intercourse, the marital duties ordained in Torah. If he performs them to appease his appetites, or for the enjoyment of his body, he should be ashamed. Even if his intentions are to have children who may later on help him and eventually take his place, he does not act in a praiseworthy manner. His intentions should be to have children who will serve his Creator; or better yet, his intentions should be to fulfill the commandment of marital duty as a man who pays a debt. [Orah Hayim 231:1]

Later, the Hasidim restored sex to a status of dignity. They saw in sexual communion, as man and woman dissolve themselves in each other through love, a refraction of the mystical union that exists between God and His people. God rejoices as His children imitate Him. He doubly rejoices when the act takes place on the Sabbath, the day of His own close communion with Israel.

Sex on Friday night was common in Jewish marriage. Regardless of the view taken of the sex act, be it as intimacy or as sacred performance, Jews never saw it as "dirty," nor would the truly pious ever eschew it. It was permitted on all holy days, forbidden only on days of penitence, such as Yom Kippur, and in mourning, including Tishah b'Av. It was, however, licit only in marriage and at those times when the woman was ritually available to her husband. This will be explained later.

The Duty of Having Children

God created the human being as man and woman and spoke to them: "Be fruitful and multiply" (Gen. 1:27–28). This was the first commandment He gave them. Man is created in God's image; the divine is made manifest in him. A failure on his part to put children into the world diminishes the divine presence in it and sheds the blood of the unborn, whom he denies life (Yevamot 63b).

Israel is God's "treasured possession among all the peoples" (Exod. 19:5). His Shekhinah dwells in the people's multitudes. A Jew failing to have children diminishes the multitude of the people and thus the Shekhinah itself:

If you have children, the Shekhinah rests upon them; if you have no children, upon whom it could rest, on wood and stone perhaps? [Yevamot 63b–64a]

A Jew renouncing children thus forfeits the fullness of life in this world and the rewards in the world to come (Berakhot 10a).

The creation of a family was regarded as so important that a man was urged to dissolve his marriage by divorce if his wife had failed to give him children over a period of ten years (Yevamot 64a).

A married couple was to have as many children as God would grant them. This is followed in Orthodox Jewry. But the Talmud sets a minimum:

Every man is commanded to bring children into the world, at least a son and a daughter. [Yevamot 61b]

Conservative Judaism has held that contraceptive measures may be permitted if this Mitzvah has been fulfilled or other compelling reasons exist.

The *Orthodox* Jew whose wife may have no more children will see his rabbi for counsel in regard to contraception.

Reform Judaism does not restrict the use of contraceptives in any way. The individual couple must be guided by their conscience.

WOMAN'S STATUS IN THE HOME

The great care advised by the Rabbis in the choice of a wife reveals their attitude toward her position in the home.

The husband must recognize that she is his equal, for without her he is nothing (Yevamot 63a). He must support her, love her as he loves himself, and honor her more than he expects to be honored himself. He may never hurt her:

Be concerned about your wife's honor; honor her, for blessing rests upon a home only on account of a man's wife. . . . Exert great care not to hurt your wife. She may weep, as tears come easy to women, and [divine] punishment for the hurt will quickly come to you. [Bava Metzia 59a]

She is his body, his helpmate (Megillah 93b). She guides her husband in all matters of the household (Bava Metzia 59a).

His fate lies in her hands, for better or for worse.

A good wife prolongs her husband's life, a quarrelsome one makes him age before his years, a shrew brings more bitterness into a man's life than death itself. [Yevamot 63a]

To a degree, it depends on him:

If he is a good man, she will be his helpmate, if he is not a good man, she will be his adversary. [Yevamot 63a]

Her dignity rests in her function:

A woman of valor, who can find, for her price is far above rubies.
The heart of her husband does safely trust in her, and he has no lack of gain.
She does him good and not evil all the days of her life.
She seeks wool and flax and works willingly with her hands . . .
She brings food from afar.
She rises while it is yet night and gives food to her household . . .
She considers a field and buys it.
With the fruit of her hands she plants a vineyard.
She girds her loins with strength, and makes strong her arms.
She perceives that her merchandise is good, her lamp does not go out at night.
She lays her hands to the distaff, and her hands hold the spindle.
She stretches out her hand to the poor.
All her household are clothed.
Her husband is known in the gates, when he sits among elders.
She makes linen garments and sells them.
She is robed in strength and dignity.
She opens her mouth with wisdom and the law of kindness is on her tongue.
She looks well to the ways of her household and does not eat the bread of idleness.
Her children rise up and call her blessed; her husband also, and he praises her;
"Many daughters have done valiantly, but you excel them all!"
Grace is deceitful and beauty is vain, but a woman that fears the Lord, she deserves to be praised.
Give her of the fruit of her hands; and let her works praise her in the gates. [Prov. 31:10–31]

The wife's domain was the home; here her rule was absolute. Her power did not extend beyond this domain except as she carried out her husband's business, allowing him "to sit with the elders" in the study of Torah. Her life was not easy, but without her, the operation of the home would collapse.

Changing times have brought new outlooks, and changing conditions have compelled us to reevaluate the traditional role of the

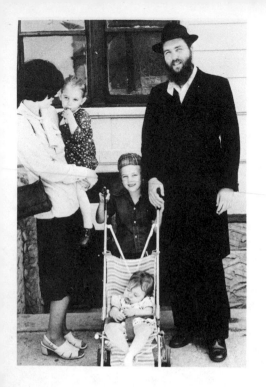

On the sidewalks of New York, a young Orthodox couple proudly pose for a family portrait. The family is central to all Jewish life. In marriage the Biblical command "Be fruitful and multiply" was made sacred.

Jewish woman and bring about those changes that are required by her right to full equality. But we ought to remember that the Jewish wife of the past saw her task as a holy calling. Moreover, the place of the woman in Judaism was secure. Though her husband could divorce her, this happened very rarely. She was part of himself, his flesh, his rib. With her departure, the Shekhinah might depart from the home, and the Temple altar itself would shed tears (Gittin 90b).

FORBIDDEN MARRIAGES, FORBIDDEN SEX

Sex taboos are as old as humanity itself. They emerged from primeval beliefs in supernatural powers, but were primarily motivated by the awareness that a peaceful community could not endure unless a man's wife were protected from encroachment by other men.

Ancient religions included sex acts in their ritual practices, engaging in orgiastic rites and sacred prostitution. Sex and idolatry were closely linked.

Torah therefore introduces sex legislation by the preamble:

I the Lord am your God. You shall not copy the practices of the land of Egypt where you dwelt, or the land of Canaan, to which I am taking you; nor shall you follow their customs. My norms alone shall you observe, and faithfully follow My laws: I the Lord am your God. [Lev. 18:2–4]

It concludes with the words:

Do not defile yourselves in any of those ways, for it is by such that the nations which I am casting out before you defiled themselves. Thus the land became defiled, and I called it to account for its iniquity, and the land spewed out its inhabitants. But you must keep My laws and My norms, and you must not do any of those abhorrent things, neither the citizen nor the stranger who resides among you. . . . All who do any of those abhorrent things—such persons shall be cut off from their people. You shall keep My charge and not engage in any of the abhorrent practices that were carried on before you, lest you defile yourselves through them: I the Lord am your God. [Lev. 18:24–30]

This passage, including a delineation of forbidden sex, is read in Orthodox synagogues on Yom Kippur afternoon. Sex is a holy act and may, therefore, be carried out only in the presence of God. Any practice that recalls the defiling ways of the heathens is forever forbidden. In addition, the creative sex act must in principle be capable of leading to a strengthening of the land through the increase of its inhabitants. It must be of the kind that produces children.

In the passage cited, Torah forbids the following sex relations: with mother, stepmother, sister, half-sister, daughter, stepdaughter, the daughter of the father's wife, the aunt, the uncle's wife, the daughter-in-law. A man is forbidden to have relations with a mother *and* her daughter, even after one of them has died. He may not have relations with two sisters as long as both are still living. A brother's wife is prohibited except when the brother died without offspring. Then the surviving brother must marry his sister-in-law to perpetuate the family. He can escape this obligation through the act of *Halitzah*, now mandatory and universally performed in Orthodoxy according to rabbinic Halakhah in place of the marriage, which in our day is no longer permitted (Deut. 25:5–10). The Rabbis added the following prohibitions: grandmother, grandfather's wife, grandson's wife.

Sexual relations with a married woman are adultery and taint the offspring of such relations, as we shall explain later.

A woman during her menstrual flow is forbidden to her husband; this, too, we shall explain below.

Marriage between cousins or between an uncle and niece is permitted. Sex with a woman incapable of having children or, for a woman, sex with a man incapable of begetting them is permitted.

The decisive factor is the principle. The preamble to the section giving the penalties reads:

You shall sanctify yourselves and be holy, for I the Lord am holy. [Lev. 20:7–21]

Among the abnormal sex activities listed in various parts of Torah we find:

MASTURBATION, the spilling of the seed that denies life to future generations. The perpetrator will be felled by God; he cannot be punished by a human court. Scripture tells us of Onan, who spilled his seed in order not to give children to his brother's widow; God killed him (Gen. 38:9–10). His name has long been attached to the practice of self-gratification: onanism. It must be remembered that Onan's act was motivated by ulterior considerations. By denying children to his brother's widow, he himself stood to inherit a portion of his brother's estate. Rabbinic injunction, however, is based on the act itself and sees it as forbidden by Torah.

INTERCOURSE WITH ANIMALS, practiced by either men or women, is punishable by death (Lev. 20:15–16).

PROSTITUTION was a cultic act; the prostitute, a cultic person. Torah, therefore, directed:

No Israelite woman shall be a cult prostitute, nor shall any Israelite man be a cult prostitute. [Deut. 23:18]

HOMOSEXUALITY was also practiced as a cultic act—possibly by heterosexuals—in heathen worship and was, therefore, forbidden. Hence it was seen as a willful defiance of the natural purpose of sex, the creation of children. It, therefore, became a capital crime for men (Lev. 18:22; 20:13). Women are not mentioned in this connection.

Torah goes even further: the characteristics of men and women may never be blurred, even in dress:

A woman must not put on a man's apparel, nor shall a man wear woman's clothing; for whoever does these things is abhorrent to the Lord your God. [Deut. 22:5]

CONTEMPORARY PROBLEMS

The severe discipline with its sanctions must be understood within the context of the situation at the time. Israel was a small nation, set apart amid a host of pagan peoples. The temptation to follow their ways was strong. As history has shown, the people perished when unity based on faith came to be undermined. Only the most determined self-control, reinforced by severe penalties, could ensure the people's survival. The act of procreation had to be exceptionally pure; any contamination spelled danger for the future.

Under contemporary conditions, many of the acts that Torah prohibits no longer have a religious character. Masturbation, for example, has been recognized as harmless to health, and anyway it is not motivated by the concerns that prompted Onan on the occasion reported in Scripture. Homosexuality, to take another example, is today not at all related to cult. Its causes are complex, but it cannot be regarded as a willful act of religious disobedience. Judaism as such cannot offer formal recognition to the bond that links homosexual persons, nor allow them any special privileges, but it also cannot deny them their Jewishness and the rights and privileges attached to it. As for the prohibitions concerning apparel, this question—raised primarily in Orthodox circles regarding the wearing of pants by women—seems to have resolved itself for most Jews; pants designed for women are women's apparel.

Premarital sex was not approved by Jewish tradition. Parents were advised to chaperone their engaged daughter and were counseled that it was better to free a slave and give him to their daughter in marriage than to expose her to premarital sex. The bachelor who lived in the city and was able to withstand temptation was daily blessed by God (Pessahim 113a).

Holiness called for the exclusive union of one man and one woman. Even polygamy, then permitted, was uncommon, and its practice was discouraged as risky for the spiritual and physical well-being of the family (Avot 2:8; Pessahim 113a). The Rabbis did not approve of a double standard for men and women.

The Jewish sex ethic has been a major force in making us a sanctified people. It has been of paramount importance in shaping our identity and will remain so in the future.

26

The Status of Women in the Religious Community

Historically, Judaism has accorded greater dignity and security to women than any other civilization. At the same time, from its very beginning Judaism has been outspokenly patriarchal. We find in Jewish tradition both expressions of deep respect for women and defamation of them.

There are, for example, two versions in Torah of the creation of woman, one giving her full equality, the other making her subservient to her husband:

And God created man in His image, in the image of God He created him; male and female He created them. [Gen. 1:27]

And the Lord God cast a deep sleep upon the man and he slept; and He took one of his ribs and closed the flesh at that spot. And the Lord fashioned into a woman the rib that He had taken from the man. [Gen. 2:21–22]

The Midrash noticed the two versions and claimed that God actually gave Adam a first wife, a "first Eve," who was equal. Pursued in desire by Adam's son, she returned to dust (Bereshit Rabba 22:8). Mystical tradition elaborated further. The first woman was Lilith. She stood before God, insisting on absolute equality with her husband, as both had been created in the same fashion and at the same time. This demand irritated God. Lilith then uttered the Name of God and became a demon to haunt mankind. In the end she will find her abode in "Edom," the land of Israel's pursuers, now forever laid waste by God's judgment (Isa. 34:14). Lilith strives to reduce man through the power of woman. She inspired the serpent in the Garden of Eden to tempt Eve.

Eve herself, though created from man, showed her superiority and power over her man. She ate of the fruit because

. . . the tree . . . was desirable . . . as a source of wisdom . . . and she gave some to her husband also, and he ate. [Gen. 3:6]

The woman, and not the man, recognized the importance of wisdom; the woman, and not the man, took the initiative; as she gave the fruit to him, he ate without objection. For this deed she was punished. Her place, power, and position were taken away from her:

In pain shall you bear children. Yet your urge shall be for your husband, and he shall rule over you. [Gen. 3:16]

The ascendancy of man over woman is here established. It came about as punishment for Eve's misuse of her power. Thus was patriarchy established.

This patriarchy was the result of a long struggle within early mankind, in which the deity was eventually conceived of as a father. Among many of the ancient religions, the female element, the mother, source of all being in nature, was originally seen as divine. With its repression, the female deities were transformed into demons, and the place of woman came to be devalued. Traces of this struggle may be recognized in the scriptural versions and their Midrashic elaborations.

But Judaism did not entirely exclude the feminine. Speaking of God's indwelling, it uses a feminine term, *Shekhinah*. Divine wisdom is called "our sister" (Prov. 7:4; Sota 11a). Women are thus closer in sensitivity to the presence and wisdom of God than are men (Berakhot 17a). They are superior to men in their loyalty to God (Berakhot 17a).

Through the merit of the loyal women were our forefathers redeemed from Egypt. [Sota 11b]

Judaism came to define the place of woman in conformity with the necessary division of duties in the family.

As duties and functions have changed through history, so has woman's place in society. Considering the spirit of Judaism, we may consider it fundamentally hospitable to recognition of women's equality.

WOMEN IN THE BIBLE

Jews believed that the position of woman was ordained by God, as was that of man in the scheme of the universe. Orthodoxy maintains this stance to this day.

If woman's place was established by divine decree, woman's endowment was not inferior to that of man. The wives of the patriarchs generally have much greater insight than their husbands; they are strong women. Moses' sister Miriam is an organizer and leader (see Exod. 15:20). Deborah acquires fame and distinction as a military leader and as the people's chief magistrate (Judg. 4–5). Huldah was a prophetess, sought out by the leaders of the people (II Kings 22:14–20). Esther was a courageous and highly skilled politician.

The case of the daughters of Zelafhad deserves special note. They were highly capable attorneys in their own case, pleading before Moses. Their father had no male heir; were they to be denied a share in the distribution of the land, because they were women? Moses did not know and had to consult God. He was told that the girls were to have their share, but were to marry cousins on their father's side, in order that the real estate remain within the clan (Num. 27:1–5; 36:6–13). The divine decision established a very important precedent: women are not chattel.

CONDITIONS DETERIORATE

In Temple days, when most of the people were farmers, work in the field brought men and women together. On the fifteenth of Av and on Yom Kippur, they met in the vineyards and in dance and merrymaking chose their partners.

Then a new ideal was established: the scholar replaced the farmer. The scholar had no contact with women. A young man had to be educated to honor and love his wife, but also to suppress the desire for women. Hence the formula, "Blessed are You, God, . . . Who has not made me a woman."

The Rabbis said: Four characteristics can be found in women: they are gluttons, eavesdroppers, lazy, and spiteful. Rabbi Judah ben Nehemiah added: they are also excitable and talkative; Rabbi Levi added: they are also thieving and run-abouts (Bereshit Rabba 45a). From childhood to the brink of the grave they deck themselves out and make themselves up and always follow the sound of any drum that invites to fun and merrymaking (Moed Katan 9b). Their yearning is for jewelry (Ketuvot 65a). This was cruel prejudice, stereotyping, most likely based on individual experience, but it had its tragic effects.

As time went on, women became more withdrawn from public life; laws and ordinances were imposed on them by the Rabbis and their successors.

Legislation Promotes Segregation

Originally, women were relieved from all those Mitzvot that called for an act of performance at a given point in time. They were not relieved from any prohibitions. The rule made sense. Women might not be able to put on Tallit and Tefillin when they were preoccupied with nursing or training their children. They might not be able to go to the Sukkah during late stages of pregnancy. But being relieved did not mean being prohibited. If they so wished, they could perform the Mitzvah. Early in history, women insisted that two of these Mitzvot be made obligatory for them: hearing the shofar on Rosh Hashanah and shaking the lulav on Sukkot. As for the rest of these Mitzvot, eventually women were *prohibited* from performing most of them.

The Women's Gallery

At the end of the first day of Sukkot, a great celebration took place in the "Court of Women" within the Temple precincts. Everybody came.

In the beginning, the women sat inside the court, the men outside. This lead to levity. It was therefore ordained that the men should sit inside and the women outside [their court]. But levity continued. It was therefore ordained that the women were to sit upstairs [in a gallery], the men downstairs . . . a gallery was built and the women were ordered upstairs, the men downstairs. [Sukkah 51b]

A modern "Women's Gallery" separated from the men's section by the *mehitzah* wall and screen. The original purpose of this separation was to avoid "levity" occasioned by the presence of women in the men's line of sight.

Later generations ordered a *mehitzah,* a wall, or at least a screen, hiding women from men. In the medieval synagogue of Worms, a complete wall separated the sexes. It had only a small window at which one of the women followed the service and sang it for her sisters.

The women's gallery and mehitzah are still required in Orthodox synagogues.

Prohibition against Studying Torah

As Eve's wisdom had not benefited her husband, it was considered desirable to exclude women from the study of Torah, although this Mitzvah is timeless and incumbent on all Jews. Support was found in Scripture; in speaking of Tefillin, Torah states as a reason for the wearing of them:

in order that God's Torah be in your mouth. [Exod. 13:9]

As the Mitzvah of Tefillin is not incumbent on women, the study of Torah is also not incumbent on them, it was held. Torah further states:

Teach them [the words of Torah] diligently unto your sons. [Deut. 11:19]

"The sons are included, the daughters excluded" (Kiddushin 29b). The Rabbis were not unanimous in their ruling, however. Some held that study of Torah was meritorious for women, whereas according to others:

He who permits his daughter to study Torah teaches her ways of licentiousness. [Sota 20a]

In modern Judaism, many of the restrictions placed on women, some instituted for superstitious reasons and some because of stereotypical thinking on the part of men, have been lifted. In non-Orthodox settings, new customs prevail: Women study Talmud, participate in the reading of the Torah, and take active roles in the prayer ritual.

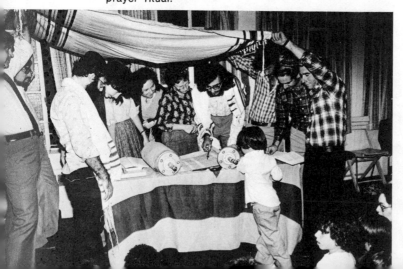

A compromise was eventually reached. Girls in the shtetl learned prayers, perhaps some portions of Scripture, and they had to be thoroughly trained in the regulations of Kashrut. But in the synagogue women used a book of meditations written in Yiddish. As for the Talmud, that was closed to women on principle. The exclusion of women from the study of Talmud has been removed even in some Orthodox circles. Among non-Orthodox Jewry, women have even become teachers of Talmud.

Prayer, Kiddush, Grace After Meals, Mezuzah

According to the Talmud, prayer, Kiddush, Grace after meals, and mezuzah are obligatory on women (see Berakhot 20b for some of the discussions surrounding these rulings).

Being Called to the Torah

The Rabbis taught:

Everyone is (called to the Torah on the Sabbath, and entitled to read his portion aloud to the congregation, if he is capable) even a minor and a woman. But the sages stated that a woman may not read publicly from the Torah in consideration of the dignity of the congregation. [Megillah 23a]

The "dignity of the congregation" was hurt if a person of inferior status (or unsuitably attired) became its Torah reader (Megillah 24b). It would be hurt if a woman read from the Torah. As she would have been excluded from the study of Torah and the men were committed to it, it reflected ill on a congregation if a woman showed a knowledge many men did not possess. Similarly, it was considered a disgrace for a man, if his wife or minor son had to recite Grace after meals for him, as he was incapable of doing so (Berakhot 20b).

The injunction against Aliyot for women thus rested on their exclusion from the study of Torah, no longer in effect. Though women may not be called up in Orthodox congregations, they may be called up in non-Orthodox congregations, as there are no reasons for their exclusion. The state of Niddah does not impede women's contact with Torah, as Torah is immune to human impurities (Berakhot 22a). The codes have so ruled; only Minhag imposed restrictions.

Wearing the Tallit

According to Halakhah, women may wear the Tallit. In Talmudic discussion the Rabbis taught all are [even] *obligated* to [put on] Tzitzit, priests, Levites, Israelites, proselytes, women. . . . According to Rabbi Simon they are relieved of this *obligation* for it is a special commandment, linked to a special time (Menahot 43a). It is recorded that Rabbi Judah the Prince made Tzitzit for the apron of his wife. But later on it was ruled:

It would not be appropriate for women to do so. A man need not put on Tzitzit, except if he wears a four-cornered garment. Women should not try to surpass their husbands by deliberately wearing such a garment with Tzitzit. [Orah Hayim: Halkhot Tzitzit 17:2]

Of course, women may wear a four-cornered garment without Tzitzit, as this is a commandment of performance, linked to daytime only. They are forbidden in Orthodoxy to wear Tzitzit, but are not forbidden to do so among non-Orthodox Jewry.

Putting on Tefillin

According to Halakhah, women may put on Tefillin. The Talmud relates that King Saul's daughter Michal put on Tefillin and the Rabbis did not object to it (Erubin 96a). Later on, however, it was ruled:

but we bar them from doing so. [Orah Hayim: Hilkhot Tefillin 38:3]

One reason given was that they were not as concerned with physical cleanliness as were men, and Tefillin have to be worn on a clean body. This certainly cannot be said of women today, if it was ever justified. Non-Orthodox Jewry permits women to wear Tefillin.

Forming a Minyan

Women do form a Minyan on one occasion. In the case of recovery from grave illness or rescue from grave danger, a blessing is to be recited before a Minyan. It is called *Birkhat Ha-Gomel,* "the Blessing of Him, Who has Accorded [great goodness]." Men speak the blessing after being called to the Torah in public reading. Women form their own Minyan for the occasion, but on no other occasion.

Being a Shohet

Women may serve as Shohet. This is clearly stated in the Mishnah (Hulin 1:1). The Shulhan Arukh declares:

We do not permit it. [Yoreh Deah: Hilhot Shehitah 1]

No reason is given.

Most recently, the Reform and Reconstructionist movements have ordained women as rabbis, and in 1979 the Conservative movement created a mechanism for doing so, though as yet no woman has been admitted to study for the rabbinate in a Conservative seminary.

RESTORATION OF RIGHTS

As early as the 1920s, the great Rabbi Anton Nehemiah Nobel of Frankfurt succeeded in gaining acceptance of a woman as candidate for a membership on the board of his Orthodox congregation, something never before regarded as sanctioned by tradition.

The women's gallery has been abolished in non-Orthodox congregations, not merely to meet a claim for equality but in order to deepen the spirit of the family through worship as a unit.

The right to study Torah and Talmud and to teach it has been restored to women in non-Orthodox Jewry, as we have seen.

Women have claimed the privilege of being *called up to the Torah, to read it in public, and to lead worship*. This may "go against the grain" of many older congregation members, but is actually a right held by women in ancient days. Many non-Orthodox congregations have restored these rights to women.

Based on ancient Halakhah, women would be permitted to *wear Tallit and Tefillin*.

As they have a Minyan on one occasion and as they are permitted to read the Torah, women can claim the right to *conduct their own service* in a form identical to the men's worship.

Non-Orthodox movements have gone beyond Halakhah. They

275

have eliminated passages from the prayer book that they regard as derogatory of women.

Counting women in the Minyan has become a practice in a number of congregations within Conservative Judaism. Reconstructionism follows the contemporary approach throughout and has often spearheaded it. The Talmud does not specify males; the Shulhan Arukh does so specify (Orah Hayim 55:1). It can be argued that whereas women stand under the obligation of prayer, as do men, women are therefore entitled to be counted as constituents of a "congregation." Reform does not require a Minyan.

Certification of women for the function of Shohet can be based on the explicit approval of the Talmud (Hulin 2a–b).

Certification of women for the function of Mohel rests on Torah itself. Ziporah, Moses' wife, circumcised her sons (Exod. 4:24–26). This may be of significance in appointing a Jewish woman pediatrician as Mohel.

Ordination of women as rabbis has become a reality in the Reconstructionist and Reform movements and was advocated in 1979 by the Conservative movement on the basis of evolving Halakhah.

The movement toward equality for women will mean that women, in addition to acquiring rights, will also acquire new duties. Judaism may have to provide opportunities under religious sanction for those who wish to have them. This may grow to include even those women who today desire no change.

27

Marriage:
Cornerstone
of Life

At his B'rit, a boy is sent into the world accompanied by three wishes: may he enter a life of Torah, a life in marriage, and a life of good deeds. Instruction in Torah begins immediately, and Bar Mitzvah publicly initiates him into full responsibility under Torah. Grown to manhood, he enters the second stage: marriage. A Jew is to marry, for only in marriage can he truly fulfill the Mitzvah of procreation. Yet marriage means more: it is life itself.

A man who has no wife is doomed to an existence without joy, without blessing, without experiencing life's true goodness, without Torah, without protection, and without peace. [Yevamot 62b]

Celibacy is not a virtue in Judaism. The High Priest had to be married in order to carry out his functions in the Temple on Yom Kippur. He had to invoke God's pardon and effect purification "for himself and for *his house*" (Lev. 16:6).

His house, his wife, she is his house. [Yoma 2a]

A Jew without a wife is homeless.

ACQUIRING A WIFE

Torah provides directives from which the Rabbis developed the legal forms of marriage. As in many ancient societies, a father had

277

A traditional Ketubah, or marriage contract, delineating the mutual obligations between husband and wife. Among its provisions is the exact amount of money to be paid to the bride in the event of her bridegroom's death or of his divorcing her. Especially among Sephardim (Jews of Spanish-Portuguese origin), the Ketubah was often highly ornamented and decorated with intricate and colorful designs.

the right to marry off his daughter in her childhood. The husband paid for her (see Deut. 22:16). It was, therefore, concluded that a grown woman could equally be acquired by a monetary transaction. The father could force his minor daughter to have sexual relations with the man to whom he had given her. Hence, the sex act constituted a legally binding marriage for adults as well. But Torah gives details about divorce.

He shall write her a bill of divorcement. . . . [Deut. 24:1]

From this statement the Rabbis deduced that marriage, dissolvable through written document, is equally contracted through such a document (see Kiddushin 2a–5aff.). They therefore ruled:

A woman is acquired in [one of] three ways, and acquires herself [as an unattached person] in [one of] two ways. She is acquired through money, contract, and sexual intercourse. She acquires herself through a bill of divorcement or through the death of her husband. [Kiddushin 1:1]

Marriage was a legal transaction. It gave the man an exclusive right over the woman, who was henceforth set aside only for him and was no longer available to anyone else. This is the original meaning of the term *Kiddushin,* to be set aside.

Evolution in Practice

Originally, a marriage could be entered into very simply. Both partners agreed to be married to each other. The man gave the woman either money or something of value. Or he might hand her a scrap of paper, on which he had written his agreement to marry her; she accepted it and became his wife. They might even consummate their marriage through sexual intercourse. Witnesses would have to attest any of these acts.

Gradually, a change took place. Rav, the great master, ordered those who legalized their marriage by intercourse to be flogged; the marriage was valid, but the method was not in accord with Jewish ideals. The marriage contract became formalized. It included stipulations for settlement in financial terms if the man died or divorced his wife. Above all, it spelled out the duties of the husband:

I will work for you, I will honor you, I will support you, as is seeming for a Jewish husband. For you, I will take my shirt off my back.

This was the *Ketubah*, the written contract.

In line with a tradition going back to Torah, the vows that bound a couple were spread over a lengthy period of time, usually a year. As a first step, the couple became betrothed. This was more than a mere engagement. It was a binding agreement that could be dissolved only through a bill of divorcement, a *Get*, but it did not confer any marital rights upon the man. The purpose of the betrothal was to give the young woman ample time to prepare her trousseau, unencumbered by worries that she might lose her fiancé.

The term *Kiddushin* acquired a new and deeper meaning. Gifts, donated to the Temple, became "set aside," or "holy" (Kiddushin 2b). Kiddushin became sanctification. The legal transaction, though necessary, had been transcended in holiness.

This was given expression by the Berakhot, the blessings at the marriage rites. After the legal proceedings have been concluded, the divine is invoked, that God may dwell upon the couple and their home and bestow His blessing upon them.

The three legal acts were combined: the ring represents the valuable; the Ketubah, a contract; and *Yihud*, being alone with each other, which is practiced in Orthodoxy, represents consummation. Non-Orthodox Jewry is satisfied with the symbolic expression of the wedding canopy, which represents the oneness of the couple under the same roof.

BETROTHAL AND ENGAGEMENT

In Talmudic days, the *formal betrothal* that bound the couple under Jewish law was a joyful celebration. The home of the girl's parents was splendidly decked out, and the groom formally expressed his pledge by giving a gift to his bride or by performing

In Orthodox and some Conservative ceremonies, the bride's face is covered before the groom is admitted to the anteroom in which she sits. The veil is lifted when the bridegroom enters, only to be replaced by him after he has repeated the ritual words announcing his approval of the bride.

some work for her; in accepting his pledge, she expressed her agreement to enter the bond. The knot was tied by a blessing of God over the cup of wine. In it, the status of the couple was firmly impressed upon them:

Blessed are You . . . He, Who has commanded us concerning forbidden relations, prohibiting us the betrothed women, the *arusot* [as partners in sex], permitting us the married, the *nesuot,* ours through *Huppah* and Kiddushin [which will follow later]. Blessed are You . . . He, Who sanctifies His people Israel through Huppah and Kiddushin.

This benediction now is part of the wedding rites.

In the shtetl, an *engagement* occurred after protracted negotiations between the families. Parents would either seek the services of a professional matchmaker, a *shadchen,* or of the rabbi or go out themselves in search of a suitable mate for their son or daughter. Yihus was of great concern; health was important; good looks were an asset. Money, too, played a significant role for a girl's parents. The lack of it might bring to nought an otherwise suitable match. When a daughter was born, the parents would begin right away to save up for her dowry.

The young people had little to say in all of this. They met but a few times. If they developed an unsurmountable aversion to each other, they would make it known, but in principle it was the parents who selected their children's partners. Love would come later, in marriage.

The formal engagement began with the signing of the *tannaim,* "conditions," setting the amount of the dowry but also providing for penalties that the prospective groom was obligated to pay should the marriage fail to materialize. The engagement had no religiously binding force.

The high point of the engagement celebration was the breaking of a plate. It had been prepared ahead of time by friends and relatives and painted in gay colors. Now it was smashed on the ground. Israel's shattered glory, the ruined Temple, dimmed every joy. There may be pagan roots: noise expels demons, loss appeases jealous gods.

During the engagement period, gifts were exchanged. The bride might give the groom a Tallit or make his kittel, which, sometimes, he would wear under the Huppah and which would be his robe on the Days of Awe and his garment in death. It beautifully expressed the sentiment that

Love is strong as death. [Song of Songs 8:6]

The groom might give the bride an engagement ring. In western Europe, he would present her with a prayer book, artistically bound in silk or velvet, in which would be recorded in later years the names of their children.

The groom bought the wedding ring, which he would place on her finger under the Huppah. As the woman does not "acquire" her husband, she did not have to get a ring for him. Traditional Judaism does not have a double-ring ceremony.

As the wedding day approached, showers were given for the bride-to-be. At this occasion, the girl's hair might be cropped. The reason? The faithful woman does not show her hair; only wantons do so (based on Num. 5:18). The Rabbis had also stated that a woman's hair is "nakedness," which only her husband was to see. From now on, her head was covered by a cap. (In the modern period, when Jews ventured out into the world, women began to wear wigs instead. Today, many Orthodox women see no reason for covering their heads with cap *or* wig, although they will cover their head in worship and when lighting the Sabbath candles.)

When and Where to Hold the Wedding

A marriage cannot be performed on a Sabbath or festival when legal transactions are not permitted. It cannot be performed on the half-holidays of Pessah and Sukkot on the principle that "we should not mix joy with joy," that of the festival and that of a wedding (Moed Katan 1:7). Similarly, there are certain periods of mourning during the year when—under ordinances established in later periods —marriage may not be solemnized.

The rites may be performed on any weekday, during daytime or at night, but not during twilight hours when the date might actually change if night falls while the ceremony is in progress.

Weddings may be performed in the synagogue, the home, or a hall. It was once common custom to conduct them in the open, often in the courtyard of the synagogue. The stars would then shine upon the couple, and their marriage be blessed with offspring as numerous and bright as the stars (Gen. 15:5).

From this practice the Huppah may have developed, as a kind of booth separating the wedding circle from the hustle of the street. Today we always use the Huppah; it is a symbol of the Jewish wedding.

The Wedding Day

On the Sabbath before his wedding, the groom is called to the Torah, a special hymn is sung in his behalf, and he is given a special blessing.

On the eve of the momentous day, groom and bride exchange the gifts they have prepared for each other.

The woman goes to the Mikvah, the ritual bath.

On the day itself, bride and groom are to fast until after the ceremony. Reviewing their life, they recite the great confession of sins, as on Yom Kippur. If a wedding is held on Hanukah or Rosh Hodesh, fasting is not required.

In the shtetl, the groom was met at his home early in the morning and escorted to the synagogue, where he was given a seat of honor. If Torah was read, he was called up. He was then escorted home, dressed in his best, to await the musicians who would lead the parade to the synagogue.

In some communities, groom and bride were given precious belts, made of gold links, which they wore for this occasion.

The bride, dressed in white, wearing her veil but leaving her face uncovered, waited in her home for the musicians to lead her and her party to her meeting with the groom.

The belief that the groom may not see the bride before the wedding is a superstition. Actually, he should see her. We remember that Laban deceived Jacob, his son-in-law, by giving him a veiled woman, whom Jacob naturally assumed to be his beloved Rachel. It was Leah (Gen. 29:16–26). The groom, therefore, looks at his bride and then places the veil over her head.

THE WEDDING CEREMONY

The ceremony is almost identical in all branches of Judaism. Conservative and Reform rites omit some of the features.

The *Synagogue* is brightly lit. Men and women assemble in the men's section, even in orthodox synagogues.

The *Huppah* stands in the center of the Bimah.

KINYAN SUDDER. In the anteroom, the groom is attended by witnesses as he performs "the acquisition through a cloth." We are reminded that a wedding is a legal transaction, the acceptance of obligations. In modern trade, an agreement is frequently sealed by a handshake. In ancient Israel, it was sealed by passing a piece of cloth from seller to buyer. The witnesses represent the bride. One of them holds a handkerchief. The groom takes it from him and raises it. The transaction has been formally completed. Sometimes the groom merely raises the corner of a witness's jacket. This ceremony is omitted in Conservatism and Reform.

BEDECKEN. The groom meets the bride in her room, where she is surrounded by her women attendants. He looks at her, then takes her veil and places it over her face, speaking:

O sister! May you grow into thousands of myriads. [Gen. 24:60—origin of veil: Gen. 24:65]

This ceremony is omitted in Reform and often in Conservatism.

THE WITNESSES. Two men (in non-Orthodox Jewry also women), not related to either bride or groom or to each other, serve as witnesses. They have to sign the Ketubah and should be able to write their names in Hebrew. The officiating rabbi can be a witness at the same time. Rabbi and witnesses now ascend the Bimah.

THE PROCESSION. The groom now enters the synagogue, escorted by his father and the bride's father. He is followed by the bride, escorted by her mother and the groom's mother. Both parents stand next to their children during the ceremony.

In modern days, wedding processions with ushers and bridesmaids have become customary. But if the parents wish it, they should be permitted to lead their children into the sanctuary and stand at their sides. This is a moment for which they have waited for years, the day when they "lead their child under the Huppah."

CIRCLING THE GROOM. A custom not widely practiced is circling the groom. The groom stands under the Huppah; the bride walks around him. In doing so, she shows that she has understood Jeremiah's injunction:

The woman shall surround the man. [Jer. 31:21]

The bride may be accompanied by the two mothers. She sometimes circles the groom seven times, thereby entering symbolically into the very core of her husband's soul, through "the seven shells" that surround it.

The Huppah may be simple or elaborate. In either case, it forms a sacred space within which the ceremony of Kiddushin is carried out.

Standing Under the Huppah

The couple now stand side by side under the Huppah, the groom at the bride's left. This will make it easier to put the ring on the index finger of her right hand.

THE WELCOME is spoken by the Rabbi in the words of the Psalm (118:26) and followed by a brief prayer for the couple's blessing. The question: "Do you take . . ." may be added here to satisfy the law of the state; it is not required by Judaism, as the man and the woman obviously have arrived by their own free will.

An address may be offered here or at some other part of the ceremony.

BIRKOT ERUSIN. The act of *betrothal* now is performed; the blessings are spoken by the rabbi over a cup of wine. The rabbi then gives the cup to the father of the groom, who puts it to his son's lips. The groom drinks. The father then gives the cup to his wife, who places it at the lips of the bride. She drinks. In symbolic action, groom and bride share the cup. If the parents do not join the couple on the Bimah, the maid of honor lifts the bride's veil, and the rabbi passes the cup first to the groom, then to the bride. This ceremony is often omitted in Reform.

THE RING is the item of value that the groom gives to the bride, and she accepts it. The rabbi once again shows the ring to the witnesses at his side; they make sure that it is an item of value. As they watch, the groom places the ring on the index finger of his bride's right hand and repeats after the rabbi the following formula:

Harei at mekudeshet li be-tabba'at zu ke-dat Mosheh ve-Yisrael.
Be you consecrated unto me by this ring, in accordance with the laws of Moses and Israel.

Even if the groom knows the formula, he must repeat it after the rabbi word for word, in order not to put to shame those who may not be able to remember it. Only the word *li*—"unto me"—is not prompted by the rabbi; there must be no doubt who speaks this decisive word.

In accepting the ring, the woman becomes the man's wife. If there is to be a double-ring ceremony, it has only sentimental value. As the bride places her ring on the groom's finger, she might recite the same words he has spoken, but in their masculine form. An often-used formula expresses her emotions:

Ani le-dodi, ve-dodi li
I belong to my beloved, my beloved belongs to me. [Song of Songs 6:3]

THE KETUBAH.   Orthodox rabbis now read the entire Ketubah, the marriage contract in its traditional form; Conservative

The wedding ceremony complete, the couple walks down the aisle in their new roles as husband and wife.

rabbis may read all or part of it; Reform has replaced it by a simple marriage certificate. The Ketubah is signed by the witnesses, not by the groom and bride. It is handed to the bride, whose rights are spelled out in it. Later on, it should be put in a safe place; it may be used in the future as a document certifying to the religious wedding.

THE SEVEN BLESSINGS. The legal acts have been performed; now God's blessing is invoked upon the couple. The rabbi (or cantor) raises the cup of wine and gives thanks to God:

for the fruit of the vine;
for creating the universe
for creating human beings;
for creating human beings in His image, in such fashion that they in turn can create life;
for His grace, as He will make Zion joyful again through [the return of] her children;
for making groom and bride joyful; may He bring gladness to them as He brought it to His creatures in the Garden of Eden;
for Him, who as Source of all joy is implored to restore speedily to the cities of Judah and the streets of Jerusalem
    the voice of mirth and the voice of joy;
    the voice of groom and the voice of bride . . .
    Blessed are You, Lord, You are He, Who makes
        the groom rejoice with the bride.

Through God "the groom rejoices with the bride." This is the only allusion to the joys of sex. It is otherwise not mentioned. But here at the end of the Kiddushin, it holds a deeper meaning. God is *Mekadesh Yisrael*, He Who sanctifies Israel. God Himself is bound to Israel by a bond of "marriage," Kiddushin. This marriage will be

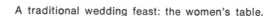

A traditional wedding feast: the women's table.

fully consummated when Israel has returned to "the cities of Judah and the streets of Jerusalem." May God bring this "wedding day" soon, and may the young couple be among those who will live to see it. *The cup is passed* to the couple in the same manner as before. They drink from it. From now on, they will share the cup of life together. May it be a "cup of salvation."

The Reform version of the Seven Blessings may vary from the traditional one.

THE PRONOUNCEMENT.   In order to meet the requirements of the state, the rabbi will now pronounce the couple to be husband and wife. He may conclude with the Biblical benediction: the Lord bless you. . . .

THE GLASS.   At the end of the ceremony, the groom steps on a glass, usually wrapped in a napkin, and breaks it. The whole assembly bursts forth: *Mazel tov,* may you stand under a good constellation! Noise had expelled evil forces.

Judaism has tied the breaking of the glass to the last of the Seven Blessings. First we express our hope that Zion may soon be restored to the Jewish people; now we express our sorrow that the day has not yet come. Our joy is diminished, as we mourn for Jerusalem and call to mind the agonies of our people.

THE RECESSIONAL is not bound to any traditional tune; yet it should be Jewish. The custom of showering the couple with rice is derived from ancient fertility rites.

YIHUD.   In Orthodoxy, the couple is led to a room in the building. The door is guarded by the witnesses. The guests are told that the newlyweds are breaking their fast, which they are doing. But the reason for Yihud is to provide the setting for the consumma-

A traditional wedding feast: the men's table.

tion of the marriage. The opportunity as such, watched over by the witnesses, is sufficient. All three ways of entering a binding marriage have thus been met: the ring, the contract, the "coming to each other."

The Wedding Feast

The Jewish wedding feast is a celebration beyond compare. The Rabbis ruled that even the study of Torah has to be interrupted in order to bring joy and honor to newlyweds (Ketuvot 17b). We are to dance before the bride and extol her beauty.

How do we celebrate the bride? The School of Shammai said: "According to her endowments." The School of Hillel said: "[One must always exclaim:] Beautiful and lovely bride!" The School of Shammai asked the School of Hillel: "What shall we do, if she is lame or blind, can we say about her 'a beautiful lovely bride,' does not Torah direct: 'Keep away from any lie'?" To which the School of Hillel replied: "In your opinion, if a person has purchased some bad merchandise in the marketplace, shall we make the merchandise look good to him by praising it, or shall we disparage it, and make it look bad to him? We surely ought to praise it." [Ketuvot 17a]

Rabbi Samuel bar Rabbi Yitzhak used to dance and juggle three [myrtle twigs]. [Watching,] R. Zera [indignantly] exclaimed: "This old man, look at him, he really makes us lose face!" Eventually, he was vindicated by a miracle, endorsing his actions.

R. Aha took the bride on his shoulders and danced with her. His disciples asked him. "May we do the same?" He replied: "If she is to you like a beam [and does not arouse you], you may, otherwise you may not." [Ketuvot 17a]

The poems recited by Western Jewry, the jokes of the jester in the shtetl—all rest on Talmudic precedents.

The dancing reminds us of Simhat Torah. Then Torah is the bride, those called to witness the reading represent the congregation as "grooms," and those who dance with it and around it feel pure joy.

In the shtetl no wedding could be with *klezmerim,* musicians. Men danced around the groom, women around the bride, and both, in the end, took them on their shoulders. If men danced with women, they would never touch; holding on to the corners of a handkerchief, the partners moved in the rhythms of the music without coming into bodily contact.

The word of Torah was never absent. Learned guests, sometimes the groom himself, offered Talmudic discourses.

Grace after dinner was opened with special thanksgiving and concluded with the Seven Blessings previously recited under the Huppah.

Joy and dancing mark the wedding celebration, just as they mark the holiday of Simhat Torah. All brides were considered beautiful and dancing
before the bride, an act of piety.

The traditional Jewish wedding lasted seven days, as Jacob had
feasted for seven days according to rabbinical interpretation of the
word of Scripture (Gen. 29:27). The couple did not go on a
honeymoon (see Chapter 28, "The Laws Affecting Women").

28

Issues Relating to Marriage

CONTEMPORARY PROBLEMS

Interfaith Marriage

The union in marriage of two people, one of whom is not a Jew by birth or conversion, endangers the very fabric of Judaism. It increases the risk of an eventual breakup of the marriage, as the unifying bond of a common faith is missing. It may create psychological problems of guilt in the marriage partners and may create similar problems in their children, who do not know where they belong and are denied the experience of a true Jewish home, to which both parents are committed in a Jewish marriage.

Can a rabbi officiate at such a union or participate in it in conjunction with a Christian clergyman? Can he do so if the couple pledge to raise their future children as Jews? Orthodox, Conservative, and Reconstructionist rabbis are forbidden to take any part in such marriage rites; Reform rabbis are discouraged from doing so. Most rabbis are prohibited from participation by the voice of their own conscience. Some Reform rabbis, however, have felt that they should officiate because rejecting a couple might bar any future hope that their children will be raised as Jews, whereas acquiescing might perhaps even lead to the eventual conversion of the non-Jewish partner.

Why are rabbis asked to solemnize interfaith marriages? A primary reason is the distress of the young Jew's parents at seeing him or her marry outside the Jewish faith. But an accommodation merely disguises the realities. Christians are married "in the name of the Father, the Son, and the Holy Spirit"; Jews are married "in accordance with the law of Moses and Israel." Whether or not these words are used, they are the foundation of the marriage bond. The marriage may be valid under the laws of the state; the religious ceremony, however, will rest on a self-deception.

We should understand the agony of parents on both sides. But we must recognize that the formality of "having a rabbi" offers no solution and may rather tend to disguise reality. It should be remembered that a couple civilly married can always adjust their religious allegiances, whereas a wedding performed by a rabbi may lull the couple into a sense of rightness that can preclude continued search and possible solution.

The couple should realize that the rabbi who refuses to solemnize their marriage has acted under the compulsion of his conscience, not for personal reasons. He will always stand ready to be their counselor and guide in all the issues of life.

Birth Control

The Mitzvah of procreation is basic (Gen. 1:28). Our need to increase is great, lest we become an "endangered species," considering the heavy losses inflicted on Jewry over the last centuries, and especially in this century.

As we have seen, the Rabbis permitted contraception under certain circumstances, but not under normal conditions. Today's parents may wish to limit their families, especially after having fulfilled the Mitzvah of having one son and one daughter. Orthodoxy permits the use of the pill, as it does not interfere with the natural process of insemination. Should other methods be required, the couple should see their rabbi. Conservative Jewry is permissive in regard to the use of other contraceptives. Reform Jewry places the decision entirely with the conscience of the individual.

Surgical interventions are regarded as a mutilation of the body and are not permitted by traditional Judaism.

Adoption

Adoption, as we know it, did not exist in Talmudic times. But the Rabbis declared:

He who raises an orphaned child is regarded by Torah as if he had given birth to the child. [Megillah 13a; Sanhedrin 19b]

The child bears the name of son or daughter of the adoptive father, though the child does not become a Kohen or Levi if the adoptive father belongs to either of these castes. By this name he or she is called to the Torah and inscribed in the Ketubah.

Adopted children mourn for their adoptive parents, and say Kaddish for them. They are the child's true parents.

If the adopted child is not Jewish, he or she has to be converted.

Abortion

All branches of Judaism oppose abortion for convenience, especially as many childless Jewish couples are waiting eagerly for a child to adopt.

Abortion for therapeutic reasons, when the mother's life is clearly in danger, is *mandatory* in Judaism. Her life takes absolute precedence over the potential life of the fetus, even at the very latest stages of development, as late as birth itself (Ohalot 7:6). The fetus is regarded as *potential* life, but not as full life, until late in the process of birth. We find the same in the ruling of Torah. A man who pushes a pregnant woman inadvertently, causing her to miscarry, is liable for damages, but not sued for involuntary manslaughter. If the *mother* were to die, the person causing her death would be sued for involuntary manslaughter (Exod. 21:22–23).

Abortion has become a significant issue in American life. For this reason we wish to quote some of the basic statements by Talmud and its interpreters—for information and insight only. The Talmud states:

If a woman has grave hardship in giving birth, we are to dissect the child in her womb and bring it out piece by piece, for her life takes precedence over its life. Has the greater part [of the child] emerged, we may not touch it, for we may not take one life for another life. [Ohalot 7:6]

If the head has emerged, we may not touch [the child]. But is [the child] not a pursuer (if a person pursues another to kill the other, we may kill the pursuer first, is this not the case here)? In this situation, God is the pursuer. [Sanhedrin 72b]

Rashi, in commenting on this passage, explains:

We are speaking of a woman who has grave hardship in giving birth and is in danger of life; as long as the [child's] head has not emerged, the midwife may extend her hand and cut the fetus, bringing it out in pieces, for as long as it has not emerged into the world, it is not a human being [literally: *nefesh*—soul], and it is in our power to kill it, in order to save its mother. But once the head has emerged, we may not touch it to kill it, for then it is regarded as having been born and we may not give preference to one life over another.

In a lucid responsum, "Teshuvah on Abortion" (*Conservative Judaism and Jewish Law*, pp. 258 ff.), Rabbi Isaac Klein has dealt with differences of opinions among the masters, whether or not the fetus is to be regarded as a person. Maimonides and the Shulhan Arukh seem to hold that way. There is no question that the life of the mother must be saved. There is, however, an issue, whether abortion may be permitted for other reasons. If we assume, as Rashi does, that the foetus is not a human being at any time until birth, we shall arrive at conclusions of wider latitude. Rashi has the cited ruling of Scripture itself as an endorsement.

Other rabbis make a distinction between the various *stages* of the fetus's *development*. (Is the fetus "but water" during the first forty days? See Rabbi Jacob J. Weinberg, *Seride Esh* 3:127 etc.)

The issue is a religious one.

But Judaism has a profound respect for life, even potential life. It has had to come to grips with situations when the mother's life was not in immediate danger but other conditions were of concern: rape, incest, danger to the mother's emotional health, expected deformities in the child, (Tay-Sachs disease, and other potentials for the child to be).

On these questions the Orthodox authorities are of divergent mind, and the Orthodox woman will have to consult her rabbi.

The State of Israel passed an Abortion Law in 1977. It rejects abortion for convenience, but is otherwise quite liberal, permitting the termination of pregnancy in regard to minors, in cases of rape and incest or of danger to the physical and mental health of the mother, and in cases when deformity or other serious ills can be anticipated in the child. This law was opposed by Orthodoxy.

Judaism has made the distinction between potential and actual life out of its own deep commitment to life. It regards potential life as sacred; its wanton destruction cannot be sanctioned. But the actually living person is sacrosanct, and the life and the welfare of this person are inviolate. To sustain the living in every way must be our lasting concern.

Insemination in Vitro

If sperm and egg have been taken from the married Jewish parents, the mother carrying the child, the procedure has been generally approved.

THE LAWS OF NIDDAH

Niddah means "she who is separated." Torah directs:

When a woman has a discharge, her discharge being blood from her body, she shall remain in her impurity seven days; whoever touches her shall be unclean until evening. Anything she lies on during her impurity shall be unclean; and anything she sits on shall be unclean. [Lev. 15:19–24]

Do not come near a woman during her period of uncleanness to uncover her nakedness. [Lev. 18:19]

If a man lies with a woman in her infirmity and uncovers her nakedness, he has laid bare her blood-flow; both of them shall be cut off from among their people. [Lev. 20:18]

Violation of this injunction thus draws severe divine sanction. The ordinance has been strictly observed in Jewish tradition.

Foundations

In human beings the forces of life and death are interwoven. Thousands of male sperm die in order that one may produce life. In woman, the forces of life and death exert their joint powers visibly. Only a woman whose blood flows and whose life force is thus diminished and replenished month after month can conceive and give life to a child. Many primitive peoples, awestruck by the mystery, were afraid that members of their society might bring pollution and contamination to the rest at a time when the forces of nature became visible on their bodies. These people had to be separated and shunned during the period of their "possession." Only after purification might they be permitted to join the group once again.

The newborn child was, therefore, kept apart for a while. The dead were removed. Women, during their menstruation, were kept separated.

These beliefs came to be rooted in Judaism as well. Thus, a person in contact with the forces of death was to be excluded from the source of life: the sanctuary. Only upon undergoing special rites would he be restored. These rites included immersion in *mayim hayim*, the waters of life—ocean, stream, Mikvah.

A dead body is *tameh*—"unclean." Those who came under the same roof with it, prepared it, and attended its burial had to be purified. The mother of a newborn child was tameh—twice as long for a daughter as for a son; it was believed that the female foetus needed twice the time of a male for development.

The Laws Affecting Women

A man need not go to the Mikvah to remain in society and join his wife in the marital bed. It is different for women, givers of life. Here the laws are very strict.

During her menstrual period and after giving birth, the "unclean" woman may not sleep with her husband and may not even touch him. When her flow has ceased, after seven days, she must purify herself in "living waters"; until then she remains Niddah, separated, removed.

A bride must go the Mikvah before her wedding to be cleansed from the Niddah status that has existed ever since her first menstruation. Newlyweds must separate after the initial consummation of the marriage, on the chance that her discharge may contain menstrual blood.

The Rabbis greatly extended the laws of Niddah. Where Torah states that a woman remains in this state for seven days, the Rabbis ordained that she remains unclean in fact for seven days *after* the flow has ceased. During this period, which lasts a minimum of twelve days every month, she may not sleep in the same bed with her husband. At nightfall, after the days of menstruation and the seven days of additional impurity have passed, she goes to the Mikvah.

A MIKVAH is a special pool, filled with "living waters" as prescribed. The water must be in contact with the groundwater of a stream or rainwater caught in a cistern. Once the required amount of "living waters" has been achieved, other water may be added, included hot water. A Mikvah should not be constructed without rabbinical guidance.

The woman may immerse herself in a stream or in the ocean.

Before entering the Mikvah, the woman takes a bath, cleansing her body thoroughly. She cleans her nails, removes all rings, bandages, anything that can be regarded as a separation between her body and the water. She brushes her hair. Then she steps into the Mikvah, nude. Spreading her arms and legs, she immerses herself fully. Even the last strand of her hair has to be under water. An attendant watches, to make certain that full immersion has taken place (see Baba Kamma 82a about this ruling ascribed to Ezra).

Upon emerging from the water, she speaks the blessing:

Barukh . . . vetzivanu al ha-Tevilah
Blessed are You . . . He Who . . . has commanded us concerning immersion.

She then immerses herself a second time.

Seven days after giving birth to a boy, fourteen days after giving birth to a girl, the young mother begins counting another seven days, immerses herself at the end of the period, and is then purified.

Importance and Effect of the Law in Jewish Tradition

Tradition has regarded the laws of Niddah as the cornerstone of *Taharat ha-Mishpahah*, the purity of the family.

The woman was spared the burden of serving her husband at a time of her discomfort.

Forbidden to touch her or to have sex with her for long periods, a husband would not tire of his wife, nor she of him.

The Jewish woman was legally dependent on her husband; yet she was independent. Without the laws of Niddah, she might not have had this dignity and independence. Through these laws, she was entitled, in effect, to say to him: "I am not your creature, or your toy. I am myself, I am God's. You may not see the workings of my most intimate nature, may not possess me then, or even touch me. I am free under God and by His will." Her husband had to learn through longing. He could not subject her to his whim. This awareness carried over into the total relationship of the partners. Thus he came to honor her, and she to appreciate him.

The wife returns to the marriage bed at the moment of her greatest physiological readiness to conceive; the end of procreation was thus served by the laws of Niddah.

Additionally, the laws of Niddah prevented the man from engaging in extramarital sex. He had to assume that any woman not his wife might be Niddah.

During the Middle Ages, Jews were often spared the ravages of epidemics that bred in dirt and came to afflict the general population. As Jewish women had to cleanse themselves and Jewish men were advised to do so under the rules of purity, Jewish law placed a protective shield about the physical health of the Jew.

The laws of Niddah impose a great restraint upon the partners and possibly result in great strains. For traditionally minded Jews, these are outweighed by the spiritual benefits they convey. The restraints are God's law and confer stability upon the family.

Reform Judaism does not feel bound by these laws. Among Conservative Jews, practice varies widely.

DIVORCE

Torah permits divorce and establishes the legal procedure for it.

A man takes a wife and possesses her. She fails to please him because he finds something obnoxious about her, and he writes her a bill of divorcement, hands it to her, and sends her away from his house; she leaves his household and becomes the wife of another man. . . . [Deut. 24:1–2]

The passage makes several important legal and ethical points:

1. A man can divorce his wife; she cannot divorce her husband.

2. There need be no blame on her part; aversion is sufficient ground for divorce.

3. Among the nations of antiquity and even under Islamic law, the husband could simply expel his wife without any formality. In

contrast, Torah, considering such an act unethical, rules that a legal act has to be performed.

This act consists of writing a formal bill of divorcement, a Get, *and* formally handing this bill to the woman.

This implies that the woman must accept the divorce paper, even against her will.

4. The woman may marry again.

5. If she has married again and been divorced from her second husband, or the latter dies, she may not marry her first husband again. This is expressed in passages following those cited (Deut. 24:3–4). If she has not remarried, she may return to her first husband in marriage.

Though the husband thus had complete freedom and the woman had none, the husband could not simply cast out his wife, nor was a divorcée automatically regarded as having any culpability.

In ancient Israel, all jurisdiction, including divorce, lay exclusively in the hands of Jewish courts guided by the law of Torah. In carrying out their jurisdiction, the Rabbis surrounded the procedure with detailed formalities. They ruled that under certain conditions, a woman could ask the court to force her husband to a divorce. If he resisted, he could be imprisoned until he was agreeable (Ketubot 61b; 77b). In the tenth century of our era, Rabbenu Gershom of Mainz put the capstone on the legislation protecting the woman: she could not be divorced against her will. If she was mentally incapable of expressing her will, one hundred rabbis, after examining her case, had to consent to her receiving the document against her will. This procedure is still followed.

Rabbinical Ordinances

The Rabbis assumed full authority to declare the conditions under which marriage or a Get, a bill of divorce, were valid. They based their power on the enunciated principle:

Anyone who enters a marriage does so in conformity with the Rabbis' rulings. [Kiddushin 3a]

The Rabbis had the power to declare it valid, invalid, or annulled.

The Get has to be given before a Jewish court. The court consists of three rabbis forming the Bet Din; in addition there have to be two witnesses and a *Sofer*, a professional Torah scribe, to prepare the instrument.

In order to give the partners a last-minute delay, the Rabbis surrounded the Get with complicated formalities. Perhaps husband and wife might change their minds, being confronted with so much "red tape."

The presiding rabbi asks several questions to ascertain the identity of the parties, to make certain that the Get is given and accepted freely and without reservations and conditions.

The Sofer then writes the Get. Each Get must be written individually in a special manner. It has exactly thirteen lines, with some letters in each line interlacing with the line above to prevent any additions between the lines. It must be done on nonerasable paper, and any error invalidates it. There cannot be any erasures, even if two letters flow into each other. The procedure takes several hours.

Upon completion, the Get is signed by the witnesses. It is then folded as a "bill." The woman places her hands together, opening them at one side to form a "V." The man places the Get into her hands. She closes them around the Get and raises them with the document in it. She is divorced.

The woman now returns the Get to the presiding rabbi. He cuts through it to invalidate it for any future fraudulent use; he will file it. Both the man and the woman receive a certificate of divorce, called *P'tur*, permission to remarry.

After ninety-two days, the woman may remarry; in this manner any possible question of paternity is eliminated, should she become pregnant very soon.

If the woman cannot be present to receive the Get from her husband, he may appoint a *Shaliah*, messenger, which has to be done before the Bet Din. This Shaliah will be permitted to hand the Get to another Shaliah. The Get may thus be mailed from Shaliah to Shaliah, if the woman lives far away. This is done by the Bet Din and certified by a covering letter under separate mailing. The woman then appears before a second Bet Din in her locale, and the Shaliah hands her the Get in the prescribed manner.

In the United States, a Get can be given only after a divorce in civil court.

In Israel, only the Rabbinical court is empowered to grant a Get. The state does not recognize any other form of divorce for Jews. It also will, to this day, imprison a husband who refuses a divorce to his wife when she should have it.

If a man remarries without a Get, he violates the ordinance of Rabbenic Gershom against polygamy. If a woman remarries without a Get, she commits adultery, and the children of this second marriage are tainted.

Contemporary Problems

REFORM JUDAISM does not require a Get for purposes of remarriage. It holds that Torah desired divorce to be a legal act and not merely the expulsion of the wife by her husband. This act is now performed in the civil courts.

CONSERVATIVE JUDAISM has had to wrestle with several problems.

If a man, after obtaining a divorce in court, refuses to give a Get to his wife, either because he "does not believe in it" or because he hates her or if he wishes to extort money from her in return for a Get, she is without recourse. These situations are not rare. The Conservative Rabbinate has, therefore, reiterated the principle of the Rabbis that any marriage entered by Jews is understood to rest on the authority of the Rabbis. The Ketubah of the Conservative Movement contains several provisions, not found in the Orthodox one, through which the husband enters a commitment, enforceable in the courts of the state, to grant a Get to his wife.

At the same time, the Conservative Rabbinate has again invoked the powers granted rabbis under Talmudic authority by assuming the right retroactively to annul marriages in extreme circumstances, such as to permit a woman to remarry, when her husband has disappeared without a trace.

ORTHODOXY sees unsurmountable difficulties in any change of the traditional Ketubah, specifically any provisions included in it. It also denies contemporary rabbis the authority held by the masters of the Talmudic period.

The Bastard: Mamzer

A child born of an illicit liaison, including that of close relations or of incest, is a *Mamzer*. The same applies to a child born of an adulterous liaison. This includes a child born in wedlock to a woman whose previous marriage was not dissolved by a Get but only in civil court. *Mamzerut* is not the same as illegitimacy, which is unknown in Judaism, though the child is surrounded by some facts of "silence" (Kiddushin 4:1–2; Yevamot 100b). The child of an unwed mother is legitimate in every way. The child of a married man, fathered out of wedlock, is not tainted if the mother was not married. The child of a married woman by any man not her husband is a Mamzer. Of such a child, male or female, Torah says:

No Mamzer shall be admitted into the congregation of the Lord; none of his descendants, even in the tenth generation, shall be admitted into the congregation of the Lord. [Deut. 23:3]

Such Jews, bound to all Jewish laws, may never marry an ordinary Jewish person, though they may marry within their own circle and will then produce another generation of Mamzerim.

Reform Judaism does not recognize the law of the Mamzer, as the Constitution of the United States declares categorically that there cannot be any "corruption of blood" (Article III, Section 3). Conservative Judaism is considering the elimination of the entire concept with all its provisions, doing so in the light of Jewish ethics, as formulated in Aggadah. We find in the Midrash that God Himself feels that He has to bring comfort to the Mamzerim, who have been oppressed without having incurred any guilt (Vayikra Rabba, Emor 32:8).

Orthodoxy places the law of Torah and the purity of the Jewish people above all personal concerns.

Agunah

A wife whose husband has vanished without trace is *Agunah,* "shut off" from life. Unless his death has been reliably witnessed or his body reliably identified, he is regarded as living, even though the courts of the land may have declared him legally dead. *Orthodoxy,* making it clear to the woman that she can never remarry, will counsel her to accept the will of God in humble submission, and to find fulfillment for her life outside of marriage. *Conservatism,* as we have seen, is in search of new Halakhic interpretations that will offer her relief. *Reform* accepts the declaration of the courts and permits her to remarry. *Reconstructionism* calls for enactment of Jewish law permitting a woman to divorce her husband. This would eliminate both Mamzerut and the status of Agunah.

Marriage to a Kohen

Orthodoxy, basing itself on Leviticus 21:7, forbids a Kohen to marry a divorcée. Non-Orthodox Jewry permits it in the spirit of ethics and resting on the fact that no Kohen nowadays "offer the bread of God," which is the reason, cited in Scripture, for the interdict. The law would actually discriminate against women.

29

Good Deeds:
The Integrated
Personality

The third of the three wishes pronounced over a child at his B'rit expresses the hope that he may enter the realm of *massim tovim,* good deeds. These become even more important after the Jew has entered fully into a life of Torah and has established a family. These are years of earning a living, of strength, understanding, and counsel, before old age begins with its own burdens and tasks (Avot 5:24). Both man and woman spend a great deal of their time at work, in the marketplace, doing chores, undertaking tasks of social leadership. *Maasim tovim* lead to personal integration during this time; they bind the strands of life into the fabric of the Jewish personality. They make the Jew into a *Tzaddik.*

Tzedakah—the striving to be a Tzaddik through deeds—is generally translated as "righteousness." Its deeper meaning is "loyalty." Loyalty springs from the heart. It is an inner quality that finds expression in many outward forms: truthfulness, uprightness, charity, piety, honesty, justice.

There are a number of things whose fruits man enjoys in this world, though their main reward is stored for him in the world to come: honoring father and mother, rendering kindness in helping others, eager and early attendance at the House of Study and Prayer, hospitality to strangers, attending the sick, endowing a [poor] bride, accompanying the dead, making peace between people; but the study of Torah outweighs them all. [Meditation in the morning prayer, based on Shabbat 127b]

There is no measure to any of these acts. They spring out of loyalty to both God and people. They are motivated by loyal faith in God's promise of a reward in the world to come and out of loyal concern with the needs of others. They confer a happiness that is its own reward. Life is good, filled with love. Rabbi Simeon, the Just, therefore used to proclaim:

The world [society] rests on three things; On Torah [study], on service [Mitzvot], and on acts of lovingkindness. [Avot 1:2]

Lovingkindness maintained the strength of our forefathers in times of oppression. It gave them emotional stability. The more insecure they became, the more they found security in mutual, loving assistance. Amid persecution and the denial of their right to exist, they were balanced, hopeful, and optimistic. In this manner, they wrought the miracle of Jewish survival.

TZEDAKAH IN PERSONAL AND SOCIAL RELATIONS

Torah and Talmud are filled with rules and directives regulating personal and social relations. To discuss them in detail would call for a major review of our spiritual heritage. We shall merely sketch some of the expectations Judaism holds for the Tzaddik, the Jew who wishes to be truly loyal.

The Tzaddik is expected to be *lifnim mi-shurat ha-din,* well within the yardstick of the law. He knows that the legal is not always the ethical, and he measures his actions and his thoughts by the standard of ethics. Torah frequently gives us ordinances that end with the statement: "I am God." By doing so it wishes to caution us: the law may offer us loopholes; God does not. The law can punish only overt acts that can be proved; God examines the heart. The Jew must be guided by the constant awareness that even enlightened self-interest falls short of the mark that God has set.

Keep in mind three things and you will not come into the area of transgression; know what is above you: an Eye that sees, an Ear that hears, and all your actions will be recorded in a book. [Avot 2:1]

PURE SPEECH is fundamental; it does not yet make the Tzaddik, but it places the Jew on the road. Slander and gossip are grievous sins, for the word, once released, can never be recalled. Torah therefore says:

Do not go about as a talebearer amid your people, do not stand by idly as your brother bleeds, I am God. [Lev. 19:16]

The Talmud reminds us that three persons will be wounded when one engages in gossip or evil talk: he who speaks it, he who hears it, and he who is the subject of the conversation (Arhin 16b).

Governing Our Feelings

We may not be able to speak out or be willing to do so when we feel our neighbor has wronged us. We wait to "get even" with him. But such pent-up hatred destroys us and destroys community. Torah firmly directs:

Do not hate your brother in your heart,
reprove, reprove your fellow
that you may not bear guilt on his account.
Do not bear vengeance, nor carry a grudge
against your kinfolk,
but love your neighbor as yourself,
I am the Lord. [Lev. 19:18]

The Rabbis add:

Three things drive a person out of the world: an evil eye [jealousy], an evil drive [selfishness], and hatred of mankind. [Avot 2:16]

Absolute honesty is commanded to us in Torah:

You shall not falsify measures of length, weight, or capacity. You shall have an honest scale, honest weights, an honest *ephah*, an honest *hin*. I the Lord am your God who brought you out from the land of Egypt. [Lev. 19:35–36]

The Positive Approach

The Jew must go out of his way. We must seek to influence our brother or sister by example and by word. To the degree that we have neglected to influence them for good, we bear a share of guilt for their misdeeds. We are responsible for them, and we have failed. We are called to

Moses Maimonides (1135-1204) listed eight degrees of charity, the highest of which was "Helping a person to help himself." This traditional portrait of the twelfth-century philosopher dates from about 1700.

The prophetic tradition calls upon us to support the cause of justice and righteousness in all our doings. Young Jews marching in protest to oppression are following in this long tradition.

love your neighbor as yourself

And as we love our neighbor, we must also love the stranger (Lev. 19:33–34), and we must even aid our enemy in his need:

When you encounter your enemy's ox or ass wandering, you must take it back to him. When you see the ass of your enemy prostrate under its burden, and would [prefer to] refrain from raising it, you must nevertheless raise it with him. [Exod. 23:4–5]

Being a Tzaddik means going all the way. On Yom Kippur, we read the call of Isaiah:

This is the fast I desire:
to unlock the fetters of wickedness,
to untie the yoke of lawlessness,
to let the oppressed go free;

304

to break off every yoke.
It is to share your bread with the hungry
and to take the wretched poor into your home;
when you see the naked to clothe him,
and not to ignore your own [human] kin.
Then shall your light burst through like the dawn. . . . [Isa. 58:6–8ff].

COURTESY AND GOOD MANNERS are the badge of the Tzaddik.

Rabbi Yohanan ben Zakkai always extended a greeting to others first, including the Gentile in the marketplace. [Berakhot 17a]

Hillel's calm and courtesy became proverbial. Hillel "loved all creatures" and thus brought them to Torah (Avot 1:12). But even the stern Shammai held:

Receive everybody with a cheerful face. [Avot 1:15]

We read in Proverbs:

A soft answer turns anger away,
an angry retort stirs up wrath. [Prov. 15:1]

CONCERN FOR ANIMALS is equally found in Torah. It forbids us to sit down at the table before we have fed the cattle. This is the interpretation the Rabbis give to the verse:

I will provide grass in the field for your cattle and [then] you shall eat and be satisfied. [Deut. 11:15]

In Proverbs we read:

The Tzaddik understands the soul of his cattle. [Prov. 12:10]

CONCERN FOR NATURE AND WORLD are enjoined at the creation of man.

The Lord God took the man [Adam] and placed him in the Garden of Eden to work it and to protect it. [Gen. 2:15]

CONCERN FOR THE STATE is clearly enunciated. In a letter addressed to the exiled in Babylonia, the prophet Jeremiah writes:

Build houses and dwell in them, plant gardens and eat the fruit of them, take wives and beget sons and daughters, and take wives for your sons, and give your daughters to husbands; and multiply there and be not diminished.
And seek the peace of the city whither I have caused you to be carried away captive, and pray unto the Lord for it; for in its peace you shall have peace. [Jer. 29:5–7]

We find in the liturgy for the Sabbath and the holy days a prayer for the government. Participation in civic affairs springs from Jewish obligation. The Rabbis are firm in stating:

Most Jewish teachers are laypeople who volunteer their time at little or no wage. Yet they are often asked to attend in-service training sessions such as the one above. In a very real sense the community sees such selflessness as Tzedakah.

The law of the State is the law. [Bava Kamma 113a]

The law of a just state has the binding power of Jewish law. It must be obeyed under the sanctions of Judaism. But the Jew must always remember that his hope may not exclusively rest with governments that change and are often fickle; it rests with God.

Put not your trust in princes,
in mortal man who cannot save.
His breath departs;
he returns to the dust;
on that day his plans come to nothing. [Ps. 146:3–4]

This is Tzedakah, of which it is said:

Tzedakah delivers from death. [Prov. 10:2; 11:4]

Abraham had trust in God:

and because he put his trust in the Lord, He reckoned it to him as Tzedakah [loyalty]. [Gen. 15:6]

Moses speaks of Tzedakah:

It will be Tzedakah for us before the Lord our God, if we guard this entire Mitzvah by doing it as He has commanded us. [Deut. 6:25]

Torah and life are here seen as *one Mitzvah*, one integrating force of life: Tzedakah, loyalty.
Isaiah proclaims:

306

Zion shall be saved by justice,
her repentent ones by Tzedakah. [Isa. 1:27]

Tzedakah is the thread that goes through our entire history.
Throughout our long pilgrimage, Tzedakah has delivered us from
death.

The Tzaddik exemplifies the beauty and nobility of Judaism to
the world. He is God's witness and proves it through his ethical
conduct. He is a personality "whose inside is like his outside"; there
is no hypocrisy in him.

TZEDAKAH AS CHARITY

In popular usage, the term *Tzedakah* has come to stand for
charity. No people or ethnic group has done more nobly than Jews
in this area. Tzedakah has saved millions and continues to sustain
them. Our giving has helped keep the State of Israel alive.

But it is not sufficient that Tzedakah be given; *how* it is given is
of the utmost importance. It must be given with joy in the opportunity and with respect for the receiver.

Maimonides, therefore, sees eight kinds of givers of Tzedakah,
each level higher than the one before:

He who gives, but grudgingly;
he who gives less than his share, but does so joyfully;
he who gives when he is asked;
he who gives without being asked;
he who gives without knowing the receiver, yet the receiver knows the
  giver's identity;
he who knows the receiver, but the receiver does not know him;
  neither party knows the identity of the other;
he who helps the other before the other suffers need, by loans, or by
  personal guidance in his affairs, or by setting him up in business or
  profession, allowing him to earn his own living. [Mishneh Torah:
  Matanot Aniyim 10:10–14]

PHYSICAL AND MENTAL HEALTH

Throughout history, Jews have always shown a remarkable affinity
for the study of medicine and the medical profession. Torah contains extended chapters dealing with contagious diseases and the
prevention of epidemics (Lev. 12–14). The priests were appointed
as diagnosticians and healers. The physician thus holds a priestly
office. Some of our greatest masters were physicians, among them
Judah Halevi and Maimonides, whose medical oath has lately come

to replace the Hippocratic oath for the graduates of many American medical schools.

Prevention of Sickness

God created man in His image (Gen. 1:27), giving him a body as vessel for his soul. The care of the body is therefore a Mitzvah. Only a healthy body can sustain a holy soul. The dietary laws are, in part, hygienic laws, according to Maimonides.

A Jew should, therefore, live prudently, avoiding excess in food and drink, in work and rest, in sleeping, sex, or any other activity, in order to keep his body strong (Maimonides, Eight Chapters). The Rabbis of the Talmud offer much sage advice in this regard: the night is created for sleep; food must be accompanied by fluids; physical exercise should follow every meal (Shabbat 41a). Change in diet may be upsetting (Ketubot 110b). As modern medicine does, the masters emphasize the importance of a good breakfast, possibly the most important meal of the day (Bava Kamma 92b, Bava Metzia 107a).

Cleanliness is strongly emphasized:

No Jew may live in a town that has no bath house. [Bava Kamma 46a]

It was a Mitzvah, according to Hillel, to take a bath, thereby keeping the divine vessel, the body, clean (Vayikra Rabba, Behar 34:3).

The Sanctity of the Body

Our bodies are the work of God. They may not be mutilated.

You are children of the Lord your God. You shall not gash yourselves or shave the front of your heads because of the dead. [Deut. 14:1]

Not only are we forbidden to mark our bodies in commemoration of the dead, as did the heathens of antiquity, but any incision that is not for therapeutic reasons is forbidden. Judaism does not permit tattooing. But asceticism that despoils the body is equally forbidden.

Healing the Body

Torah rules that if a person strikes another and injures him, the assailant has to pay damages, including the physician's fees. This will

let him be healed, fully healed. [Exod. 21:19]

From this statement the Rabbis deduced that medical help was to be sought.

Torah also states:

As part of an outreach program, young rabbinical students volunteer a part of their time to helping the aged, the sick, and the poor. Tzedakah, once practiced, soon becomes a way of life. The joy that it brings to others reflects in one's attitude toward self.

You shall keep My laws and My norms, by the pursuit of which man shall live: I am the Lord. [Lev. 18:5]

This means to say, the Rabbis explain:

He shall live by their pursuit, not die by it. [Yoma 85b]

We are, therefore, commanded to do everything necessary in the preservation of life, even if it entails a violation of the law of Torah. The Rabbis, therefore, ruled:

No Jew may live in a town that has no physician,

and if a Jew feels ill, he must immediately consult the physician (Bava Kamma 46a).

The medical knowledge of the Rabbis was extensive, and many modern works have been written about Talmudic medicine.

Mental Health

Mental health is equally the Rabbis' concern. It was safeguarded by Mitzvot, by joy ordained in Torah, by laughter found in Jewish life. Laughter was never silenced among Jews; it sprang from faith. Caring for others frees us from an undue preoccupation with ourselves and reveals to us that we are needed; it is a great cure for self-pity and depression.

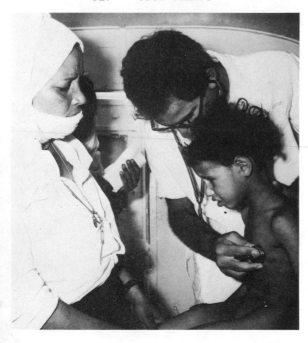

When it comes to acts of Tzedakah, there are no enemies.
Here, Israeli doctors visit Bedouins in the Sinai to treat their
sick.

Torah tells us:

You shall love your neighbor as yourself. [Lev. 19:18]

In these words it reveals that we cannot love others unless we have
come to love ourselves decently. The Rabbis, therefore, warn against
disparagement of self:

Be not wicked in your own sight. [Avot 2:18]

Avoidance of Danger

Torah directs:

When you build a new house, you shall make a parapet for your [flat]
roof, so that you do not bring blood guilt on your house, if anyone should
fall from it. [Deut. 22:8]

"Anyone" can be ourselves. We may not place ourselves in danger
of limb and life, nor expose ourselves to unnecessary health risks
or danger. S'kanak, avoidance of danger, is enjoined more categorically than observance of religious law (Hulin 10a–Taanit 20b).

Suicide

Suicide is forbidden in Judaism; it is "murder." The body we
possess is not ours; it belongs to God. For Jews, the supreme commandment is to live. Self-preservation is fundamental.

CARING FOR THE SICK

Sickness is trial, test, and symbol. It is a trial no human being can escape, it is a test of our spiritual strength, and it is a symbol of God's presence. The afflictions that come to the individual reflect those that have come to the Jewish people, and both are ultimately dispensations of divine love.

Abraham's greatest physical pain was directly caused by an act of divine love: the commandment of circumcision, sign of the covenant. God, therefore, visited Abraham to alleviate his suffering (Gen. 18:1; Bava Metziah 86a). Job's affliction was a divine test; his friends immediately dropped everything they were doing to bring him aid and comfort (Job 2:11ff.).

Sickness has its physical causes, but its cure calls for a healing of soul as well. Nothing is as hard for a patient as the feeling that he has to bear his suffering alone. As Jews, we know about this, for we have had to bear our collective suffering all by ourselves. The suffering Jew will find strength in knowing that God is with him: thereby he gains the will to fight for his health. God stands at his head; family, friends, and community stand at his side.

Visiting the sick is a sacred duty—so important that even the scholar must lay aside his sacred book and the leader of the community must abandon his pressing obligations to visit the poor and the lonely.

Once a disciple of Rabbi Akiva fell sick. Not one of the Rabbis came to visit him, but Rabbi Akiva paid him a visit. The young disciple had received the best of medical care and attention, yet, as he recovered, he said to Akiva: "Master, *you* have saved my life!" Henceforth, Rabbi Akiva publicly taught: "He who fails to visit the sick is as one who has shed blood." [Nedarim 40a]

Each visit brings dual blessing: healing to the sufferer and faith to the visitor, which will aid him or her when he himself or she herself comes to be afflicted. Our visits must offer us a true picture of the patient's condition in order that we may do what is required for his or her recovery through prayer and action. The Talmud advises us not to pay a visit early in the morning, when a patient usually feels better. We may conclude that his or her sickness is not so serious after all. Neither should we visit him or her at nighttime, when he or she may be in such a poor state that we feel justified in abandoning all our efforts of help. We must attend to him or her when we can see his or her true condition in order that we apprehend his or her need for help (Nedarim 40b).

Our visit must be equally thoughtful in regard to the patient's comfort. We may not overtax him or her. We must constantly remain sensitive to the patient's condition and wants, with the length of our visit depending on his or her comfort or needs. Our talk must be cheerful and not depressing; our presence must convey to the patient our readiness to do for him or her what he or she at present is unable to do for himself or herself (see Nedarim 45a–b). Unless our help is indispensable, we should not visit patients with contagious diseases, lest we spread them.

Our duties toward the sick are both collective and highly personal. We must find for the sick the best possible medical care and hospitalization, if needed. In some cases, this may be a communal obligation, if the ill are unable to afford such care. In addition, we must become the patient's personal physician of the soul by our individual concern.

Then the miracle of healing will come to pass. The Rabbis see in the restoration of a person to health a miracle greater than that wrought by God to the three men who remained unscathed in a fiery furnace (Dan. 3). Its fire was made by man and could be conquered by men; sickness is inflicted by God, a fire only God can quench (Nedarim 41a). In caring for the sick, we truly become God's co-workers.

We may pray with the sick, if he or she so wishes. Lengthy prayers are not required. When Miriam, Moses' sister was afflicted, her brother spoke the shortest prayer in Scripture:

O God, pray heal her. [Num. 12:13]

On leaving the bedside, we offer a traditional greeting:

Ha-Makom yerahem alekha (for a woman: *alayikh*) *veyishlakh lekha (lakh) refuah shelemah b'tokh sh'ar holei Yisrael*
The All-Present have compassion upon you and send you complete healing together with all the other sick in Israel.

The Rabbis were initially reluctant to permit visiting the sick on the Sabbath, lest their woe destroy our Sabbath peace and cause us to speak in prayer of needs that should be forgotten on this day. Eventually, they permitted it, recognizing the value of the visits. Our greeting on Sabbath is different:

Shabbat hi mi-lisok u-refuah kerovah lavo im sh'ar holei Yisrael
The Sabbath keeps us from voicing any plaintive plea, but healing is well on the way, soon to come to you amid all the other sick in Israel.

The same greeting is expressed on holy days, with the name of the festival replacing the word *Shabbat*.

Before an operation, the Jew goes to the synagogue to invoke God's help. He may be called to the Torah. He will then enter the hospital knowing that, together with God, the hearts and prayers of the congregation are in tune with him, their souls at his side. On recovery from sickness, the Jew again goes to the synagogue to give thanks. He testifies to God's graciousness before the assembled congregation. This is an occasion when tradition calls for a women's Minyan if a woman is to speak the blessing. After the completion of the Torah section, to which he is called, the convalescent speaks *Birkat Ha-Gomel*, Blessing to Him Who Bestows Good.

Barukh . . . hagomel l'hayavim tovot, she-g'malani kol tov
Blessed are You . . . He, Who bestows good unto the unworthy, Who has bestowed all this good unto me.

The congregation responds:

Mi sh-g'malkha kol tov, Hu yig'mlakha kol tov selah!
May He who has bestowed upon you all this good continue to bestow every good upon you—Selah!

Sickness shared becomes more tolerable. A Jew who celebrates his or her Judaism is armed against the attacks of sickness that medicine alone cannot cure.

30

Old Age
and Death

OLD AGE

Everyone prays to attain old age; length of years is a blessing. But old age presents us with many problems as well. The Mishnah we quoted at the beginning of this part of our book does not disguise the fact that at the age of sixty we enter the period of our senior years, at seventy that of old age. We have arrived at a definite stage of life; to deny it would be both futile and foolish.

When Moses stood before Pharaoh in Egypt to express to him Israel's determination to follow God's call to freedom, he stated clearly:

We will go with our young and our old. [Exod. 10:9]

The young would be at the head of Israel's pilgrimage.

The prophet Joel, speaking of Messianic days, proclaims:

Your sons and daughters shall prophesy,
your old men shall dream dreams,
your young men shall see visions. [Joel 3:1]

As Rabbi Meir Loeb ben Yehiel Michael Malbim (1809–1879) explains in his commentary to the verse, each statement relates to a different level of prophesy. Youth will have the full power of divine, prophetic inspiration; youthful adults will still be endowed with visions; to the aged there will be granted only the lowest level of sight, dreams.

To some "elect," true Tzaddikim, continued productivity may be granted.

In old age they still produce fruit,
they are full of sap and freshness,
attesting that the Lord is upright,
my Rock in whom there is no wrong. [Ps. 92:15–16]

Yet strength in old age may not be taken for granted. We can only hope that God may listen to the prayer so fervently voiced on Yom Kippur:

Do not cast us away from Your Presence,
and do not take Your holy spirit from us.
Do not cast us aside at the time of old age,
do not desert us, when our strength has vanished.

Old Age as Distinction

Judaism has regarded old age as a distinction and has demanded that we respect it. Torah ordains:

You shall rise before the aged and show deference to the old; you shall fear your God: I am the Lord. [Lev. 19:32]

This injunction has a double thrust: We are tempted to cast aside the aged, claiming that they have had their day. This is hard and cruel; we may not do it. We must rise to their assistance.

In a wider sense, the *Zaken,* the aged, is seen as a person endowed with wisdom.

Who is called Zaken? He who has acquired Torah. [Kiddushin 32b]

The term is, therefore, used in Scripture as a connotation for masters, leaders, and judges. The Talmud follows this definition:

Moses received the Torah at Sinai, and transmitted it to Joshua, Joshua transmitted it to the *Zekenim,* the elders, masters of the people. [Avot 1:1]

The facial and body features of the aged are regarded by our masters as a badge of merit. We should not be ashamed of them, nor try to hide them.

Problems: Old and New

No one likes to relinquish power. Every parent wishes to spare his children the errors of youth, the mistakes that life has revealed. But youth must find out for itself.

The Mishnah, as we have seen, relegates the aged to advisory positions. As we get older, we must accept this status. We may regret the lost chances of imparting our philosophy of life to our

Judaism has never viewed old age as an impediment. Indeed, the stress placed on the link between generations gives cause to respect and honor the old as a repository of wisdom. And, too, there are those special moments that only the difference in age can bring.

children, now that time is running out. We may even feel that our children are not yet ready to take over. But we need not worry. In most cases we shall have succeeded in giving our children that which is best in us. They will find their way, guided by our earlier example, and will reflect honorably upon us after we have departed.

Modern life has added to our problems the problems of the young who must deal with the aged.

We have permitted the aged to suffer want, loneliness, deprivation, and neglect. The aged are no longer needed. Here lies tragedy. We have to find creative outlets for the aged, as long as they live, to meet the basic human need to be needed.

The proper care of the aged, granting them the dignity to which they are entitled, making "beautiful their faces" in old age, has remained one of the challenges facing the Jewish community.

Concern for the aged and contact with them hold a reward for both young and old. Throughout history, traditions have been transmitted from grandparent to grandchild (parents are often too deeply engaged in earning a living). In the shtetl, the aged had the function of praying for the family. For us, they are a source of oral history that must be tapped while it is still flowing. Loving and frequent contact between the generations may bring deep joy and satisfaction to the young as well as to the old.

DEATH

We wish to live, but know that we shall die. We have to cope with death throughout life, an unknown of which we have no experience. In our own time, more than ever before, death has become the concern of psychologists and writers. How can we meet it? Judaism offers us answers that rest on faith, but also on deep psychological insight.

Without death there can be no life. From the moment of our birth, cells must die for new ones to be created. The grain must die to give us a new harvest. Without death, there might be no desire to propagate, and human life would not come into being. Without death there would be no incentive to gain knowledge, for its acquisition could be postponed indefinitely. The awareness of death permeates all our knowing and translates it into wisdom, leading to ethical conduct. The Psalmist declares:

The span of our life is seventy years,
or, given the strength, eighty years . . .
Teach us to count our days rightly,
that we may obtain a wise heart. [Ps. 90:10, 12]

A definite number of years is here set for us, allowing us to count their days; were they without limit, we could not number them, nor gain wisdom. But we can use them foolishly. The faithful Jew will not do so. With the Psalmist he speaks:

The dead cannot praise the Lord,
nor any who go down into silence
But we shall bless the Lord
now and forever. . . . [Ps. 115:17–18]

Aware of our finiteness, we bring God's blessings into the world now and, as a people, forever.

Judaism has as its goal to make us aware of death, in order that we may transcend it in life. Maimonides holds that the increasing proximity of death sensitizes our awareness of God and our love for Him (Guide of the Perplexed, ch. 51). We, therefore, do not find in Judaism a great preoccupation with the hereafter. The task is here and now. Death is to be conquered through faithfulness to God's command, Mitzvah.

The Fear of Death

We would deceive ourselves were we to assume that these principles have succeeded in overcoming the fear of death in Jews. We know that it means not-being, and the thought frightens us.

There is great reluctance among Jews to mention death among

the living; we use circumlocutions instead. But Jews have shown an equal hesitation to ascribe the execution of death to God. We know that we die by God's judgment; He sets the limit to our days. But Jewish tradition speaks of *Malakh Ha-Mavet*, the Angel of Death; *he* is the executioner. A loving God may inflict trials, but He "does not have the heart" to take life. In the end, God will destroy the angel of death:

He will destroy death forever,
My Lord God will wipe the tears away from all faces
and will put an end to the humiliation of His people
throughout all of the earth,
for it is the Lord, who has spoken. [Isa. 25:8]

Death is equated with our oppressors, who have made Jews die a thousand deaths over and over again. Israel will be redeemed from both. A reflection of these thoughts is found in our last table song at the Seder: "*Had Gadya*." "The little kid my father bought" represents Israel; nation after nation attacks it and then all attack each other, bringing destruction on one another. In the end, the "butcher" is killed by the angel of death, and the angel of death is destroyed forever by God Himself.

We are afraid of death. But we are told that each death, each generation, leads us forward to the day of freedom. There is meaning in death. Even the child, for whom "Had Gadya" is designed, is here exposed to death and is given comfort. There is fear of death in many a child, perhaps in a subconscious recollection of his or her state of "not yet being" in the womb of his or her mother. Education in facing death has to start early. It is achieved through religion.

Resurrection and the World to Come

We might simply consider death as rest for the weary, peace after toil. A more powerful antidote to fear of death is found in the Jewish belief in resurrection and the world to come. Judaism does believe in resurrection. It even speaks of a form of purgatory; this purgatory lasts but one year, and relief is given the sufferers on the Sabbath. Judaism does not emphasize this concept, however, for we are to follow the Mitzvot not for the sake of a reward or in fear of punishment, but for love of God (see Maimonides: Mishneh Torah, Sanhedrin 10:1; also Avot 1:3). The belief has been widely abandoned in non-Orthodox Judaism.

Judaism also holds a firm belief in the hereafter, the world to come. It offers great consolation.

The day of death is the moment of encounter of two worlds in a kiss: This world is departing, the world to come is entering. [Yerushalmi, Yevamot 15:2]

Rav Kuk, chief rabbi of Palestine (1864–1935) could, therefore, proclaim:

Death is but illusion, symbolized by the state of uncleanness imparted to it by religious law. . . . What people call death is rather an intensification and renewed invigoration of life. [Orot Hakodesh, p. 392]

But the character of *Olam haba,* the world to come, is beyond human comprehension. It would be an error to regard it as an earthly paradise, transposed into heaven.

. . . of the world to come it is said:
No eye has seen it but Thine. [Isa. 64:3] [Berakhot 34b]

This concept of the world to come is a late arrival to Judaism. In the time of the Second Temple the Pharisees emphasized it as an essential of faith, whereas the Sadducees denied it. But the belief struck such firm roots that the daughter religions of Judaism, Christianity, and Islam built entire structures of faith around it.

In Holy Scripture we do not learn of the world to come. But there are intimations that the life of a person is not wiped out at death. We read of the patriarchs that each of them

died and was gathered to his kin. [Gen. 25:17; 35:29; 49:33]

Upon death they entered the pantheon of the nation.

In the same vein it is stated:

The memory of the Tzaddik will be for a blessing. [Prov. 10:7]

This statement is enlarged by the Rabbis:

The Tzaddikim are called living even after their death. [Berakhot 18a]

It was inconceivable even to the pessimistic author of Ecclesiastes that the divine in man should perish with his body:

The dust returns to the earth as it was, the spirit returns to God, who gave it. [Eccles. 12:7]

The departed form a reservoir from which Jewish strength replenishes itself; the traces of their life on earth are eternal.

LEARNING THE FACTS OF DEATH

Judaism does not gloss over the ever-closer approach of death. It prepares us for it.

Regret at lost opportunities is assuaged by the knowledge that it is not our duty to complete the work if we have done our best (Avot 2:21). We may come to accept that which we clearly know: we are not immortal. We have to face the loss of our friends; it touches us deeply. But Judaism assures us that we live and die at God's behest.

If we follow the guidance of our tradition, we will be prepared; but at no stage will we lose our grip on life, even in suffering. Life becomes more concentrated with every day, bringing its own rewards:

Grandchildren are the crown of the aged. [Prov. 17:6]

Torah can still be studied; *maasim tovim*, still performed:

If you have studied much Torah, you will receive much reward; the Master of your work is faithful; He will give you the wages for your labor, but know that the main reward for the Tzaddikim is in the world to come. [Avot 2:21]

Preparations

Wisdom dictates that we spare our children and relatives as much as possible during the inevitably traumatic period of bereavement.

We should make our will and review it periodically. We should acquire a plot in a Jewish cemetery. We should give clear directions regarding our funeral. If it is conducted in accordance with Jewish tradition, it will save our relatives the expense involved in showy caskets and other ostentatious forms that are often dictated by a sense of guilt.

If we own our own burial garments, *Takhrikhim*, we should tell the family where they are stored.

We should not make special requests of the family for the funeral; they may impose burdens on the bereaved. The traditional Jewish funeral has been tested through the ages; it brings peace to the soul. If there exists a *Hevrah Kadishah*, it can bring aid and peace of mind to the bereaved.

The Hevrah Kadishah: Holy Fellowship

Hevrah Kadishah is an organization that serves the dying and the dead and that ought to exist in every Jewish community. In former days, the members never received any remuneration for their work, but paid dues that were used to defray the cost of funerals for poor people. There never was any charge for their service, irrespective of the person involved.

The members of the fellowship were called as soon as a Jew entered the last stages of life. Taking turns, the men or women, as the case might be, sat by the bedside day and night, making sure that the dying one recited the confession of sins and uttered "*Sh'ma Yisrael*" with his or her last breath. If the patient was unable to do so, they did it for him. After death had been confirmed, they moved the body to the ground. It was then taken away to be prepared for burial. At no time was the body left unattended. The men of the

Müller inv: P. IV.   *et fculpfit.*

An engraving by J. C. Bodenschatzen, 1748. The last precious moments of life, shared by family and friends. A last blessing of the children and grand-children; the last recitation of the Sh'ma prayer; the moment of death and its aftermath—the body dressed in shrouds and the Hevrah Kadishah (keeping watch through the night).

Hevrah made the coffin of unpolished boards. This was done in the basement of the synagogue. Then they performed the *Taharah*, the washing and clothing of the deceased; women did the same for departed women. They placed the body in the coffin and closed it.

At the cemetery, another fellowship, *Hevrah Kabranim*, the Society of the Gravediggers, had in the meanwhile dug the grave. After the funeral service, the members of the Hevrah Kadishah were the first to carry the body to the grave. After it had been lowered, they were the first to pour three shovelfuls of earth on it, before the relatives did so. After the assembly and the members of the Hevrah Kabranim had filled the grave and formed the mound, the members of the Hevrah Kadishah padded the soil, giving it symbolic firmness. It was the last act in honor of the dead.

At no time, from the moment of death to the conclusion of the burial, was the body handled or served by any paid personnel or undertaker.

THE ARRIVAL OF DEATH

At the Deathbed

We are born alone and we die alone; no one can share these ultimate moments of life with us. But a Jew knows that he or she will not enter the portals of death unattended. As he or she was received by attendants on emergence from the mother's womb, thus will the Jew be accompanied by attendants on the eventual return to the womb of eternity.

As the patient's condition becomes critical, the members of the Hevrah Kadishah arrive. They will be with him or her until the grave has been closed.

The men or women of the Holy Fellowship will offer Psalms. If the patient is conscious, they will prepare him or her for the last Mitzvah in life: to die as a Jew. They will urge him or her to bless the children assembled at the bedside, to confess the sins committed during life, to commit himself or herself to God. With the last breath left, the Jew is to pronounce the affirmation of faith: *"Sh'ma Yisrael,"* so timing it that the word *Ehad*—"One"—is uttered with the last breath.

Such occasions, when a Jew is conscious enough to perform these sacred acts, are extremely rare. Most often the attendants have to speak the words for him.

A number of manuals have been prepared by the various branches of Judaism, containing selections to be read at the bedside visit. At the beginning of their vigil, the attendants pray for the patient's recovery. They choose verses from Psalm 119, whose first letters spell out the patient's name. There comes a moment, however, when the patient's condition changes. The breath becomes rasping, indicating a congestion that is the result of a rapid cessation of organic functions. At this moment, the attendants abandon their prayers for recovery, but plead for a speedy release from struggle:

Go, for God has sent you!

They bless him or her with the scriptural blessing.

In the Synagogue

In the shtetl, where ties among members of the community were so strong as to make them into a family, the congregation would be assembled to pray for the critically ill. The congregation recited selected Psalms, ending with verses of Psalm 119 that spelled out the sufferer's name. As a last and desperate measure, they would change the person's name, reasoning that God may have ordained that a person by the name of, say, Abraham was to die, but His judgment did not extend to a person by the name of, say, Isaac. A copy of Hebrew Scriptures would be opened at random, and the first name of a meritorious Jew that appeared would be bestowed upon the patient. If he recovered, he would carry this name from then on.

We may regard this act as a superstition, but we may also see in it an expression of the Jewish faith that God is so merciful He waits for a "loophole" to allow Him to extend His mercy and, above all, that His providence rests on every individual person.

When Death Comes

During the last stages of life, unnecessary ministrations are forbidden, as they may shorten the divinely allocated span. Even when they are reasonably certain that death has come, the attendants wait another fifteen minutes and then place a feather to the deceased's nostrils; if it fails to move, they are assured that all life has fled. Today, the physician makes this determination.

Each of the bystanders make a small tear in his or her clothes, speaking:

Barukh Dayan ha-Emet
Blessed are You, the True Judge.

They close the deceased's eyes, then tie a cloth around the head from crown to chin to keep the mouth from opening. They prepare some straw on the floor and remove the body from the bed to the ground (reversing the raising at Holegrasch, p. 226). The body is so placed that the feet face the door through which he or she will depart from the house or room. The attendants put a pillow under the head; straighten out arms, hands, legs and feet at the side; and cover the body with a black cloth. A light is kindled and placed at the deceased's head. An attendant will keep watch.

In the shtetl, the water in the house of death and the neighbors' houses was poured into the street, a mute announcement of death, which no one wished to spread by word of mouth, in allusion to the Biblical verse that in death we are indeed like water spilled (II Sam. 14:14).

Death in Dignity

The advances of modern medicine have produced tools for shortening life without pain and prolonging life by artificial means. Our ancestors could not envision these developments. They have created issues for contemporary Jews.

EUTHANASIA is a Greek word meaning "beautiful death." Its advocates promote laws that would permit a physician to bring about a patient's earlier and easy death, especially when he or she suffers unspeakable pain from a disease that can no longer be cured. Judaism strictly forbids euthanasia, regarding it as murder. We may not, through active interference, shorten a human life by even one hair's breadth.

We cannot leave the decision on death to human beings, for we do not know where it will lead.

LIFE-PROLONGING DEVICES, invented by modern medical science, have brought many blessings and restored many a life. But they have also caused problems. It is possible today to keep a body alive even after all brain functions have stopped and the individual, plugged in to a battery of apparatuses, no longer is a person.

In several states legislation has been passed allowing a patient to make a "living will." In it, he or she declares that there are to be no mechanical life-prolonging devices if and when, in the judgment of a council of physicians, life in its true sense, namely a functioning brain, has ceased.

This raises several questions from the Jewish point of view: Are we permitted to refrain from *attaching* life-prolonging devices? Are we permitted to *remove* them, once they have been attached?

Modern medicine, having found ways of measuring the waves of the brain, has held that life actually stops when the brain is destroyed and no longer working. Jewish tradition has maintained that the cessation of the vital functions of *heart* and *lungs* constitute death. It is possible to keep these organs alive even after the brain is dead. Whether or not we *must* attach mechanical devices to the body in order to preserve life and whether or not we may remove them once they have been attached are questions that have been answered differently by the various branches of Judaism. *Reform* Judaism holds that Jewish ethics *forbids* us to prolong a life that has been reduced to the status of "vegetable."

Orthodox and *Conservative* Jewry look to Halakhah to arrive at their positions. The *Shulhan Arukh* rules that we may remove obstacles to death as long as no direct death-producing action is involved. (Yore Deah 339:1; in Ketubot 104a, Rabbi Judah's maid is praised for "pulling the plug" of the attending Rabbis' incessant prayer that prevented Rabbi Judah's death. She tossed a jar out of a window. The startled Rabbis interrupted their prayer; Rabbi Judah's soul entered into its rest.)

When the time to die has arrived, we need not try to postpone it. *Orthodox* Rabbis, nevertheless, are not in agreement. Though some hold that it is permitted to discontinue the use of artificial devices, even after they have been attached, the weight of opinion seems to veer in the direction of the ruling that it is not required to use special devices initially, but that we may not disconnect them once they have been attached.

Conservative opinion seems to move in the direction of the idea that it is permissible to detach such devices and permit nature to take its course.

As these issues affect life and death, a Jew should surely consult his rabbi before authorizing action. He should also be mindful that artificial life preservers have indeed restored many a life, as in heart attacks. Only after the most searching consultation with physicians and rabbi should action be permitted.

DONATIONS OF ORGANS seems to be permitted by all branches of Judaism, as it directly aids other human beings. The rabbi should be consulted. *Dissection* of the corpse is permitted in Orthodox Judaism only if a person *presently* suffering from the same disease that felled the deceased can be helped. The other branches of Judaism takes the position that it is permitted even if it merely expands our knowledge, enabling us to help others at some time in the future. The dissected parts of the body have to be buried with the rest.

In the House of Mourning

In earlier days, the deceased was prepared in his own home, where he had died. All mirrors were veiled. Reflected in a mirror, the dead might be "captured," his ghost retained to haunt the survivors. We have kept this custom. Mourners should not be compelled to view themselves in the ghastly state of their distress, nor their home be mirrored in its emptiness.

We kindle a light at the head of the departed and in the home to which he or she brought so much light in the past.

The soul of man is a light of God (Prov. 20:27).

Tumah and Taharah

The body of the dead is *tameh*, unclean, and makes unclean those who touch it and those who are under the same roof with it (Num. 19:11–16ff). A Kohen may not be in contact with the dead. Only for his closest relatives may he expose himself. These are: wife, mother, father, son, daughter, unmarried sister (Lev. 21:1–3). He may not go to the cemetery, nor may he be a member of the Hevrah Kadishah. This law is observed by Orthodoxy.

Taharah

Before the body is laid to rest, it is cleansed and dressed by the members of the Holy Fellowship. They wash it in lukewarm water through a sheet placed over it, pare the nails and groom the hair. This is called *Taharah*, the cleansing. At the end of the cleansing, they perform a symbolic act of pouring water over the body beneath the sheet, and speak the words of purification:

Rabbi Akiva said: "Happy are you Israel. Who is it before Whom you cleanse yourselves and Who cleanses you? It is your Father, Who is in heaven. As it is said:
I shall sprinkle upon you clean water and you shall be clean from all your uncleanness and all your fetishes will I cleanse you. [Ezek. 36:25]
The Holy One Blessed Be He purifies Israel." [Yoma 85b]

The body is then dried by using another sheet. The body is dressed in the white Takhrikhim (from *kharakh*, to wrap). First a cap is placed on the head; it will be pulled over the face. Now follow the undergarments: shirt, trousers, linen shoes, and finally the kittel worn on Yom Kippur. (A Kohen is dressed in two kittels.) The belt worn on Yom Kippur is placed about the body.

The coffin is of unplaned wood. In it is placed a large shroud, which eventually will cover and hide the entire body. Next, over the shroud, the Tallit is put into the coffin, in order that it may rest on the body's shoulders when it is lowered into the coffin or over the head, just as the deceased has worn it in life. All ornaments are removed from the Tallit; one of the Tzitzit is cut: the dead are not subject to Mitzvah, merely honored.

The body is lowered into the coffin. The linen bag used throughout the years to hold the Takhrikhim is filled with earth and placed

Fig. XVII.   Von der Begræbniß.   pag. 179

P. IV.   G. P. Nusbiegel sculp.

At the cemetery. An engraving by J. C. Bodenschatzen depicts traditional rites of burial: the funeral procession, burial in a simple wooden coffin, and the covering of the grave by the mourners.

under the head. A small stone is put under the chin. Earth from Eretz Yisrael is sprinkled over the body; symbolically at least, the Jew is buried in the soil of the Holy Land. Here resurrection will commence.

The Tallit is adjusted. The shroud is wrapped around the entire body to cover it. Then the coffin is nailed shut. Judaism does not approve of open caskets. A black pall is put over it. A light burns. Attendants watch over it until the moment of the funeral. Before the members of the Hevrah Kadishah depart, they step to the feet of the coffin and in silent prayer ask forgiveness of the departed soul if they have shown any inadvertent neglect or made any mistake.

Stepping outside, they wash their hands.

Embalming is not approved of in Judaism, unless state law or special conditions require it. If the body has been embalmed, the extracted blood must be placed in the coffin.

Anything attached to the body at the time of death must be buried with it. On the other hand, nothing may be given the dead in the coffin. In death we must all be equal.

Simplicity and Equality

By rabbinical ordinance Jewish funerals are distinguished by the most austere simplicity. The garments are the same for every person, for all are alike in death. The coffin of unpolished wood reveals this equality to the assembled funeral congregation. Flowers are frowned upon; the money should rather be given to charity. There is no need for professionals. The Jew who gives his departed ones the simplest of funerals lives up to the noblest ideals of Judaism. An ostentatious funeral violates the spirit of Judaism (see Moed Katan 27a, b; Ketubot 8b). There is no reason to feel "guilty" about such simplicity. The personal affection we give our dear ones in life and in death is the real honor we bestow upon them.

31

Funerals
and Mourning

THE FUNERAL

Torah states:

> . . . dust you are and to dust you shall return. [Gen. 3:19]

It is our duty to perform the Mitzvot commanded us as quickly as possible. As the deceased cannot fulfill the commandment of returning to the dust, we must do it for him or her as soon as possible. In this manner we honor the departed. The ancient Jews and our ancestors in the ghetto and the Pale saw to it that the body was buried within twenty-four hours. Later on, when the state prohibited early funerals, the Jews had to yield, but did so only after stiff conflicts with the authorities. To this day, we arrange funerals at the earliest possible moment. We may delay a funeral in compliance with state law or to permit relatives to arrive. A postponement that is motivated by concern for the honor of the departed is permitted; otherwise, it is to be avoided.

The injunction of Torah also makes it clear that man must return to "the dust." Cremation is, therefore, prohibited under traditional Jewish law; Reform does not object to it. The flimsy coffin we make is designed to speed decomposition of the body, its return to the dust. We find that Jews were at times buried merely in a shroud, placed in direct contact with the soil.

The Character of the Funeral

Many peoples of antiquity surrounded a funeral with great ceremony. In Egypt the annual funeral of Osiris lasted for seven days, and Jews have a similar period of deep mourning. Grief was powerfully expressed and even induced by professional "lamenters," women who raised their voices in agonizing shrieks, tore their hair and garments, and sometimes incised their bodies. Incisions are forbidden by Torah. Public lamentation was an accepted part of ancient Jewish funeral rites.

Judaism is motivated by the desire to reveal the stark reality of death, permitting the bereaved to express their grief fully, encouraging its actual eruption. The wound is opened in order that it may eventually develop a healthy scar and no aftereffects.

The Mitzvah of "Levayat ha-Met"

Levayat ha-Met, accompanying the dead to their last resting place, is a great Mitzvah, an act of love that bears its own reward and is compensated by God in the world to come (Peah 1:1).

The Rabbis declare:

One must abandon the study of Torah to carry the dead [to their resting place]. [Ketubot 17a]

Books containing God's name in Hebrew are not destroyed when they grow old and ragged. Instead, they are given a funeral such as this one held at the cemetery of Hebron, Israel, for prayer books desecrated during an Arab raid.

The Funeral Rite

Before cities grew, the procession would start at the home of the deceased and wind its way to the cemetery.

On weekdays, a eulogy is delivered, followed by praise of God. It begins with the words *Hatzur tamim*:

The Rock!—His deeds are perfect, yea all His ways are just. A faithful God, never false, true and upright is He. [Deut. 32:4]

It comes to its conclusion with the words:

The Lord has given and the Lord has taken away, Blessed be the Name of the Lord. [Job. 1:21]

If funeral services are held in a chapel, Hatzur Tamim is recited in the cemetery. On festive days, no eulogy is offered, and Hatzur Tamim is not recited. In most congregations, a prayer for the eternal rest of the departed follows: the *El Male Rahamim*.

Psalms and other prayers have come to be added.

Now the coffin is carried to the grave. Friends render this service. During the walk, Psalm 91 is recited. The coffin is set down several times as bearers are exchanged. Each time the coffin is set on the ground, it is lifted again to the words:

He will order His angels
to guard you wherever you go.
They will carry you in their hands
lest you hurt your foot on a stone. [Ps. 91:11–12]

The grave is reached; the body is lowered into it. This is the moment of the most tearing grief. It must be given outlet. The relatives tear their garments, perform *Keriah*. As they do so, they bless God even in their affliction. They speak:

Barukh attah . . . Dayan Ha-Emet
Blessed are You . . . the True Judge

Earth is poured on the coffin. The children and then relatives are the first to whom this final honor is given. The assembly fills the grave and shapes the mound. There is no deception: the end has come. But there is also comfort: the dead one is not left above ground as the relatives return home.

The children now recite the Kaddish. Together with the Berakhah at Keriah, this is their first prayer since the moment when death struck (see below, Aninut and Shivah). In the Kaddish, the mourners invite the congregation to "sanctify and magnify the Name of God." They honor their departed by testifying to God's holiness even in the moment of their most bitter grief.

The assembly forms two rows of comforters; the mourners walk through the aisle thus created, and the people speak:

Ha-Makom yenahem etkhem betokh shear avele Zion ve-Y'rushalaim
The-All-Present-in-Every-Place comfort you amid those who mourn for
Zion and Jerusalem.

In some congregations, the assembled individually pull a blade of
grass at the border of the cemetery, expressing the hope of resurrection:

May they sprout from this place as the grass sprouts from the earth!
[paraphrasing Ps. 103:15]

Outside the cemetery, all participants wash their hands by pouring
water over them.

The mourners return home. *Avelut,* the period of mourning,
begins.

Funerals are not permitted on the Sabbath or on the first day of
the festivals. They may be conducted on the second day, but without eulogy or pouring of earth or Keriah. If no non-Jewish attendants can be found to do all the work on such days, the funeral has
to be postponed.

Keriah

The nearest relatives must tear their garments at the moment of
their most pronounced grief. This is done at the graveside or, in
some congregations, at the beginning of the funeral service.

Children perform Keriah on the left, over the heart. Brothers,
sisters, parents, husband, and wife must also perform Keriah, but
do so on the right. An attendant makes a small cut; then the mourners tear about one hand's breadth.

The tear for relatives may be mended after the period of mourning is over; the Keriah for parents may never be mended.

It has become customary in Conservative Jewry to attach a ribbon to the lapel of the jacket or to the dress, and this is then torn
instead of the garment itself.

The garment or ribbon is to be worn throughout the period of
mourning. Reform Judaism does not require Keriah.

If a funeral takes place on the second day of a festival, the rite
of Keriah is postponed until the end of the festival.

FORMS AND STAGES OF MOURNING

In establishing the formal rules of mourning, the Rabbis were
guided by the emotions of the bereaved both before and after
burial. Before the departed has been laid to rest, his or her relatives
are in a state of shock. This is the period of *Aninut.* With the com-

pletion of the burial, the healing process begins. It extends over a lengthy period and through several stages: *Shivah, Sheloshim,* and, for parents, *a whole year.*

Aninut

Death creates a trauma. Momentary numbness leads to outcry, defiance of God's justice and cruel fate. In this state, the bereaved, *Anen,* is incapable of accepting consolation, and we may not try to comfort him or her.

Do not console your friend at a time when his dead lies before him. [Avot 4:23]

Eventually, his or her thoughts begin to center about the urgent tasks of providing for the funeral. Nothing may be forgotten, for the moment is unique and irreplaceable, and time is short. Concern with the practical preparations numbs pain.

The Rabbis, therefore, ruled that the Anen may not pray, may not put on Tefillin, may not speak any blessings. In his state, blessing would be a mockery and prayers would turn into rebellious curse.

Neither may he pursue his regular occupation. He must devote all of his time and energy to the preparations for the dead. Activity will be therapy for him. Later on, he will derive comfort from the knowledge that, in single-minded thought and action, he saw to the needs of the dead without permitting any intrusions, not even comfort.

The Funeral serves as catharsis. Emotions are expressed fully. The bereaved tears his garments and, in doing so, pronounces the first blessing since death has struck. The grave is filled in; the mound is shaped. Now healing may set in. The mourner returns to life with the Kaddish, the sanctification of God. He receives the words of comfort from his friends. He becomes a "mourner," and mourning is therapy. *Shivah* begins, the "seven days."

Shivah

For seven days the bereaved is in the deepest mourning. As Jews rejoice for seven days of wedding, they mourn for seven days of sorrow. At both occasions, they are surrounded by friends.

The mourner returns from the cemetery to a home where the mirrors are veiled and a light burns in honor of the departed.

He has to take off his leather shoes, and he sits on a low stool or on the ground, if he wishes to sit down at all. In antiquity, the beds and couches were turned over. Marital relations are forbidden. He does not shave his beard or cut his hair, and he reduces his care for his body to a minimum. He may not study Torah, except for those passages that deal with woe, as do the books of Job and Lamentations. He does not extend greetings to visitors. In ancient days, he would cover his face. His thoughts center on the departed.

But he is not alone. Returning from the funeral, he finds that friends have prepared his first meal. They bring it to him: eggs or lentils, traditional symbols of mourning. The friends urge him to eat, for he must restore his strength. In consuming food that symbolizes mourning, he finds the task easier; he gains strength while honoring the dead.

The rites of Tishah b'Av are derived from these rites of mourning. There is meaning in it. The Jew knows that his brothers and sisters, come to comfort him, understand the agony of loss and have true empathy with his emotions. Every Jew is a mourner, as long as Zion and Jerusalem lie desolate, their possession not secure to the Jewish people, their glory not restored. The visitors express this in their greeting on parting:

Ha-Makom yenahem otkha [plural: etkhem], betokh shear avele Tziyon ve-Y'rushalaim.

The-All-Present-in-Every-Place comfort you amid those who mourn for Zion and Jerusalem.

Every morning and every evening, throughout the Shivah period, services are conducted in the house of mourning. A Torah is placed there for the ordained readings on Monday and Thursday. We omit those passages of the service that deal with our regret for our sins; the mourners might feel that *their* sins brought death to a dear one, and wounds that had scarcely begun to heal would be torn open again. After each service the mourners speak the Kaddish.

The first three days are a period of unrelieved grief, and we do not count the mourners among the Minyan, for they are not yet ready to take their place in the community. From the fourth day on, the mourner must be on his way to life. He is counted in the Minyan.

The prohibition against leather shoes and the burning light evoke associations with Yom Kippur. For the mourners this is a period of Teshuvah. It must end in an affirmation of God and of life.

Duties of Friends

We should listen to the sometimes unspoken needs of the mourners. They may wish to repeat over and over again the virtues of the departed. We should add, of our own knowledge of the deceased, items that may lift their spirit. They may feel guilt at having failed their dear one in his last illness or throughout life. This is a normal reaction. We have to bring them assurance that they have been good and true and loving and have not failed. They may need the comfort that comes from the knowledge of the world to come. We have to give them the surety that their dear one is indeed sheltered in a loving God's eternal realm of peace and bliss.

Sabbath During the Shivah and the Length of the Shivah

The Sabbath of the week is counted among the seven days. But there is no mourning. On Friday evening, unless services are held in the home, the mourners go to the synagogue. They wait in the entrance hall until the congregation has completed the welcoming Psalms and hymns. They do not join the congregation until Shabbat has fully arrived. Then the rabbi and cantor receive them at the door and welcome them with a greeting, in which the congregation joins:

Ha-Makom yenahem . . .
The-All-Present-in-Every-Place comfort you . . .

During his entire period of mourning the bereaved does not take his accustomed seat but moves farther back: he has relinquished a part of his standing within the community; he is diminished. During the Shivah, the mourner is not called to the Torah.

The Rabbis have a principle: part of the day counts as a whole day. The day of the funeral counts as one day, even if the funeral was held in the afternoon, provided Shivah began before nightfall. The afternoon of Erev Shabbat removes part of the mourning, and the bereaved may go to the synagogue. On the last day, mourning is to be observed for two hours in the morning only.

By ruling of the Conservative rabbinate, three days constitute the minimum of deep mourning and satisfy the requirement in case of special conditions. This means that mourning is observed immediately upon the return from the cemetery (one day), a full second day, and for two hours on the third day. People in doubt should contact their rabbis in individual situations.

Sheloshim

A period of thirty days, beginning with the completion of the burial, has been appointed in the case of the death of any close relative to complete formal mourning except for parents, for whom it lasts a full year.

During the period the mourner does not cut his hair or beard and may not attend festivities or be wed. Then life must return to its normal state.

The Rabbis explained:

Weep you not for the dead, neither bemoan him. [Jer. 22:10]
Do not unduly weep for a dead person, nor mourn him beyond measure.

How long [shall mourning last]? Three days for weeping, seven days for lamentation, thirty days for bleached garments and for [the prohibition of the] cutting of hair.

From then on, the Holy One Blessed Be He speaks: "You may not be more compassionate and more affectionate than I am." [Moed Katan 27b]

We read in Torah:

And the Israelites bewailed Moses in the steppes of Moab for thirty days. [Then] the wailing period in mourning for Moses came to an end. Now Joshua son of Nun was filled with the spirit of wisdom . . . [Deut. 34:8–9f.]

Life must be resumed, we must become "Joshua." Undue mourning is a rebuke to God.

The Year

Mourning for parents continues for a whole year. The children attend worship every morning and evening and recite the Kaddish. In this manner, the bereaved gradually adjust to life and society. In the synagogue they find out that others bear equal sorrow and an equal pain of loss. Mutually the worshipers serve as a source of strength, as all of them find consolation in the beauty of Jewish tradition, bequeathed to them by their ancestors, who have gone to their eternal rest.

Actually, Kaddish is said for only eleven months. Tradition holds that after this period, all, except outspoken evildoers, are irrevocably admitted to their reward.

During this period, the mourners are not to visit the grave. It may open wounds, and such visits may also become habitual, something that is psychologically undesirable.

At the end of the year, the stone is set. From now on, the children observe *Yahrzeit* for their parents. They will remember them for as long as they themselves will live. As they mention their names, they add:

Zikhrono l'Brakhah (or *Zikronah*, for a woman)
May his [her] memory be for a blessing.

Festivals Cancel the Mourning Period

Both Shivah and Sheloshim are canceled out by the major festivals.

If the burial took place on the afternoon of Erev Rosh Hashanah, and the bereaved have begun Shivah, it is canceled out by the feast and need no longer be observed afterward. The following Yom Kippur cancels out the Sheloshim. If the burial takes place on Erev Sukkot and Shivah was begun before nightfall, the Sukkot feast

An eastern European cemetery. Since the days of Abraham, Jews have purchased and set aside special areas of land in which to bury the dead. The Jewish cemetery is consecrated as a sacred space, and it is customary among many Jews to leave a pebble or small stone resting on the top of a tombstone as a sign that the tomb has been recently visited.

cancels out the Shivah and Sh'mini Atzeret, being a separate festival, cancels out the Sheloshim. Pessah and Shavuot cancel out only one stage of the mourning period, being but one feast. If the burial takes place on the holy day, such as the second day of a festival, or Hol Ha-Moed of Pessah or Sukkot, the mourning period begins after the festival is over. There is then no cancellation.

The Conservative rabbinate has ruled that if burial has taken place during the holidays, or on Hol Ha-Moed, no Shivah may be observed during the festival period, but relatives and friends may be received as long as no outward signs of Avelut are observed.

At the end of the festival, the mourners should observe one full day after the holy days and a short period on the following day. In this manner, the basic obligation is met. The last day of the festival, whose observance is not commanded by Torah, counts as the first day, although no open observance of Avelut is to be practiced; together with the day following the festival and the period of a few hours on the following day, this meets the minimum requirement of three days of deep mourning.

In this manner, mourners are not compelled to undergo the pain of a full period of Shivah after a lengthy postponement required by law. At the same time, the comforting presence of friends carries the bereaved over the immediate period when open mourning is not permitted.

Recent and Delayed News of Death

A person who receives the news of the death of a relative within thirty days after it occurred, even on the thirtieth day, must observe full mourning, beginning with the day he got the message.

If the news reaches the person *after* thirty days, only one hour of symbolic mourning is required. The mourner takes off his or her shoes and sits on the ground for one hour. Then life returns to normal.

Children should be informed right away of the death of a parent, in order that they may say Kaddish.

The mourning year for a parent begins with the time of death, even if the news has arrived late.

The regulations on Avelut may create difficulties for Jews in earning a livelihood. In such circumstances, the person should consult the rabbi.

The Tombstone

Traditional Jewish cemeteries reflect the spirit of equality. They have no flowers, but wild flowers grow in abundance. Eventually, the grave merges with the soil around it. There is great beauty in this simplicity.

The stone we choose should be simple but of the very best quality; it has to withstand time and elements. A Hebrew inscription is appropriate. Up to modern times, we find only Hebrew inscriptions on stones. Later, the secular name of the person came to be inscribed on the back of the stone, or at the bottom. On many modern stones we find hardly any Hebrew. But a stone should at least carry the letters פ״נ on top. They are an abbreviation of: *Po Nikaver [et]*, "Here is buried." At the bottom should be the letters תנצב״ה , an abbreviation for: *Tehee nafsho[h] tzerurah bitzror ha-hayim*—May his [her] soul be bound up in the bond of life.

In order to enable future generations to observe *Yahrzeit*, the stone should give us the Hebrew name and Hebrew day of death.

Burial vaults have come to be accepted in Conservative and Reform Judaism. We are not permitted to move a body once buried, except for highly compelling reasons.

The setting of the stone marks more or less the end of the period of mourning; there is finality to the act. It has, therefore, become customary to mark the moment by a ceremony of *unveiling*. This rite was not known in western Europe. It is a simple ceremony: a

Psalm is read; a word of comfort spoken; the children or closest relatives remove the cover that up to now has hidden the inscription. Kaddish and El Male Rahamim are recited.

Yahrzeit: Visiting the Graves

We should always remember the example set us by our departed. On special occasions, we call forth their memory in the congregational service. This is *Yizkor,* the memorial service, observed on the last day of the Pilgrimage Festivals and on Yom Kippur.

In Talmudic times, the people would visit the graves on all fast days. The purpose of these visits was to evoke the spirit of contrition, as before God "we are but dust, the dust of the dead"; in addition, its purpose was to "evoke the dust of Isaac [his sacrifice] in order that the dead might intercede for the living" (Taanit 16a). We are warned, however, not to pray to the dead. Our plea must be addressed to God alone.

Later custom appointed the ninth of Av and the days before Rosh Hashanah and Yom Kippur as additional days of visitation. In conjunction with each of our visits, we are to give to charity. By appointing special days, our masters may have wished to warn us against too frequent visits that make us dependent on our departed and impede our development as authentic individuals in our own right.

There is also a special day we must observe individually: *Yahrzeit.* The term is Yiddish and means "anniversary." Yehrzeit is observed on the Hebrew date of a parent's death. If he or she died after nightfall, the following calendar date counts as day of death. To observe Yahrzeit correctly, we must have a Jewish calendar.

Yahrzeit is a day of Teshuvah. From evening to evening, we light a candle. The children of the departed may fast, perhaps at least for half a day. They attend synagogue worship and recite the Kaddish. They should study Torah and give to charity.

We should also attend worship on the Sabbath before and after the Yahrzeit day and be called to the Torah.

On Yahrzeit, we visit the graves of our departed. We address our prayers to God, pleading that the example of our dear ones may aid us to walk in His ways and find grace before Him. A simple prayer, offered by one of the masters, was:

May it be Your will that the rest of this departed be with honor, and his [her] merit stand up for me.

Tenderly, the visitor will place his or her hand on stone and grave. Upon leaving, the visitor places a small stone on the tombstone as an act of love, his or her "visiting card." (For these Minhagim and prayer, see Baer Hetev, note 8, to Orah Hayim 224:12.) The custom

This stone, found in the Jewish cemetery of Mainz, Germany, tells much about Jewish life and destiny. It is the stone of my father of blessed memory.

On top the letters: פ״נ here lies enshrouded, on the bottom the letters: תנצב״ה may his soul be bound up in the bond of life (based on Samuel I, 25:29). The size of the stone is the largest the Nazis would allow; the stone was set four months after burial in fear that eventually no stone for Jews would be allowed. The inscription is entirely in Hebrew; the German names were added later by me, in order that those unacquainted with Hebrew might find it. Note the small stones on top of the stone, placed there by visitors. I also had added the name of my mother of blessed memory with the note: deported. This is her tombstone, too, as we do not know where she died. Her Hebrew name could not be added; there was at the time no stonemason capable of doing the work.

It was customary in Germany for the rabbi to bestow the title Haver—distinguished fellow—on members of special dedication, scholarship, and devotion.
The inscription reads:
Here lies enshrouded
A man, "Tzaddik"
in all his ways
The "Haver" Rabbi Meir ben Yehudah Trepp
All his days did he occupy himself
with Torah, Mitzvot, and good deeds.
His sons also did he direct on the road of Torah
and the fear of Heaven.
He left behind him a good name and blessing.
He died on the tenth of Av 5701
May his soul be bound up in the bond of life.

of placing a stone on the grave developed because originally only a stone mound marked the grave; the visitor who placed a stone on it helped maintain it.

On visiting the cemetery, we may not step on the graves. Originating in fear of demons, the ghosts of the departed that hover over the graves, it has become a simple expression of respect. We are careful not to step over our departed.

We may not pluck flowers from the gravesides. They may have been nourished by the bodies of those buried here; to take them with us would be wrong under Jewish tradition. We may not gain from any human remains, even indirectly, even "for memory's sake." We may, however, take plants from the edges of the cemetery, where there are no graves.

The Kaddish

Only children are required to say Kaddish for a parent. We are not obligated to speak it for any other relative, but may do so. The Kaddish is not a prayer for the dead; it is an affirmation of God's holiness.

Actually, Kaddish is offered throughout the service. Except in the morning service, it introduces the Amidah; an abbreviated version is also offered at the end of the Torah reading. Every public worship finds its climax in the Kaddish. After communal study of Torah or Talmud, Kaddish is offered. In each case, a middle paragraph relates to the activity that is to be "sanctified" through Kaddish. In this form and use the Kaddish is old, going back to Talmudic times. In the Middle Ages it came to be the affirmation of mourners as well.

Kaddish is a call to the congregation to affirm God's holiness. It can, therefore, be offered only in public worship when a Minyan is present. The mourners exemplify their faith by inviting their friends to praise God and do so while they themselves stand under divine trial. The dead are not mentioned at this occasion. (Reform has introduced a paragraph pleading for the departed's eternal rest.)

The source of the Kaddish can be found in Ezekiel, where we read:

I will magnify Myself and sanctify Myself, and I will make Myself known in the eyes of many nations; and they shall know that I am the Lord. [Ezek. 38:23]

The Kaddish is a proclamation spoken by the leader with response by the congregation.

Leader: Magnified and sanctified be His Great Name throughout the world, which He has created according to His will. May He establish His Kingdom during your lifetime and during your days, and during the lifetime of the entire House of Israel. To this say ye: Amen [so be it].

Congregation: Amen! His Great Name be blessed for ever and unto all eternity.

Leader: Blessed, praised, exalted, elevated and lauded in every way be His Holy Name. Blessed be He!

Congregation: Blessed be He!

Leader: He is above all blessings, hymns, and praises that can be spoken in the world. To this say ye: Amen.

Congregation: Amen!

Leader: May there be abundant peace from heaven and life unto us and unto all of Israel. To this say ye: Amen.

Congregation: Amen!

Leader: May He, who makes peace in His [heavenly] heights, make peace for us and for all Israel. To this say ye: Amen.

Congregation: Amen!

Kaddish is the summation of Israel's faith.

Epilogue

I n following the course of life we have concluded by speaking of death. According to tradition, however, no book should end on a tragic note.

This work has been designed to open a gate to the study of Judaism that we may come to cherish it, learn ever more about it, and make it our way of life.

It may be appropriate to end with words included in the Kaddish when it is recited after the study of Torah. They are my personal wish and prayer for my readers and for all Israel:

Unto Israel, its teachers, their disciples and all their disciples' disciples, and unto all who occupy themselves with Torah, here or at any place, may there be granted unto them and unto you abundant peace, grace, and loving kindness, and compassion, and long life, and abundant sustenance, and redemption, from Him, our Father, who is in Heaven.

To this, may you join me in saying:

Amen!

Bibliography

GENERAL WORKS

Baeck, Leo. *The Essence of Judaism.* New York: Schocken Books, 1961.

Baron, Salo W. *A Social and Religious History of the Jews,* 16 vols. New York: Columbia University Press, 1960 and following.

Finkelstein, Louis, ed. *The Jews, Their History, Culture and Religion,* 4 vols. Philadelphia: Jewish Publication Society, 1949.

Fox, Marvin, ed. *Modern Jewish Ethics.* Cincinnati: Ohio State University Press, 1975.

Janowsky, Oscar, ed. *The American Jew: A Reappraisal.* Philadelphia: Jewish Publication Society, 1964.

Kaplan, Mordecai M. *The Meaning of God in Modern Jewish Religion.* New York: Reconstructionist Press, 1962.

Roth, Cecil, ed. *Encyclopedia Judaica,* 16 vols. Jerusalem, Israel: Keter, 1972.

Sklare, Marshall, ed. *The Jew in American Society.* New York: Behrman House, 1974.

Sklare, Marshall, ed. *The Jewish Community in America.* New York: Behrman House, 1974.

Trepp, Leo. *A History of the Jewish Experience.* New York. Behrman House, 1973.

Waxman, M. *A History of Jewish Literature* (Second Edition). New York: Thomas Yoseloff, 1960.

THE BIBLE

Cohen, A., ed. *The Soncino Books of the Bible*, 14 vols. London: Soncino Press, 1947 and following.

Hertz, J.H. *The Pentateuch and Haftorahs* (Second Edition). London: Soncino Press, 1970.

Plaut, Gunther W. *The Torah, A Modern Commentary: Volume I, Genesis*. New York: Union of American Hebrew Congregations, 1974.

TALMUD AND CODES

Appel, Gersion. *Concise Code of Jewish Law*. New York: Ktav, 1977.

Cohen, Abraham. *Everyman's Talmud*. New York: Schocken Books, 1975.

Danby, H. *The Mishnah*. London: Oxford University Press, 1933.

Epstein, Isidore, ed. *The Babylonian Talmud with Introduction and Commentary*, Vol. 1-36. London: Soncino Press, 1935-1952.

Freedman, H. and Simon, Maurice, ed. *Midrash Rabbah*, Vol. 1-10. London: Soncino Press, 1939.

Freehof, Solomon B. *Responsa Literature*. Philadelphia: Jewish Publication Society, 1955.

Freehof, Solomon B. *Reform Responsa*. Cincinnati: Hebrew Union College Press, 1960.

Freehof, Solomon B. *A Treasury of Responsa*. Philadelphia: Jewish Publication Society, 1963.

Ganzfried, Solomon and Goldin, Hyman E. *Code of Jewish Law*. New York: Hebrew Publishing Company, 1963.

Herford, J. Travis. *The Ethics of the Talmud: Sayings of the Fathers*. New York: Schocken Books, 1962.

Jacobs, Louis. *Jewish Law*. New York: Behrman House, 1968.

Montefiore, C.G. and Loewe, H. *A Rabbinic Anthology*. New York: Schocken Books, 1960.

Newman, Louis I. and Spitz, Samuel, ed. *The Talmudic Anthology: Tales and Teachings of the Rabbis*. New York: Behrman House, 1945.

Siegel, Seymour, ed. *Conservative Judaism and Jewish Law*. New York: The Rabbinical Assembly, 1977.

Twersky, Isadore. *A Maimonides Reader*. New York: Behrman House, 1972.

RELIGIOUS MOVEMENTS AND ZIONISM

Diamond, Malcolm L. *Martin Buber, Jewish Existentialist.* New York: Oxford Press, 1960.

Herberg, Will. *The Writings of Martin Buber.* New York: Meridian Press, 1956.

Kaplan, Mordecai. *The Greater Judaism in the Making.* New York: Reconstructionist Press, 1960.

Laqueur, Walter. *A History of Zionism.* New York: Holt, Rinehart and Winston, 1972.

Learsi, Rufus. *Fulfillment, the Epic Story of Zionism.* Cleveland: World Publishing Co., 1951.

Levinthal, Israel H. *Point of View.* London and New York: Abelard Schuman, 1958.

Minkin, Jacob S. *The Romance of Hassidism.* New York: Thomas Yoseloff, 1955.

Naamani, Israel. *The State of Israel.* New York: Behrman House, 1979.

Rubenstein, Aryeh. *Hassidism.* New York and Paris: Leon Amiel, 1975.

Rudavsky, David. *Modern Jewish Religious Movements* (Third Edition). New York: Behrman House, 1979.

Sachar, Howard M. *A History of Israel.* New York: Knopf, 1976.

HISTORY

Dawidowicz, Lucy S. *Holocaust Reader.* New York: Behrman House, 1976.

Dawidowicz, Lucy S. *The War Against the Jews 1933-1945.* New York: Holt, 1975.

Eban, Abba. *My People: The Story of the Jews.* New York: Behrman House and Random House, 1969.

Learsi, Rufus. *Israel: A History of the Jewish People.* Cleveland: World Publishing Co., 1949.

Learsi, Rufus. *Jews in America.* New York: Ktav, 1972.

Levin, Nora. *The Holocaust.* New York: Thomas Crowell, 1968.

Roth, Cecil. *A History of the Jews: From Earliest Times Through the Six Day War.* New York: Schocken Books, 1970.

Sachar, Howard M. *A History of Israel.* New York: Alfred A. Knopf, Inc., 1976.

Sklare, Marshall. *The Jew in American Society.* New York: Behrman House, 1974.

OUT OF THE PAST

Ayalty, Hanan J. *Yiddish Proverbs*. New York: Schocken Books, 1949.

Dobroszki, Lucjan, and Kirschenblatt-Gimblet, Barbara. *Image Before My Eyes: A Photographic History of Jewish Life in Poland, 1864-1939*. New York: Schocken Books, 1975.

Howe, Irving, and Greenberg, Eliezer. *Voices from the Yiddish*. New York: Schocken Books, 1975.

Howe, Irving. *World of Our Fathers*. Philadelphia: Jewish Publication Society, 1976.

Rosten, Leo. *Leo Rosten's Treasury of Jewish Quotations*. Philadelphia: Jewish Publication Society, 1972.

Sachs, A. S. *Worlds That Passed*. Philadelphia: Jewish Publication Society, 1943.

Zborowsky, Mark and Herzog, Elizabeth. *Life Is With People*. New York: Schocken Books, 1976.

DEATH AND BURIAL

Abrahams, Israel, ed. and tr. *Hebrew Ethical Wills*. Philadelphia: Jewish Publication Society, 1976.

Lamm, Maurice. *Jewish Way in Death and Mourning*. Middle Village, New York: Jonathan David, 1972.

Lauterbach, Jacob Z. "Burial Practices," in *Studies in Jewish Law, Customs and Folklore*. New York: Ktav, 1976.

Riemer, Jack, ed. *Jewish Reflections on Death*. New York: Schocken Books, 1974.

THE CONTEMPORARY JEWISH WOMAN

Koltun, Elizabeth, ed. *Jewish Woman: New Perspectives*. New York: Schocken Books, 1976.

Lerner, Ann Lapidus. "Who Hast Not Made Me A Man," in *American Jewish Yearbook*, Vol. 77. New York: The American Jewish Committee; Philadelphia: Jewish Publication Society, 1976.

Priesand, Sally. *Judaism and the New Woman*. New York: Behrman House, 1975.

JEWISH TRADITIONS AND RITUALS

Dresner, S. *The Dietary Laws*. New York: Burning Bush Press, 1959.

Gutman, Joseph. *Beauty in Holiness: Studies in Jewish Ceremonial Art.* New York: Ktav, 1970.

Kaplan, Mordecai. *Questions Jews Ask.* New York: Reconstructionist Press, 1956.

Kayser, Stephen. *Jewish Ceremonial Art.* Philadelphia: Jewish Publication Society, 1959.

Kertzer, Morris. *What is a Jew?* (Revised Edition). New York: Macmillan, 1969.

Kraus, Samuel. "The Jewish Rite of Covering the Head," in *Hebrew Union College Annual,* Vol. 19. Cincinnati: Hebrew Union College Press, 1945.

Schauss, Hayyim. *The Lifetime of a Jew.* New York: Union of American Hebrew Congregations, 1976.

Waxman, Meyer. *Judaism, Religion and Ethics.* New York: Thomas Yoseloff, 1958.

Wouk, Herman. *This is My God.* New York: Doubleday and Co., 1960.

MARRIAGE AND THE FAMILY

Feldman, David M. *Marital Relations: Birth Control and Abortion in Jewish Law.* New York: Schocken Books, 1974.

Goodman, Philip and Goodman, Hannah. *The Jewish Marriage Anthology.* Philadelphia: Jewish Publication Society, 1965.

Gordis, Robert. *Love and Sex: A Modern Jewish Perspective.* New York: Farrar, Straus & Giroux, 1978.

Lauterbach, Jacob Z. "The Ceremony of Breaking a Glass at Weddings," in *Studies in Jewish Law, Custom and Folklore.* New York: Ktav, 1970.

Routtenberg, Lilly S. and Seldin, Ruth R. *Jewish Wedding Book: A Practical Guide to the Tradition and Social Customs of the Jewish Wedding.* New York: Schocken Books, 1969.

Schneid, Hayyim, ed. *The Family.* Philadelphia: Jewish Publication Society, 1974.

THE SYNAGOGUE

Kampf, Avram. *Contemporary Synagogue Art.* Philadelphia: Jewish Publication Society, 1966.

Kaploun, Uri, ed. *The Synagogue.* Philadelphia: Jewish Publication Society, 1966.

Levy, Isaac. *The Synagogue: History and Functions.* London: Vallentine and Mitchell, 1963.

Rosowsky, Solomon. *The Cantillations of the Bible*. New York: Reconstructionist Press, 1957.

Wischnitzer, Rachel. *Synagogue Architecture in the United States*. Philadelphia: Jewish Publication Society, 1955.

PRAYER BOOKS

Harlow, Jules, ed. *Mahzor for Rosh Hashanah and Yom Kippur* (Conservative). New York: Rabbinical Assembly, 1972.

Hertz, J. H. *The Authorized Daily Prayer Book* (Orthodox). New York: Bloch, 1948.

High Holy Day Prayer Book, Vol. I and II (Reconstructionist). New York: Jewish Reconstructionist Foundation, 1948.

Jewish Reconstructionist Foundation: Sabbath Prayer Book (Reconstructionist). New York: Jewish Reconstructionist Foundation, 1945.

Pool, David de Sola, ed. *The Traditional Prayer Book*. (Prepared under direction of Rabbinical Council of America.) New York: Behrman House, 1960.

Rabbinical Assembly: Sabbath and Festival Prayer Book (Conservative). New York: Rabbinical Assembly, 1947.

Silverman, Morris, ed. *High Holy Day Prayer Book*. Hartford: Prayer Book Press, 1959.

Stern, Chaim, ed. *Gates of the House, the New Union Home Prayer Book* (Reform). New York: Central Conference of American Rabbis, 1977.

Stern, Chaim, ed. *Gates of Prayer, the New Union Prayer Book* (Reform). New York: Central Conference of American Rabbis, 1975.

Stern, Chaim, ed. *Gates of Repentance, the New Union Prayer Book for the Days of Awe*. New York: Central Conference of American Rabbis, 1978.

ON JEWISH PRAYER AND LITURGY

Agus, Jacob. "The Meaning of Prayer," in Millgram, Abraham E., ed. *Great Jewish Ideas*. Washington, D.C.: B'nai B'rith Department of Adult Jewish Education, 1964.

Arzt, Max. *Justice and Mercy*. New York: Holt, Rinehart and Winston, 1963.

Garfiel, Evelyn. *Service of the Heart*. New York: Thomas Yoseloff, 1958.

Glatzer, Nahum N., ed. *Language of Faith: A Selection from the Most Expressive Jewish Prayers.* New York: Schocken Books, 1974.

Greenberg, Simon. *The Jewish Prayerbook: Its Ideals and Values.* New York: National Academy for Adult Jewish Studies of United Synagogue of America, 1957.

Heinemann, Joseph. *Literature of the Synagogue.* New York: Behrman House, 1975.

Heschel, Abraham J. "The Mystical Element in Judaism," in Finkelstein, Louis, ed. *The Jews: Their Religion and Culture,* Vol. II. New York: Harper & Row, 1949.

Isaacs, Nathan. "Study as a Mode of Worship," in Millgram, Abraham E., ed. *Great Jewish Ideas.* Washington, D.C.: B'nai B'rith Department of Adult Jewish Education, 1964.

Millgram, Abraham. *Jewish Worship.* Philadelphia: Jewish Publication Society, 1971.

Petuchowski, Jacob. *Understanding Jewish Prayer.* New York: Ktav, 1972.

SABBATH AND FESTIVALS

Agnon, Shmuel Y. *Days of Awe.* New York: Schocken Books, 1965.

Bronstein, Herbert, ed. *A Passover Haggadah* (Reform). New York: Central Conference of American Rabbis, 1975.

Gaster, Theodore H. *Festivals of the Jewish Year.* New York: Wm. Morrow & Co., 1952.

Goldschmidt, E. D. *The Passover Haggadah.* New York: Schocken and Farrar, Straus and Young, 1953.

Goodman, Philip, ed. *Hanukkah Anthology.* Philadelphia: Jewish Publication Society, 1976.

Goodman, Philip, ed. *Passover Anthology.* Philadelphia: Jewish Publication Society, 1961.

Goodman, Philip, ed. *Purim Anthology.* Philadelphia: Jewish Publication Society, 1949.

Goodman, Philip, ed. *Rosh Hashanah Anthology.* Philadelphia: Jewish Publication Society, 1970.

Goodman, Philip, ed. *Shavuot Anthology.* Philadelphia: Jewish Publication Society, 1975.

Goodman, Philip, ed. *Sukkot and Simhat Torah Anthology.* Philadelphia: Jewish Publication Society, 1973.

Goodman, Philip, ed. *Yom Kippur Anthology.* Philadelphia: Jewish Publication Society, 1971.

Kaplan, Mordecai M., ed. *The New Haggadah* (Reconstructionist). New York: Behrman House, 1942.

Klein, M., ed. *Passover.* Philadelphia: Jewish Publication Society, 1961.

Millgram, Abraham E., ed. *Sabbath: The Day of Delight.* Philadelphia: Jewish Publication Society, 1944.

Schauss, Hayyim. *The Jewish Festivals.* New York: Schocken Books, 1974.

Szyk, Arthur. *Passover Haggadah.* Jerusalem: Massada, 1967.

Yerushalmi, Yosef Hayim. *Haggadah and History.* Philadelphia: Jewish Publication Society, 1975.

Index